INSIGHT GUIDES

QUEENSLAND

& THE GREAT BARRIER REEF

D0709111

Part of the Langenscheidt Publishing Group

✖ INSIGHT GUIDE
QUEENSLAND
& THE GREAT BARRIER REEF

Commissioning Editor
Rebecca Lovell
Series Manager
Rachel Lawrence
Publishing Manager
Rachel Fox

Distribution

UK & Ireland
**Dorling Kindersley Ltd, a Penguin
Group company**
80 Strand, London WC2R 0RL, UK
customerservice@dk.com

United States
Ingram Publisher Services
One Ingram Blvd, PO Box 3006
La Vergne, TN 37086-1986
customer.service@ingrampublisher
services.com

Australia
Universal Publishers
PO Box 307
St. Leonards NSW 1590
sales@universalpublishers.com.au

New Zealand
Brown Knows Publications
11 Artesia Close, Shamrock Park
Auckland, New Zealand 2016
sales@brownknows.co.nz

Worldwide
**Apa Publications GmbH & Co.
Verlag KG (Singapore branch)**
7030 Ang Mo Kio Avenue 5
08-65 Northstar @ AMK
Singapore 569880
apasin@singnet.com.sg

Printing

CTPS-China

ABOUT THIS BOOK

The first Insight Guide pioneered the use of creative full-colour photography in travel guides in 1970. Since then, we have expanded our range to cater for our readers' need not only for reliable information about their chosen destination, but also for a real understanding of the culture and history of that destination. Now, when the internet can supply inexhaustible (but not always reliable) facts, our books marry text and pictures to provide those much more elusive qualities: knowledge and discernment. To achieve this, they rely heavily on the authority of locally based writers and photographers.

How to use this book

The book is carefully structured to convey an understanding of the region, and to guide readers through its sights and activities:

◆ The **Best of Queensland** section at the start of the book gives you a snapshot of the island's highlights, helping you prioritise what you want to see and do.

◆ To understand Queensland today, you need to know something of its past. The **Features** section covers the state's people, history and culture in lively, authoritative essays written by specialists.

◆ The **Places** section provides a full rundown of all the attractions worth seeing. The main places of interest

LEFT: learning to surf at a Queensland beach.

◆ Photographs are chosen not only to illustrate the landscape and buildings but also to convey the moods of the region and the life of its people.

The contributors

This edition of *Insight Regional Guide: Queensland and the Great Barrier Reef* was updated throughout by **Lindsay Brown**, an experienced travel writer and Australia resident, who is knowledgeable about all things Australian. It was commissioned by **Astrid de Ridder** and managed by **Rebecca Lovell** at Insight Guides.

This edition builds on the work of previous contributors. These include **Jerry Dennis**, commissioning editor of the first edition, who also took many of the photographs, and original writers **David Bentley**, **Anna King Murdoch**, **Tim Baker** and **Christine Long**.

The book was edited by **Cathy Muscat**, proofread by **Hildegarde Serle** and indexed by **Helen Peters**.

are coordinated by number with full-colour maps. Margin notes provide background information and tips on special places and events.

◆ **Photo features** illuminate multiple aspects of Queensland culture, such as reef conservation, the wildlife of the rainforest and local sports.

◆ The **Travel Tips** listings section provides full information on transport, hotels, restaurants (located at the end of the relevant Places chapter), shopping and activities, from culture and festivals to bushwalking and surfing. Information can be located quickly by using the index printed on the back cover flap – and the flaps are designed to serve as bookmarks.

CONTACTING THE EDITORS

We would appreciate it if readers would alert us to errors or outdated information by writing to:

Insight Guides, P.O. Box 7910, London SE1 1WE, England.
email: insight@apaguide.co.uk

NO part of this book may be reproduced, stored in a retrieval system or transmitted in any form or means electronic, mechanical, photocopying, recording or otherwise, without prior written permission of *Apa Publications*. Brief text quotations with use of photographs are exempted for book review purposes only.

Information has been obtained from sources believed to be reliable, but its accuracy and completeness, and the opinions based thereon, are not guaranteed.

www.insightguides.com

Left: Cape
Tribulation.

Maps

THE BEST OF QUEENSLAND: TOP ATTRACTIONS

Discover the best of Queensland's attractions – nature parks, island resorts, family outings, historic towns... Here, at a glance, are our top recommendations

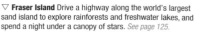

▽ **Fraser Island** Drive a highway along the world's largest sand island to explore rainforests and freshwater lakes, and spend a night under a canopy of stars. *See page 125.*

△ **The Great Barrier Reef** One of the most spectacular natural wonders on the planet, the magnificent Great Barrier Reef is Queensland's, if not Australia's, don't-miss experience. *See page 53.*

△ **The Sunshine Coast** Nature excels herself with golden beaches, the Glasshouse Mountains, and whale-watching in Hervey Bay; and another world awaits in the chic boutiques and restaurants of Noosa Heads. *See page 115.*

◁ **Cairns** Cairns is not just a gateway to the Great Barrier Reef. Its man-made lagoon, indigenous attractions and scenic railway to the rainforest village of Kuranda make it a destination in its own right. *See page 175.*

△ **The Gold Coast and Surfers Paradise** The glittering pleasure zone southeast of Brisbane where condominiums crowd the beaches, theme parks buzz with excitement, and, you can learn to surf in Surfers Paradise. *See page 90.*

▽ **Daintree and Cape Tribulation** Lush rainforests are the draw, whether exploring Mossman Gorge or cruising the Daintree River. Cross the river to remote Cape Tribulation, where the rainforest meets the reef. *See pages 188–9.*

▽ **Cape York** The sleepy village of Cooktown marks the start of the Cape York Peninsula, a wild area of croc-infested rivers, rainforest and savannah woodlands that modern-day adventurers can 4WD all the way to the tip. *See page 195.*

◁ **The Outback** For a full immersion into the Outback, take the Matilda Highway from north to south (or vice versa), from the mining town of Mount Isa *(page 217)* or Karumba on the Gulf of Carpentaria *(page 212)*, through an ever-changing landscape, stopping at hospitable country towns such as Winton *(page 222)*, Longreach *(page 228)* and Barcaldine *(page 229)*.

▽ **The Whitsunday Islands** Sail among coral-fringed islands, snorkel over an undersea garden, stroll along a brilliant white beach or simply laze about in a luxurious resort. It's all possible in the wonderful Whitsundays. *See page 151.*

▽ **Brisbane** From the sophisticated cultural precincts and parklands of Southbank to the natural playground of Moreton Bay, Queensland's stylish yet relaxed capital wraps itself around the meandering Brisbane River. *See page 71.*

The Best of Queensland: Editor's Choice

Setting priorities, making choices, unique attractions... here are our suggestions, plus some tips and tricks even Queenslanders won't always know

Best Islands

- **The Whitsundays** Charter your own sailing boat, paddle a sea kayak, or join an organised island-hopping tour. *See page 151.*
- **Magnetic** Just over the water from Townsville, but a world away. *See page 161.*
- **Stradbroke** Or rather Stradbrokes: North for relaxed DIY holidays, perhaps taking a tent; and South for the eco-friendly luxury of Couran Cove Resort. *See page 101.*

- **Lizard** The furthest north of a handful of islands that are home to a single exclusive resort. Save up. *See page 198.*
- **Great Keppel** Mostly National Park and unspoilt; there's a holiday village to stay in and white beaches to lounge on. *See page 139.*
- **Thursday** Up at the top of Cape York, this former base for pearl divers is a sleepy outpost with a largely Aboriginal population. *See page 203.*

Best Surfing

- **Surfers Paradise** Not always the best waves but a good place for lessons and plenty of après-surf options. *See page 94.*
- **Burleigh Heads** Seriously good waves; a popular spot among experienced surfers. *See page 97.*
- **Noosa** A surf centre before its gentrifica-

tion and the perfect waves are still there. *See pages 121–2.*
- **Coolangatta** Great spot at the bottom of the Gold Coast, and home of the Superbank. *See pages 98–99.*
- **Moreton Island** Close to Brisbane but not too crowded. *See page 84.*

Above: paddling a sea kayak near Cairns.
Right: surfing at Kings Beach, Caloundra, Sunshine Coast.

BEST KIDS' STUFF

- **Gold Coast** Theme parks, dolphin shows, movie characters and hair-raising rides are sure to entertain the kids and the kids-at-heart. See pages 92–4.
- **Australia Zoo** The zoo made famous by the celebrated Crocodile Hunter, the late Steve Irwin. See page 117.
- **Cairns Lagoon** Lifeguards patrol this serene and safe swimming spot right on the waterfront. See page 176.
- **Lark Quarry** Budding Attenboroughs will be astounded by the tracks left by a dinosaur stampede. See page 223.
- **Streets Beach, South Bank, Brisbane** Building an artificial beach just kilometres away from real beaches may seem misguided, but this inner city oasis works. See page 77.

ABOVE: artificial Streets Beach in South Bank Parklands. **LEFT:** Lone Pine Koala Sanctuary. **BELOW:** the Queensland Gallery of Modern Art, Brisbane.

BEST WILDLIFE AND NATIONAL PARKS

- **Glass House Mountains** Extraordinary volcanic-rock formations in the Sunshine Coast hinterland. See page 115.
- **Whale watching in Hervey Bay** It's awe-inspiring to see your first whale breaching metres away from your boat. See page 125.
- **Platypus at Eungella National Park** Settle beside a river bank just after dawn or before dusk to catch a glimpse of these elusive creatures. See page 149.
- **Lone Pine Koala Sanctuary** More than 130 koalas frolic close to Brisbane. OK, they sleep a lot, but there are other, more active animals, too. See page 84.
- **Hinchinbrook Island** Unspoilt wilderness, sheer granite mountains and empty beaches make this irresistible to walkers. See page 167.
- **Daintree** If the environmental wonder of the rainforest isn't enough, there's also dramatic Cape Tribulation. See page 188.
- **Australian Butterfly Sanctuary** Hundreds of butterflies flutter here, in the hills above Cairns at Kuranda. See page 179.

BEST CULTURAL QUEENSLAND

- **Queensland Art Gallery/Gallery of Modern Art, Brisbane** Outstanding exhibition space and world-leading modern-art gallery gracing the South Bank Parklands. See page 76.
- **Tjapukai Cultural Park, Cairns** Australia's largest cultural park celebrating the history of the Aboriginal people of the rainforest. See page 186.
- **Judith Wright Centre of Contemporary Arts, Brisbane** A platform for cutting-edge performance arts, including dance, music and multimedia. See page 83.
- **QANTAS Founders' Outback Museum, Longreach** Hangars filled with exhibits and a jumbo jet parked outside, in the airline's home town. See page 228.
- **Australian Stockman's Hall of Fame, Longreach** An award-winning museum, also in Longreach, devoted to all things Outback. See page 228.

THE BIG COUNTRY

A vast state as varied and remarkable
as a small country, blessed with natural wonders
and a personality all of its own

Queensland is certainly special. For southern Australians, it has a reputation for producing larger-than-life characters, including archetypal stockmen, world-champion surfers, overexcitable politicians and entrepreneurs of dubious moral fibre. Of course, none of that detracts from Queensland's chief reputation as Australia's pre-eminent holiday destination. It's easy to think of this state as one huge playground because there is just so much on offer.

In Queensland you can discover the Dreamtime of an ancient culture, learn to surf in Surfers Paradise, explore World Heritage rainforests, sail among tropical islands, snorkel over coral gardens or strap on the scuba gear and enter the world of the Great Barrier Reef. Stretching for over 2,000km (1,240 miles) from the tip of Cape York towards the Tropic of Capricorn, the Reef truly is one of the wonders of the natural world and a must-see.

Now size isn't everything, but it is a factor when considering Queensland. Its 1.73 million sq km (667,000 sq miles) would comfortably swallow an assortment of European countries. However, within this vast area there are only 4.6 million people – equivalent to the population of Sydney – and most of those are crowded into the southeast corner. This leaves thousands of kilometres of coast where anyone can find his or her own little piece of paradise – a rare and precious opportunity on a crowded planet.

But if it's bright city lights that beckon, whether you are seeking to discover world-class art galleries, sophisticated eateries, lively nightclubs, thrilling theme parks or indulgent shopping, Queensland also has these well covered.

The flipside to the cityscape is found inland. For many, this is where the real Queensland begins – in the vast Outback. You don't have to go as far west as Birdsville or Mount Isa. And you don't need to navigate the rough, often impassable tracks of Cape York in the Far North to feel the Outback spirit. Just move in from the coast and, within an hour or so, the landscape and light changes. Time slows down, the beer is colder, the stars are brighter and the stories in pubs get more outlandish. ❑

PRECEDING PAGES: aerial view of the Great Barrier Reef; Millaa Millaa Falls, north Queensland.
LEFT: the parched red earth of southwest Queensland.

QUEENSLAND PEOPLE

Before the European invasion, over 100,000 indigenous Australians representing more than 200 tribes occupied the land we call Queensland today. The Europeans had a tough start, and the clash of the two cultures was hardly amicable, but Queenslanders have developed into a relaxed, friendly group with a strong sense of state pride

A Melbourne journalist once observed that Queensland was so different from the rest of Australia that it was always a surprise that you didn't need a visa to go there. The houses on stilts, the tropical vegetation and flowering trees with musical names – frangipani, jacaranda, poinciana, bauhinia – the heat, the vivid light, the vast distances and the people themselves – so much more laid-back, friendly and direct than southerners, made it seem like another country.

In a typical Queensland childhood, a baby will be placed in a hole at the water's edge on the Sunshine Coast or the Gold Coast and sit with the waves pounding beside it. Several holidays a year may be spent playing on these long, wide, white beaches. Surfing the waves, with your body or your board, becomes as natural as breathing. To the Queenslander, the Pacific Ocean is a necessity of life.

In Queensland, there is 1 sq km of space for every 2.7 people – possibly the most space per person anywhere on Earth.

Space is also something that Queenslanders take for granted. In 1901 there were just half a million people in an area of 1,734,189 sq km (670,000 sq miles), two-and-a-half times the size of Texas. More than a century later, there are over four-and-a-half million people

and with around three million living in the greater Brisbane area, that leaves just 1.6 million spread around the cities, rural towns and estates.

Queensland had a rough start. When it was separated from New South Wales in 1859 and became an independent colony, this vast state had a population of only 23,520 (although the indigenous population was not counted!). Brisbane was originally the Moreton Bay penal colony for the toughest of convicts.

Nature could be harsh and threatening. The Queensland Club in Brisbane, an elegant colonial sandstone building, is a bastion of the old established WASP families, yet in the entrance

LEFT: trader at Eumundi Market, Sunshine Coast. **RIGHT:** surfing is a way of life for ocean-loving Queenslanders.

lies a stuffed crocodile – a reminder of the country's primordial nature, a symbol of how different this state is from the milder south.

In the early days, Queensland was a multicultural melting pot. Joining the indigenous Australians and Torres Straits Islanders were English, Irish, Scottish and German settlers, Chinese miners, and South Sea Island "Kanakas", who were indentured to work in sugar-cane fields. All that ended with the White Australia Policy of 1901, which saw deportation of "foreign" workers and a selective immigration programme introduced.

The pioneers, threatened by a harsh, immense bush and often hostile Aboriginal people, had to be resourceful, with a sense of adventure

> *Brisbane is Australia's third-largest city and has long since discarded the moniker of "country town". Visitors to the state capital will discover a cosmopolitan, forward-looking city.*

attitudes to the Aboriginal people and their fellow migrants. There was a time when those in industry and big business down south considered it good training to send talented youth up north for a bit of toughening experience in the tropics.

But although southerners could be patron-

and an independent spirit. This developed into a kind of patriotism. Even as recently as the 1980s, during the State of Origin rugby league matches against New South Wales, whenever they were under the cosh, one of the Queensland team would yell out, "Queenslander! Queenslander!", and immediately they would be galvanised. They won decisively.

Although outstanding Queenslanders have often left the state in search of greater opportunities, they can never forget it. As local writer Hugh Lunn says: "There's no such thing as an ex-Queenslander, only a lapsed Queenslander."

In the south, Queenslanders have often had a reputation for being uncultured, with "redneck"

ising, there was a sense that, with its mineral wealth, size, diversity and its sheer beauty, Queensland was a place of immense potential. In the last 20 years, it has been living up to that sense of promise in unforeseen ways.

A fast-growing state

Queensland has only recently been overtaken by resource-rich Western Australia as the fastest-growing state in Australia. But it shares with Western Australia the blessing of a resources boom economy. People do arrive as a result of immigration, but it is the interstate migrants – here for the greater opportunities, the climate and the relaxed atmosphere – who have changed

Queensland most dramatically. They include a lot of young job seekers, entrepreneurs eager to take advantage of the mining boom, and southern baby-boomers and retirees bringing their life savings north to settle on the coast.

Brisbane has become a city that is full of people from somewhere else, each making a contribution to its vibrant, multifaceted scene. Adjunct Professor Allan Paull, of the School of Mechanical Engineering at the University of Queensland, is researching technology that will help make international travel faster and provide an inexpensive method for launching satellites. He says that while failure means death to projects in some parts of the world, in

the long-term Jo Bjelke-Petersen government; and a new period of Labor rule began. Brisbane started to be seen as a place that was moving ahead and yet getting the balance right: it was neither hidebound by tradition like Melbourne nor street-tough like Sydney.

Despite its rapid growth, Brisbane still offers a slower and less complicated lifestyle than Sydney or Melbourne. In summer, it is normal to see people watering their gardens at sunrise or taking a quiet walk around the streets. Brisbane children are still more carefree than in the southern cities, and are often seen walking barefoot in the streets and parks.

Nature has a powerful presence even in the

Queensland "it is part of the course of learning – the first failure doesn't mean doom".

The capital

In the 1970s, Brisbane was hardly more than a large country town from which every young person with nous or ambition wanted to escape. But then came the 1982 Commonwealth Games and the '88 Expo – a celebration of the bicentenary of the First Fleet, attracting tourism and interest from all over the world. The Fitzgerald Inquiry exposed the corruption of

LEFT: sinking a cool one in a Queensland bar. **ABOVE:** Brisbane children lead a sun-filled life.

middle of the city, where there are thriving mangroves on the river banks, and seagulls, hawks, cormorants and pelicans on and around the river. In bush suburbs only 20 minutes' drive from the city centre, there are poisonous brown snakes. Backyard hens' eggs can be taken by carpet snakes, while the redback spider can live in gardens and under houses in the inner city.

And there is another natural danger. Living in some of the most intense sunlight on Earth, Queenslanders have the world's highest rate of skin cancer. But the fair-skinned are learning. In the south of the state, at least, you no longer see the same number of baked-brown faces.

Brisbane people are less conservative than their

rural cousins, though opportunistic politicians still routinely tap age-old prejudices surrounding immigration and indigenous Australians. Family values are very strong. And although the city has many more fashion designers, including the international duo Easton Pearson, the general community still tends to dress down. Thongs (flip-flops) and shorts remain a common sight.

The regions

Queensland is Australia's most decentralised state. Large communities live on the Gold Coast (the state's second-largest city was formed in 1959 to unite several small centres along the strip), on the Sunshine Coast, and

Hmong from Laos in northern Queensland.

The further north you go, the hotter and more humid it gets and the more extreme the accent. Speech gets slower and each comment invariably ends in "eh". Cape York Peninsula has some of the country's biggest cattle stations, some up to 400,000 hectares (1 million acres) or more.

The west – roughly a three-hour drive in every direction from Longreach, home of QANTAS – has a special spirit. Flat and dry, with huge skies, the landscape can be interpreted as harsh, but the space generally brings a profound sense of freedom and peace. The stars out there seem brighter than anywhere else on Earth.

Families have run farms in the west for

in Rockhampton, Townsville, Mackay, Cairns, Gladstone, Toowoomba and Mount Isa. With huge distances between them and with populations of varying ethnic mixes, these areas have developed their own distinct identities.

The primary farming produce and industries – wheat, tropical and temperate fruit, cattle, cotton, sugar cane, viniculture, wool, bauxite, coal, copper, silver, lead and zinc – have largely depended on the hard work of immigrants from more than 200 nations. Some have congregated to great effect: the Germans on the Darling Downs; Australia's largest population of South Sea Islanders in Mackay; the Italians of Innisfail; the Finns and Yugoslavs of Mount Isa; and the

generations and continue to do so, despite the economic pressures, whereas in other areas of the country the population turnover is much greater. Western Queenslanders are known for their hospitality, humour and trustworthiness.

Queensland's indigenous people

According to the 2006 census, about 146,000 Aborigines and Torres Strait Islanders live in the state. There is no escaping the fact that the Aboriginal people of Queensland have had a tragic existence since white settlement: killed in huge numbers through deliberate shootings and poisonings, and living at the mercy of discriminatory laws and imported diseases, alcohol and drugs.

European historians told of family communities living on the stations of their employers, who valued their skills as stockmen and trackers. But, generally, the relationship was not one of respect, let alone equality. There have been decades of government assistance and many dedicated people working to improve conditions – prominent among them the poet and activist Kath Walker (whose traditional name is Oodgeroo Noonuccal, *see below*) – and although many policies have been misguided, and Aboriginal people still have a shorter life expectancy than that of the white community, there are plenty of inspiring stories that tell of a revitalised people and culture.

Counted among Queensland's indigenous

style. In 2010 it was reported that Queensland's population could rise to seven million by 2042. Brisbane resident Dr Aila Keto, an environmentalist with a global reputation, has devoted her life to preserving Queensland's natural heritage. It is thanks to her and her husband, Keith Scott, that the Wet Tropics of Queensland, Fraser Island and the central-eastern rainforest of Australia are World Heritage-designated. But she says that her joy at seeing so much preserved has been "tinged with a sense of tragedy" at the amount of destruction in the southeast of the state. Meanwhile, the economists and politicians continue to encourage growth and the concrete continues to flow.　　❑

success stories are the world-renowned didgeridoo virtuoso, William Barton, the artist Judy Watson, the Olympic gold medallist Cathy Freeman, the rugby league legend Arthur Beetson, and the actor and television personality Ernie Dingo.

The future

There are fears that overdevelopment and too rapid a rate of population increase could destroy much of the state's great natural beauty and life-

LEFT: flying the flag; a pineapple seller. ABOVE LEFT: Kath Walker, poet and activist, who died in 1993. ABOVE RIGHT: Arthur Beetson, rugby league legend.

NOTABLE QUEENSLANDERS

Out of this state have come the Nobel Prize-winning scientist Peter Doherty, the poets Kath Walker, Judith Wright and Peter Porter, the writer David Malouf, the painters Margaret Olley and William Robinson, the actor Geoffrey Rush, the didgeridoo player William Barton, the band Powderfinger, and many great sports people: cricketers Matthew Hayden and Andrew Symonds, tennis players Rod Laver (the Rockhampton Rocket), Roy Emerson and Pat Rafter, golfer Greg Norman (the Great White Shark), rugby union player Michael Lynagh and captain John Eales, Olympic gold medal runner Cathy Freeman, and rugby league player Wally Lewis (King Wally).

DECISIVE DATES

c.50,000 BC
The first Aborigines arrive overland from present-day New Guinea.

1606
Dutchman Willem Janszoon is the first European to discover Australia when he lands on the west coast of Cape York.

1644
Dutchman Abel Tasman charts the coast from Cape York to Port Hedland.

1770
Lieutenant James Cook explores Australia's east coast, claiming the land for the British Crown.

1788
The First Fleet arrives at Sydney Cove with a cargo of convicts.

1790
Ill-equipped Second Fleet arrives. The colony nearly succumbs to starvation.

1793
Free settlers arrive in the colony.

1797
The first merino sheep are brought to Australia from South Africa.

1799
Matthew Flinders names Red Cliffe Point, the site of Queensland's first European settlement.

1802
Flinders sails through the Whitsunday Passage and charts the inner edge of the Great Barrier Reef.

1823
Surveyor-General John Oxley locates and navigates the mouth of the (now) Brisbane River.

1825
A convict settlement is established on the present site of Brisbane.

1828
The rich pastoral land of the Darling Downs is discovered.

1842
Brisbane is declared open for free settlement.

1844
Ludwig Leichhardt leads an expedition from Brisbane to Port Essington, near to what is now Darwin.

1848
Queensland's first immigrant ship, the *Artemisia*, reaches Moreton Bay. Edmund Kennedy sets out from Tam O'Shanter Point to chart a land route up the Cape York Peninsula.

1859
Statehood comes with the separation from New South Wales and the naming of Queensland.

1860s
Sugar is planted at Redland Bay, providing a ready source of rum.

1861
Burke and Wills perish on their return south from the Gulf of Carpentaria.

1868
Queensland's pearling industry is established in the Torres Strait.

1871
Gold is discovered near Charters Towers, sparking a rush and rapid growth in the area.

1875
Cobb & Co. initiates a coach service linking Brisbane with Nerang Heads.

1876
A party reaches Trinity Bay and the new town of Cairns is proclaimed.

1882
Tea and coffee trees are

planted at Bingil Bay, and sugar cane is cultivated at Gordonvale, south of Cairns.

1885
Legislation is passed to discontinue the "recruiting" of Pacific Islanders for Queensland's tropical agriculture.

1887
Brisbane is connected by rail to Sydney.

1890s
A shearers' strike at Barcaldine is a catalyst for the organisation of labour and a trade union movement.

1891
The Cairns to Kuranda railway line opens.

1901
The six independent colonies are federated into the Commonwealth of Australia.

1914
The first Australian troops leave home to join the Allies in World War I.

1920
Qantas is founded at Longreach.

1928
The Royal Flying Doctor Service (RFDS) is established in Cloncurry by John Flynn.

1933
The Surfers Paradise town-

LEFT: Burke, Wills and companions set out on their ill-fated expedition to the interior in 1860.
RIGHT: Townsville in the early 1970s.

ship is named after James Cavill's hotel of the same name.

1941
Brisbane becomes a base for thousands of American servicemen fighting the Japanese.

1942
Catalina flying boats operating from Cairns attack Japanese positions in the Pacific islands.

1947
Airline owner Reg Ansett boosts tourism to the Whitsundays with his acquisition of Hayman Island.

1962
Queensland Aborigines get the right to vote in Commonwealth elections.

1965
Queensland Aborigines get the right to vote in state elections.

1968
Joh Bjelke-Petersen begins a 19-year reign as state premier, and a ruthless, ultimately corrupt, period of government ensues.

1976
The Great Barrier Reef Marine Park Authority is established.

1982
The 12th Commonwealth Games are held in Brisbane.

1988
Amid Australia's bicentenary celebrations, Brisbane

hosts World Expo '88.

1992
The Australian High Court rejects the *terra nullius* (empty land) concept and rules that native title exists.

2001
Centenary of Australian Federation.

2006
Cyclone Larry devastates the state's northeast coast around Innisfail.

2007
Anna Bligh becomes Queensland's first female premier.

2008
Prime Minister Kevin Rudd apologises to the Stolen Generation.

2011
Queensland is devastated by floods covering over 1 million sq km (386,000 sq miles) and three-quarters of the state are declared a disaster zone.

THE MAKING OF QUEENSLAND

Aborigines lived here for more than 50,000 years before the arrival of James Cook and the colonists who followed in his wake. They paved the way for an energetic population – the intrepid explorers, emancipated convicts and free settlers who carved out a life in Queensland's fertile hinterland

About 15 million years ago, the Australian continent broke away from an ancient land mass known as Gondwanaland and gradually drifted northwards to its present location. Due to periodic ice ages, sea levels were lower than today – so low that anyone reaching New Guinea from eastern Asia could continue the journey to north Queensland on foot. These first eastern Asian migrants, ancestors of Australia's Aborigines, dispersed along the Gulf of Carpentaria, spreading south and west until, with the warming of the planet, the sea rose to isolate them from the rest of the world.

The original inhabitants evolved a nomadic way of life based on hunter gatherer methods and seasonal migration. Tribes traded with one another and also with Torres Strait Islanders. Their life in the harsh landscape of Australia consisted of the men hunting and the women

Human history in Queensland began at least 50,000 years before the arrival of colonising Europeans, with the settling of migrants from eastern Asia – the ancestors of Australia's Aborigines.

fishing and gathering. A good hunter knew intimately the habits of the creatures he stalked, was an expert tracker and understood the seasons

LEFT: an early European impression of an Aboriginal camp. RIGHT: a Dutch crew in the *Duyfken* (Dove) discover the Gulf of Carpentaria.

and the winds. He took only what he needed to feed himself and his people, and hence was able to keep in balance with his supply. Conservation was the Aborigine's way of avoiding starvation; in a country that would cause the death of many white pioneers, the Aborigine was perfectly at home.

The first Europeans

Some historians argue that Portuguese mariners charted the northern coastline of Queensland as early as the 16th century, but that they kept their maps secret lest they fell into the hands of the Spanish. Nonetheless, Dutchman Willem Janszoon, who sailed the *Duyfken* into the Gulf of Carpentaria in 1606, is generally cited as the first European to "discover" Australia.

Another Dutchman, Abel Tasman, visited the Australian coastline twice – in 1642, when he charted parts of Tasmania, and in 1644, when he traced the northern coast from Cape York to Port Hedland. English buccaneer William Dampier sailed to the west Australian coast in 1697 and 1699. However, credit for charting the eastern coastline goes mostly to Lieutenant James Cook, whose 1770 voyage opened the way to colonisation. Initially, however, the new continent was seen by the British government as more useful as a dumping ground for Britain's criminal element *(see box below)*.

The penal years

In 1788 and 1790, fleets of convict ships arrived at Port Jackson, Sydney's great harbour-to-be, and the colony stumbled into life. Poor soil and harsh conditions overrode thoughts of further exploration until 1799, when Governor Hunter dispatched Lieutenant Matthew Flinders in the *Norfolk* to look more closely at the north.

Flinders charted much of Moreton Bay, in southern Queensland, but failed to notice the mouth of the Brisbane River that emptied into it. The honour of "discovering" the Brisbane River fell to three convicts – John Finnegan, Thomas Pamphlet and Richard Parsons – whose boat washed up on Moreton Island in 1823 after

Captain James Cook

James Cook (1728–79), who may have been informed by a Portuguese map, followed the shore from Cape Everard on the Victorian coast to Botany Bay, then northwards to Cooktown and the Torres Strait. The place names he left behind give a clue to his travails – Point Danger and Mount Warning at the southern extreme of Queensland and Cape Tribulation and Weary Bay to the north. Specifically, the names express Cook's dismay at having hit a coral reef, a misfortune that obliged him to beach the *Endeavour* for repairs in the river that now bears its name.

He remained at present-day Cooktown for nearly seven weeks. Having restored the *Endeavour* to seaworthiness,

he continued to Possession Island at the tip of Cape York where, on 22 August 1770, he claimed the east coast for King George III.

His report was positive, but incited no rush to establish a colony. As far as the British government was concerned, the new continent was mainly useful as a repository for felons, whose numbers exceeded the ability of British jails to accommodate them. Of around 1,300 people who left Britain aboard the First Fleet, more than half were convicts. The new arrivals set up camp at Port Jackson on 26 January 1788 – an occasion of dubious celebration to the original inhabitants.

being swept northwards in a gale. With no idea where they were, these marooned ticket-of-leave men paddled to the mainland in a makeshift canoe, and followed the Brisbane River as far as Oxley Creek before retracing their steps to Moreton Bay.

They were a motley crew. Parsons made several attempts on Finnegan's life, then wandered off on his own. The other two ended up on Bribie Island, where they were spotted by surveyor-general John Oxley. He had been sent to locate the site for a northern outpost where fractious convicts might be exiled. Having investigated Port Curtis and found it unsuitable, he called into Moreton Bay on his return journey to

ruled the fledgling colony with a severity bordering on the sadistic, while devoting his leisure hours to the gentlemanly pursuit of exploration. In October 1830, while mapping the headwaters of the Brisbane River, Logan disappeared. After a four-day search, his body was found, face-down, in a shallow grave. Investigators supposed that Aborigines had ambushed Logan. But the captain had made a great number of enemies, and many believed that he had been ambushed and beaten to death by escaped convicts exacting revenge. Either way, Logan's demise was like an epitaph to an era of hardship, merciless discipline and relentless toil, when convicts were whipped to death and prisoners cast lots to slit

Penal station at St Helena, Moreton Bay, Queensland

Sydney. When Finnegan showed him the Brisbane River, Oxley was impressed. So, too, was Governor Brisbane, who, in the following year, despatched Oxley to establish a new penal settlement in Moreton Bay.

Oxley's party comprised Lieutenant Henry Miller, botanist Allan Cunningham, various assistants and family members, plus 14 soldiers and 29 convicts, including Finnegan.

For five years, until his death in 1825, Moreton Bay commandant Captain Patrick Logan

LEFT: Captain Cook taking possession of the Australian continent on behalf of the British Crown. **ABOVE:** penal station at St Helena, Moreton Bay.

one another's throats to escape torment.

Logan's reputation for cruelty eclipsed his work as an explorer. Posterity rarely remembers him for locating the river that bears his name, nor for his significant contribution to the exploration of the Tweed.

The land rush

As the penal years receded into history, free settlers would reap the benefit from the sweat and misery of the lash-scarred wretches who cleared the bush, established farms and erected public buildings. Nonetheless, Brisbane's progress was slow compared with that of the rural areas around it.

Surveyor-general Allan Cunningham's discovery of a pass to the Darling Downs in 1828 encouraged pastoralists to push north, a land rush spearheaded by brothers Patrick and George Leslie, who drove 5,000 sheep from New England. By the late 1840s, more than 45 stations were established on the Downs, with only slightly fewer on the eastern side of the Great Dividing Range. The first sheep farmers were "squatters", illegally occupying Crown grazing land. But by the late 1840s, the authorities recognised their economic worth for the colony, and issued them leases for their sheep runs. Soon, squatters outnumbered Brisbane's meagre population of 540 people, and many became wealthy landowners.

military explorers named rivers and mountains after government luminaries who might forward their careers, Leichhardt honoured benefactors who had given practical help. The Burdekin River was named after a woman who helped to outfit his expedition; Charley's Creek, near Chinchilla, immortalised his tracker; and Kent's Lagoon celebrated the quartermaster who supplied him with chocolate.

The expedition was fraught with setbacks. Hostile Aborigines killed one of his party and badly injured two others, while packhorses drowned, forcing him to jettison scientific experiments. Yet he won through – 14 months after their departure and long after being given

Leichhardt's great expeditions

As gentlemen graziers carved out dynasties on the Downs, they wondered whether greener pastures lay beyond. In 1844, a Prussian adventurer, Ludwig Leichhardt, set out from Moreton Bay to find out. Unlike many early explorers, Leichhardt was not a career soldier. He viewed exploration as a spiritual quest, and his journeys were financed not by the government, but by land-hungry squatters.

Once he had found sufficient backers, he gathered an expedition team of 10 companions, Aboriginal guides and a bullock herd, and set off on a 5,000km (3,000-mile) trek from Brisbane to Port Essington in the Northern Territory. Where

up for dead, Leichhardt and his party staggered into Port Essington. Returning by sea to Sydney, these "men from the grave" were fêted as national heroes.

Generous government grants and public subscriptions encouraged Leichhardt to explore further. In 1847, his next expedition, which he said would take him "through the interior of Australia to the Swan River on the west coast", foundered after seven months. His bid to cross central Australia to the west in the following year fared worse. The party of six whites and two Aborigines left Mount Abundance in April 1848, never to be seen again. By that time, Aboriginal attitudes to white intruders had hardened. Even outlying tribes knew that white men herding livestock (as Leichhardt's party did) intended to seize rivers and hunting lands for themselves. A form of guerrilla warfare prevailed. Squatters drove off Aborigines by fair means or foul, and, when Aborigines

> Ironically, Leichhardt's lost expedition succeeded in opening up vast tracts of Queensland. Rescuers searching vainly for the explorer returned with glowing reports of the terrain that had swallowed him up.

retaliated, native policemen from other tribal areas exacted retribution, massacring entire communities.

It may be that Aborigines mistook Leichhardt, his men and livestock for settlers come to steal their land. It may also be that Leichhardt inadvertently stumbled on to sacred ground – and paid the ultimate price.

So dramatic were Leichhardt's journeys that the expedition of his rival, Sir Thomas Mitchell, to find a route from Sydney to the Gulf of Carpentaria paled almost to insignificance, and as Leichhardt pressed on into Port Essington at the triumphant conclusion of his journey, Mitchell turned back. He gave up too soon. He had located pastoral land in interior and southern Queensland, but stopped tantalisingly short of valuable grazing country that Leichhardt's route had bypassed.

Kennedy's expedition

Edmund Kennedy, who had been Mitchell's deputy on the Queensland expedition, attempted to consolidate the work of Leichhardt and Mitchell by sailing to Rockingham Bay on Cape York's eastern seaboard, then overlanding to meet supply ships at Princess Charlotte Bay and Port Albany. Tragically for Kennedy, the marine surveyors who recommended Rockingham Bay had made their assessment from the deck of a ship. What they took to be gently wooded hills were, in fact, impenetrable tropical jungles.

Landing in May 1848, Kennedy found steep mountains blocking the way north and mangroves blocking the way west. He had to lead 12 men, 27 horses, 11 sheep, three carts and a ton of flour through trackless rainforest. Six months later, having survived skirmishes with Aborigines and trudged through the rough terrain, the exhausted explorers reached Weymouth Bay, where eight of the men, too sick to travel, stayed behind with a supply of provisions. The expedition was further depleted near Shelbourne Bay, when one man could go no further, and the party's blacksmith accidentally shot himself in the chest. Kennedy left a third man to care for them until help arrived,

and pressed on with his Aborigine guide, Jacky Jacky, for Port Albany.

After hacking through scrub for a month, they sighted their destination just 30km (19 miles) away. It was here, in a swamp by the Escape River, that Aborigines who had been tracking them moved in for the kill. Kennedy was killed but Jacky escaped with a head wound. He struggled through the jungle to the Cape and informed the waiting schooner of the whereabouts of the other survivors who were stranded on the coast. Of the eight men at Weymouth Bay, two survived. The three at Shelbourne Bay were never seen again. Jacky Jacky enjoyed a brief glow of celebrity but died

LEFT: the start of the Leichhardt search expedition.
RIGHT: explorer Edmund Kennedy is killed by Aborigines.

six years later after falling into a camp fire. Kennedy's remains were never found.

Burke and Wills

In August 1860, Robert O'Hara Burke embarked on a hugely ambitious expedition – his intention was to lead the first party to cross the continent from coast to coast, south to north. The explorers were given a ceremonious send-off by gold-rich Melbourne burghers who felt it their patriotic duty to lift the mantle of mystery shrouding the Australian interior. However, the pomp of departure soon turned to dust. Morale plummeted in the eight weeks that it took to reach Menindie. When deputy

leader William Landells dropped out, Burke appointed 26-year-old surveyor William Wills as his second-in-command.

Burke left some of his party at Menindie while he forged ahead. In theory, the Menindie group would bring the stores to Cooper Creek, but after five weeks nothing had arrived, and Burke lost patience. Leaving William Brahe and three others at the Cooper, he set out for the Gulf with Wills, John King and Charlie Gray. The monsoons hit in January. Burke's camels slithered into the quagmire, until, on 17 February, Burke and Wills left King and Gray at their last camp and sloshed through mud until they reached the Gulf of Carpentaria.

On the return journey, Gray died of exhaustion. In April, the three emaciated survivors, Burke, Wills and King, staggered into the base camp on the Cooper, where they found the warm ashes of a fire and the words "Dig.3ft.N.W.April.21, 1861". Wills and King unearthed meat, rice, flour, sugar and a letter from depot leader William Brahe, who said that, since no one had arrived with supplies, he was turning back. Brahe had waited four months – a month longer than his orders. He had left just seven hours before Burke, Wills and King returned. Burke and Wills died of starvation. Only King, cared for by Aborigines, survived to tell the story.

An independent Queensland

The first half of the 19th century saw a change in European settlement in Australia. The transportation of convicts was phased out, and by 1860, the continent had been divided into seven colonies, one of which was Queensland. At that time the European population numbered only 23,520, and no industry had yet been established, although gold had been discovered in 1858.

Labour shortages continued, despite the conscientious efforts of Henry Jordan, the colony's immigration agent in London, who, by 1865, had enticed 50,000 British workers to try their luck in Queensland. At about the same time, cotton grower Captain Robert Towns embarked on a scheme to recruit indentured Kanakas from the Pacific Islands to do the work that white men could not or would not do.

Kanakas provided muscle for sugar plantations along the tropical seaboard, particularly in Maryborough, Mackay, Bundaberg and Innisfail, where they died in alarming numbers. The system trod a fine line between indenture and slavery. The Kanaka system thrived for another decade until 1904, when the new Federal Government prohibited entry of Kanakas to Australia, and initiated a programme of repatriation.

The Queensland gold rushes

Queensland's progress to this point had been characterised by reckless optimism, alarming setbacks and lucky breaks, exemplified by the 1866 bank crash that caused funds for railway projects and public buildings to dry up. Workers went unpaid, and riots erupted in the streets. Only a miracle could save Queensland. It came in the form of a gold strike near Gympie, where, in 1867, prospector James Nash made a major find, sparking a rush that would last for five decades. Finds were reported at Cape River, inland from Bowen; at Ravenswood, 130km (81 miles) southwest of Townsville; and, in 1871, at the Charters Towers goldfield, which at one point attracted a population of 27,000.

More gold was found the following year in the Palmer River, southwest of Cooktown, sparking another major gold rush that attracted large numbers of Chinese immigrants. By 1876, Chinese miners outnumbered European ones, who expressed their displeasure by burning down Chinese dwellings. The government

Towards the end of the century, the increase in population, the advance of social legislation in Europe and the depression of the 1890s encouraged the growth of trade unionism and led to the emergence of a Labor Party with well-defined policies. In 1891, the Shearers' Union organised a seven-month strike in Queensland after the ranch-owners began to employ non-union labour at lower wages. The strike was finally broken, but subsequent legislation provided shorter working hours and improved working conditions. In December 1899, Queensland had for six days the first Labour government in the world (though a minority one).

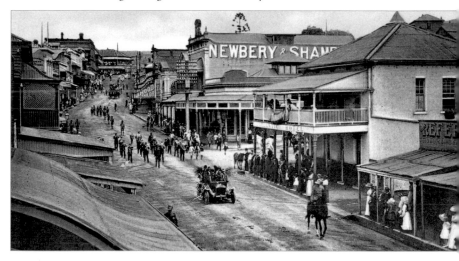

eventually legislated against the Chinese, banning them from new goldfields for the first three years.

Station hands sinking postholes at Croydon, in the Gulf of Carpentaria, made discoveries that sparked the last of the big Queensland gold rushes. Despite its isolation, Croydon at its zenith had 36 hotels catering to a population of 7,000. The get-rich-quick gold-mining era was dwindling by the 1890s, but mineral wealth remained important to the economy.

LEFT: the exploring party of Burke and Wills comes upon an Aboriginal encampment. **ABOVE:** residents attending a parade in Upper Mary Street, Gympie.

Federation and war in Europe
In September 1900, Queen Victoria regally proclaimed that, on 1 January 1901, a new nation would be born – the Commonwealth of Australia, which included the state of Queensland. The 1901 census recorded 498,129 inhabitants in the state, excluding Aborigines. Brisbane was proclaimed a city in 1902.

When Britain declared war on Germany in August 1914, Australia, as a member of the British Empire, was automatically at war, too. Of the 330,000 troops despatched to Europe to fight, 226,000 were casualties, a greater percentage by far than had been suffered by any other country among the Allies.

In 1923, vast silver-lead-zinc deposits were found at Mount Isa, but the Depression of the late 1920s and early 1930s was hard on Queensland. In 1929, amid rising unemployment, falling incomes and social distress, the Labor government was ousted by the Country Party.

During its five-year tenure, the Country Party was unable to stem the tide of the Depression, and was replaced in 1934 by the Labor Party, which attempted to stimulate the economy through large capital improvement projects, including the Story Bridge, the Stanley River Bridge and the construction of the University of Queensland at St Lucia. By now, the worst of the Depression was over, and many social services, suspended during the bad economic times, were reinstated.

War and peace

When Britain went to war against Germany in September 1939, Australia once more automatically entered the conflict. Of the one million Australian servicemen and -women who had enlisted, almost 10,000 died in Europe and more than 17,000 in the Pacific. Of those taken prisoner by the Japanese, 8,000 did not survive the terrible privations and humiliations to which they were subjected. Meanwhile, in Queensland, a free hospital service was introduced in 1946, and the government began large-scale irrigation projects, which included the Burdekin and Tully hydroelectric scheme.

The 1950s also saw the rapid development of the coastal strip south of Brisbane. Originally a secluded holiday destination for the Brisbane middle classes, its property values soared in the post-war period, leading one journalist to dub the area the "Gold Coast". There was a rush to build large beach-front holiday apartments and hotels, to support the rapidly growing tourist market. In 1958, the South Coast Town Council was renamed "Gold Coast Town Council": it now administers Australia's sixth-largest city. By the 1960s, the beach front was almost completely developed, and the urbanisation of the surrounding farms and wetlands began.

Modern politics

The long tradition of Labor politics in Queensland fell apart in the mid-1950s, with fiercely conflicting views on the influence of communism in the Labor Party and the trade unions. After 25 years in power, the party split into competing factions, and promptly lost the next election, ushering in 32 years of rule by the National Party.

For two decades, politics in Queensland was dominated by one man, Sir Joh Bjelke-Petersen. The eccentric, despotic and sometimes naive reign of this fundamentalist farmer has left an indelible imprint on the state – as much for his ruthless silencing of dissent as for his unsentimental approach to development. Yet Sir Joh accomplished much. The 1982 Commonwealth Games and the building of the Cultural Complex at South Bank were achieved under his government. World Expo '88 – arguably the

THE BRISBANE LINE

On 19 February 1942, after Japanese planes bombed Darwin, the Allies expected a full-blown land invasion, starting in north Queensland. The Japanese dropped bombs in the Torres Strait, Townsville and Mossman, and the area north of Rockhampton was designated a war zone. American troops arrived to defend the "Brisbane Line" against the anticipated Japanese invasion. As it turned out, the only conflict was between the American and Australian servicemen, due to friction over supplies and amenities. The "Battle of Brisbane" was fought on 26 November 1942. It escalated into an ugly riot, in which one Australian was shot and 14 others wounded.

event that elevated Brisbane from country town to cosmopolitan city – was another of his initiatives. But although he built up Queensland into an economic power, he also demonstrated arrant chauvinism, hostility to social and environmental concerns, and disregard for alleged police corruption. His era ended badly, amid accusations of bribery and corruption. The Fitzgerald Inquiry, which was set up to investigate police corruption, also uncovered corruption linked to senior government members. Even when he was deposed by his own National Party in 1987, he at first refused to vacate the premiership. He finally yielded to reality, relinquishing both the premiership and the parliamentary seat

Goss, a solicitor, enacted many of the reforms recommended by the Fitzgerald Inquiry under Bjelke-Petersen. He won a second term but lost Green Party support in 1995 over a government plan to destroy koala habitat for road widening. A re-count in the Townsville seat of Mundingburra, in the narrowly contested election, led to a hung parliament. When the Gladstone-based Independent Liz Cunningham gave her support to the Rob Borbidge-led National-Liberal Coalition, Goss resigned as premier.

The lacklustre Borbidge government lost office in 1998, and Labor's Peter Beattie began his reign as premier. Like others in the rough and tumble of Queensland politics, Beattie has

he had held for 41 years. His 1991 trial for perjury ended with a hung jury.

Bjelke-Petersen's successor, Mike Ahern, adopted a moderate approach that displeased Nationals accustomed to Sir Joh's bulldozer tactics. In September 1989, Ahern was toppled as leader by hardliner Russell Cooper, a cattle breeder who remained premier for just six weeks. His defeat at the hands of Labor leader Wayne Goss in the 1989 state election ended 32 years of continuous National Party rule in Queensland.

had to weather scandal. In 2000, a number of prominent Labor Party figures were implicated in electoral fraud, but Beattie was perceived as having handled the crisis fearlessly and with honesty – emerging victorious in the 2001 and 2004 elections. He went on to weather more political storms and win another election in 2006, before announcing his retirement in September 2007.

Beattie was replaced by his deputy, Anna Bligh. When her government was re-elected in 2009 she became the first popularly elected female premier. Her focused and unstoppable performance during the devastating 2011 floods saw a positive turnaround in her popularity stakes. ❑

LEFT: Australian plane destroyed during the Japanese raid of Brisbane. **ABOVE:** Surfers Paradise in the 1960s, a boom time for Queensland.

ABORIGINAL AUSTRALIA

Despite two centuries of cultural attrition, the Aboriginal people have retained a strong sense of identity and a fierce pride in their heritage. The land is a crucial part of their being, and the fight for 'land rights' goes on

When James Cook took possession of the eastern coast of Australia in the name of King George III on 22 August 1770, he created a minefield of perplexing landownership issues. According to 18th-century law, the ways to gain legal sovereignty over new lands were by conquest, by the indigenous populace ceding sovereignty, or by declaring the land *terra nullius*. The first two options carried an obligation to negotiate just reparations for the alienated occupants of the lands. The third option was based on the notion that the territory lacked human habitation and could therefore be obtained for free.

The British government went for the last option. The first settlers to arrive on Australia's remote shores could not understand the Aboriginal people's nomadic lifestyle or their profound connection to their tribal lands. It seemed that they came and went without rea

When the first settlers arrived in Australia, the number of indigenous people was estimated at 300,000. By 1888, the Aboriginal population had been reduced to around 80,000.

son across the sparse landscape. Ignoring the presence of an estimated 300,000 indigenous people who had been pursuing their culture for

more than 50,000 years, the British government conveniently declared Terra Australis to be a *terra nullius* – an uninhabited void that could be occupied without further thought. The results were devastating for Aboriginal culture.

The colonial curse

When the First Fleet arrived, no war was declared. White settlers simply occupied land and Aboriginal resistance was met with savage reprisals. Those living in the vicinity of Port Jackson were the first to lose their territory. As white settlement expanded, so began the cycle of attack and reprisal. Previously unknown European diseases brought death and misery,

PRECEDING PAGES: dirt road in the Queensland Outback. **LEFT:** Torres Strait Islander in traditional dress. **RIGHT:** an early European depiction of an Aboriginal camp.

while survivors were reduced to living in abject squalor around the periphery of white settlements. An ugly war of attrition prevailed, and massacres were exacted upon people who often had taken no part in any transgressions.

As the spread of settlement increased, Aboriginal people ejected from their tribal lands were forced into territory belonging to their neighbours – adding internal conflict to an already difficult situation. Either way, spears stood no chance against bullets, and, sadly, some of the worst atrocities were carried out by native police trained by the settlers in the use of carbines. Last of the tribes to succumb were the Kalkadoons, whose territory once encompassed

consideration, but, for the most part, graziers paid Aboriginal people subsistence wages and denied them basic human rights.

By 1888, Australia's Aboriginal population had been reduced to around 80,000 – but, to the disappointment of white supremacists, it showed no sign of dying out completely. The Queensland government embarked on a policy to isolate and "protect" the surviving Aboriginal people from white society – a strategy designed to keep the Aboriginal "problem" hidden.

Nonetheless, in the late 1890s, it became apparent that ruthless whites were preying on indigenous women, exploiting their children, paying subsistence wages to their men.

the land on which the mining city of Mount Isa now stands. The Kalkadoons engaged native police and squatters in wily guerrilla warfare for more than a decade, striking unexpectedly then melting into the hills. Lured into open conflict at Battle Mount, north of Cloncurry, in 1884, they were finally mown down by native police.

Australia's apartheid

Survivors of this colonial holocaust lived as refugees – marginalised in wretched shanties on the outskirts of white settlements or occupying squalid *humpies* (temporary shelters) on pastoral properties. Some graziers treated Aboriginal stockmen and servants with kindness and

The government reacted by passing the Aboriginal Protection and Restriction of the Sale of Opium Act 1897, which made the majority of Aboriginal people wards of the state. People were relocated from their traditional lands to government reserves and church missions, and families dispersed to different reserves. Few freedoms applied. Permits were required in order to work outside the reserves; income was managed by the state; and Aboriginal people wishing to marry required permission from the chief protector.

Dissent

There is a perception that Aboriginal dissent did not surface until the 1960s and 1970s. In fact, an

Aboriginal-rights association existed in Sydney as early as 1924. Indeed, the Melbourne-based Australian Aborigines Advancement League petitioned King George V for special indigenous electorates in 1932. If white Australians believed (as many did) that Aboriginal people owed them a debt of gratitude for having brought civilisation to *terra nullius*, they were disabused by the Aboriginal Progressive Association manifesto of 1938. Issued on the 150th anniversary of the landing of the First Fleet in Botany Bay, this document declared 26 January a "day of mourning" – a theme that would be repeated over ensuing decades. "You took our land away from us by force," the manifesto said continuing: "You have almost exterminated our people, but there are enough of us remaining to expose the humbug of your claim as white Australians to be a civilised, progressive, kindly and humane nation. By your cruelty and callousness towards the Aborigines you stand condemned in the eyes of the civilised world."

World War II brought white Australians and Aboriginal people into closer communion, particularly within the armed forces. At the same time, better communications made it harder to get away with abuses in remote areas. By the 1940s, various lobby groups were championing Aboriginal political rights, and in 1949 the Chifley government passed an Act confirming that those who could vote in their states could vote for the Commonwealth. Interestingly, Aboriginal people in all states except Queensland and Western Australia had been entitled to vote in state elections from the 1850s. They didn't vote because no one told them their rights. (Queensland accorded state voting rights to Aboriginal people in 1965 – the last Australian state to do so.)

The Stolen Generation

If Aboriginal people were hazy about their rights, so, too, were the police and welfare officers who forcibly removed up to 100,000 children from their parents between 1910 and 1970. The idea was to "assimilate" mixed-blood Aboriginal children into European society over one or two generations. They were fostered into white homes and forbidden to speak their own language. Most were given menial jobs, many suffered abuse, and nearly all experienced psychological damage. They became known as the Stolen Generation.

Aboriginal activists

The 1967 referendum, in which 90 percent of Australians voted to allow the Commonwealth to make laws for Aboriginal people, marked the turning point in attitudes to Aboriginal rights. The previous year, Aboriginal stockmen at Wave Hill Station, 600km (375 miles) southwest of Katharine, staged a historic "walk-off", sparking

DREAMTIME

Dreamtime is the basis for all traditional Aboriginal thought and practice, informing their cultural and ancestral heritage. Dreamtime was the dawn of all creation, when the land, the rivers, the rain, the wind and all living things were generated. The individual exists within an eternal dreaming, only attaining physical embodiment through a mother and briefly existing on Earth before returning to the Dreamtime. The place of birth is the key in relating an individual to a specific region or clan. Tribal elders maintain a clan's identity through totems. Each clan forms a bond with a specific totem, usually an animal or plant that is seen as a protector.

LEFT: Aboriginal servicemen, 1943. RIGHT: still from the 2002 feature film *Rabbit-Proof Fence*, a moving testimony to the suffering of the Stolen Generation.

the land-rights movement. Previous Aboriginal protests had been easily crushed, but the Gurindji people stood firm for nine years, expanding their cause from a plea for fair treatment to a demand for the return of traditional lands.

Having "walked off", the tribe set up camp at Wattie Creek, naming the new settlement Daguragu, and pursued a campaign that would lead to the Commonwealth Land Rights Act (Northern Territory) 1976. The build-up to all of this was characterised by 1960s radicalism. Inspired by the US civil-rights movement, Aboriginal activist Charles Perkins led a series of "freedom rides" through Outback Queensland and northwest New South Wales, bringing his

mining company Nabalco had established a bauxite project. In support of their claim, activists set up a "tent embassy" outside Parliament House, demanding legal title of mining rights on existing reserve lands, preservation of sacred sites and A\$6 billion compensation. The judge ruled against the Yirrkala people in the subsequent court action, but their bold stand signalled new confidence among Aboriginal activists.

Towards self-determination

This new-found political consciousness forced the Federal Australian Government to come up with a new policy, "self-determination". This allowed Aboriginal people to make decisions

message to the most remote communities. At a time when feelings were running high over apartheid in South Africa and racial discrimination in the American Deep South, Perkins visited Australian towns where Aboriginal people were banned from pubs, RSL (Returned and Services League) veterans' clubs and community pools. By highlighting Australian discrimination, Perkins did much to eliminate it.

Later that year, Aboriginal poet Kath Walker (aka Oodgeroo Noonuccal) toured the country speaking in favour of land rights. In 1971, the Yirrkala people on the Gove Peninsula, in the Northern Territory, mounted a land claim to win back control of traditional land where the

affecting their own future, retain their cultural identity and values, and achieve greater economic and social equality.

The Department of Aboriginal Affairs was established in 1972, followed by the Aboriginal Development Commission (ADC) in 1980. The concept was to develop programmes that would bring economic independence to Aboriginal people by fostering the development of business enterprises – but it didn't happen overnight. Since the 1970s, Aboriginal people have become involved in the development of government policies that affect them, and in the delivery of services. More importantly, a wide range of organisations, from medical and legal services to Land Councils (which govern the affairs of different regions), have been established; there are now more than 2,500 Aboriginal community organisations.

In 1988, while the rest of Australia celebrated 200 years of white settlement at the Bicentennial, Aboriginal activists staged peaceful protest marches. The international media carried their

> *The land is a crucial part of the Aboriginal being, and the responsibility for protecting significant sites is central to their spiritual life.*

message around the world, and white Australians were forced to admit that Aboriginals had very little to celebrate. The events of 1988 pushed Aboriginal issues to the forefront of the political agenda.

Land rights

For all Aboriginal groups, "land rights" have always been the top priority. It has been a source of profound distress that they have been pushed from their traditional homes, and seen sacred sites mined, built on, flooded or otherwise destroyed. The Northern Territory Land Rights Act, passed in 1975, allowed Aboriginal people to make claims to vast swaths of the Outback on the basis of traditional ownership. The Act also gave them significant control over mining and other activities. Royalties from mining operations were distributed to Aboriginal groups throughout the territory.

Land-rights Acts have been passed in various states, and in 1985, the Federal Government attempted to introduce national land-rights legislation. There was strong opposition – particularly in Queensland and Western Australia, where mining lobbies are powerful – and Canberra backed down, agreeing that a state-by-state approach was more appropriate.

Perhaps the most symbolic change occurred in 1992, when the High Court of Australia overturned the legal fiction of *terra nullius* – the assumption that people previously living in

the region had been too primitive to qualify as human beings. The judges agreed that "native title" had always existed for land that had been continuously occupied by Aboriginal people. Where a traditional connection to land and waters had been maintained and where government Acts had not removed it, the law recognised this as native title.

In 1993, the government set up a Native Title Tribunal to regulate claims. As time went on, however, it appeared that the tribunal would achieve little in practice: since 19th-century missionaries had moved indigenous peoples around, often splitting up clans and lumping them together again in remote areas, few Aboriginal

groups could prove continuous occupation of their lands. In 1998, however, the Western Yalanji people of north Queensland were formally recognised as the native titleholders of a pastoral property called Karma Waters, although their rights are limited because of the government's pastoral lease and other actions in the past.

In 2008, Prime Minister Kevin Rudd issued a formal apology to the Stolen Generation on behalf of the Government of Australia. It was a significant admission of past wrongs. Meanwhile, land rights remains a sticking point for reconciliation, and the social problems facing Aboriginal communities, both remote and urban, continue to defy simple solutions. ❑

LEFT: "Freedom Ride" bus tour led by Charles Perkins.
RIGHT: a wake-up call for white Australia.

CULTURAL QUEENSLAND

Queensland has a rich cultural heritage and a vibrant contemporary arts scene. From ancient rock art to eclectic street art, and from the bustling capital to the sleepy regional centres, there is always a performance or exhibition revealing this state's energy and identity

Concerts, festivals and celebrations punctuate the Queensland events calendar, and galleries and theatres along the coast and far inland host the state's artistic talent. Not surprisingly, the vibrant capital is the focal point for many of these cultural activities.

The Queensland Performing Arts Complex, at South Bank in Brisbane, regularly features performers of international renown, and blockbuster exhibitions are the norm rather than the exception at the Queensland Art Gallery. The city is home to a fine symphony orchestra, an accomplished ballet company, professional opera and theatre companies, as well as an active art and literary scene.

To complement – and to some extent challenge – mainstream cultural events, the city has nurtured alternative venues devoted to cutting-edge performances and exhibitions, notably the Brisbane Powerhouse and the Judith Wright Centre of Contemporary Arts. Queensland, particularly Brisbane, also demonstrates a knack for producing internationally successful actors and musicians. Diane Cilento, Bille Brown, Geoffrey Rush and Mount Isa-born Deborah Mailman have all achieved prominence. Home-grown musicians include Kate Miller-Heidke, Christine Anu, Pete Murray, Emma Louise, Savage Garden, Powderfinger, george, The Go Betweens and The Saints.

The desert blooms

Queensland was somewhat unfairly perceived as a cultural desert from the 1950s to the 1970s, but its cultural scene has blossomed visibly over recent decades. It would be an exaggeration to portray mainstream Queenslanders as voracious culture vultures. Thanks to a sunny outdoor lifestyle and the hero worship accorded to sporting stars, the arts play second fiddle to sport. Nonetheless, Brisbane has a lot to offer, a change largely brought about by Expo '88, coupled with clever programming on the part of former Queensland Performing Arts Complex director Tony Gould and former Queensland Art Gallery supremo Doug Hall.

Gould successfully enticed people out of their homes and into the QPAC for sell-out seasons of musicals, plays, ballets, operas and concerts. Hall, for his part, lent entrepreneurial zest to the QAG, attracting massive crowds to blockbuster exhibitions. In a sense, the gallery's 1982 opening symbolised a watershed for the arts. Until then, the state gallery had been without a permanent base since its beginnings in 1895. Today, QAG not only has its own impressive headquarters but also a sister gallery, the Queensland Gallery of Modern Art, exhibiting 20th- and 21st-century art and often outshining its sibling, and many other Australian galleries, by attracting notable and provocative international shows.

There are also many significant regional galleries around the state, notably Artspace Mackay, the Bundaberg Arts Centre, the regional galleries of Cairns, Caloundra, Gladstone and Rock-

artists, continued to work in his Glasshouse Mountains studio until 2010.

Cairns-based Ray Crooke, winner in 1969 of the Archibald Prize, Australia's oldest and most prestigious visual-arts award, produces paintings in the style of Gauguin that are much sought-after. His works are in major collections, including the National Gallery of Australia and the Vatican Collection in Rome. Fellow Archibald Prize winners include William Robinson (1987 and 1995) and Davida Allen (1986), known for her images of female sexuality; while William Robinson has also been awarded the Wynne Prize for landscape painting (1990 and 1996).

hampton, and the Perc Tucker Regional Gallery and the Umbrella Studio of Contemporary Arts in Townsville.

Queensland painters

In the 1950s and 1960s, Brisbane nurtured an important school of painters, including such acclaimed artists as Lawrence Daws, Margaret Olley, Charles Blackman, Andrew Sibley and Jon Molvig. A number of these pioneers have died or moved on, but the brilliant Daws, one of the state's most revered and recognisable

Aboriginal artist Rosella Namok, whose work has been featured in more than 30 national and international exhibitions, maintains her close association with the Lockhart River Art Gang, which generates some of the most exciting Aboriginal paintings in Australia.

Regional arts

Inevitably, the primary cultural focus falls on Brisbane, but with more than 35 percent of the state's 4.6 million population living in regional, rural and remote centres, touring has become an essential aspect of taxpayer-funded arts organisations. Part of the Queensland Ballet's annual funding is spent on touring the company's 26

LEFT: Brisbane-born singer Kate Miller-Heidke in concert.
ABOVE: Queensland Gallery of Modern Art, Brisbane.

dancers around Queensland – Cairns, Townsville, Mackay and Maryborough. Every other year, the company tours smaller Outback centres – Chinchilla, Roma, Stanthorpe, Milmerran, Emerald and even further afield.

As well as delivering four to six major productions and concerts in Brisbane annually, Opera Queensland takes productions to regional centres around the state in alternate years. In addition it pursues a state-wide programme of about 60 community concert tours extending deep into far north Queensland and spilling south into northern New South Wales.

Similarly, the Queensland Theatre Company's play-reading tours cover vast tracts of

southeast Queensland, with performance artists travelling as far afield as Weipa and Cairns to mentor local productions.

The biennial Queensland Music Festival is an inclusive, state-wide celebration, which is held in over 33 regional locations, from the Gold Coast to Winton and even Thursday Island. No wonder it claims to be the largest musical festival in the world.

At the same time, regional centres have established their own events. Townsville's annual Australian Festival of Chamber Music, for example, presents nine days of concerts by distinguished soloists and chamber musicians from around the world.

Alternative venues

In Brisbane, it is entertaining to compare the delightfully old-fashioned Brisbane Arts Theatre (210 Petrie Terrace) with the stylishly grungy Brisbane Powerhouse (119 Lamington Street, New Farm) and the lively Judith Wright Centre of Contemporary Arts (420 Brunswick Street, Fortitude Valley).

BAT, as the community Arts Theatre is popularly known, has been churning out amateur drawing-room comedies, Agatha Christie-style mysteries, musical comedies, children's plays and pantomimes in a crowd-pleasing manner since 1936. It's light years away from the Powerhouse, which operates within a formerly derelict building where graffiti and industrial machinery lend an edge to performance spaces mainly dedicated to the avant-garde. The Brisbane Pride Festival is orchestrated here each June, and a range of events, from alternative drama to children's workshops, take place throughout the year.

Literature

As for literature, the Brisbane Writers Festival (www.brisbanewritersfestival.com.au), held annually in September, features prominent writers in five days of panel sessions, performances, book launches, discussions and interviews. The festival brings renowned international authors to a city with a long literary pedigree.

Within Toowong Cemetery, in Brisbane's inner west, a visitor may like to track down the red-granite headstone that marks the final resting place of Arthur Hoey Davis, aka Steele Rudd, creator of the immortal rural characters Dad and Dave (look for his grave in portion 29a, off Fourth Avenue). Davis died on 11 October 1935. His best-known book, *On Our Selection*, sold more than 250,000 copies, and all 21 of his titles were reprinted a total of 239 times. In his time he matched the popularity of Henry Lawson (1867–1922), who wrote about life in the Australian bush, and Andrew Barton (Banjo) Paterson (1864–1941), renowned for penning the poem, *The Man from Snowy River*, as well as Australia's unofficial national anthem, *Waltzing Matilda*.

If anything, the absence of cultural celebration in early Brisbane appears to have inspired its writers to fresh heights. Certainly, it stimulated David Malouf's well-known quotation about the city in which he was born in 1934 in his acclaimed novel, *Johnno*: "Brisbane is so sleepy, so slatternly, so sprawlingly unlovely! I have taken to wandering about after school looking for one simple object in it that might be romantic, or appalling even, but there is nothing. It is simply the most ordinary place in the world." Such is the confidence of modern Brisbane that these words have been enshrined on a pavement plaque in the inner city, as if to demonstrate how much things have changed since the 1940s.

To pursue Brisbane's literary legacy further, it is worth obtaining a copy of *Words to Walk By: Exploring Literary Brisbane*, by Todd Barr and Rodney Sullivan. It includes a literary map of the landmarks that provided backdrops for stories by local authors such as Hugh Lunn, Matthew Condon, John Birmingham, Nancy Cato, Nick Earls, Bruce Dawe and Andrew McGahan. Lunn is Brisbane's best-known author, most famous for his tales of growing up in Queensland, while Condon has produced a tapestry of personal reflections and local history in *Brisbane*.

Outside the principal conurbations, literature can take on quite a different hue. An evening of bush poetry in an Outback pub may not satisfy literary purists, but it can tell you as much about life as it's lived in Queensland as any of the garlanded writers competing for space in the bookshops.

Music

Musically, Brisbane is something of a smorgasbord, where live rock bands feature in pubs, string quartets and jazz groups play intimate venues, and indigenous music may be heard on a street corner or in a concert hall. The Queensland Orchestra delivers a programme of more than 70 concerts annually, from classics, new commissions and baroque recitals through to cinema favourites.

Brisbane also has a thriving jazz scene, partly centred around the Brisbane Jazz Club at Kangaroo Point, partly in Fortitude Valley bars such as Ric's, The Press Club and The Bowery *(see page 83)*. Public radio station 4MBS conducts a Festival of Classics annually in May, when hundreds of local classical musicians perform around Brisbane.

Cairns has produced two award-winning female artists in Christine Anu, whose version of Neil Murray's *My Island Home* tapped her Torres Strait Islander roots and took the 1995 ARIA award for Best Indigenous Release, and Emma Louise, who took the 2011 Queensland Music Award for Song of the Year with the haunting *Jungle*.

To find out about all kinds of cultural and entertainment events in Brisbane, visit www.my247.com.au/Brisbane. For more information on galleries, theatres, performance venues and events in Queensland, *see pages 263–7*. ❑

THE QUEENSLAND BALLET

Interestingly, the Queensland Ballet was not established with government patronage but by expatriate Frenchman Charles Lisner, who danced with Edouard Borovansky's ballet company and the Royal Ballet in London before arriving in Brisbane in 1953 to found the Queensland Ballet, remaining at its helm until 1974.

The company's major performances are staged at QPAC's Playhouse, but the thrice-annual Vis-à-Vis performances at the company's heritage-listed headquarters are a must for lovers of dance (424 Montague Road, West End, Brisbane; www.queenslandballet.com.au; tel: 3013 6666).

LEFT: culture in the Outback. RIGHT: Clare Morehen of the Queensland Ballet performs in *Swan Lake*.

SURF CULTURE

Introduced to Australia in 1914 by Duke Kahanamoku of Honolulu, surfing has become a way of life for many of the continent's coastal dwellers. With ideal waves and weather, southeast Queensland is a surfer's paradise that has produced both champions and dropouts

If you hit the southeast coast of Queensland when the surf's up you may wonder if anyone here goes to work or school. On a good day at Noosa Heads, Burleigh, Snapper Rocks or dozens of other Queensland surf beaches, thousands of surfers of all ages and on all kinds of equipment clog the line-ups. From Brisbane, drive for an hour north to the Sunshine Coast, or south to the Gold Coast, and you can't help but be struck by the all-pervasive surf obsession.

The lure of warm water, long point breaks, sand-bottomed tube rides and a balmy subtropical climate have drawn surfers here for generations. Australian surfing may have begun at Sydney's Freshwater Beach, when visiting Hawaiian champion Duke Kahanamoku put on his historic display in 1914, but the surfing lifestyle seems to have reached its zenith here in Queensland.

The idea of a life spent lolling under pandanus trees on a grassy headland overlooking a glistening Pacific Ocean, in between idyllic surf sessions, is rooted deep in the Australian surfer's psyche.

The history of surfing

Early European settlers initially frowned upon surf bathing, as both physically and morally

dangerous. Mixed genders in minimal clothing frolicking in the surf were regarded as an almost certain prelude to the breakdown of civilisation. Slowly but surely, however, the surf's siren song proved irresistible. Surf life-saving clubs were formed in the early 1900s to protect public safety, and quickly grew as social hubs for the emerging beach culture.

There is some evidence of a surf culture among pre-European, indigenous Australians. They were adept at fishing, even enjoying the aid of dolphins to herd schools of fish shorewards, and they fashioned canoes out of bark that were seaworthy even in rough surf. Indigenous Australians were almost certainly competent and

LEFT: riding a tube. **RIGHT:** Hawaiian champion Duke Kahanamoku.

confident in the surf – the foundation meeting of the Greenmount Surf Club in 1908 paid tribute to a local Aboriginal man, called Churaki, for the many daring rescues he carried out in the surf prior to the club's formation.

Early surfcraft were cumbersome, 5-metre (16ft) "toothpicks", hollow plywood paddleboards, nicknamed for their narrow, pointed appearance. Surfboats were built for ocean rescues and manned by teams of earnest scullers, but proved poorly designed for rough ocean conditions, and probably caused as many casualties as they prevented. More successful was the belt and reel, introduced to Queensland by a pair of Sydney visitors, the Bennett brothers, in 1915.

gave rise to rock'n'roll inspired a rebellious new surf culture. Freshly inspired surfers rejected the stuffy, regimented conservatism of the surf clubs and ditched their voluntary beach patrols for the freewheeling lifestyle of the wave-chasing surfie. Simmering tensions between the life-savers (or clubbies) and the surfers occasionally boiled over, with surfers claiming the life-savers erected their swimming flags where the waves were best, or steered their unwieldy surfboats through packs of surfers. Life-savers claimed surfers were endangering public safety and often confiscated their boards.

The late 1960s "shortboard revolution" further exacerbated tensions, as surfers began

Surf clubs remained unchallenged as the seat of beach culture until the 1950s, when a group of Americans visited Australia to coincide with the 1956 Melbourne Olympics. Their surfriding displays at Torquay in Victoria, and Manly and Avalon in Sydney, on revolutionary, short, light Malibu boards, reverberated around the country.

Surfers of the 1960s

The introduction of a new, radical style of surfing on more manoeuvrable equipment coincided with the emergence of a new culture of independence and social revolution among Western youth. The same circumstances that

SURFING LINGO

The following is a short glossary of surfing terms to help the uninitiated:

Bodyboarder: one who surfs on their belly on a short body (or boogie) board.

Grommet: a young surfer still learning the ropes.

Lineups: areas where waves are ridden at a surf break.

Pointbreak: a wave that breaks along a point of land, or headland.

Shorebreak: where waves dump abruptly on to the beach.

Superbank: the man-made break comprising previously separate breaks from Snapper Rocks to Kirra.

to chop a foot or more at a time off their old longboards, in the quest for ever lighter, more manoeuvrable equipment with which to enact the new "hotdog" style of surfing.

Queensland's Noosa Heads, with its long, perfectly peeling pointbreak, provided the perfect test track for surfing's new experimentalists. American kneeboarder and filmmaker George Greenough, surfboard shaper Bob MacTavish, and 1966 world champion Nat Young formed the vanguard of this revolution, enjoying long, uncrowded sessions at Noosa to push the limits of wave-riding. A new generation of freedom-seeking surfers grew their hair, defied the austere post-war work ethic of their parents and were ready, in the words of acid guru Timothy Leary, to "turn on, tune in and drop out". Queensland's beaches provided the perfect environment to do just that.

In the late 1960s and early 1970s, surfing's public image reached an all-time low, associated as it was with laziness, drug use and anti-social behaviour. Vagrancy laws were enacted to lock up surfers who weren't carrying a specific amount of money. Drug raids on surfer households were commonplace, carried out by a Queensland police force renowned for their heavy-handedness.

But the waves kept on rolling in, and this period is still revered today as a golden era of uncrowded surf, with consistent, ruler-edged cyclone swells pouring into the pointbreaks. In Queensland, under an ever-shining sun, it was all too easy to surf all day and not worry about tomorrow.

Going professional

Beneath the hippy trappings, however, a new revolution began bubbling away in the quiet Queensland town of Coolangatta. The dream of professional surfing, to be paid to ride waves as a legitimate sporting career, took hold of a small group of top practitioners. Intense rivalry between Coolangatta's top three 1970s surfers, Michael Peterson, Peter Townend and Wayne "Rabbit" Bartholomew, provided the spark for this hyper-competitive push. Coolangatta's neighbouring pointbreaks

LEFT: surfing at Kings Beach, Caloundra, Sunshine Coast.
RIGHT: pristine surfing conditions at Snapper Rocks, Gold Coast.

of Snapper Rocks, Greenmount Point and Kirra were the scene of ground-breaking performances in the new hotdog surfing and the advent of deep tube-riding. While the three vied for the title of the best surfer in town, they were also pushing each other to heights that would ultimately see them acclaimed as the very best in the world.

A loose collection of surf contests scattered around the globe were first cobbled together into a unified world tour in 1976, to anoint Peter Townend, the Coolangatta Kid, as pro surfing's first world champion. But the real birth of pro surfing was at Burleigh Heads in 1977, when former Queensland and Australian

champion Peter Drouyn masterminded the first Stubbies Classic. Under his innovative man-on-man format (still used today), judging was made fairer, and a major mainstream sponsor put up serious cash for the winners. Thousands of spectators crammed Burleigh Heads to see all the giant surfing talents of the day do battle in Burleigh's perfect barrels. Peterson emerged victorious, with a then staggering A$5,000 prize, and swiftly vanished into a drug-and-paranoia-fuelled oblivion. It was left largely to Townend, Rabbit and a handful of their contemporaries to steer professional surfing towards mainstream acceptance and respectability.

Rabbit went on to claim the world title in

1978, and hold down a top-five world ranking until 1984, as a new era of big money and media coverage dawned. But, strangely, few of Rabbit's Queensland peers seemed ready to follow in his wake. The most common theory is that the Queensland surfing lifestyle is so pleasant, the living so easy, with the lure of generous unemployment benefits, frenetic nightlife, a great climate and sheer overindulgence, that the typical Queensland surfer of the day was rendered unsuited to, or simply uninterested in, the demands of world travel and elite competition. Queensland's surfing history is littered with monumental talents who burnt out on a "too-much-too-young" trajectory. It seems you

and worldwide superstardom beckon. Legions of success-hungry grommets (junior surfers) vie for supremacy in their wake. The worldwide boom of the surf industry means that professional surfers have the opportunity to set themselves up financially for life. Young surfers barely out of their teens drive luxurious 4WD vehicles and buy million-dollar mansions. Home-grown surf label Billabong, started on the kitchen table of a rented Gold Coast apartment some 30 years ago, is now a publicly listed, Top 100 company on the Australian Stock Exchange. And its founder, Gordon Merchant, a nomadic surfboard shaper, and a handful of his senior management, are

can have too much of a good thing. Queensland's status as the skin-cancer capital of the world seems to stand as a kind of metaphor for flying too close to the sun while enjoying this alluring lifestyle.

Surfing today

Yet a new generation of talented Queensland surfers seems to have learnt the cautionary lessons of their elders well. Today, a new trio of gifted Coolangatta Kids – Mick Fanning, Dean Morrison and Joel Parkinson – is mimicking the rivalry of their predecessors, pushing themselves towards surfing greatness. Lucrative careers with million-dollar salaries

wealthy beyond their wildest dreams.

Surfing today is as mainstream as tennis, golf, cricket or football, regularly splashed all over local newspapers. The Association of Surfing Professionals, presides over a multimillion-dollar world tour from its Coolangatta head office overlooking the waves. Government departments undertake weighty studies of the economic and social value of surfing. The Quiksilver Pro and Roxy Pro at Snapper Rocks are estimated to inject more than A$16 million into the local economy each year.

The old surfer/clubbie rift has long since healed. Queensland's twin surf cultures now co-exist and overlap, and local kids grow up riding every kind of surfcraft imaginable. If you come across a Saturday morning "nippers" (junior) surf life-saving session, with kids who look as if they're barely out of nappies charging in and out of the waves, you would swear they're breeding a new, genetically modified amphibious race here. Webbed hands and feet and gills are surely only a few generations away.

Those old surf clubs, with their prime beachfront positions, are still the social hubs of the Queensland coast, where you can enjoy a cheap meal, a cold beer, or succumb to the dreaded "pokies" (fruit machines), all with unmatched ocean views. The old, framed black-and-white photos of past surf champions peer down curiously, echoing earlier, simpler times. Surf clubs act as village square, public house, gymnasium and ceremonial site for rites of passage into adulthood.

Or you can walk around those mighty headlands at Noosa, Burleigh, Kirra, Greenmount or Snapper, and watch new generations of surf-crazed kids or ageless grown-ups happily feeding an unstoppable addiction. On a full moon, you'll even find a few hardy souls surfing it up in the silvery light, just to escape the incessant crowds and threat of melanoma.

For the quintessential Queensland surf experience, have a surf lesson, sit under a pandanus tree with a pie and a chocolate milk, go for another surf, then retreat to the surf club for a steak and a beer as the sun sets over the mountain hinterland. Just see if you don't feel strangely good about the world. Then go to bed, wake up and do it again. Ad infinitum.

Wave etiquette

More than 1,000 Australians move to southeast Queensland every week, and, along with a couple of million tourists a year, it seems as if they all want to surf. If you plan on entering the fray, think about a surf lesson first, and learn some of the basic rules. Unwritten codes of conduct govern the safe functioning of a busy surf spot, and you are advised to respect them. The surfer on the wave has right of way. The surfer closest to the curl (the breaking part of the wave) has first priority. Learn to handle your board, to paddle and duck-dive away

from more experienced surfers and challenging waves. Find a little beachbreak to yourself to flounder around in while you learn the basics, rather than being one of the hundreds of visiting surfers who paddle out at Snapper Rocks, or Burleigh, or Kirra, just so they can tell the folks back home they did it. Give space to more experienced and local surfers. Don't drop in on someone else's wave. Never throw your board in the face of an oncoming wave if it's going to endanger others. And one last thing. You would hardly credit that it needs saying (but it clearly does): make sure you can swim proficiently before you try to surf. Stay safe and have fun.   ❑

LEFT: champion professional surfer Mick Fanning. **RIGHT:** surf schools can be found at all major surf beaches.

THE GREAT BARRIER REEF

A protected World Heritage Area, the Great Barrier Reef is one of the most beautiful and diverse natural sites in the world. With good reason, it is Queensland's top attraction

The Great Barrier Reef, one of the Seven Natural Wonders of the World, is an aquatic wilderness bigger than the UK, Holland and Switzerland put together. The reef extends over 250,000 sq km (96,500 sq miles) and comprises some 3,000 individual coral reefs and 940 islands, running along the Queensland coast from north of Cape York Peninsula to just north of Fraser Island.

Declared a World Heritage Area in 1981, it is an extraordinarily complex ecosystem, a dazzlingly beautiful universe of low-wooded islands, mangrove estuaries, seagrass beds, algae and sponge gardens, sandy and coral cays, mud floors and deep ocean troughs.

At the heart of this astounding ecosystem is the coral polyp, a tiny animal consisting of little more than a tentacle-surrounded mouth and a limestone carapace into which

> *The Great Barrier Reef brings over A$5 billion into the Australian economy from more than two million tourists who visit each year, and more than 60,000 people earn a living from it.*

it withdraws. Within its tissue are tiny protozoa, zooxanthellae, that photosynthesise in sunlight and provide the coral polyp with increased nutrition.

LEFT: Great Barrier Reef, Whitsunday Islands. **RIGHT:** school of yellowfin goatfish.

The largest structure built by living organisms on Earth, the reef contains one-third of the known species of soft coral and more than 360 hard corals. It is also the home of 1,500 species of brilliantly coloured and patterned fish (of which the most prized are the long-lived coral trout, red emperor and red-throat emperor), dugongs, marine turtles, dolphins, whales, sea snakes, seals, crocodiles, sea horses, sea dragons, pipefish, birds, sharks, rays and skates *(see page 56)*.

The Great Barrier Reef Marine Park Authority was set up to protect this unique wonderland of colour and life forms. And in July 2004 the Australian government increased the area protected from fishing from 4.6 percent to 33.3

percent of the 344,000-sq-km (133,000-sq-mile) park, making it the largest protected marine area in the world.

Visiting the reef

There are numerous ways to experience the reef: you can stay dry in a semi-submersible or glass-bottomed boat; view the immensity of the reef on a scenic flight; or enter the underwater world and be surrounded by all the vibrant colour and life. And there are several gateways to choose from, ranging from resort towns with exciting nightlife and sophisticated dining to wilderness islands where back-to-nature is the theme.

Cairns and Port Douglas are the best known gateways, and at these ports you will be spoilt for choice. At Cairns' Reef Fleet Terminal, all the operators are grouped in one building, which makes choosing your ideal experience easy. Over a dozen operators offer a range of tours, including day cruises to pontoons moored on the reef; overnight sailing adventures; and, for the keen, professional diving courses. Everyone is catered for, from the novice upwards, and all you need do is check where the vessel is heading to and what activities and meals are included in the price. Another thing worth checking is the maximum number of guests on each trip. This can vary from little over a dozen on a leisurely

sailing boat to several hundred squeezed into a wave-piercing catamaran. But don't necessarily be put off by the crowds: the big boys run well-oiled operations, with sophisticated and comfortable pontoons and professional staff. Just up the coast in Port Douglas, the reef is even closer. Several operators run reef trips to the nearby Low Isles or further out to the pristine Agincourt ribbon reefs.

In Townsville and other centres further south, reef exploring is less commercialised and sophisticated, and none the worse for that. In the waters of Townsville, as well as visiting the reef, you can dive Australia's best wreck dive, the SS *Yongala*, visit the acclaimed Reef HQ aquarium, and base yourself in the resorts of Orpheus or Magnetic islands.

The Whitsunday Islands are probably the most celebrated of Queensland's treasure trove of tropical islands. From the mainland gateway of Airlie Beach you can make day trips to island resorts to use the snorkelling and other water-sports equipment. Alternatively, you can overnight on one of the islands offering wilderness campsites or stay at a resort, ranging from low-key Hook to five-star Hayman.

For those who wish to get closer to nature, the coral cays of the southern reef, including Heron, Lady Elliot and Lady Musgrave islands, offer spectacular reef diving and snorkelling. Access to these remote and amazing islands is from Gladstone, Bundaberg, and Town of 1770, respectively.

Threats to the reef

Of the many threats to the reef, the worst is coral bleaching. Some marine scientists are now warning that the Great Barrier Reef could be nothing more than a vast skeleton by 2030 if global warming, caused by increases in greenhouse gases (most significantly carbon dioxide owing to deforestation and the burning of fossil fuels), continues. If the clear, tropical waters remain too warm for too long, corals expel their photosynthesising zooxanthellae and become colourless. Bleached corals are not necessarily dead and can regain their original algae if not too stressed, but if the water does not cool within about a month, the coral will die.

Maximum summer sea temperatures only 2–3 degrees centigrade above normal can kill corals. The summer of 1997–8 was the hottest recorded on the reef since records began in the late 19th century. Then, in the summer of 2002, the worst bleaching ever recorded occurred, with 60–95 percent of the marine park affected.

Up to 5 percent of the Great Barrier Reef has been severely damaged during each of the last two major bleaching events, and this process has revealed that many of the corals are now living at the top of their temperature tolerance. Increased temperatures from global warming are also thought to cause more violent tropical storms, but fortunately the reefs are resilient and do recover from storm damage. Cyclones – there have been 130 in Queensland waters over the past 30 years – have one

most sought-after by fishermen and collectors). Line fishing, which puts the most pressure on reef fish, is at least being controlled by licensing, gear restrictions, size and bag limits, and seasonal closures.

The dugong and all six of the reef's marine turtle species are threatened, with the loggerhead most in danger because of the loss and degradation of its habitat, and commercial and traditional fishing nets, shark nets and illegal nets, as well as foxes taking their eggs on land. The loggerhead-turtle population has dropped by up to 90 percent since the 1960s. Turtles are long-living and slow-growing, and it can take decades to perceive changes in

of the most powerful natural impacts on the reef, albeit indirectly. Flooding onshore results in millions of litres of earth-laden fresh water flowing into the sea, and this has a detrimental effect on the balance of the reef.

Direct human use of the reef can also cause significant damage. Corals are damaged by anchors; the dredging of harbours and channels for boats and marinas; sewage from resorts; divers and snorkellers; commercial reef lines; recreational and charter-boat fishing; and aquarium fish collecting (the coral trout is the

LEFT: crown-of-thorns starfish, predator of coral. **ABOVE:** diver watching a graceful bullray.

THE ISLANDS

The resort islands offer a great variety of ways to experience the Great Barrier Reef. Accommodation varies from five-star hotels with every conceivable luxury to family-friendly, low-key resorts to backpacker lodges and camp grounds. Most provide reef-viewing opportunities on fringing reefs, and all manner of water-borne activities. The major islands from south to north are: Lady Elliot *(see p134)*, Lady Musgrave *(see p134)*, Heron *(see p137)*, Great Keppel *(see p139)*, Brampton *(see page 151)*, The Whitsundays *(see p151-5)*, Magnetic *(see p161)*, Orpheus *(see p165)*, Hinchinbrook *(see p167)*, Dunk *(see p169)*, Green *(see p185)* and Lizard *(see p198)*.

A Reef Experience

Every morning, dozens of sleek boats head out to a marine wonderland, carrying expectant passengers on the one-hour journey to a unique encounter

The easiest way to visit the reef is to take a day trip from Cairns or Port Douglas. You can also take reef trips from Cape Tribulation and coastal towns further south such as Townsville and Town

of 1770. These tend to be less commercialised and more relaxed.

Because the water above the reef is generally so shallow, snorkelling is perfectly satisfactory for seeing the colourful marine life. In fact, many people prefer the freedom and ease of snorkelling to scuba diving; even so, most boats offer tanks for experienced divers and supervised "resort dives" for novices.

When you reach your destination it can be disconcerting. Above the waves, there may be nothing to see: only a sand cay crowded with sea birds might break the turquoise expanse. But as soon as you

poke your mask underwater, the world erupts. It's almost sensory overload: there are vast forests of staghorn coral, whose tips glow purple like Christmas-tree lights; brilliant blue clumps of mushroom coral; layers of pink plate coral; bulbous green brain coral. Tropical fish with exotic names slip about as if showing off their fluorescent patterns: painted flutemouth, crimson squirrel fish, hump-headed Maori wrasse, cornflower sergeant-major. Take it all in with the eyes, but avoid damaging the reef by touching it. You definitely don't want to pick up the conus textile shells: they shoot darts into anything that touches them, with enough venom to kill 300 people.

Most reef trips follow a similar format. There's a morning dive, followed by a buffet lunch; then an afternoon dive. There should be a marine biologist on board, who will explain the reef's ecology. Before you book, ask about the number of passengers the boat takes: it varies from several hundred on the famous Quicksilver fleet of catamarans to fewer than a dozen on smaller craft.

As a general rule, the further out the boat heads, the more pristine the diving. Green Island, near Cairns, and the Low Isles, near Port Douglas, have suffered from over-visitation. But don't be overly concerned by hype about the "Outer Reef" – as the edge of the continental shelf, it may be the "real" reef, but it looks pretty much the same as other parts.

Weather will play an important part in your enjoyment of the Great Barrier Reef's scenic attractions. From late April to October, it's at its best, the clear skies and moderate breezes offering perfect conditions for coral-viewing, diving, swimming, fishing and sunbathing. In November the first signs of the approaching "Wet" appear: variable winds, increasing cloud and showers. By January it rains at least once most days. Even in the winter months, the water here is never cold, but it is worth paying a couple of dollars extra to hire a wetsuit anyway; you can go on snorkelling for hours in this extraordinary environment. ❏

LEFT: fusiliers schooling over coral reef.

their population. The correlative is that it can take decades to recover from any downturn. But thankfully, since the incorporation of turtle-excluding devices on trawlers in 2001, the number of breeding adults visiting nesting beaches has slowly increased.

The reef's human history

Many shipwrecks in the reef's waters, ruins and lighthouses on the cays and islands, and relics from World War II tell of the European presence. But the shell middens, rock paintings, artefacts and story sites suggest that the reef has been of great importance to Aboriginal tribes all along the coast.

the sediment and chemical run-off from farming, and from the loss of the coastal wetlands that have acted as a natural filter in the past.

About a fifth of Queensland's population lives along the coast adjacent to the reef, and with the current interstate and overseas migration to the state, communities continue to grow. How to manage water quality, tourism and commercial and recreational fishing is a major concern.

Limiting the damage

In response to the enormous threat of climate change, the Australian government has said it is committed to reducing annual greenhouse-gas

When the Europeans settled, they cleared forests, mined, engaged in agriculture and established towns. It is unfortunate that, unlike most other reefs, the Great Barrier Reef runs along a string of major centres – Cairns, Townsville, Mackay, Rockhampton and Gladstone. Coastal wetland forest is still being cut down to make room for the beef cattle, sugar cane, cotton industries and banana plantations close to the coast, which result in large quantities of fertiliser running into the sea.

Hundreds of reefs are currently at risk from

Above: scuba diving in Cairns reveals all manner of underwater delights.

emissions by 85 million tons, although, given that it has not signed up to the Kyoto Protocol, there are some who question how serious it is about this commitment.

What is more, the Great Barrier Reef Marine Park Authority has established a A$2-million programme to boost the resilience of the reef, while also sustaining the industries and communities that depend on it. Using a combination of satellite imagery and aerial and underwater surveys, the country's best marine scientists can quickly determine the extent of coral bleaching and analyse the effects on the reef. It is to be hoped that these measures are not too little, too late. ❑

PROTECTING THE REEF

The world's largest living entity, the Great Barrier Reef is top of most tourist itineraries, but its fragility means that it's important to minimise visitor impact

The Great Barrier Reef may be the largest collection of living organisms on Earth, but it is also extremely fragile. Rising sea temperatures have added to the already considerable threat posed by tourism, pollution and natural enemies such as the crown-of-thorns starfish. Protecting the reef from its natural and man-made enemies has become more important than ever, as we learn about the biodiversity under the waves. The reef's astonishingly complex and diverse ecosystem will disappear if precautions aren't taken.

The appeal of the Great Barrier Reef to visitors is undeniable, and tourism is big business. But should you decide to visit the park, there are a number of things you can do to limit your environmental impact. Scuba diving is one of the main tourist draws to the reef, but it can take an average of 25 years for coral to recover from an accidental knock and scrape from an inexperienced diver. The main way to avoid causing damage to the reef is to take scuba lessons before you travel, and then choose a recognised dive operator to take you to the site. Smaller groups of divers are also preferable as they are less likely to cause disturbance to the coral and its inhabitants.

If you fish, make sure you utilise the Marine Park Authority's zoning maps, which will let you know of any restrictions in force in the area. Be sure to return any unwanted or undersized fish to the water as quickly as possible. Use official campsites and take all litter, including fishing lines, with you when you leave.

LEFT: a juvenile regal slipper lobster *(Arctides regalis).*

ABOVE: clownfish live at the bottom of the sea in sheltered reefs or in shallow lagoons, usually in pairs. In the wild, they live in a symbiotic relationship with the sea anemone.

ABOVE: a diver contemplates a sea fan, or gorgonian. A colony can be several metres high and across, but only a few centimetres thick. There are more than 500 species of gorgonian in the ocean.

THE REEF'S GREATEST ENEMY?

For years, the worst threat to the Reef was thought to be the crown-of-thorns starfish *(above)*, an ugly creature that clamps on to coral and effectively spits its stomach out. Its digestive juices dissolve the polyps and leave great expanses of coral bleached and dead. The crown-of-thorns is poisonous to other fish and is almost indestructible: it can regenerate to full size from only a single leg and small piece of intestine.

With only a few around, it was easy to ignore their depredation of the reef, but in the early 1960s the pattern changed. Instead of a few crown-of-thorns starfish, suddenly there were millions. Green Island was the first to see the plague in 1962. From there it spread southwards, reaching the reefs around Bowen by 1988. Surveys between 1985 and 1988 established that about 31 percent of the reefs examined had been affected. Even after millions of dollars' worth of research, no one knows what caused the proliferation of the starfish. Furthermore, no economic way to get rid of the pest has presented itself.

Recently, however, marine biologists have decided to let the crown-of-thorns infestation run its destructive course. The latest wisdom posits that it is a natural, if poorly understood, part of the reef's life cycle and that the reef can return to pre-outbreak levels of coral in 10–15 years. Only time will tell if this scientific theory is correct.

ABOVE: a yellow crinoid *(Phylum echinodermata)* waves in the waters of the Great Barrier Reef. The name "crinoid" comes from the Greek word for lily, although this is an animal, not a plant.
BELOW: the potato cod *(Epinephelus tukula)* is native to Australia.

RIGHT: six species of sea turtle call the Great Barrier Reef home, and there are two distinct genetic groups of the green sea turtle: one at the north end of the reef, and one at the south.

PLACES

Queensland is a vast state with a staggering array of attractions, including empty Outback vistas, technicolour coral gardens, ancient rock-art galleries, golden-sand beaches and sophisticated cities

Today, the Queensland capital of Brisbane exudes a sparkle that many other cities envy. A mini-Manhattan sprouts from its centre, well-tended parklands border its river banks, and its galleries and cultural spaces are cutting-edge.

Few destinations can boast such a diversity of surf beaches, coral cays and islands as the Queensland coast. Surfers Paradise is as famous for its glitter as for its surf beaches. Noosa, to the north, offers gastronomy and fashion in addition to its perfect waves. Of course, a good proportion of the billions of dollars generated by tourism each year stems from the Great Barrier Reef. Many resorts cling to the peripheries of this spectacular ecosystem, and three of them – Green Island off Cairns, Heron Island off Gladstone, and Lady Elliot Island off Bundaberg – stand on the reef itself.

In the Far North, it's not all about the reef and the resorts. Here you can also find swathes of pristine rainforest, a bounty of tropical fruit, and a vibrant contemporary Aboriginal culture.

The Outback offers quite different rewards to travellers willing to get off the beaten track. Sights that would attract thousands elsewhere, such as the Aboriginal rock paintings in Laura, the breathtaking Lawn Hill Gorge, the site of the dinosaur stampede at Lark Hill Quarry – all of these can be enjoyed in peace, often with just a handful of other travellers. Sing in the bar at the North Gregory Hotel where Banjo Paterson first banged out *Waltzing Matilda* on the pub piano in 1895. Take in the Stockman's Hall of Fame in Longreach. Seek out the Burke and Wills Dig Tree on the desert border with South Australia. Or have a well-earned beer in the Birdsville pub.

There's a lot on offer in this huge state, and while size isn't everything, it is certainly a factor when planning your Queensland holiday. Choose a corner or two, and there will be plenty left for the next trip.	❑

PRECEDING PAGES: climbing Story Bridge in Brisbane; aerial view of Surfers Paradise Beach, Gold Coast. **LEFT:** Palm Cove, Queensland. **ABOVE:** a view of Brisbane from the river.

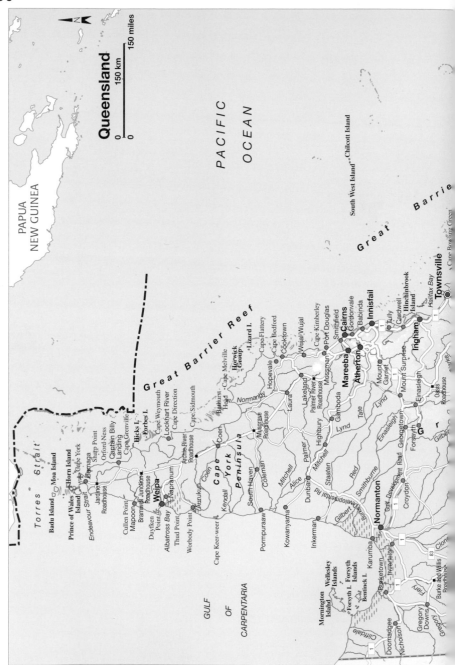

Queensland

150 km
0   150 miles

PAPUA
NEW GUINEA

PACIFIC

OCEAN

South West Island Chilcott Island

Great   Barrier

Great Barrier Reef

Torres   Strait

Cape Bowling Green

Townsville
Halifax Bay
Hinchinbrook
Island
Cardwell
Tully
Ingham
Babinda
Innisfail
Gordonvale
Cairns
Mount Surprise
Mareeba
Atherton
Mount
Garnet
Oasis
Roadhouse
Einasleigh
Georgetown
Forsyth
Lynd
Smithfield
Port Douglas
Cape Kimberley
Mossman
Wujal/Wujal
Cooktown
Cape Bedford
Cape Flattery
Lizard I.
Horwick
Group
Cape Melville
Bathurst
Head
Cape Sidmouth
Cape Direction
Lockhart River
Cape Weymouth
Forbes I.
Hicks I.
Gr
Cloncurry
Einasleigh
Palmer River
Roadhouse
Lakeland
Gamboda
Laura
Lynd
Tate
Highbury
Palmer
Mitchell
Staaten
Red
Smithburne
Gulf Developmental Rd
Croydon
83
Gilbert
Gilbert
Normanton
Inkerman
Dunbar
Alice
Kowanyama
Pormpuraaw
Coleman
Seven-Haven
Coen
Archer River
Roadhouse
Musgrave
Roadhouse
Normanby
Hopevale
Great Barrier Reef
Cape
York
Peninsula
Coen
Kendall
Aurukun
Cape Keer-weer
Worbody Point
Thud Point
Albatross Bay
Duyfken
Point
Mapoon
Cullen Point
Napranum
Weipa
Bramwell Junction
Roadhouse
Cape Grenville
Captain Billy
Landing
Orford-Ness
Jardine
Roadhouse
Sharp Point
Bamaga
Cape York
Endeavour Strait
Prince of Wales
Island
Horn Island
Moa Island
Badu Island
Karumba
Normanton
Burketown
Inverleigh
Bentinck I.
Forsyth Islands
Forsyth I.
Wellesley
Islands
Mornington
Island
Burke and Wills
Roadhouse
Fiery
Gregory
Downs
Gregory
Nicholson
Doomadgee
Cliffdale
1
1
1
1
1
1
1
1
1
1
1

GULF

OF

CARPENTARIA

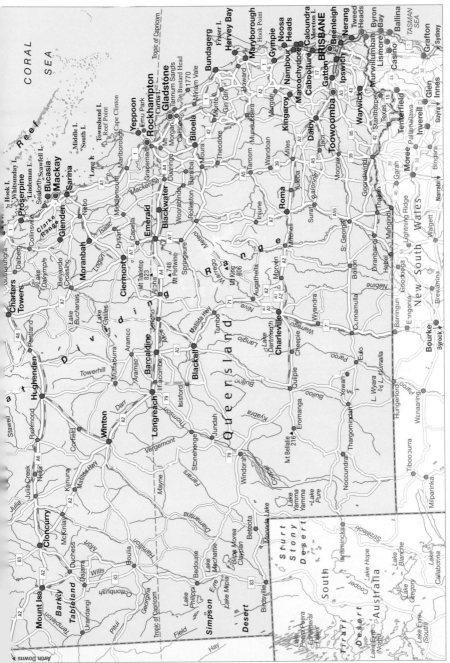

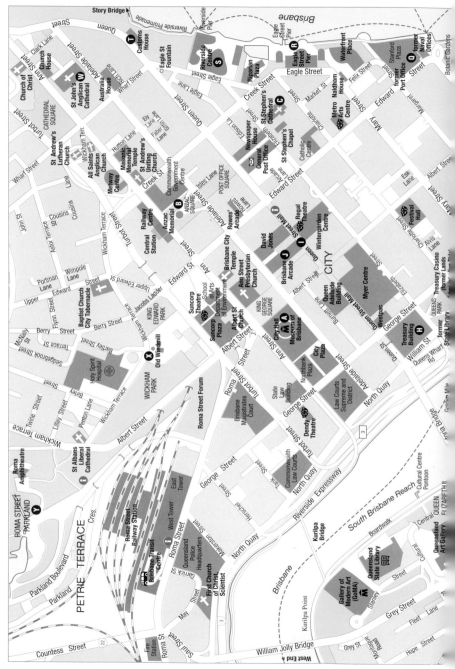

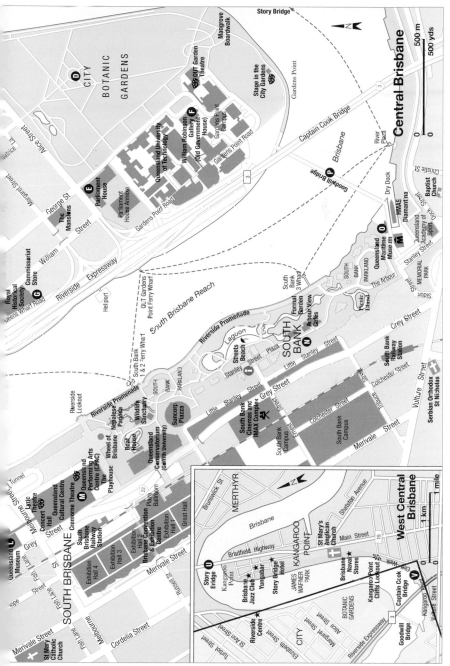

Story Bridge

N

500 m
500 yds

Central Brisbane

Mangrove
Boardwalk

C I T Y

B O T A N I C

G A R D E N S

D

QUT Garden
Theatre

Stage in the
City Gardens

Gardens Point

William Robinson
Gallery
(Old Government
House)

F

Queensland University
of Technology

Gardens Point Campus

Captain Cook Bridge

Brisbane

Goodwill Bridge

P

River
Plazz

Dry Dock

HMAS
Diamantina

Christie St

Dock Street

Baptist
Church

Queensland Academy
of Sport

Queensland
Maritime
Museum

O

M

Stanley Street

MEMORIAL
PARK

Alice Street

Beatrice

Margaret Street

George St

William   Street

The
Mansions

E

Parliament
House

Parliament
House Annexe

Gardens Point Road

Gardens Point Road

Riverside Expressway

Helport

QUT Gardens
Point Ferry Wharf

SOUTH
BANK
PARKLAND

South
Bank
3 Wharf

SOUTH

The Arbour

Picnic
Island

Sidon   Street

Stanley Street

Royal
Historical
Society

Queens Wharf Road

Commissariat
Store

G

Riverside
Lookout

South Brisbane Reach

South Bank
1 & 2 Ferry Wharf

Riverside Promenade

Formal
Garden

Arbour View
Cafes

Crey Street

Serbian Orthodox
St Nicholas

Tunnel

Melbourne Street

Grey   Street

Riverside Promenade

Nepalese Peace
Pagoda

Wildlife
Sanctuary

Boat
House

Wheel of
Brisbane

Queensland
Conservatorium
(Griffith University)

SOUTH
BANK
PARKLAND

Laguon

Streets
Beach

Plazz

Stanley   Street

Little   Stanley   Street

Suncorp
Plazza

Grey   Street

SOUTH
BANK

N

Little   Stanley   Street

South Bank
Railway Station

Colchester Street

Lyric
Theatre

Concert
Hall

Queensland
Cultural
Centre

Cremorne Theatre

Queensland Performing Arts
Centre (QPAC)
The
Playhouse

South Bank Cinemas and
IMAX Complex

South Bank
Campus

Colchester   Street

Colchester   Street

Ernest   Street

Merivale   Street

Vulture   Street

SOUTH BRISBANE

Queensland
Museum

L

Grey   Street

Melbourne   St

Fish   Lane

Fish   Lane

South
Brisbane
Railway Station

Brisbane Convention
& Exhibition
Centre

Exhibition
Hall 4

Exhibition
Hall 3

Exhibition
Plaza
Hall

Exhibition
Hall 1

Plaza
Ballroom

Great Hall

Merivale   Street

Grey   St

Cordelia   Street

Merivale   Street

St Mary's
Catholic
Church

Russell   St

22

South Bank
Campus

South Bank
Railway Station

West Central Brisbane

N

1 km
1 mile

BrunswickST

MERTHYR

Brisbane

Shafston Avenue

KANGAROO
POINT

St Mary's
Anglican
Church

Main Street

Bradfield Highway

Story
Bridge

U

Kangaroo
Point

Brisbane
Jazz Club

Yungaba

Story Bridge
Hotel

JAMES
WARNER
PARK

Brisbane
Naval
Stores

Kangaroo Point
Cliffs Lookout

Riverside
Centre

St Ann Street

Elizabeth Street

Turbot Street

BOTANIC
GARDENS

C I T Y

Margaret Street

Alice Street

Goodwill
Bridge

Captain Cook
Bridge

Kangaroo Point

Riverside Expressway

Vulture   Street

BRISBANE

Brisbane has shaken off its image as a sleepy backwater and emerged as a cosmopolitan city, with a thriving arts scene, vibrant nightlife and world-class cuisine. But Australia's third-largest city still retains something of a country heart

Brisbane●

T he southern approach to Brisbane presents a striking picture: rounding a bend on the Pacific Motorway you see weatherboard stilt houses on leafy hills, with the thrusting towers of the Central Business District (CBD) beyond. Crossing Captain Cook Bridge, you catch glimpses of the serpentine Brisbane River, bordered by skyscrapers on one side and lush parkland on the other. It's hard to believe that, only a few decades ago, this impressive waterway was polluted and neglected. Today's sparkling river is at the hub of city life and is the pride of its inhabitants. It serves as an aquatic highway for ferries connecting riverside suburbs, and is the focal point for festivals and celebrations. The motorway follows the river's edge, swooping above the bank and through luxuriant mangroves – an unexpected sight deep in the heart of a modern city.

Nearly half of Queensland's population of 4.6 million lives within Brisbane's statistical boundaries – a sprawling 4,673 sq km (1,800 sq miles) – one of the reasons why the city's reputation as "the world's biggest country town" lingered for so long. The catalysts for change were

the 1982 Commonwealth Games and Expo '88, which put Brisbane on the cultural map. Inevitably, something of the city's laid-back character has been lost in the transition to cosmopolitan hub. The new Queenslander may wear board shorts and thongs, but, in business, he or she is as hard-nosed as anyone from Sydney or Melbourne. More than likely, the new Queenslander *is* from Sydney or Melbourne. Yet there remains some truth to the old saying: "In Melbourne they ask what school you went to, in Sydney

Main attractions
BRISBANE CITY HALL
CITY BOTANIC GARDENS
QUEEN STREET MALL
QUEENSLAND CULTURAL CENTRE
SOUTH BANK PARKLANDS
STORY BRIDGE
ROMA STREET PARKLAND
BRISBANE BOTANIC GARDENS
FORTITUDE VALLEY
MORETON BAY

LEFT: McWhirters old department store (1912), a historic landmark. **RIGHT:** the riverside skyscrapers of Brisbane's CBD.

Within City Hall is a museum "for and about the people of Brisbane". Free concerts are also enjoyed here throughout the year.

BELOW: soldiers preparing for an Anzac Day ceremony in Anzac Square.

they ask how much you earn, in Brisbane they ask if you'd like a beer."

Rough edges remain, but there's also a worldly sophistication, as evidenced by a multicultural restaurant scene and the growing number of cafés and wine bars. Add Brisbane's young generation, who have only known the city as vibrant and forward-looking, to the mix and you have one sassy, confident city. Young people no longer feel the imperative to leave. This, plus the constant interstate migration, has seen Brisbane's population outpace that of most other Australian state capitals. The climate – subtropical summers and mild winters – has undoubtedly played a part in Brisbane's rise.

Brisbane's recognition of the value of its architectural heritage came too late to save many iconic buildings, destroyed during the development frenzy of the 1980s. Still, enough historic architecture remains to show what used to be. Many of the city's distinguished colonial-style residences were wrenched from their stumps in leafy Ascot or Hamilton and relocated, iron-lace and all,

to exclusive outer suburbs such as Brookfield and Pullenvale.

Brisbane City Hall

A suitable place to begin exploring the city is **Brisbane City Hall** Ⓐ (Mon–Fri 8am–5pm, Sat–Sun 10am–5pm; free; guided tours Mon–Fri; tel: 3403 8888) on King George Square. Designed on grand neoclassical lines, with massive sandstone columns, City Hall held the record as Brisbane's tallest building until the early 1960s – and even now provides excellent views from the soaring 92-metre (300ft) clock tower. Installed in 1929, it features a cast-iron tower bell weighing 4.32 tons and four smaller bells of more than 3 tons apiece. Initially, these massive bells chimed 24 hours a day and were audible in faraway Wynnum, leaving the citizenry bleary-eyed. Nowadays the bells peal during daylight hours only.

The **Museum of Brisbane** (daily 10am–5pm; free), on the ground floor, is dedicated to the city's social and cultural history, as well as contemporary visual art, crafts and design.

City Hall flanks **King George Square**, a public space notable for its eclectic collection of statuary. Works include a 1938 statue of King George V on horseback and a 1988 tableau depicting early Brisbane pioneers, the Petrie family.

Anzac Square

From King George Square, proceed along Ann Street (away from North Quay) to **Anzac Square** Ⓑ and the **Shrine of Remembrance** – taking time to marvel at one of the more intriguing examples of Australia's farsighted urban design. Position yourself at the shrine's upper level, looking across Anzac Square and neighbouring Post Office Square to the clock tower of the **General Post Office** (261 Queen Street) two blocks away, erected between 1871 and 1879. Now take a 180-degree turn and you'll see

the **Central Railway Station** clock tower, opened in 1901. Both towers stand in perfect alignment with the sacred flame and war memorial in the square directly below.

Descend the curved steps beside the shrine, past commemorative bottle trees and symbolic date palms, to **Post Office Square**. Legend has it that a secret tunnel once connected the post office with the former AMP (Australian Mutual Provident society) building at the corner of Edward Street and Queen Street, now known as MacArthur Chambers (and converted into an upmarket apartment hotel). US Army General Douglas MacArthur commanded the Allied forces in the southwest Pacific from this building during World War II. The **MacArthur Museum Brisbane** (Tues–Thur and Sun 10am–3pm; entry by gold-coin donation), containing MacArthur memorabilia, has been established on the eighth floor of his former HQ.

Having given the GPO's colonnades and Corinthian columns the once-over, follow the narrow lane flanking the building to Elizabeth Street and **St Stephen's Cathedral** **C** (tours Mon–Fri 10.30am, Sun 9am, 11am, 1pm; free; tel: 3336 9111). Within this precinct you will find the gracefully weathered Pugin's Chapel, also known as **Old St Stephen's Church**, completed in 1850 to a design by the celebrated neo-Gothic architect Auguste Welby Pugin. Beside it, the more imposing cathedral replaced the church as Brisbane's seat of Catholicism in 1874.

City Botanic Gardens

Wander through the church precinct, passing the large bell, into Charlotte Street. Turn right into Charlotte Street, then left at the next junction, following Edward Street to the **City Botanic Gardens** **D** (entrance in Alice Street). Covering 20 hectares (50 acres) and laced with footpaths and trails, these remarkable gardens offer a peaceful oasis amid the inner-city bustle. Established in 1828 to provide vegetables for the penal settlement, the gardens boast a row of weeping figs planted by the first gardens director, Walter Hill, in the 1870s. There are open

TIP

The Brisbane Council Translink Loop operates a free bus service that circles Brisbane's CBD every 10 minutes (weekdays approx 7am–6pm). Stops include Central Station, Queen Street Mall, City Botanic Gardens, Riverside Centre, QUT and King George Square. Visit www.translink.com.au (tel: 13 12 30).

BELOW: City Botanic Gardens.

Visitors will need to find a member to vouch for them if they are to get beyond the front door of the illustrious Queensland Club.

BELOW: the Mansions.

spaces, an ornamental lake bordered by palms and bamboo, and a **mangrove boardwalk** skirting the river.

Parliament House precinct

Overlooking the gardens is one of Queensland's best-loved landmarks, **Parliament House ❺** (corner of George and Alice Streets; Mon–Fri 9am–4pm; free; www.parliament.qld.gov.au; guided tours hourly during non-sitting times). The grand French Renaissance-style building, designed by Charles Tiffin, eloquently expresses Queensland's satisfaction at having achieved separation from New South Wales in 1859. Nearby, **Old Government House ❻**, another grand Tiffin design, was built in 1862. The porphyry-and-sandstone structure remained the governor's official residence until 1910, when it became the first University of Queensland. The building is now administered by the Queensland University of Technology and houses the **William Robinson Gallery** (Mon–Fri 10am–5pm, Sun 10am–4pm; free).

Opened in 1884, the **Queensland Club** (intersection of Alice and George Streets) exudes an air of superiority. The Italianate three-storey building, with its spacious verandas and cast-iron balustrading, was designed by Francis Stanley as a bastion of gentility – and so it remains today.

Further along George Street, **The Mansions** is an ornate row of terrace houses built in 1889 as residences for the gentry. Here you'll find Augustine's restaurant *(see page 86)*, a favourite haunt of high-ranking politicians.

Near the river, another historic landmark is the **Commissariat Store ❼** (William Street; Tues–Fri 10am–4pm; free). It was built in 1829, one year before Moreton Bay's tyrannical commandant, Captain Patrick Logan, was struck down and killed on a mapping expedition in Brisbane River headwaters *(see page 27)*. Built as a government store, the Commissariat also houses a museum documenting the early history of Brisbane, as well as local Aboriginal history.

The array of authentic convict memorabilia includes shackles, lashes and a macabre glass tube containing

convicts' fingertips, sliced off by the convicts to avoid having to work.

Treasury Casino

On the corner of Elizabeth Street and William Street stands the former **Treasury Building** ❾, converted in to a casino in 1995. The main entrance is in Queen Street Mall, but no one will mind if you slip in by the rear door to try your luck at the 80 gaming tables and 1,300 slot machines that occupy this formerly dignified space. The casino is open 24 hours a day, with a selection of bars, restaurants and even hotel rooms for those who can't tear themselves away. There's a nearby pawnshop where high rollers hock cars and watches for another round with Lady Luck. Despite sincere attempts to preserve the building's heritage values, the strident casino culture overwhelms the building's sombre architecture. For the record, work on the Treasury began in 1886 and was completed in 1928, when it was deemed one of the state's most notable buildings.

Queen Street Mall

The retail heart of Brisbane is the **Queen Street Mall** ❶, a pedestrian area with more than 600 shops, 45 cafés and restaurants, two cinema complexes and 11 shopping zones. At first glance, the bustling mall appears completely modern from street level – but look above the awnings and you'll see old-fashioned shop facades that have been faithfully preserved. Embedded in walls decorated with neoclassical columns, archways and keystones, you can still make out the names of hotels and stores that once thrived here.

The precinct throbs with offbeat vitality. Professional acts perform in the rotunda, but the spirit of the mall is best expressed by its buskers and street performers: a soupy sax wobbling through *Waltzing Mat-ilda*, trained poodles playing dead

for loose change, or maybe a clown coaxing animal shapes from balloons for the amusement of small children. Pause for a coffee or lunch in one of the sidewalk cafés, and take it all in.

Pop in to at the **Regent Theatre** (167 Queen Street) to admire the grand marble staircase, ornate ceilings and gilded walls in the lobby, which remain virtually unchanged since 1929. The intermission organist, who magically appeared at the console of a Wurlitzer, disappeared for ever during the 1970s refurbishment that carved the large cinema up into four small ones.

Another slice of history remains in the refined Edwardian-style **Brisbane Arcade** ❸, built in 1924 and now the city's oldest surviving shopping arcade. This charming row of shops, on two levels, connects Queen Street Mall with Adelaide Street. Upmarket boutiques occupy the lower level. The mezzanine floor has been colonised by milliners and fashion designers.

Similarly intact is the classical-revival architecture of the former **Bank of NSW** (now Westpac) at the corner of Queen and George streets.

TIP

Brisbane has embraced the bicycle with the City Cycle bike-sharing scheme (tel: 1300 229 253; www.citycycle.com. au). You can download a map when you subscribe and pick up a bike from one of over 130 stations. You will need to be over 17 years of age and have access to a helmet.

BELOW: Brisbane Arcade.

The present Victoria Bridge, opened in 1969, is the third bridge to be built on this site. As a consequence of floods and problematic foundations, early attempts at bridging the Brisbane River were short-lived. A leftover pylon from bridge number two, built in 1897, carries a poignant memorial to a boy killed during the World War I victory celebrations.

BELOW: sculpture in front of Queensland Art Gallery.

Queensland Cultural Centre

Having browsed in the mall, cross **Victoria Bridge** to **South Bank**, where the **Queensland Cultural Centre** rises impressively. On one side of the street is the Queensland Performing Arts Complex, on the other the Queensland Art Gallery and the Queensland Museum South Bank (joined by a walkway). The opening of the Cultural Centre coincided with the opening of Expo '88 – an event that stimulated a burst of community confidence.

The **Queensland Art Gallery** Ⓚ (Mon–Fri 10am–5pm, Sat–Sun 9am–5pm; free; tel: 3840 7303; www.qag.qld.gov.au) is one of the most prestigious art galleries in the country. In addition to its extensive permanent collection of Australian, Aboriginal, European and Asian works, the gallery has a reputation for putting on outstanding international exhibitions. It's sister gallery, the **Queensland Gallery of Modern Art (GoMA)** (same visiting hours and contact details as the Queensland Art Gallery), at nearby Kurilpa Point, is

the biggest and foremost gallery of modern art in Australia.

The **Queensland Museum South Bank** Ⓞ (daily 9.30am–5pm; free; tel: 3840 7555; www.southbank.qm.qld.gov.au) tells the region's history through a fascinating display of exhibits, from a Muttaburrasaurus, the most complete dinosaur skeleton found in Australia, to the tiny aeroplane that Bert Hinkler flew from England to Australia in 1928. Kids love the **Sciencentre**'s hands-on interactive displays and the life-size models of humpback whales in the Whale Mall. Under the same roof, the **Dandiiri Maiwar** centre provides an insight into the Aboriginal and Torres Strait Islander cultures.

Also part of the complex, the **State Library of Queensland** (Mon–Thu 10am–8pm, Fri-Sun 10am–5pm; free) holds important archives relating to the history of Queensland.

The **Queensland Performing Arts Centre** Ⓜ (www.qpac.com.au), across the elevated walkway, is a superb facility; it hosts a wide range of world-class theatrical productions in four theatres, and includes restaurants, bars and a gift shop.

Savouring South Bank

Following the great flood of 1893, much of the South Bank neighbourhood fell into dereliction and languished for decades. South Bank's present incarnation dates from the late 1980s when, except for a handful of historic buildings, the site was flattened for Expo '88. The venerable Plough Inn, built in 1885, is one of the few survivors and is still a good place to quench a thirst. South Bank's makeover has continued over recent decades and the area has blossomed with cultural, recreational and culinary attractions. Several former Expo pavilions have been converted into riverfront restaurants, and Little Stanley Street is lined with with bars and casual pavement dining options.

South Bank Parklands

The parklands take over where the Cultural Centre ends. Sprawling across the revamped Expo '88 site, **South Bank**  has become an inner-city playground of tropical gardens, lagoons, restaurants and boutiques. You could easily spend a whole day or more here without finding yourself in the same place twice.

Towering almost 60 metres (197ft) above the parklands, the **Wheel of Brisbane** (Mon–Thu 11am–9.30pm, Fri–Sat 10am–11pm, Sun 10am–10pm; charge) is worth a spin. Inside the air-conditioned pod you will hear an informative commentary while enjoying the great view of the city skyline.

From the wheel, follow the bouganvillea-draped walkway, the **Arbour,** to the Rainforest Walk and search out the **Nepalese Pagoda**, which was constructed for the 1988 World Expo.

The precinct's most popular attraction is **Streets Beach**, a large swimming lagoon where the essential elements of beach culture have been replicated. white sand, lapping water, lifeguards, tanned and toned bikini-wearers and small children with buckets and spades.

Behind the beach, Stanley Street Plaza hosts the **South Bank Visitor Centre** (daily 9am–5pm) and, at weekends, the vibrant **Lifestyle Markets** (Fri 5–10pm, Sat 10am–5pm).

Queensland Maritime Museum

Meandering south, either along the promenade that skirts the river or following the Arbour, you come to the **Maritime Museum** (daily 9.30am–4.30pm; charge; tel: 3844 5361; www.maritimemuseum.com.au) in Sidon Street. Ever since the Dutch explorer Willem Janssen and the crew of the *Duyfken* landed on Cape York Peninsula in 1606, the sea has shaped Queenslanders' lives. The museum features a wealth of artefacts reflecting the state's maritime history. These include a Royal Australian Navy frigate snug within a 19th-century dry dock, a Torres Strait pearling lugger, and the 1925 steam tug, *Forceful.*

Near the museum is the **Goodwill Pedestrian Bridge** , connecting

BELOW: the artificial Streets Beach in South Bank Parklands.

Queensland Maritime Museum has a fascinating collection of vessels to investigate, including a Torres Strait pearling lugger and the Royal Australian Navy frigate, Diamantina.

BELOW RIGHT: Eagle Street Pier.

South Bank with the CBD and continuously streaming with cyclists, rollerbladers and commuters. Having reached the CBD side, retrace your steps past Parliament House and into Alice Street, where huge figs grow beside, and in some places engulf, the iron railings of the City Botanic Gardens.

Old maritime precinct

Within the CBD, roughly bounded by Edward, Eagle, Felix and Charlotte streets, the historic architecture of Brisbane's dockland stands remarkably intact. The **Former Naval Offices** and the next-door **Port Office** have been immaculately restored and subtly incorporated into the Stamford Plaza Hotel. The former headquarters of the Australian United Steam Navigation Company, **Naldham House** (Mary Street), now provides premises for the Brisbane Polo Club. Flood markers on the side of the building are reminders of Brisbane's vulnerability to inundation.

In the 19th century, the maritime precinct was a rumbustious blend of warehouses, engineering works, mercantile agencies, brothels, boarding houses and residences amid busy wharves, rough hotels, a ferry terminal and the Botanic Gardens. The raffish cosmopolitanism of those days finds a muted resonance in the array of fine-dining restaurants lining **Eagle Street Pier** , where Brisbane's expense-account set congregates to sluice and trough.

Riverside

From Eagle Street Pier, follow the boardwalk to Harry Seidler's remarkable **Riverside Centre** . This bold tower inspired Brisbane's mini-Manhattan, and it is widely admired within the architectural fraternity. But another Seidler design, the **Riparian Plaza**, and **One One One Eagle Street** have now eclipsed it. Seidler once described his own design as "before its time and, above all, an Australian building with a capital A". The Royal Australian Institute of Architects, which has honoured Seidler's vision with three of its most prestigious awards, clearly.

Across Eagle Street, at its junction with Queen Street, stands the **Eagle**

A Culinary Revolution

A couple of decades ago, Brisbane was something of a gastronomic desert. The city's culinary development began in the early 1980s, with a food movement led by a group of young chefs who, having toiled in the fine hotels of Europe, returned home to fire up Brisbane's food revolution. They called themselves The Five Chefs and became Brisbane's culinary superstars. Three of the five – Philip Johnson (E'cco), David Pugh (Restaurant Two) and Russell Armstrong (Seasalt at Armstrongs) – continue to run successful restaurants. Younger chefs have followed in their footsteps. The appearance in the city of accomplished European chefs such as Romaine Bapst (Drift) and Romeo Rigo (Romeo's) has confirmed its culinary coming of age. It can now be said that the best restaurants of Brisbane have hit international standard.

Along with the many formal restaurants, you'll find an array of very good ethnic places (including Thai, Indian and Vietnamese). And Brisbane-ites still love steak and fish-and-chips – two of the city's most successful restaurants (Brett's Wharf and Pier Nine) have turned these popular staples into art forms *(see pages 86–7 for restaurant listings).*

Street Drinking Fountain, completed in 1880 as part of a beautification project. At some point in time, the public arrived at the mistaken conclusion that the fountain commemorated James Mooney, a volunteer fireman killed on active duty in 1877. The myth became so embedded in the public consciousness that, in 1988, the Brisbane City Council turned folklore into reality, adding a tablet honouring Mooney and other firemen.

Nearby, the copper-domed **Customs House** ❼, at 399 Queen Street, lends a splash of colonial pomp to both the street and the river front. Once a source of maritime tax revenue, the building is now owned and operated by the University of Queensland as a heritage facility, offering boardrooms, a ballroom, an art gallery and a waterside brasserie. And its influence hasn't ceased, at least in the architectural sense, with copycat domes crowning several neighbouring towers.

Story Bridge

Of the many bridges spanning the Brisbane River, none holds a more lasting place in Queenslanders' affection than the iconic **Story Bridge** ❶. Tram tracks were removed in 1959, but otherwise this elegant structure, joining Kangaroo Point with the CBD, stands unchanged since its opening on 6 July 1940.

At the time, it symbolised progress in an era of political and economic uncertainty. Hundreds of tradesmen and engineers worked on the project during the six years from design to completion – a task made perilous because the sandy river bed necessitated unusually deep foundations. Tragically, four men died during construction.

Today, the Story Bridge carries around 100,000 vehicles daily. Lit by night, it is Queensland's most photographed landmark, appearing in countless books, brochures and postcards of the region. For a remarkable 360-degree view of the city, sign up for a Story Bridge Adventure Climb (170 Main Street, Kangaroo Point; charge; tel: 1300 254 627; www.storybridgeadventureclimb.com.au). Supervised ascent of the arches takes around two-and-a-half hours.

TIP

Eagle Street Pier is the departure point for paddle-wheeler cruises on board the *Kookaburra River Queen I* and *II*. Lunch cruises depart Tue, Thu-Sun at noon; dinner cruises Tue, Thu–Sun 7pm (tel: 3221 1300; www.kookaburrariverqueens.com).

BELOW: Story Bridge at night, seen from the Riverside Centre.

Examples of public art decorate the parkland around Brisbane Naval Stores.

Kangaroo Point precinct

The **Kangaroo Point Cliff Walk** offers great views of the city as it winds from South Bank to Dockside and beyond. Formed by convicts quarrying porphyry for building with, this serene sliver of riverside parkland hums with wildlife: scurrying possums, long-legged sea birds, posturing lizards, jumping fish and, in the dead of night, soaring fruit bats. By day, it belongs to joggers, rollerbladers, rock climbers and cyclists. As shadows lengthen, picnickers, lovers and, occasionally, fire twirlers take over.

The 130-year-old **St Mary's Anglican Church** (455 Main Street, Kangaroo Point) clings to the cliff edge. Nearby, a ramshackle set of stairs tumbles down the cliff to the **Brisbane Naval Stores**, built in 1887 to supply the Queensland Navy. The old stores are now the HQ of the Riverlife Adventure Centre (tel: 3891 5766; www.riverlife.com. au), where, among other pursuits, you can have a go at kayaking, abseiling, rock climbing and rollerblading. To get there, catch the ferry to the Thornton Street Ferry Terminal, then follow the signs along the river.

Whimsical examples of public art are dotted along this stretch of the parkland – among them Christopher Trotter's scrap-metal fish, Mona Ryder's sculpture of rowers at Thornton Street Ferry, and a solar sunflower that doesn't work. Elsewhere, the park serves as a repository for a series of one-dimensional sculptures, huge buoys, ancient anchors, rusty chains and unidentified nautical bits and bobs. Gazebos, follies and jetties jut from the boardwalk.

As for Kangaroo Point itself, few traces remain of the gracious houses that lined River Terrace and the waterfront. **Yungaba**, built to accommodate immigrants from 1885–7, still stands, as does the **Story Bridge Hotel**, at least 120 years old, tucked under the bridge's approach ramp, and one of Brisbane's most popular watering holes.

A short walk away, in a creaking boathouse on priceless riverfront real estate, stands the **Brisbane Jazz Club** (1 Annie Street, Kangaroo Point; tel: 3391 2006) – last bastion of main-

stream jazz, traditional dixieland and big-band swing. This brave little club, with its alarming sloping floor, has battled for survival for 40 years – and shows no sign of surrendering.

St John's Cathedral and Wickham Terrace precinct

Head back to the CBD and the grand, Gothic-revival **St John's Cathedral** **W**, Ann Street. Work started here in 1901, but the final touches weren't applied until 2009. St John's is impressive in design, scale and lighting, and it's worth entering to appreciate the stained-glass windows and colonnades. The cathedral also boasts Australia's only example of a vaulted ceiling constructed entirely of stone.

Within the grounds stands the **Deanery**, a two-storey porphyry building that served as the governor's residence from 1859 to 1862. Nearby, in Ann Street, stands **All Saints' Church** – the oldest Anglican church in Brisbane, founded in 1862 to minister to the spiritual needs of residents in what was then Windmill Hill. Cross into **Wickham Terrace** and discover a shady boulevard that

has attracted specialist medical practitioners since the 1920s.

Many historic buildings line its length, but none so historic as **The Old Windmill ❌** – built in 1828 and one of only two convict buildings surviving from the first wave of construction. Small and unprepossessing, the windmill has been many things since the convict era: a signal station, a fire lookout and, in 1935, the scene of Brisbane's first television broadcast. Its original purpose was to grind the grain cultivated on the surrounding land. It was powered, partly by sails, partly by convicts slaving on a treadmill for up to 14 hours a day. Its designer, a convict miller named John Oseland, absconded within a couple of days of the sails turning and was never seen again.

An offbeat modern building in this precinct is the **Wickham Terrace Car Park**. Car parks are rarely seen as iconic, but this one continues to excite comment (*see margin, right*).

Roma Street Parkland

Wickham Terrace provides an entry point to **Roma Street Parkland ❓**,

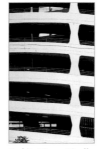

Architect James Birrell won an award for the heritage-listed Wickham Terrace Car Park, designed for Brisbane City Council in 1958. Contemporary architects are still full of praise for Birrell's ingenious use of concrete.

BELOW: Roma Street Parkland.

TIP

Spring Hill Baths (14 Torrington Street, Spring Hill; Sep–Apr Mon–Thur 6.30am–7pm, Fri 6.30am–6pm, Sat–Sun 8am–5pm; charge; tel: 3831 7881), a heritage-listed swimming pool, opened in 1886 and claims to be the oldest municipal baths in Australia.

the world's biggest subtropical inner-city garden. Formerly a railway shunting yard, the 16-hectare (40-acre) site has been planted with more than 100,000 varieties of shrub and 1,200 mature trees. The floral displays are breathtaking, with themed gardens that include a topiary maze, a lilly-pilly garden and a "wall" of epiphytes. Seasonal plants scramble over Wendy Mills' stainless-steel sculpture, and the massed displays of azalea, camellia and tropical rhododendron are spectacular. Anyone with even a passing interest in horticulture could spend a whole day enjoying the orchids, ferns and lilies of the forest and of Fern Gully walk. The bridge across Fern Gully is just one of several vantage points for superb views over the parklands to the city centre.

Brisbane Botanic Gardens, Mount Coot-tha

Quite different in character to the Roma Street Parkland, but no less visually arresting, are the **Brisbane Botanic Gardens ❶** in Mount Coot-tha Road. Just 10 minutes from the city centre, these gardens contain Australia's largest display of subtropical flora, spread over 57 hectares (140 acres), including lakes and streams. Among its attractions are a climate-controlled dome filled with rare tropical plants, a planetarium and formal Japanese garden. Further up Mount Coot-tha Road, a popular lookout provides a panoramic view of the city and glimpses of Moreton Bay.

Fortitude Valley and Brunswick Street Mall

For urban recreation, head for **Fortitude Valley ❷** – once Brisbane's premier commercial and retail hub, now reborn as a cosmopolitan precinct of trendy bars, clubs and residential apartments. The area is especially lively at weekends, with most of the action concentrated around the pavement cafés and bars in and around

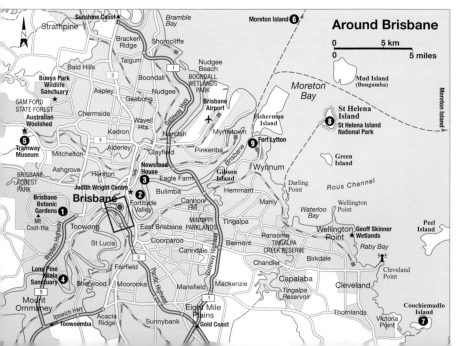

Brunswick Street Mall. One of the area's busiest clubs, the **GPO** (corner of Ann and Ballow streets), occupies the former Fortitude Valley Post Office, an ornate Victorian structure built in 1887 to reflect the area's burgeoning importance *(for more night-life venues, see box, below right)*.

Other noteworthy buildings include **The Empire Hotel** (1880s), **McWhirters Department Store** (1912), both in Brunswick Street, and the **Valley Police Station** (1936), corner of Wickham and Brooke streets. The Empire is now given over to chic bars and thumping music. McWhirters has become residential apartments. Only the police station is used for its original purpose.

Adding to the Fortitude Valley mix is the **Judith Wright Centre of Contemporary Arts**, at 420 Brunswick Street. Named after the late Queensland poet and environmental activist, the contemporary arts centre incorporates a 300-seat performance space, art gallery, artists' studios, screening room, workshops and theatre, music, dance and circus rehearsal spaces.

Also integral to the Fortitude Valley precinct is **Chinatown Mall** in Duncan Street, where dining choices cover a wide range of Asian cuisines, including Thai, Malaysian, Korean and Japanese... but not so much Chinese. Excellent Chinese restaurants do operate within Chinatown but, in general, Chinese restaurateurs and shopkeepers have gravitated to **Sunnybank**, a well-to-do fringe suburb with a large expatriate Chinese community.

Newstead House

For more early Brisbane history, head to **Newstead House** ❸ (Newstead Park, Breakfast Creek Road, Newstead; Mon–Thu 10am–4pm, Sun 2pm–5pm; charge; tel: 3216 1846; www.newsteadhouse.com.au). Brisbane's oldest surviving residence has been quietly dominating Breakfast Creek since 1846, when pioneering Darling Downs pastoralist Patrick Leslie built the then two-storey house for his father William. Neither Leslie appears to have spent much time there. In the year after its completion, the government resident, Captain John Wickham moved in, establishing the building as

Inside Mount Coot-tha Botanic Gardens.

BELOW LEFT: mixing it at the Wickham Hotel.

Party Brisbane

Brisbane's annual celebration, the **Brisbane Festival** (www.brisbanefestival.com.au), is a major event attracting a bevy of international and Australian acts. For three weeks in September, the city is in party mode and its meandering river becomes a platform for cutting-edge performances and family fun. Many events are free, including the spectacular opening fireworks display. It's colourful, it's loud and, even if you don't feel like partying, the spectacle is reason enough to visit **Fortitude Valley** – the city's hotspot for music, food and fun. Wickham and Ann streets, and the Brunswick Street Mall linking them, offer a profusion of clubs and bars. At **Family** (8 McLachlan Street), the crowd raves to a pounding 33,000-watt sound system. Sunday is gay night, but not exclusively so. The **Press Club** (339 Brunswick St) is less noisy and more upwardly mobile than many of the bars and clubs in the valley. Live-music venues include **Ric's Bar** (Brunswick Street Mall) and **The Zoo** (711 Ann Street), where many a famous Brisbane band made its start. Brisbane's gay scene centres on the **Wickham Hotel** (308 Wickham Street). Another gay-friendly venue is **The Beat Mega Club** (677 Ann Street), which offers themed bars on several levels.

TIP

On an upstream loop of the Brisbane River, Lone Pine can be reached by taxi or bus. Better still, at least in one direction, take a leisurely and scenic 19km (12-mile) cruise up the river on *Mirimar*, a stately, 60-year-old timber vessel that departs daily at 10am from the Cultural Centre pontoon (tel: 0412 749 426; www.mirimar.com).

BELOW: a number of sanctuaries in Queensland, including Lone Pine, keep wombats.

the unofficial Government House. Across Breakfast Creek is the **Breakfast Creek Hotel**, famous for beer "off the wood", and excellent steaks.

Lone Pine Koala Sanctuary

In such a sprawling city, it's impossible to see everything in one visit. Still, visitors who stay in Brisbane more than a day or two usually wind up nursing a koala at **Lone Pine Koala Sanctuary ④** (Jesmond Road, Fig Tree Pocket; daily 9am–5pm; charge; tel: 3378 1366; www.koala.net). Open since 1927 and noted in the *Guinness Book of Records* as the world's first and biggest koala sanctuary, Lone Pine also keeps kangaroos, wombats, birds, bats, reptiles, echidnas, Tasmanian devils and dingoes.

Tramway Museum

At Ferny Grove, just northwest of Brisbane, you'll find the **Tramway Museum ⑤** (Tramway Street; Sun 12.30–4pm; charge; tel: 3351 1776; www.brisbanetramwaymuseum.org), where tram aficionados maintain a fleet rendered obsolete by the City Council's 1968 decision to end a tradition of

transport that began with horse-drawn trams in 1885. Many of the exhibits here are true collectors' items – from the 1901 Californian-built Car 47 that ran between Edward Street and the City Botanical Gardens, to Car 554, the last car to run officially on the tram system.

Moreton Bay

In many respects, **Moreton Bay** is Brisbane's best natural asset – stretching 160km (100 miles) from Caloundra in the north to Southport, and encompassing some 360 islands. On **Moreton Island ⑥**, Tangalooma Resort (tel: 3268 6333; www.tangalooma.com), built on the site of a whaling station where more than 6,000 humpback whales met their deaths between 1952 and 1962, now promotes whale-watching and dolphin studies. Just 75 minutes by catamaran from the CBD, it's close enough to call by for lunch. Departures are from Tangalooma Launch Terminal at Holt Street Wharf, Pinkenba, on the lower Brisbane River. A transfer coach (tel: 3637 2000, A$20/10 per adult/child, booking essential) operates daily

from most CBD hotels and the Roma Street Transit Centre. The transfer coach connects with the 10am service to the resort and the 4pm service from the resort only. The day tour that includes hand-feeding dolphins costs adult/child A$175/130.

James Cook named the bay as he sailed past in 1770, but Matthew Flinders was the first European to enter its waters in 1779 – an event re-enacted annually by the residents of **Coochiemudlo Island ❼**. Flinders was followed by John Oxley, who, with the assistance of three castaway convicts, explored the Brisbane River in 1823 *(see page 26)*. Located 40km (25 miles) southeast of Brisbane, Coochiemudlo is accessed by ferry. From Brisbane, take Cleveland Road towards Victoria Point; follow the sign at the main traffic lights in Victoria Point. (Contact Redlands Tourism, Shore Street West, Cleveland; tel: 3821 2730 for details.)

Stradbroke Island *(see page 101)*, meanwhile, has been identified by Brisbane's prosperous middle classes as a good place to build weekenders. Historically, the bay's most interesting

island is **St Helena ❽**, 6km (4 miles) southeast of the river mouth, where crumbling walls form the outline of a self-sufficient prison farm that, at its zenith, held 300 prisoners – among them Captain Starlight (the sobriquet given to legendary hustler Henry Readford, who entered folklore in 1870 when he and two others stole around 1,000 head of cattle from Longreach). The oldest ruins date from 1866. The prison was finally abandoned in 1933. (To get there, contact Cat-o-Nine-Tails, tel: 1300 438 787, or Brisbane Cruises, tel: 3630 2666.)

Fort Lytton

Visitors interested in military history should plan a visit to **Fort Lytton ❾** (South Street, Lytton; Sun and public holidays 10am–4pm; charge; tel: 3906 9111), near the mouth of the Brisbane River. Built to repel a feared Russian invasion in the late 19th century, the fort is shielded by earthworks and surrounded by a moat, with underground passages connecting its chambers. Invading navies would be met by a combination of heavy guns and controlled river mines. ❏

If you're not at Tangalooma during the whale-watching season, try your hand at sand tobogganing.

Below: watching the humpback whales in Moreton Bay.

Best Restaurants, Bars and Cafés

Restaurants

Prices per person for a three-course dinner with house wine:

$ = A$60 and under
$$ = A$60–100
$$$ = A$100–120
$$$$ = A$120 and over

Most Brisbane precincts have at least one formal dining space and a selection of ethnic restaurants, the most common being Thai, Indian and Vietnamese. The cafés and bistros of Park Road, Milton; Brunswick Street, Fortitude Valley; Merthyr Road, New Farm; and Little Stanley Street, South Bank, offer excellent fare in often sophisticated settings. Asian restaurants are mainly concentrated in Fortitude Valley, West End and Sunnybank.

Ahmet's
10/164 Grey Street, South Bank
Tel: 3846 6699
www.ahmets.com
Open: L & D daily. $$
Be transported to a Turkish bazaar in this atmospheric restaurant. Attention to detail extends to the tasty dishes that are best shared.

Augustine's on George
40 George Street
Tel: 3229 0014
Open: L Mon–Fri, D Mon–Sat. $$
Hong Kong expatriate Augustine Tso has been a flag on Brisbane's fine-dining map for more than 26 years. The quality at this snug restaurant in historic George Street has never wavered: thoughtful, flavoursome dishes that sit lightly on the palate. Entrées such as braised wagyu beef cheeks with baby beets and goat curd, tempura courgette flower and basil oil set the scene for mains such as pan-seared barramundi, bouillabaisse featuring Morton Bay bug, and char-grilled loin of lamb.

Aria
Eagle Street Pier
Tel: 3233 2555
www.ariarestaurant.com
Open: L Mon–Fri, D daily. $$$
With spectacular views over Story Bridge and the Brisbane River, Aria has an elegant contemporary menu devised by celebrity chef Matt Moran. Seafood and steaks dominate, but there are excellent vegetarian options and delicate Asian interpretations.

Breakfast Creek Hotel
2 Kingsford Smith Drive, Albion
Tel: 3262 5988
www.breakfastcreekhotel.com
Open: L & D daily. $$
The Brekkie's steaks are virtually the size of a dinner plate, and consistently thick, juicy and flavoursome. Choose your own premium cuts at the grill in the Staghorn Beer Garden or visit the Spanish Garden Steakhouse for full table service and other (non-steak) dishes.

Brett's Wharf
449 Kingsford Smith Drive, Hamilton.
Tel: 3868 1717
Open: L & D daily. $$$
Located beside the Brisbane River, with pelicans perched on the pylons outside, this is one for seafood-fanciers. The menu reflects what's biting, and on a good day the fare is absolutely stunning. Restaurateurs Francis and Marilyn Domenech also own Baguette in nearby Racecourse Road – another Brisbane institution.

Il Centro Restaurant
Eagle Street Pier
Tel: 3221 6090
www.il-centro.com.au
Open: L Sun–Fri, D daily. $$$
One of a selection of upmarket restaurants overlooking the Brisbane River at Eagle Street Pier. The menu at Il Centro is Italian-inspired and makes great use of Queensland's amazing variety of seafood.

Cha Cha Char
5 Waterfront Place
Tel: 3211 9944
www.chachachar.com.au
Open: L Mon–Fri, D daily. $$$
Owner John Kilroy takes steak very seriously. His menu discusses the history of the beef you're about to eat, its age, provenance and the pasture on which it was raised. Regulars discuss steak as they do wine.

E'cco
100 Boundary Street (corner Adelaide Street East)
Tel: 3831 8344
www.eccobistro.com
Open: L Tue–Fri, D Tue–Sat. $$$
One of Brisbane's most awarded bistros. Philip Johnson's mantra is simplicity, simplicity, simplicity. Essentially, his food relies on fresh ingredients and unfussy preparation. Settle in for field mushrooms, olive toast, rocket and parmesan, or try seared scallops, white polenta, sauce Romesco and flaked almonds. And that's just for starters.

Gambaro's Seafood Restaurant
33 Caxton Street
Tel: 3369 9500
www.gambaros.com.au
Open: L Mon–Fri, D Mon–Sat. $$$
The Gambaro family has been in the seafood business since 1953, and Gambaro's has been a Brisbane institution since it opened in 1972. The seafood platters are gastronomic delights, and from the tanks you can select Moreton Bay bugs, lobster and mud crabs.

The Green Papaya

898 Stanley Street,
East Brisbane
Tel: 3891 5000
Open: D Tue–Sun. $$
The Green Papaya earned its reputation as an excellent Vietnamese restaurant but has undergone a facelift and been reborn under chef Kesinee Sae-Jung as a Balinese and Thai blend showcasing local ingredients. BYO.

Jade Buddha

Eagle Street Pier
Tel: 3221 2888
www.jadebuddha.com.au
Open: L & D daily. $$$
With its pan-Asian and modern-fusion cuisine, which for the most part employs fresh Queensland seafood, the "Buddha" attracts Brisbane's glitterati. Kick off the night with colourful cocktails in the chic Shadow Lounge, and enjoy the delicious views of the Brisbane River.

Moda

12 Edward Street
Tel: 3221 7655
www.modarestaurant.com.au
Open: L Mon–Fri, D Mon–Sat. $$$
Award-winning restaurant offering innovative but accessible cuisine conceived by Javier Codina to a dedicated inner-city following. Excellent wine cellar.

Montrachet

224 Given Terrace,
Paddington
Tel: 3367 0030
www.montrachet.com.au
Open: L Mon–Fri, D Mon–Thu. $$$
Lyon-born chef Thierry Galichet has been a significant presence on the Brisbane scene for years, operating a series of memorable restaurants across the city. Montrachet is his best yet. Main courses include baked rack of lamb with Morbier cheese soufflé, and a wonderful bouillabaisse.

Ortiga

446 Brunswick Street,
Fortitude Valley
Tel: 3852 1155
www.ortiga.com.au
Open: D Tue–Sun. $$$
Chef Pablo Tordesillas brings Iberian influence to Simon Hill's latest creation. The exciting menu is designed to be shared, from the tapas to mains such as *arroz caldoso de marisco*. The wine list is excellent and the service swift and unobtrusive.

Port Office Hotel

Corner Margaret and Edward streets.
Tel: 3221 0072
Open: L & D Mon–Sat. $$
The Heritage Port Office Hotel has a great mix of dining styles. Choose between the casual Marble Bar, tapas in the Fix Wine Bar, or more elegant dining in the Fix Restaurant. There are pizzas cooked in wood-fired ovens, seafood and vegetarian options, although the steaks from the grill enjoy pride of place.

Restaurant Two

2 Edward Street
Tel: 3210 0600
www.restaurant2.com.au
Open: L Mon–Fri, D Mon–Sat. $$$$
Classic dining in a lovely high-ceilinged room with a stylish bar. Owner-chef David Pugh, one of Brisbane's "Five Chefs", emphasises freshness and natural flavour in his elegant dishes.

Seasalt at Armstrongs

Incholm Hotel
73 Wickham Terrace
Tel: 3832 4566
www.armstrongsrestaurant.com.au
Open: L Mon–Fri, D Mon–Sat. $$$
Russell Armstrong has been a stalwart of the Brisbane food scene for more than two decades – feisty, uncompromising, and one of the most experienced chefs in Australia. Seasalt has a small, Modern Australian menu that features a range of meats and is not, as it sounds, dominated by seafood.

Bars and Cafés

Cru Bar & Cellar (22 James Street, Fortitude Valley; tel: 3252 2400; www.crubar.com; open: L & D daily; $$) serves great wine and tapas and is a pleasant place to while away an hour. Part-bottle shop, part-bar and part-café, Cru is run by one of Brisbane's most successful food-and-drink teams. There are plenty of quiet corners for people-watching while enjoying a snack and a glass of wine. For something altogether different, try **Belgian Beer Café Brussels** (Mary and Edward streets; tel: 3221 0199; open: L & D daily; $$), where you can wash down authentic Flemish dishes with a selection of Belgian beers on tap.

RIGHT: acclaimed bistro, E'cco.

SPORTS

It's difficult to tune into the local psyche without some grasp of local sports. In Queensland, there are plenty to choose from

ABOVE: Outback horse racing at the annual Birdsville Cup races. Every September the remote town of Birdsville hosts one of Australia's most famous bush racing carnivals.

ABOVE: the State of Origin series between Queensland and New South Wales is the highlight of the rugby league calendar. The matches are played as a best-of-three every June and inspire passionate support from inhabitants of both states.

ABOVE: Broadbeach, on the Gold Coast, hosts the annual Australian National Lifesaving Titles. The summer contest attracts thousands of competitors from clubs in every state, and a vast number of spectators.

No nation's population is more passionate about sport than Australia's, whether as participants or spectators. And no region is more passionate than Queensland. Certainly some sports are favoured, but give Queenslanders something to cheer about and there's no stopping them, even if it's not a "local" game. The Brisbane Lions story *(opposite)* is testimony to this.

But if there is a number one sport for Queenslanders, it's rugby league. The Brisbane Broncos, Gold Coast Titans and North Queensland Cowboys are the state's National Rugby League (NRL; www.nrl.com.au) teams, and attract passionate support. However, it's that the State of Origin games between the Maroons (Queensland) and the Blues (New South Wales) that really stir the blood in deep winter. Suncorp Stadium (Milton, Brisbane ; tel:3331 5000; www.suncorpstadium.com.au) hosts Queensland's rugby league, rugby union and soccer matches. Soccer is growing as a participation sport, its profile raised by the A-league set up in 2005; Brisbane Roar is the local team.

In summer, cricket is king, with tests, limited-over, and interstate games at the "Gabba" (named after the suburb Woolloongabba; tel: 1300 843 422; www.the-gabba.com.au) in Brisbane. Basketball is popular, country rodeos have their own appeal, and, if flamboyant Outback horse racing is your thing, head to the famous Birdsville Races (www.bridsville-races.com) in September.

AUSSIE RULES

For years, Australian Rules Football was the preserve of Victoria, until it was decided that if the sport was to survive, it would need to build up its fan base. As part of this process, the Fitzroy Lions from inner Melbourne merged with the Brisbane Bears in 1996 and the Brisbane Lions were born. Similar moves, overseen by the Australian Football League (AFL; www.afl.com.au), saw teams established in the other mainland states, but for some time the dominant clubs still came from Victoria. This began to change when the West Coast Eagles from Perth won championships in 1992 and 1994, but the real shift in attitudes came with the astonishing success of the Brisbane Lions, when the team won three consecutive Grand Finals, from 2001 to 2003. With success came loyalty from local fans, and nowadays the team can attract thousands of diehard fans to the Gabba in Brisbane. In 2011, the Gold Coast Suns, with star Victorian recruit Garry Ablett Jnr, joined the fray. The season runs from March to September, and there's always a willing local to explain the arcane rules to an overseas visitor.

ABOVE: Matthew Hayden, from Kingaroy, is one of the greats of world cricket. Known for trading records for highest scores with the West Indies' Brian Lara for many years, he made 380 in a test match in 2003. The left-hander played for Queensland and debuted for Australia in 1993. He was the first man to make over 1,000 test runs in five seasons. He retired from the sport in 2009.

RIGHT: Ian Thorpe may be the international poster boy of Australian swimming, but it's Queenslander Grant Hackett who has quietly broken records and secured championships at a steady rate during the last decade. As winner of the 1,500 metres freestyle at both the 2000 and 2004 Olympics (and silver medalist in 2008), Hackett has established himself as one of the greats of distance swimming. He was made team captain of Australia as well, before his retirement in 2008.

Gold Coast

Brisbane

Welcome to the subtropical pleasure zone, home of the bronzed, the toned and the proudly hedonistic. Away from the flash and the hoopla, you can still find tranquil waterfalls, verdant rainforests and rolling cane farms

South of Brisbane, the 32km (20-mile) stretch of coast from Coolangatta to Surfers Paradise – bushland just two generations ago – is one of the fastest-growing tourist and residential areas in Australia. The Gold Coast is superficial and showy in parts, beautiful in others, but never dull. The beaches, particularly Burleigh Heads, set in national parkland, are strikingly gorgeous, while the high-rise skyline of Surfers Paradise, holiday headquarters of Australia's rich and hedonistic, must now rank with Ipanema, Miami and Cannes for architectural overkill: famously, the skyscrapers at Surfers cast shadows over the beach every afternoon. But that no longer matters by night, when the partygoers take over the streets, restaurants and nightclubs.

Soaring residential towers and conurbations line almost the entire length of this coastal stretch. Successive waves of development have all but obliterated the original shoreline. Only the sea remains untamed, as beach-front residents become painfully aware whenever turbulent seas threaten the dunes.

It's appropriate that this bright and brassy strip should be known as the Gold Coast – a headline dreamt up in the 1940s by journalists writing about the post-war real-estate boom (a boom, apparently, without end). The name stuck and became official in 1959. Ever since, the Gold Coast – Surfers Paradise in particular – has taken perverse pride in its embracing of glitz and pizzazz.

Gold Coasters live for the moment. They are fascinated by glamour. They love to flaunt. It's a happy hunting ground for wealthy retirees and divorcees. Tummy tucks and face-lifts are *de rigueur*. The young go surfing.

LEFT: the entrance to the extravagant "6-star" Palazzo Versace.

The young-at-heart go partying. This is a proudly hedonistic society that sees no contradiction in working extremely hard to maintain outward impressions of leisurely, designer-clad affluence.

Main Beach

Just north of Surfers Paradise, on the Gold Coast highway, lies **Southport.** When Governor Sir Anthony Musgrave built a summer retreat here in the late 1880s, the town became all the rage. The cream of Brisbane society braved an arduous coach journey, ferry crossing and horseback ride to be close to the action. Nowadays, Southport is a relatively low-key residential area. The action long ago shifted across the Broadwater to **Main Beach ❶**, with its glittering hotels, resorts, theme parks, bars, boutiques and restaurants. The Spit is a 3km (2-mile) sandbar running north of Main Beach, separating the Broadwater from the Pacific Ocean. On one side of the main street running south to north stands **Sheraton Mirage**, the airy Honolulu-style resort. On the other is the decadent

"6-star" **Palazzo Versace**, where the floors are laid with fine Italian marble, the bellboys dress better than the clientele, and guests can choose from six types of pillow.

Within the nearby **Marina Mirage Shopping Complex**, a twice-monthly farmers' market brings jolly cheese makers and weathered crayfish farmers into incongruous communion with boutique owners pandering to the Louis Vuitton set. Spice blenders, emu ranchers, beekeepers, sausage makers, organic fruit growers and others set up shop around the faux-Renaissance fountain – making it one of the few places you can buy silk socks and smoked eel under one roof.

The precinct is also a fine-dining zone. Both Palazzo Versace and Sheraton Mirage maintain excellent restaurants. One of the Gold Coast's more elegant Italian eateries, **Ristorante Fellini**, occupies premises within Marina Mirage. For most visitors, however, it's enough to slip into one of the casual cafés lining the boardwalk, order something Mediterranean and watch the yachts

TIP

If the surf's up, as it almost always is on the Gold Coast, an international brigade of surfing devotees will be riding the waves from dawn. Main Beach, at the northern end of the high-rises, is particularly popular with surfies, but you'll find them performing almost anywhere along the strip. The yellow lookout towers are for the lifeguards, who regularly perform rescues, even on the mildest days.

BELOW: the beach at Surfers Paradise.

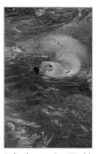

Polar bear at Sea World, a big theme park on the Southport Spit.

scud gracefully across the Broadwater, with the towers of Southport beyond. At nearby Tedder Avenue in Main Beach, trendy bars, alfresco cafés and restaurants cater to a less pretentious crowd who nonetheless take pleasure in seeing and being seen.

Sea World

Beyond the upmarket shopping mall, crowds flock to the theme park **Sea World ❷** (Seaworld Drive, The Spit; daily 10am–5pm; charge; tel: 5588 2222; www.seaworld.myfun.com.au). Attractions on offer include choreographed water-skiers, performing dolphins, polar bears in a replicated Arctic tundra, sharks swimming in a purpose-built lagoon system, and king, gentoo and fairy penguins zipping around in their cool-water enclosures.

For safe thrills, take a ride on **The Sea Viper**, a triple-loop roller-coaster, or snorkel amid benign reef sharks and colourful fish in the tropical reef lagoon.

Dreamworld and Whitewater World

The Gold Coast has no shortage of theme parks. Apart from Sea World, they are concentrated at the north-western end of the coastal strip, off the Pacific Motorway.

Dreamworld ❸ (daily 10am–5pm; charge; tel: 5588 1111; www.dream world.com.au) at Coomera combines gentle fun with adrenalin-pumping rides. The **Tower of Terror II** hurls passengers 120 metres (395ft) vertically into the firmament. If you can bear to open your eyes, there is, momentarily, a marvellous view of the surrounding countryside as the gondola teeters at the upper limit of its trajectory. **Wipeout** is another ride for thrill-seekers: a spin on this roller-coaster is likened to "windsurfing in a washing machine". Among the gentler attractions are a carousel, bumper cars, the big red car ride at **Wiggles World**, and interactive entertainment shows for kids. There

are wildlife attractions, too – Bengal and Sumatran tigers, two cougars and Australian fauna.

Whitewater World (daily 10am–5pm; charge; www.whitewaterworld.com.au) is right next door and under the same management (joint tickets are available). Here the name says it all, with various slides and tubes to ensure you get drenched, and a wave pool.

Wet'n'Wild

For more water-based spills and thrills, head to **Wet'n'Wild Water World ❹** at Oxenford (daily 10am–5pm, 27 Dec–15 Jan until 9pm, 16–22 Jan until 7pm; charge; tel: 133 386; www.wetnwild.myfun.com.au). Spread over 10 hectares (25 acres) of subtropical garden, this giant water-sports park makes a genuine attempt to please everyone. Activities run from the scary to the therapeutic. Eligibility for the more exciting rides is regulated by height, not age. Thus, you must be 110cm (3ft 7in) tall for the **Kamikaze** or the **Blackhole**, but only 100cm (3ft 3in) tall for the **River Rapids** or **Mammoth Falls**.

Movie World

Not to be outdone, the nearby **Movie World ❺** (daily 10am–5pm; tel: 5573 8485; charge; www.movieworld.myfun.com.au) features the **Wild West Falls Adventure Ride**, an "action-packed, six-minute adventure propelled by more than a million litres of wicked water to a 20-metre (65ft) heart-stopping final splashdown". One of Australia's biggest theme-park attractions, the ride is built in and around an artificial mountain, itself part of a Wild West movie set, complete with Native American reservations, ghost towns and wagon trains.

Movie World is interesting because it combines the functionality of a working film studio – not open to the public, by the way – with high-tech rides, staged stunts, animatronics and pyrotechnics. Clint Eastwood set the tone at the opening in 1991 when he pulled the first beer in the Dirty Harry Bar. While visitors are unlikely to spot any Hollywood stars, their chances of bumping into Daffy Duck or Yosemite Sam are quite good.

High tech exhibits reflect Warner Bros. cinema hits. The **Scooby Doo**

The Superman Escape ride at Movie World promises 0–100km per hour in 2 seconds.

BELOW: Wet'n'Wild's Super 8 Aqua Racer.

TIP

The Aquaduck Gold Coast Tour (7a Orchid Avenue, Surfers Paradise; tel: 5539 0222; www. aquaduck. com.au) offers an innovative and popular city-sights guided tour on an amphibious vehicle equipped to travel on land and water. Book an early trip – preferably the first of the day – at least a day ahead.

Spooky Coaster, for instance, is a A$13-million indoor ride inspired by the 2002 film shot at the Gold Coast. Lethal Weapon delivers "drops, dives, rollovers, side-winders, double spins, loops" and fast, upside-down thrills.

Movie World's gnarliest roller-coaster, **Superman Escape**, accelerates from 0 to 100kmph (62mph) in two seconds, traversing 760 metres (2,500ft) of vertical climbs, weightless drops and giant G-force turns.

At **Kids WB Fun Zone**, the little ones can have fun on the **Road Runner Rollercoaster**, get wet in the **Splash Zone**, and hop on board for the Looney Tunes river ride.

Australian Outback Spectacular

Finally, for "a genuine Aussie Outback experience", there is Warner's **Australian Outback Spectacular 6** (Tues–Sat 7.30pm; charge; tel: 5573 8289; www.outbackspectacular.myfun.com.au), located between Movie World and Wet'n'Wild. Tuck into a three-course barbecue while watching stockmen deal with wild horses and stampeding cattle. The extravaganza comes complete with audio and visual effects, an array of bush vehicles and a mustering helicopter.

It's a short drive from here to **Sanctuary Cove 7** (tel: 5577 6175), an enclave of mega-mansions and maxi-yachts belonging to the super-wealthy Gold Coast elite. The late crooner Frank Sinatra launched this resort, which boasts two excellent golf courses, a country club, a "village" of bars, boutiques and restaurants, and the sumptuous Hyatt Regency Hotel.

To reach Sanctuary Cove, take exit 57 from the Pacific Motorway near Coomera, then drive down Casey's Road for 10 minutes, or until you catch the whiff of money.

Surfers Paradise

Surfers Paradise 8 has meretricious charm, as befits the Gold Coast's iconic city. The surf rolls in. Tanned musclemen and beautiful women strut their stuff on the beaches and in the bars. A sense of suntanned *joie de vivre* prevails.

You see faces from Asia and the Middle East, and hear American

BELOW: attractions at Movie World.

accents. Visionaries who dreamt that Surfers Paradise would one day become an international destination are having their day. It's cosmopolitan and saucy. **Orchid Avenue**, one of several busy thoroughfares within the main hub of the area, is a heady mix of luxury hotels, clubs, bars, strip joints, hot-dog stands, smart restaurants and boutiques selling Prada and Cartier.

Older locals speak wistfully of the 1950s and 1960s, when Surfers blossomed as a friendly resort filled with Runyon-esque characters with names such as Cherokee Bill and the Mutton Bird Man. Pragmatists realise that Surfers Paradise has long since passed the point of no return. Its future lies as a party town, a place where people let their hair down. School-leavers descend en masse every November to carouse and celebrate the end of exams in "schoolies' week". Sometimes, on the nightclub strip, their antics tread a fine line between high jinks and sleaze.

Meanwhile, a surge of luxury development has created a new generation of upmarket restaurants, boutiques and spas – edging out the tacky arcades, gaudy signage and seedy shops that infested the CBD through the 1990s. Massive developments such as the **Renaissance Towers** on Surfers Paradise Boulevard and the 80-storey **Q1** residential tower in Hamilton Avenue have set the tone for the future. The magnificent sand and surf of the foreshore play a curiously secondary role to the high-rise apartment blocks that overshadow them. Surfers continue to catch the waves, but thanks to successive skin-cancer awareness campaigns, Queenslanders spend less time on the beach than they used to.

Surfing and amusements

Ironically, it's for the entertainment more than the surfing that people flock to Surfers Paradise, even though it has several surf schools and is a good place for novices to get started.

Former world surfing champion Cheyne Horan (Cheyne Horan School of Surf, corner Hanlan Street and The Esplanade, Surfers Paradise; tel: 1800 227 873; www.cheynehoran. com.au) promises to get his students riding in their first lesson. Beginner classes are daily 10am–noon, 2–4pm,

TIP

The Australian National Life Saving Titles attract thousands of competitors from clubs in every state, and a vast number of spectators. Competitions are held most frequently during the summer months, from around mid-September to the end of April. For information on contests, call the Queensland Surf Life Saving Association (tel: 3846 8000; www.life saving.com.au).

BELOW: this way to Paradise.

The Fly-Coaster: apparently part of a Gold Coast traders' initiative to part punters from their lunches so they have to go and eat again.

BELOW RIGHT: aerial view of Surfers Paradise.

and the school offers complimentary hotel pick-up. Another recommended surf school is Gold Coast Surfing Centre (154 Marine Parade, Rainbow Beach, Coolangatta; tel: 0417 191 629 5495), where former professional surfer Dave Davidson gives lessons for beginners daily 10am–noon (8am in summer); 2pm–4pm daily. *(See page 272 for more about surf schools.)*

For a blast of old-fashioned hoopla, check out **Ripley's Believe It Or Not! Museum** (Cavill Mall; daily 9am–11pm; charge; tel: 5592 0040; www. ripleys.com). Within the museum's 12 themed galleries are displayed such bizarre items as "a rare shrunken head" and "a real Fiji mermaid". Visitors are invited to "stand next to the tallest and biggest men who ever lived".

Thrill-seekers are well catered for in Surfers Paradise. Heart-stopping attractions include **The Vomatron** – a device based on astronaut training equipment that puts participants through 4Gs of force – and **The Sling Shot** (6 Palm Avenue; daily; tel: 5570 2700; www.funtime.com.au) – a 52-metre (170ft) high catapult that

propels two passengers 80 metres (260ft) into the air at speeds of more than 160kmh (100mph) aboard an open-seat gondola attached using steel cables.

Back on terra firma, **The Infinity Funhouse** (Chevron Renaissance, corner Surfers Paradise Boulevard and Elkhorn Avenue; daily 10am–10pm; charge; tel: 5526 8935; www. infinitygc.com.au) is a disorientating but captivating series of futuristic mazes filled with special effects and illusions.

Broadbeach

A short drive from Surfers Paradise is **Broadbeach** ❾ – a rapidly developing precinct of residential towers, snazzy shopping zones and trendy eat streets. As the name suggests, Broadbeach has a top surf beach. Locals promenade along this sandy strip from 5.30am onwards. Broadbeach is also home to the **Kurrawa Surf Life Saving Club**, host of the annual Australian Surf Life Saving Championships.

More family-orientated than Surfers Paradise, Broadbeach surged

The Rise and Rise of the Gold Coast

In the 1840s, cedar getters pushed into the Nerang Valley, setting up their loading stations on the Logan and Coomera rivers. In their footsteps came graziers and cane farmers, whose agricultural methods irrevocably altered the hills, rivers and wetlands that the Aboriginal inhabitants had known. Nerang, the first town, was surveyed in 1865. The stagecoach operators, Cobb & Co., ran services to Southport in 1878, while steamers made regular voyages to and from Brisbane. The completion of a coast road in 1923 coincided with the arrival of dashing English surfing instructor James Cavill, who built a hotel at Elston that became known as The Surfers Paradise Hotel. It proved so popular that, in 1933, the entire township was renamed Surfers Paradise. By the mid-1950s, thanks to the post-war economic boom and nonexistent building regulations, the Gold Coast's destiny was already clear. The first high-rise, Kinkabool, went up in 1959.

At 322 metres (1,056ft), the Q1 is currently the highest building and Skypoint, on level 77, is one of Queensland's top attractions, providing breathtaking coastal views from Brisbane to Byron Bay (www.skypoint. com.au, Sun–Thur 9am–9pm, Fri–Sat 9am–midnight; charge).

ahead during Surfers Paradise's period of stagnation and decline in the 1990s and now prospers as its more conservative twin. Broadbeach may seem less racy and frenetic than Surfers, but it still offers plenty of sun and fun, with crowd-pulling attractions of its own.

More than 13,000 people daily pass beneath the rippling neon facade of **Jupiters Casino, Broadbeach Island** (tel: 5592 8100) to try their luck at the tables. The 24-hour casino has five restaurants, nine bars, a 600-room hotel and a 2,000-seat theatre. There's no need to leave until the money runs out. A monorail connects the Jupiters with the Oasis complex across the Gold Coast Highway. Yet more alfresco eateries and wine bars line **Surf Parade**.

Burleigh Heads

Driving south from Surfers Paradise, the atmosphere becomes more laid-back as thrill-a-minute diversions give way to natural attractions in the form of nature reserves, wildlife parks and bird sanctuaries.

Burleigh Heads ⑩, 89km (55 miles) south of Brisbane, is the Gold Coast's premier family destination and has been insulated from the excesses of development by preservation of the terrain around the Tallebudgera Creek Estuary. It is also a mecca for surfers, whose skills have become something of an attraction in themselves – sometimes observed by hundreds of spectators on **Burleigh Headlands** as they ride the southeasterly swell to the beach.

The small **Burleigh Heads National Park** embraces coastal rainforest and heathlands. A 3km (1¾-mile) walking trail around the rocky headland departs from the Burleigh Heads Information Centre (1711 Gold Coast Highway, on northern side of Tallebudgera Creek). It leads past mangroves, eucalypts and pandanuses, which shelter reptiles, wallabies, bandicoots and koalas – all a world away from the concrete coastal jungle. The track emerges at Goodwin Terrace, at which point you can either follow the boardwalk along the foreshore or head back to the information centre via a steep rainforest walk.

BELOW: catching a wave at Burleigh Heads.

TIP

A short circular walk affords marvellous views of the natural arch over Cave Creek *(pictured below)*. Look out for noisy pittas, rainforest dragons and rainbow lorikeets in the forest. At night, you can see the large colony of glow-worms inside the cave under the rock arch. Natural Bridge is 30km (18 miles) from Nerang.

BELOW: Cave Creek, Springbrook National Park.

Wildlife sanctuaries

West of Burleigh Heads, the **David Fleay Wildlife Park** ⓫ (Kabool Road, West Burleigh; daily 9am–5pm; charge; tel: 5576 2411) is well worth a visit. The park functions both as a research centre and a sanctuary for endangered and injured wildlife. Now operated by the Queensland Parks and Wildlife Service, it continues the work of the late naturalist and platypus breeder Dr David Fleay, who established the park in the 1950s. It comprises five distinct habitats, from tropical rainforest, the habitat of tree kangaroos and cassowaries, to a nocturnal / arid zone, home to lesser-known species such as the great bilby and the yellow-bellied glider. It's a wonderful place to familiarise yourself with native Australian species.

Heading south towards Coolangatta is **Currumbin Wildlife Sanctuary** ⓬ (28 Tomewin Street, Currumbin; daily 8am–5pm; charge; tel: 5534 1266; www.cws.org.au), the Gold Coast's longest-running attraction, famous for its rainbow lorikeets. The story goes that founder Alex Griffiths began hand-feeding these chattering, brightly coloured parrots in the late 1940s to distract them from his favourite cultivated flowers, which they would attack in search of nectar. His feeding sessions attracted so many visitors that he formalised it into a business.

The sanctuary has evolved significantly since then. Run by the National Trust of Queensland since 1976, it now holds Australia's biggest collection of native animals, including 1,500 species of mammal, reptile and bird. Nearly half-a-million visitors pass through the turnstiles annually to see birds of prey, cuddly koalas, crocodiles and wildlife shows featuring venomous snakes. It's a natural haven amid the Gold Coast's surfeit of artificial splendours and excess.

Coolangatta

Coolangatta ⓭ is at the easy-going end of the Gold Coast, a border town that melds seamlessly with **Tweed Heads**, its twin on the southern side of the Queensland–New South Wales border. The Gold Coast's international airport is located at nearby Bilinga, but, thus far, Coolangatta has

been spared the full brunt of high-rise development. Located 102km (63 miles) south of Brisbane, the laid-back resort remains popular for family holidays and is a top surfing destination. It has great beaches, rolling surf and is well positioned for day trips to the hinterland.

Local landmarks Point Danger and Mount Warning are among the few places that Captain Cook felt inspired enough to name along this part of the coast. The town is named after the *Coolangatta*, an 88-ton brigantine that came to grief in 1843. Views from the Point Danger headland along the coast are lovely, plus it's a great spot to watch the surfing action. There's a memorial at the lighthouse to Captain Cook made of cast-iron ballast jettisoned from his ship, the *Endeavour*.

Springbrook National Park

Less than an hour's drive west of the Gold Coast, the **Springbrook National Park ⑭** (tel: 5533 5147; www.derm.qld.gov.au/parks) offers a cool and tranquil refuge from the noisy, urbanised lowlands. The park occupies the northern rim of an ancient volcano, which was once centred on Mount Warning in New South Wales. It is made up of three reserves: the **Springbrook Plateau** section, the **Mount Cougal** section and the **Natural Bridge** section, remarkable for an intriguing rock-arch formation over Cave Creek *(see Tip, left)*. Listed as a World Heritage Site, the park preserves subtropical rainforest, eucalypt forest and montane heath. It's a stunning landscape of ancient trees, gorges and waterfalls.

An extensive network of walking paths has been cut through all three sections of the park. The Springbrook Plateau section, in particular, has lookouts affording spectacular views, albeit shrouded in cloud on overcast days. There are information displays at all major track entrances, and a small information centre operates from the historic Springbrook schoolhouse, where you can pick up a booklet of the park's trail network.

Two bitumen roads lead to Springbrook Plateau, which is 29km (18 miles) from Mudgeeraba and 34km (21 miles) from Nerang.

Thanks to an hour's time lag between New South Wales and Queensland (the latter does not observe daylight saving in summer), New Year's Eve attracts big crowds, with revellers surging across the border in order to celebrate twice.

BELOW LEFT: Purlingbrook Falls, Springbrook National Park.
BELOW RIGHT: Currumbin Wildlife Sanctuary.

Walking in Lamington National Park.

BELOW: the Couran Point Island Beach Resort.

Lamington National Park

The sheer beauty of **Lamington National Park** , another World Heritage Site, defies description. The park lies in the McPherson Ranges directly behind the Gold Coast, about a 90-minute drive inland. This vast and dramatic park of subtropical rainforest, wildflower heath, tall open forests and splashing waterfalls offers some of Australia's best bushwalking, with several appealing mountain lodges to stay in.

The park is also the natural habitat of a realm of rarely seen birdlife – a place of pilgrimage for "twitchers", who come here in search of both the rare and the exotic. British television naturalist David Attenborough has filmed here, drawn by the usually elusive black-and-yellow regent bowerbirds that descend en masse to be hand-fed. Satin bowerbirds, collectors of all things blue, also flutter amid the guests, vying with king parrots that perch on the heads, hands and shoulders of bemused visitors in noisy expectation of food.

Tamborine Mountain

Tamborine Mountain 🔟, 40km (25 miles) from Southport, comprises three distinct settlements – Mount Tamborine, North Tamborine and Eagle Heights – dispersed around a compact mountain plateau (550 metres/1,800ft) with stunning views. These heritage communities have been taken over by craft shops, galleries and tearooms, set up to cater for the Gold Coast tour buses. The real attraction of the area is the natural beauty of the surrounding rainforests, streams and waterfalls within the 12 reserves that make up the Tamborine National Park.

There are well-marked walking tracks at scenic Joalah, Cedar Creek, The Knoll, MacDonald Park, Palm Grove and Witches Falls. Contact Tamborine Mountain Visitor Information Centre (tel: 5545 3200) or Queensland Parks and Wildlife Service (tel: 5576 0271; www.dermqld.gov.au/parks).

Thanks to rich volcanic soil and cooler temperatures, the region supports avocado, kiwi fruit and rhubarb farms – and is an emerging wine district, with half-a-dozen cellar-door outlets and a distillery selling schnapps.

North and South Stradbroke Islands

These attractive bay islands were connected when Captain Cook sailed past in 1770 – and remained that way until 1896, when a storm caused a breakthrough at Jumpinpin. **South Stradbroke ⑰** is the smaller and less populated island, with 22km (14 miles) of ocean beach fringing national park containing remnant livistona rainforest and melaleuca wetlands. Apart from camping sites and private rental of former resort bungalows, the best place to stay or visit is the Couran Point Island Beach Resort (tel: 5501 3555; www.couranpoint.com.au), midway between the Gold Coast Seaway and Jumpinpin. Access to the island is by ferry from Marina Mirage at 10am and the resort at 2.45pm, or by water taxi.

Activity on **North Stradbroke Island ⑱** – "Straddie" to locals – focuses around the townships of Dunwich, Amity Point and Point Lookout. Barges and ferry offload visitors at **Dunwich**, a settlement dating to 1827, when convicts were deployed to load and unload ships unable to navigate the shallow waters of Moreton Bay. While in Dunwich, pick up maps and information from the Stradbroke Island Tourist Information Centre (8.30am–4.30pm; www.stradbroketourism.com). The island's resorts are mainly clustered around **Point Lookout** and **Main Beach. Amity Point**, on the island's northern tip, retains the atmosphere of a fishing village.

North George and South Gorge, high above the rocky headland at Point Lookout, Queensland's most easterly point, afford sightings of migrating humpback whales from June to November. Turtles, manta rays and dolphins are seen all year round.

The stunning 5,000-hectare (12,355-acre) national park, the **Naree Budjong Djara**, which means "My Mother Earth", occupies 20 percent of the island. Its main attraction is the two-hour return walk to Kaboora (Blue Lake), 10km (6 miles) east of Dunwich. The gin-like waters lap clean white sand and turn sapphire blue as the waters deepen. Vehicle and passenger ferries and water taxis link Straddie to Cleveland, 35km (22 miles) southeast of Brisbane CBD. ❑

Stradbroke Island-born Aboriginal poet and activist, the late Oodgeroo Noonuccal, formerly known as Kath Walker, led often-heated confrontations over mining damage to the environment. The Noonuccal Nughie Centre in Ballow Road conducts cultural tours and sells arts and crafts made by the island's Aboriginal community.

BELOW: shallow mid-off. The thrills of beach cricket.

BEST RESTAURANTS, BARS AND CAFÉS

Restaurants

Prices for a three-course dinner per person with a half-bottle of house wine:

$ = A$60 and under
$$ = A$60–90
$$$ = A$90–120
$$$$ = A$120 and over

The Gold Coast has over 500 restaurants, but a high proportion of these are decidedly average – which makes the standout venues really stand out. Avoid the franchises. Rather, seek out the smaller, owner-operated dining venues that cater for locals as well as tourists. There are plenty of these along the coast, beyond the most concentrated shopping areas. Here are a few recommendations.

Absynthe
Q1 complex, 9 Hamilton Avenue, Surfers Paradise
Tel: 5504 6466
www.absynthe.com.au
Open: L Mon–Fri, D Mon–Sat. **$$$**
Celebrated French chef Meyjitte Boughenout lends a dash of Gallic élan to the 80-storey Q1 building. He has become famous for juxtaposing the most unlikely of flavours to create taste sensations that are as beguiling as they are unexpected. His mascarpone sorbet, warm strawberries, white chocolate and black pepper tuile is one such culinary delight.

The Broadbeach Tavern
Old Burleigh Road, corner of Charles Avenue, Broadbeach
Tel: 5538 4111

www.broadbeachtavern.com.au
Open: L & D Mon–Sat. **$**
Good food from an extensive and surprisingly inexpensive menu. However, most people come here for the live entertainment, on seven nights a week. Check the website for details.

The Fireplace
Hyatt Regency
Sanctuary Cove
Tel: 5530 1234
www.thefireplacerestaurant.com.au
Open: L & D daily. **$$$**
If you're not deterred by the expense, the Fireplace offers a wonderful gastronomic experience. Succulent grilled meats and seafood are the speciality of the house, and the ambience is reminiscent of a private dining room in a large manor house. Chefs are on show, interacting with diners while meticulously preparing the freshest local produce.

Moo Moo Wine Bar & Grill
2685 Gold Coast Highway, Broadbeach
Tel: 5539 9952
www.moomoorestaurant.com
Open: L & D daily. **$$**
A superlative steakhouse that tells you everything you need to know about what you are eating – cattle breed, age and diet are all detailed on

the menu. The restaurant's signature dish is a 1kg wagyu rump roast, carved at the table and served with a trio of sauces.

Northcliffe Surf Club Bistro
Corner Garfield Terrace and Thornton Street, Surfers Paradise
Tel: 5539 8091
www.northcliffesurfclub.com.au
Open: L & D daily. **$**
Surf life-saving clubs are iconically Australian. At this one you can watch the action on the beach while enjoying a casual and extensive menu that includes everything from burgers, baguettes, sandwiches, pasta and pizza to char-grilled meats and seafood dishes.

Omeros Brothers Seafood Restaurant
Marina Mirage, 74 Seaworld Drive, Main Beach
Tel: 5591 7222
www.omerosbros.com
Open: L & D daily. **$$**
Ideal for expertly cooked seafood with a minimum of fuss. The decor is lavish and the bill of fare is laced with retro favourites such as oysters mornay, mussels á la parisienne, steak Diane and spaghetti marinara.

Oskars on Burleigh
43 Goodwin Terrace, Burleigh Heads
Tel: 5576 3722

LEFT: the interior of the celebrated Absynthe.

www.oskars.com.au
Open: L & D daily. **$$$**
Oskars has been a Gold
Coast institution for more
than 30 years – and it's
easy to see why. The sea-
food-dominated menu
changes daily, but the
twice-baked sandcrab
soufflé with tomato com-
pote, rocket and walnut
salad is a frequent
entrée. The beach loca-
tion, with sweeping ocean
views north to Surfers
Paradise, is a strong com-
ponent of its appeal.

Ristorante Fellini
Marina Mirage, Seaworld
Drive, Main Beach
Tel: 5531 0300
www.fellini.com.au
Open: L & D daily. **$$**
Carlo Percuoco and his
sister Anna Cacace,
along with chef Richard
Burt, dish up superb
Italian cuisine within
their elegant, award-
winning restaurant. Try
the pasta *linguette allo
zafferano* – saffron-in-
fused long, flat pasta
cooked with Moreton
Bay bug meat in a light
cream sauce. Like other
entries on the menu,
the dish makes a virtue
of simplicity, and is a
perennial favourite with
regulars. The restaurant
looks across the South-
port Broadwater, and
behind it stands the
pasta shop, Pastificio
Fellini, where the available lines include ravioli
with fresh deep-sea
ocean trout cooked in
Sauvignon.

Shuck
20 Tedder Avenue,
Main Beach
Tel: 5528 4286
www.shuck.com.au
Open: L & D daily. **$$**
As the name implies,
Shuck is noted for oys-
ters. The kitchen also
churns out excellent sea-
food chowder, crab lasa-
gne and bouillabaisse
dishes… as well as
steaks. Seating is mainly
alfresco, with courtyard
tables overlooking a
passing parade of
poseurs. The Mod Oz
cuisine, open-air setting,
and general feeling of
relaxation make it exact-
ly right for this trendy
Gold Coast precinct.

**Yellowfin Seafood
restaurant**
6/20 Queensland Avenue,
Broadbeach
Tel: 5504 5335
Open: L & D daily. **$**
Yellowfin serves up
appealing dishes in styl-
ish but relaxed surround-
ings. Try the salt-and-
pepper calamari or the
mixed seafood platter for
two. There's also a great
kids menu.

Bars and Cafés

**Charlie's 24-Hour
Café, Restaurant &
Bar**
Cavill Avenue,
Surfers Paradise
Tel: 5538 5285
Open: 24 hours a day. **$**
Everyone ends up at
Charlie's sometime
during their stay in

Surfers Paradise. Well
located and affordable,
Charlie's hasn't closed its
doors since 1976. Fare
includes pasta, pizzas,
grilled fish, steaks, sal-
ads and sandwiches.

**Dee and Paul's Rain-
bow Bay Café**
13 Ward Street,
Rainbow Bay
Tel: 5536 4999
Open: 7am–6.30pm daily. **$**
One block from the
beach, the Rainbow Café
offers generous break-
fasts and filling snacks,
including scrambled
eggs, bacon and toast;
and mixed grill of steak,
sausages, eggs, bacon,
tomato, toast and chips.
The café is decorated
with surfing memorabil-
ia, much of it contributed
by the clientele. You
could well find yourself
rubbing shoulders with
well-known surfing per-
sonalities such as Joel
Parkinson, Mick Fanning
and Dave Davidson.

Melba's
46 Cavill Avenue,
Surfers Paradise
Tel: 5592 6922
www.melbas.net.au
Open: 7.30am–5am daily.
$$
Wild nights have been
known to begin and end
in Melba's horseshoe-
shaped bar and upstairs
nightclub. Melba's res-
taurant offers steak, seafood and pizza. Breakfast
is popular, but the place
doesn't really start to
pump until the lunch
crowd surges in. Locals
who drop by for after-
work drinks often stay
until the wee small hours.

Sage
Shop 5, 20 Queensland
Avenue, Broadbeach
Tel: 5538 9938
Open: L & D daily. **$$**
Sage enjoys a central
location. It offers good
food, efficient service –
and makes a fine place
to watch Gold Coasters
promenade.

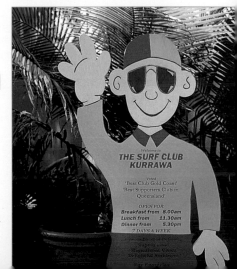

RIGHT: good-value food can be found in the clubs.

DARLING DOWNS

Inland from Brisbane, the countryside is almost entirely ignored by tourists. Here, the tablelands give way to the Darling Downs, a vast area of beautiful rolling plains and rich soil, and a centre for the dairy, beef, wool and horse-stud industries

Brisbane ●

Fat cattle, sheep farms, booming wineries and stately homes mark this fertile region, stretching north to Kingaroy in the South Burnett, west to Roma on the Warrego Highway, and south to Goondiwindi and Stanthorpe, the only place in the world that celebrates Christmas twice. It's prime motoring territory, studded with bed and breakfasts and pretty towns – and, for bushwalkers, highland rainforest parks with surreal granite outcrops.

Ipswich

Thanks to a fast motorway, **Ipswich ❶** lies within easy commuting distance of Brisbane (about a 40-minute drive). As Queensland's oldest provincial city, it has a rich history and is renowned for its impressive architectural and cultural heritage.

Rivalry with Queensland's capital goes back to the 1860s, when Ipswich challenged Brisbane as the colony's pre-eminent city. The influential squatters' lobby favoured Ipswich as the starting point for a railway. The first section to Grandchester was opened in 1865, reaching Toowoomba and the Darling Downs a couple of years later.

For 130 years, the North Ipswich Railway Workshops remained a major economic and cultural force – employing more than 1,500 people at any one time, and reaching a peak of 3,000 after World War II. The complex has now been reborn as the **Workshops Rail Museum** (North Street, North Ipswich; daily 9.30am–5pm; charge; tel: 3432 5100; www.theworkshops.qm.qld.gov.au) and comprises a streetscape of robust brick industrial buildings in late-Victorian style, the oldest of which date from 1878. Among the exhibits

Main attractions

IPSWICH
WARWICK
STANTHORPE
GIRRAWEEN NATIONAL PARK
GOONDIWINDI
ROMA SALEYARDS
TOOWOOMBA
BUNYA MOUNTAINS NATIONAL PARK

LEFT: the joey of an eastern grey kangaroo.
RIGHT: trained sheepdog in action.

The stylish municipal incinerator, built in 1936 in Queen's Park, was converted to a theatre in 1969 and is now home to the Ipswich Little Theatre (tel: 3812 2389).

is Australia's oldest operating engine (from 1865) and a vice-regal car built in 1903 for the exclusive use of the governor of Queensland and visiting royalty. There's a scale model railway of Queensland's rail network, and a working blacksmith's shop.

Ipswich has 54 National Trust-listed buildings spread about the city, all described in the *Ipswich City Heritage Trail* pamphlets, available from the tourist information centre (Queen's Park, 14 Queen Victoria Parade (Brisbane Road); tel: 3281 0555). Heading along Burnett, Limestone or Milford streets, you'll see some of the fine old houses featured. **St Paul's Church**, in Brisbane Street, dates from 1859, making it the oldest Anglican church in Queensland, with the colony's first pipe organ.

After languishing for decades, the city has come to life, relishing its past glory and enjoying its relaxed contemporary lifestyle, despite the fact that it has been engulfed by Brisbane's urban sprawl. The population of 164,000 includes a strong multicultural component, which is reflected in the burgeoning art scene. Located in the Old Town Hall, the **Ipswich Art Gallery** (d'Arcy Doyle Place; daily 10am–5pm; free; tel: 3810 7222) offers a dynamic programme of visual arts, and has a popular children's gallery.

An alternative form of family entertainment is on show at **Willowbank Raceway** (Champions Way, Willowbank; charge; tel: 5461 5461; www.willowbank-raceway.com.au), which stages year-round drag-racing events.

Warwick

Warwick ❷, 162km (100 miles) southwest of Brisbane, promotes itself as the "Rose and Rodeo City" – after the signature rose that grows in its parks and because of its well-attended rodeo, held every October. The arrival of the railway from Ipswich in 1871 sparked a boom that, by 1936, had

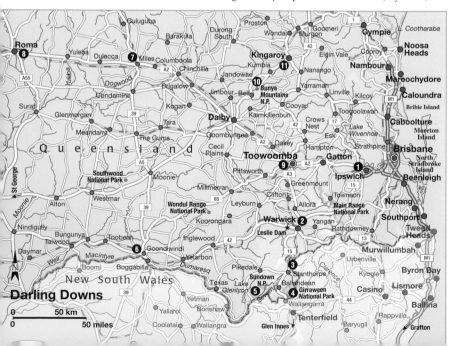

established Warwick as the second-biggest city on the Darling Downs. Essentially, it is an agricultural centre in a pleasant location with interesting architecture. Modern sprawl has obscured some of the town's early grandeur, but fine examples of colonial timber and sandstone architecture – churches, public buildings and grand residences – survive.

Something of the flavour of 19th-century Warwick can be gleaned from the former **St Mary's Church**, 163 Palmerin Street – dating from 1865, and the city's earliest sandstone church. However, the best way to begin an appraisal of Warwick's 30 heritage-listed sites is to visit **Pringle Cottage** (open Wed–Fri 10am–noon, 2–4pm, Sat and Sun 11am–4pm) in Dragon Street, within the grounds of the **Warwick and District Historical Museum** (tel: 4661 3234 for heritage trail booklets and tours by arrangement). This two-storey cottage, dating from the 1870s, is filled with an interesting collection of old contraptions, costumes, telephones and photos; it was the residence of John McCulloch, the mason responsible for most

of the district's sandstone buildings – including the Court House (1885), St Mark's Anglican Church (1874), St Andrew's Presbyterian Church (1869), the Methodist Church (1875) and the Central School (1874).

Warwick Railway Station (mid-1880s), in Lyons Street, is also worth looking at, as are Warwick's fine old hotels. O'Mahoney's (1890), formerly the National Hotel, in Grafton Street, and the Criterion Hotel (1917), in Palmerin Street, are still good for a beer.

The **Jackie Howe Memorial**, on the corner of Glengallan Road and the Cunningham Highway (notable for the large shears on top) honours Warwick's favourite son; legendary shearer Jackie Howe, born on Canning Downs Station in 1861, still holds the record (established in 1892) of having shorn 321 sheep with a set of hand shears in under eight hours.

Excursions from Warwick

A popular local excursion is to **Leslie Dam** – 13km (8 miles) west of Warwick along the Cunningham Highway on the road to Goondiwindi

TIP

The Warwick Visitor Information Centre, at 49 Albion Street (Mon–Sat 9am–5pm, Sun 9am–3pm; tel: 4661 3122), has plenty of material on the "Rose and Rodeo City", and neighbouring South Downs towns.

BELOW: giant sculpture evoking an Aboriginal legend in Warwick.

BELOW: filling up for a road trip.

– where you can go fishing, swimming and boating; there are picnic areas for day visitors and camping areas for longer stays.

About 50km (31 miles) northeast of Warwick on the Cunningham Highway, the **Main Range National Park** (www.derm.qld.gov.au/parks) forms the western part of a semicircle of mountains known as the Scenic Rim. This impressive wilderness is mostly dense rainforest, but there are areas where picnic tables, wood barbecues and toilets are provided. Have a bush picnic beside West Gap Creek near Cunningham's Gap; at the Pioneer Picnic Area at Spicer's Gap; or at Queen Mary Falls. Around these areas are walking tracks – the rest of the park is suitable only for experienced, well-equipped bushwalkers. For spectacular views, head for Governor's Chair, Sylvester's and Fassifern lookouts.

Stanthorpe

The pleasant highland town of **Stanthorpe** ❸ is best known for its climate, which the inhabitants have turned into a tourist attraction. Sitting at 915 metres (3,000 feet), bracing winters have inspired a mid-year Christmas complete with crackling hearths and festive hoopla, known as the Brass Monkey Festival, part of a whole Brass Monkey season.

The four-season climate means that fruit and vegetables flourish in the Granite Belt region just south of town, around the village of **Ballandean**, especially wine grapes: there are around 50 wineries within 20km (12 miles) of Stanthorpe (see box opposite). If you plan to tour the wineries, it's a good idea to sign up with a tour operator, such as the Grape Escape Tour Company (tel: 1300 361 150) or Granite Highlands Maxi Tours (tel: 4681 3969) – for a winery crawl with lunch.

The temperate climate also appeals to sun-baked Brisbane residents, who make the 220km (137-mile) journey to attend the numerous seasonal festivals. The Apple and Grape Harvest Festival is held in the early spring in even-numbered years, with street parades, sheep shearing and grape crushing. The Spring Wine Festival takes place every October, while wine maker Angelo Puglisi organises

"Opera in the Vineyard" concerts every May Day weekend.

The town has a good number of heritage buildings. The Federation-style **Post Office** sports an illuminated clock installed in 1903; the **Railway Station** (1881) recalls Stanthorpe's moment of eminence as a railhead; and the **Central Hotel** is everything you would expect of an old-fashioned pub.

For a comprehensive rundown of where to go, and a copy of the district's *Cultural Heritage and Historic Building Trail* booklet, contact **Stanthorpe Visitor Information Centre** (28 Leslie Parade; daily 9am–5pm; tel: 1800 762 665).

Girraween National Park

About 20km (12 miles) south of Stanthorpe, on the border with New South Wales, a lovely place to enjoy the great outdoors is **Girraween National Park ❹**. Surreal granite outcrops, pristine forests and amazing wildlife are the highlights here, and there are plenty of walking trails to explore. Perhaps the best is the 10km (6-mile) trek to the top of Mount Norman (1,265 metres/4,140ft). Contact the visitors centre (tel: 4684 5157) for information on camping and fees.

Sundown National Park

Another great place to explore is the **Sundown National Park ❺** (tel: 6737 5235), further west along the border with New South Wales (80km/50 miles southwest of Stanthorpe); it's a stunning wilderness area with spectacular steep-sided gorges, sharp ridges and towering granite rocks. Conventional vehicle access is at the southern end of the park. A four-wheel-drive route leads 16km (10 miles) from Ballandean to the park's eastern boundary, followed by a rough 20km (12½-mile) track to campsites at Burrows' Waterhole and Reedy Waterhole. Sundown has a history of grazing and mining – pastoral relics and old surface diggings remain.

Goondiwindi

West of Warwick, and still on the New South Wales border, **Goondiwindi ❻** is a rural community of

TIP

Goondiwindi means "resting place for birds", and the area is true to its name, with over 200 species identified. Pick up a route guide from the tourist office to find the best bird-watching sites in and around town.

BELOW LEFT: bottles at a Stanthorpe winery.

Granite Belt Wines

All good wine starts with the soil, and the typically well-drained granitic soils around Stanthorpe are ideal for viticulture. The 250-million-year-old granite is everywhere, most obvious in the giant outcrops erupting from the hills and the coarse sandy soil. The local geology has always had an influence – even the name Stanthorpe is derived from its beginnings as a tin-mining centre (*Stannum* is Latin for tin). But like all mining booms, the good times soon ended and the locals turned to agriculture. The local wine-making tradition can be traced back to the settlement of Italian immigrants in the region in the 1920s. But the metamorphosis to a prestigious wine-producing region was slow. It wasn't until the 1980s that wine connoisseurs began to sit up and take notice. There are now over 50 wineries in the region, most of which are small, family-owned and -operated. Apart from the soil, the unique climate plays an important part in the process. These are Australia's highest vineyards, the altitude providing the necessary cool climate at such a low latitude. While there's an assortment of grape varieties planted, it's the full-bodied Shiraz and fruity Verdelho wines that are getting rave reviews.

Goondiwindi's Victoria Hotel is one of the best-preserved colonial pubs in Queensland. Built in 1898, it has a display of memorabilia linked to a phenomenally successful racehorse: Gunsynd, the "Goondiwindi Grey".

Below: sheep farmers at auction.

about 5,000 people, whose main distinguishing feature is a collective obsession with the racehorse Gunsynd, winner of races in the late 1960s and early 1970s. A **Monument to Gunsynd**, also known as the Goondiwindi Grey, stands beside the MacIntyre River in Apex Park. In the main street is the "Digger" statue, erected in 1922, and memorial gates (from 1949) in honour of the thousands of Australian soldiers who died in the two world wars.

Other eye-catchers are the **Victoria Hotel** and the **Customs House** – two well-preserved relics of Goondiwindi's 19th-century heyday. The refurbished pub features ornate verandas and a grandiose tower that dominate the streetscape. Inside you will find the Gunsynd Lounge (named after the legendary racehorse) and several other bars. The **Customs House Museum** (1 MacIntyre Street; Wed–Mon 10am–4pm; free; tel: 4671 3041) has a small collection of historical artefacts and a lovely flower-filled garden.

For more information, contact the Goondiwindi Visitor Information Centre (Bowen and McLean streets; tel: 4671 2653; daily 9am–5pm).

Miles

In the small rural centre of **Miles ❼**, 220km (137 miles) north of Goondiwindi, the highlight is the **Historical Village** in Murilla Street (daily 8am–5pm; charge; tel: 4627 1492). A 19th-century streetscape, including relocated heritage buildings, has been created by members of the local historical society, and includes a general store, post office, bakery, barber shop, bootmaker, saddlery, café and bank.

The eccentric Prussian explorer Ludwig Leichardt (*see page 28*) established a crossroads here in 1844, and named it Dogwood Crossing after a locally occurring wild flower. It was still known as Dogwood Crossing in 1878 when construction of the railway from Brisbane came to an unscheduled halt at Dogwood Creek. The delay dragged on so long that Dogwood Crossing became a temporary railhead for the west, complete with shops, stores and pubs. At about this time, the town's name was

changed to honour William Miles, the Queensland Colonial Secretary.

Today, **Dogwood Crossing@ Miles** (Mon–Fri 8.30am–5pm; Sat–Sun 9am–4pm; free; tel: 4627 2455) is a community project illustrating how this small town was born, developed and prospered; it comprises a museum, art gallery, library and multimedia resource centre, and gives a colourful insight into the growth of this little patch of the Downs.

Roma

If you want to see how 10,000 head of cattle are sold in one morning, head for **Roma ❽**, 140km (87 miles) west of Miles, which has Australia's largest cattle-selling centre – the **Roma Saleyards** (Warrego Highway; Tues and Thur only; tel: 4624 0402).

Roma came to national attention in 1900 when a crew drilling for water hit gas by mistake. It was the first strike in Australia – and, to this day, sheep and cattle farms surrounding Roma are studded with oil and gas installations. Roma's main tourist draw is **The Big Rig** (Riggers Road; daily 9am–5pm; charge; tel: 4622 4355), which traces the development of the industry through a series of interpretive panels and audiovisual presentations. Exhibits include a 1929 steam powered oil- drilling rig that stands 45 metres (148ft) high. The **Roma Visitor Information Centre** (tel: 1800 222 399) is in the same complex.

Toowoomba

Hilly **Toowoomba ❾** sits impressively on the rim of the Great Dividing Range, 700 metres (2,300ft) above sea level, with the Darling Downs laid out before it. It's a pleasant place, with a passion for floral displays and an incredible 230 parks and gardens – hence its sobriquet, the "Garden City". It is colourful all year, but sensational in the springtime, when flowers bloom.

At street level, Toowoomba is very much a modern city, yet to raise your eyes above the awnings is to see facades little altered since the early decades of the 20th century. Toowoomba's beginnings date from around 1850, but it was the arrival of the railway in 1867 that brought prosperity, tree-lined streets and elegant Victorian buildings and the gardens it is so proud of. You can pick up a heritage trail brochure from the **Toowoomba Visitor Information Centre** (86 James Street; daily 9am–5pm; tel: 1800 331155 or 4639 3797).

Toowoomba **Railway Station** opened in the 1870s and is a classic piece of Queensland architecture. The only thing that seems to have changed over time is the volume of passengers. In 1945, more than 230,000 people passed through the station; these days, the human flood has reduced to a mere trickle, with only two trains per week connecting Toowoomba with Brisbane. The historic **Railway Refreshment Room** functions as well as ever, offering morning tea and lunch. It is elegant, old-fashioned and frequently booked up.

BELOW: an old petrol pump at Miles' Historical Village.

*One council
thoughtfully provides
signs for those not
blessed with a car full of
impatient children.*

BELOW: floral displays
are lovingly maintained
in Toowoomba, the
"Garden City".

Bunya Mountains National Park

Northwest of Toowoomba, the forested peaks of the **Bunya Mountains National Park** ⑩, 1,000 metres (3,300ft) above sea level, are home to a wide variety of wildlife, including wallabies, crimson rosellas and king parrots. The park is named after the bunya pines that thrive here. Every few years, these trees produce a crop of huge edible bunya nuts. But if you're walking in the forest during the nut season, between late January and April, beware of the falling fruit – they are heavy and the size of a pineapple. There's an extensive network of paths, ranging from a gentle discovery walk to a 10km (6-mile) trek to the Big Falls Lookout.

The three main camping and picnic areas are Dandabah, Burton's Well and Westcott. Dandabah has coin-operated barbecues and hot-water showers. Burton's Well has bush showers, Westcott does not. Cabins and guesthouses are available near the park. Call in at the Queensland Parks and Wildlife Service in Towoomba (173 Hume Street) to obtain a camping permit, or buy one online (www.qld.gov.au/camping).

Kingaroy

Kingaroy ⑪, 56km (35 miles) northeast of the Bunya Mountains National Park, is the centre of Australia's most important peanut-growing area, and peanuts seem to dominate every facet of life in the town. Among Australians, the town is best known as the home of Queensland's notorious ex-premier, Sir Joh Bjelke-Petersen. The twice-weekly tours of his property, **Bethany** (Peterson Drive, Kumbia; Wed, Sat 2pm; charge; tel: 4162 7046) remain a top attraction.

Kingaroy is also the centre of a promising wine industry; the region produces award-winning wines and is rapidly challenging the Granite Belt's reputation as the state's premier wine area. The Kingaroy Information Art and Heritage Precinct (1–8 Haley Street; tel: 4162 6272) has details of noted wineries and other attractions – including the gastronomic pleasures of the district's olive groves, aquaculture farms and cheese factories. ❑

BEST RESTAURANTS, BARS AND CAFÉS

Prices for a three-course dinner with house wine per person:

$ = A$60 and under
$$ = A$60–100
$$$ = A$100 and over

Ballandean

Barrel Room Café
Ballandean Estate
354 Sundown Road
Tel: 4684 1226
Open: L daily, D Fri–Sun. **$$**
Pleasant Italian food graciously served amid 130-year-old barrels filled with port and liqueur. Taste wines grown on Stanthorpe's oldest estate, established by the Puglisi family in 1930 and still operated by them.

The Vineyard Cafe
Vineyard Cottages, New England Highway
Tel: 4684 1270
Open: L daily, D Wed–Sun. **$$**
In an old church and surrounded by gardens and vineyards, this restaurant forms part of a five-star resort. Book ahead.

Bunya Mountains

Cider Gum Restaurant
20 Bunya Avenue
Tel: 4668 3131
Open: L daily, D Wed–Mon. **$$**
The menu incorporates bush tucker-based dishes such as quondong aïoli with bunya nut and capsicum relish.

Goondiwindi

Gibbsy's Restaurant
Jolly Swagman Motor Inn,
1 Anderson Street
Tel: 4671 4560
Open: D Mon–Sat. **$$**
On the outskirts of town, with an extensive menu.

The Townhouse Motor Inn Restaurant
110 Marshall Street
Tel: 4671 1855
Open: L Tues–Fri, D Mon–Sat. **$$$**
A popular place for special occasions.

Ipswich

Cottons
Peppers Hidden Vale, 617 Mount Mort Road,
Grandchester
Tel: 5465 5900
Open: L & D daily. **$$$**
A 30-minute drive southwest of Ipswich, this elegant restaurant is part of an up-market resort.

Fentons Restaurant
17 Limestone Street
Tel: 3812 0424
Open: L Mon–Fri, D Mon–Sat. **$$**
Delicious dishes showing Western, Asian and French influences.

Kingaroy

Accents Restaurant and Café
30 Alford Street
Tel: 4162 2990
Open: L & D Tues–Sat. **$$**
Award-winning yet unpretentious restaurant with an excellent European menu that makes the

most of local produce. Great breakfasts, too.

Booie Bello Vista Restaurant
Corner of Schellbachs and Haydens Road, Booie
Tel: 4162 7632
Open: L Wed–Sun, D Thu–Sat. **$$$**
Located 6km (4 miles) from Kingaroy, this stylish restaurant commands fantastic views.

Roma

Golden Dragon Restaurant
60 McDowall Street
Tel: 4622 1717
Open: L Mon, Wed–Fri, D daily. **$$**
Traditional Chinese cooking adapted to Outback tastes with happy results.

The Overlander Homestead Motel
44,767 Warrego Highway,
Tel: 4622 3555
Open: D daily. **$$$**
No-frills Outback restaurant with good chargrilled steak.

Stanthorpe

Anna's Restaurant
1 O'Mara Terrace
Tel: 4681 1265
Open: D Mon–Sat. **$$**
The Pompetti family's old-fashioned eatery is a Stanthorpe institution.

Toowoomba

Burke's Bar & Bistro
Burke and Wills Hotel
554 Ruthven Street
Tel: 4632 2433

Open: D daily. **$$**
This well-run bistro is just the place to unwind with a drink and some excellent comfort food.

Fire+Ice
Ruthven Street
Tel: 1800 008 269
Open: L & D Mon–Sat. **$$**
A sleek restaurant that has been garnering awards from day one.

Gip's Restaurant
120 Russell Street
Tel: 4638 3588
Open: L & D Mon–Sat. **$$**
Tasty Asian and Western fusion food.

Picnic Point Café and Restaurant
164 Tourist Road
Tel: 4631 5100
Open: L daily, D Fri–Sat. **$$**
Eclectic Mod-Oz menu and scenic location.

Warwick

Café Jacqui's
8 Albion Street
Tel: 4661 9022
Open: L daily. **$**
Light meals featuring great preserves and ice creams from Stanthorpe's Bramble Patch berry farm.

Spring Creek Mountain Café
1503 Spring Creek Road,
Killarny
Tel: 4664 7101
Open: L Thur–Sun, D by appointment. **$$**
40km (25 miles) south of Warwick, this appealing café offers great views and gourmet food.

SUNSHINE COAST

This area lives up to the promise of its appealing name. There are golden beaches stroked by warm, blue Pacific waters under usually sunny skies. Behind the beaches are volcanic peaks, verdant forests and towns that marry affection for the past with a devotion to the easy life

Brisbane

The Sunshine Coast, about an hour's drive north of Brisbane, is one of the most gorgeous stretches of Queensland's coastline. The region extends from Caloundra at the tip of Bribie Island, beyond Noosa Heads to Rainbow Beach, its northernmost point. It is backed by the dramatic Glass House Mountains to the west, which rise sheer from the grassy plains. Less brash and commercial than the Gold Coast, its mix of high-rise development and relaxed beach accommodation is characterised by long expanses of golden beach. Laid-back resorts such as Maroochydore and Coolum fill up with families during the school holidays, but it's the chic resort of Noosa that exemplifies the lifestyle of the Sunshine Coast. Inland, the national parks and mountain resorts – "the green behind the gold" – offer a refreshing alternative to the sea and sand.

Glass House Mountains National Park

Motoring north from Brisbane on the Bruce Highway, you'll catch your first glimpses of the **Glass House Mountains** ❶ – a cluster of craggy

volcanic peaks towering over a scenic patchwork of bushland, pine plantations and small farms. The steep-sided and heavily eroded mountains were formed by volcanic activity millions of years ago. They are so named because of tricks of reflected light on the rain-dampened peaks, first noted by Captain Cook from the sea, and the stuff of Aboriginal legend *(see box on page 117)*.

The well-drained slopes of rich volcanic soil are ideal for growing pineapples, which are sold at numerous

Main attractions

GLASS HOUSE MOUNTAINS
   NATIONAL PARK
AUSTRALIA ZOO
MOOLOOLABA AND
   MAROOCHYDORE
NOOSA
GREAT SANDY NATIONAL PARK
HERVEY BAY
FRASER ISLAND
THE HINTERLAND
EUMUNDI MARKETS

LEFT: the Sunshine Coast lives up to its name. **RIGHT:** climbing a dune in the Great Sandy National Park.

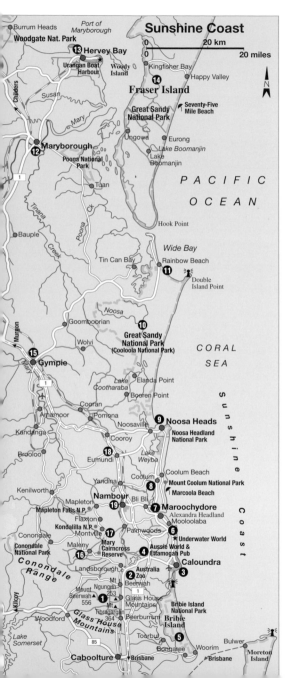

roadside stalls, along with avocados and other locally grown fruit. The region is also the home of the Queensland nut, now better known worldwide as the macadamia nut.

Eight of the 16 peaks fall within the 920-hectare (2,270-acre) **Glass House Mountains National Park** (tel: 5494 3983), where remnants of eucalypt woodland and mountain heath provide shelter to rare and threatened plants.

For the best views of the region's geological showpiece, come off the Bruce Highway and join the slower scenic roads that snake their way among them. The Aboriginal owners, the Gubbi Gubbi people, regard the mountains as sacred, frowning on attempts to climb them, so trails have been created within the national park, presenting walkers with various levels of difficulty. The circuits on **Mount Beerwah** (556 metres/1,824ft) and **Mount Tibrogargen** (364 metres/1,194ft) are for experienced bushwalkers only. The track on **Mount Ngungun** (253 metres/830ft) is less taxing, though with challenging sections. Other tracks have been cut at **Mount Beerburrum**, **Wild Horse Mountain**, **Glass House Mountains Lookout** and the **Beerwah Forest**.

An excellent campground at Coochin Creek is accessed via a forestry track off Roys Road, east of Beerwah. For general information about national parks in Queensland, visit www.derm.qld.gov.au. For specific information about Glass House Mountains National Park, contact the Queensland Parks and Wildlife officer at 61 Bunya Street, Maleny (tel: 5494 3983). For campground permits, tel: 13 74 68; or book online at www.qld.gov.au/camping.

Whilst here, it's worth checking out the **Spirit of Cobb & Co.** complex (tel: 5496 9588) at the corner of Old Gympie Road and Mount Beerwah Road, in the township of Glass

House Mountains. Built around an authentic 1860 Cobb & Co. changing station, the operation includes a working blacksmith's shop, where horse-drawn carriages are built from scratch. Visitors also learn how to make "damper", Australian bush bread made from a simple water and flour dough, cooked in coals or a camp oven.

Australia Zoo

One of Queensland's top tourist attractions is the **Australia Zoo ❷** (daily 9am–5pm; charge; tel: 5436 2000; www.australiazoo.com.au), on the Steve Irwin Way at Beerwah. This was the home of the late Steve Irwin, whose famous television show, *The Crocodile Hunter*, earned him an international reputation *(see margin, right)*. Steve and his family translated that success into a multi-million dollar wildlife park. Australian wildlife is well represented in the park, though you will also find tigers, cheetahs, Asian elephants, camels, Komodo dragons, and even South American macaws alongside native species. It's all about spectacle, and there are feeding and handling shows

throughout the day (including koala cuddling and elephant feeding). The 5,000-seat outdoor stadium, the Croco-seum, hosts crocodiles, tigers, elephants and more, always with a conservation message behind the hoopla.

Caloundra

The first major town at the southern end of the Sunshine Coast is **Caloundra ❸**, a pleasant resort with a sparkling coastline and dramatic hinterland parks. Its magnificent beaches draw surfing and fishing fans, while a variety of man-made attractions, including Australia Zoo, Aussie World and the Ettamogah Pub, make it popular with families.

Caloundra has been transformed from a sleepy backwater into one of the fastest-growing cities in Australia. In 1961, the population of the municipal area stood at less than 3,000. By 2011, it had passed 100,000, a good percentage of which is made up of commuters working in Brisbane. Given the town's proximity to Brisbane – about an hour's drive it's surprising that the population explosion took so long to ignite.

In 2006, Australian conservationist and TV personality Steve Irwin, known for his work with native Australian wildlife, was tragically killed after being pierced in the chest by a stingray barb while filming a documentary in the Great Barrier Reef. He was just 44 years old.

BELOW: a view over the Glass House Mountains.

Mountain Spirits

Named by Captain Cook in 1770, the Glass House Mountains hold great significance for the Gubbi Gubbi Aboriginal people. According to legend, each peak represents one member of a family of mountain spirits, the offspring of Tibrogargen and his wife Beerwah. Fearful of flooding and the safety of his pregnant wife, Tibrogargen appealed to his eldest and strongest son, Coonowrin, to protect his mother, but the frightened boy abandoned her. Tibrogargen beat his son and cast him off, hence the wide valley between father and son. The many streams coursing through the mountains are the tears shed by the family over the disgraced Coonowrin.

TIP

Thrill-seekers can
explore the Sunshine
Coast on a Harley
Davidson bike or
souped-up trike.
Freedom Wheels (tel:
5485 3513; mob: 0413
606 241; www.
freedomwheels.com.au)
offers excursions lasting
from an hour to a full
day.

Bulcock Street, in Caloundra's Central Business District (CBD), has morphed into a busy food and retail precinct of boutiques, coffee bars, pavement cafés, pubs and restaurants. Residential towers have sprouted along the coastline, and property values in hinterland villages have skyrocketed.

While senior citizens continue to fish in Pumicestone Passage, the picturesque channel that separates Caloundra from nearby Bribie Island, Caloundra's recreational emphasis rests on the excellence of its surf beaches. Life Savers patrol Golden Beach, Bulcock Beach, Kings Beach, Dicky Beach, Currimundi, Wurtulla and Buddina. A coastal path from Golden Beach to Buddina has been designed to link with similar paths in Maroochydore and Noosa.

The **Old Lighthouse** on Canberra Terrace is the city's oldest building and one of the few historic structures still standing amid all the new development. First erected in 1896, this venerable structure used a kerosene lamp to guide shipping into Moreton Bay until 1942, then electricity until 1968, when it fell into disuse after being replaced by a new signal tower.

At the **Queensland Air Museum** (7 Pathfinder Drive, Caloundra Airport; daily 10am–4pm; charge; tel: 5492 5930; www.qam.com.au), aviation buffs will find 40 historic aircraft, including a collection of post-World War II de Havillands and Australia's oldest DC3.

To find out more, contact the Caloundra Visitor Information Centre, 7 Caloundra Road, Caloundra (tel: 5420 6240; www.caloundratourism.com.au).

Aussie World and the Ettamogah Pub

For those who enjoy old-fashioned fun parks, a visit to **Aussie World ❹** (daily 9am–5pm; charge; tel: 5494 5444; www.aussieworld.com.au) – off the Bruce Highway at Palmview, northwest of Caloundra – is just the ticket. This low-key park of about 30 rides and games is reminiscent of a 1960s fairground. Set in native gardens, it sells didgeridoos, dot paintings and other Aboriginal-themed merchandise.

The distinctive **Ettamogah Pub**

BELOW: the Ettamogah Pub tilts in all directions.

next door is a working tavern built to resemble the imaginary Outback hotel made famous by cartoonist Ken Maynard in *Australian Post* magazine. Maynard's drawings pictured the building tilting crazily in all directions. The real-life Ettamogah Pub has been built exactly as Maynard drew it, only to larger-than-life scale.

Bribie Island

Across the Pumicestone Passage from Caloundra is the northern tip of **Bribie Island** ❺. Until the opening of a bridge in 1963, Bribie Island was mainly known as a destination for Brisbane-based excursion ferries bringing day-trippers to a place of peaceful isolation. Today, the island, which measures 34km (21 miles) from end to end, functions as a dormitory suburb for commuters and a haven for retirees. Most of its 17,500 residents are gathered at the southern end, 70km (43 miles) north of Brisbane, accessed via a turn-off from the Bruce Highway, near the Caboolture exit. The remaining 80 percent of its area is taken up by the bushland and beaches of **Bribie Island National Park** (Visitor Information Centre: 48 Benabrow Street, Bellara; tel: 3408 9026; www.tourismbribie.com. au). This is a truly beautiful reserve. More than 350 bird species have been identified within it, and sightings of turtles, dugongs and dolphins are frequent in the adjoining Moreton Bay Marine Park.

Mooloolaba and Maroochydore

North of Caloundra, the residential towers of **Mooloolaba** ❻, painted in Mediterranean hues, signal a brave new resort, quite literally on the way up. Just about every other prime site along Mooloolaba's esplanade has been redeveloped, with apartment towers offering the standard street-level mix of pavement cafés, boutiques and designer shops. Locals who have lived through Mooloolaba's pressure-cooker transition from fishing village to high-rise resort seem bemused by the changes, but they are outnumbered by new settlers smitten by the gloss. Few café precincts in the world are better positioned to take advantage of crashing waves

The first European to set foot on Bribie Island's sandy shore was Matthew Flinders in 1799. The township of Bongaree is named after Flinders' Aboriginal companion.

BELOW: Caloundra Head.

Life of a Recluse

Scottish-born Ian Fairweather (1891–1974), arguably Australia's greatest painter, lived the life of a recluse on Bribie Island. After serving in the British Army in India, he voyaged from Darwin to Indonesia on a home-made raft in 1952, settling on the then remote Bribie Island the year after. After Fairweather's death, vandals burned his Polynesian-style grass hut. A stone and plaque commemorates the site at the corner of First Avenue and Hunter Street, long since engulfed by suburbia.

THIS MEMORIAL IS IN HONOUR OF
INTERNATIONALLY RENOWN ARTIST
IAN FAIRWEATHER
WHO LIVED AND PAINTED ON THIS SITE
FROM 1953 UNTIL HIS DEATH IN 1974

ERECTED BY THE PEOPLE OF BRIBIE ISLAND

*Boats for hire,
Maroochydore.*

and spectacular sea views. The local council, for its part, has landscaped the seafront, installing fanciful bollards and surfboard-shaped benches. Fine views are offered from any balcony or pavement café. The eye follows the tree-lined arc of the sandy Spit to Point Cartwright lighthouse. Trawlers chug down Mooloolaba Harbour, past canal developments and marinas. It's particularly picturesque when yachts taking part in the annual Sydney–Mooloolaba or Auckland–Mooloolaba races weave among pleasure craft and charter boats coming and going.

Within the harbour, **Underwater World** (Parkyn Parade, Mooloolaba; daily 9am–5pm; charge; tel: 5448 6280; www.underwaterworld.com.au) is an aquarium displaying sharks, rays, moray eels, turtles, octopi, reef fish, groupers and other sea critters. Visitors are invited to handle starfish and hermit crabs, swim with seals and scuba dive in the shark tank. There's also a 2.5-million-litre oceanarium containing thousands of reef fish.

The complex, spread over four levels, is itself part of a retail/res-taurant precinct called **The Wharf**. While you are in the vicinity, do as the locals do and buy fresh prawns from the trawlermen's outlets near the Fisheries Board.

To Maroochydore

A few kilometres north of Mooloolaba is **Alexandra Headland** – a tower-strewn but relaxed coastal community known to locals as "Alex", where nothing much happens and that's the way they like it.

Alexandra Headland's beach segues into **Maroochydore Beach** and the estuary of the Maroochy River – which, in turn, flows through **Maroochydore ⑦**, seat of local government and the commercial hub of the Sunshine Coast. Located 98km (61 miles) north of Brisbane, Maroochydore (pop: 18,000) is a pleasant place that keeps its feet firmly on the ground. As with most of the settled areas along the coast, the town has experienced a development boom – which, if nothing else, has brought good restaurants along with inflated real-estate values. The city's best asset is the **Maroochy**

River, an easy-flowing waterway that imparts a sense of calm. **Cotton Tree Park**, on the south bank, is a sweet place to picnic. Conservation parks occupy the northern bank.

Coolum

Laid-back **Coolum**  has two assets: the unspoiled **Marcoola Beach** and **Mount Coolum National Park**. The beach is overlooked by the swish 5-star Hyatt Regency hotel, complete with 18-hole championship golf course. The hotel grounds adjoin Mount Coolum National Park, which contains coastal wallum, paperbark wetlands and rainforest remnants that have virtually disappeared from the surrounding lowlands. Peregrine falcons nest along the cliff faces. After rain, waterfalls cascade down the sides. You can clamber up and down the craggy 208-metre (680ft) peak. For more information, contact Noosa National Park (tel: 5447 3522).

Noosa

Nestling beside the usually tranquil waters of Laguna Bay, **Noosa**  has been called the Cannes of Australia,

a heady blend of beauty, sophistication and high finance. Noosa Heads is the chic, high-density heart of the Noosa region. It comprises the iconic Hastings Street strip, nearby Noosa Hill and the adjacent national parks. Its real estate is highly sought-after, with prices that reflect exclusivity and scarcity.

Only slightly less valuable is the real estate in Noosa proper – a region that begins at Peregian Beach, extending north through Marcus Beach, Sunrise Beach and Sunshine Beach to Noosa Heads, then along the southern bank of the Noosa River through Noosaville to Tewantin.

Noosa is the town that pioneered alfresco dining, fusion food and good ecological practice at a time when such ideas were considered dangerously radical. Locals now lament that Noosa's aestheticism has yielded to ostentation, its idealism to pragmatism – and that too much of its distinctive architecture has been bulldozed for pretentious mansions.

Hemmed in by sea and national parks, Noosa can't get bigger, only more elitist. As the population

TIP

Noosa Visitor Information Centre (61 Hasting Street, Noosa Heads; tel: 5430 5000) provides information about accommodation, as well as events such as the Noosa Long Weekend in June, the Celebration of Food and Wine in May, and Noosa Jazz Festival in September.

BELOW: the beach at Noosa.

TIP

Before going to Great Sandy National Park, visit the QPWS Great Sandy Information Centre (240 Moorindil Street, Tewantin; tel: 5449 7792), which provides information on park access, tide times, fire bans, campsites and camping permits for the park.

approaches saturation, this formerly bohemian enclave increasingly resembles an exclusive realm of the Sydney and Melbourne plutocracies.

For battle-scarred veterans of the Noosa Parks Association, it's a cruel irony. Having shielded Noosa from rampant development, they discover themselves to be caretakers of a playground for the rich. Thanks to the association's quiet persistence, 35 percent of the shire's 875 sq km (340 sq miles) has been amalgamated into national park, state forest, fauna reserve and vacant government land.

All that said, Noosa remains an undeniably charming and atmospheric place. Hastings Street, its central hub, is a leafy, cosmopolitan thoroughfare of enticing restaurants and smart apartment buildings, thronged by the designer-clad well-to-do. The street leads down to a patch of sandy beach occupying reclaimed woodland on **Noosa Spit**, where children paddle and rainbow lorikeets screech in the she-oaks.

Whatever else may happen, Noosa Heads will always enjoy the saving grace of the adjoining 477-hectare

(1,180-acre) headland section of the **Noosa National Park**, with its craggy cliffs, sheltered beaches, heathlands and rainforest.

Great Sandy National Park

About 30km (19 miles) to the north of Noosa Heads is Lake Cootharaba, a wide expanse fed by the Noosa River – and an entry point to the 50,000 hectares (123,553 acres) of unspoilt tranquility that is the Cooloola section of the **Great Sandy National Park ❿**. Here, at Boreen Point or Elanda Point, it is possible to rent a canoe and paddle along the glassy waters of Noosa River, cutting through rippling reflections of reeds, cabbage palms, cyprus, cotton trees, bloodwood and banksias.

Camping grounds lining the stream provide designated areas, some with basic amenities, others without. Motorised vessels are not permitted beyond a certain point. One of the sites, Harry's Hut, is accessible by road – but only by 4WD.

North from the Noosa River to Rainbow Beach, the Cooloola section of the park is characterised by

BELOW: Noosa Spit.

sand dunes, coloured sand cliffs, sweeping beaches, sand blows, freshwater lakes, tall forests, paperbark swamps and wild-flower heath. Plants and animals whose habitats have been compromised by coastal development – the Cooloola acid frog, for example – have found sanctuary here. The park is also home to one of Queensland's few remaining emu populations.

Providing you have a 4WD and a permit, it is possible to drive the 50km (31 miles) from the north shore of Noosa Heads to Rainbow Beach and Inskip Point, which is a terminus point for barges to Fraser Island. Migrating humpback whales pass offshore between August and October. By way of relics, you'll see **Double Island Point Lighthouse**, built in 1884, and the now vestigial remains of the *Cherry Venture*, wrecked on **Teewah Beach** in 1973.

For permits and more information about the Great Sandy National Park, contact the information centre at Tewantin (240 Moorindil Street; tel. 5449 7792) or visit www.derm.qld.gov.au.

Rainbow Beach

Rainbow Beach  is a cross between frontier town and fishing village – with a salty, come-what-may ambience that is most refreshing after prolonged immersion in the espresso-and-high-rise culture to the south. Originally established to serve the sand-mining industry, Rainbow Beach gradually turned into a fishing and retirement retreat, and now offers motel and caravan-park accommodation to thousands of visitors annually. It takes its name from the amazing multicoloured sand cliffs nearby, which offer a sweeping panorama from Fraser Island in the north to the lighthouse at Double Island Point in the south.

Scuba diving, surfing, boating and windsurfing are popular pursuits here. A good spot to watch the sunset is the **Carlo Point Marina**, which doubles as a restaurant and centre for charter boats and houseboat hire.

The Rainbow Beach office of the QPWS (tel: 5486 3160) is located on Rainbow Beach Road, as you enter town. The Rainbow Beach Tourist

Pelicans on the Noosa River.

BELOW: hiking through the sand dunes of Fraser Island, part of the Great Sandy National Park.

Maryborough's 19th-century Post Office, with its ornate tower

BELOW: Brennan & Geraghty's Store, Maryborough.

Information Centre is at 8 Rainbow Beach Road.

Maryborough

Maryborough ⓬ is a venerable Queensland city with much of its colonial architecture intact, and the placid Mary River flowing through it. Located 264km (164 miles) north of Brisbane, Maryborough creates a sense of unhurried permanence – due, perhaps, to its reliance, not on tourism, but on local industries based around timber, sugar and engineering.

First settled in 1847, Maryborough was already a busy immigration port when the Maryborough Sugar Company was established in 1865. The gold rush at nearby Gympie shortly afterwards assured its future. Grand public buildings erected during the late 19th and early 20th century express the optimism of the time. The 1866 **Post Office**, in particular, is an exercise in colonial gravitas, complete with arcaded verandas and clock tower. The original tower was equipped with a time ball that, at the stroke of 1pm, dropped noisily on the roof of the postmaster's residence. To the postmaster's relief, the time ball was jettisoned in 1869, and replaced by a clock in 1872.

Telling the time remained an issue until 1877, when Queensland premier John Douglas gave the city an 18th-century cannon, fired daily at 1pm for the benefit of ships' captains, and to alert Kanakas – South Pacific Islanders press-ganged into virtual slavery on the area's sugar plantations during the latter decades of the 19th century – that it was time for lunch. The actual gun, cast for the Dutch East India Company, is displayed in Maryborough's **Bond Store Museum**. A replica is fired at Heritage City Markets on Thursdays at 1pm.

Another Maryborough gem is **Brennan & Geraghty's Store**, 64 Lennox Street. Built in 1871 and restored in 1990, this remarkable museum, with its shuttered windows and Victorian facade, is a rare example of a late 19th-century retail outlet. The store traded continuously for 100 years until 1972, when its second-generation owner George Geraghty closed the doors

on his treasure trove of merchandise, some of which had remained unsold since the store's opening.

To learn more about Maryborough's historic buildings, call into the Maryborough Fraser Island Visitor Information Centre (Bruce Highway; Mon–Fri 9am–5pm, Sat–Sun 10am–4pm; tel: 4121 4111); or Maryborough City Hall Visitor Information Centre (Kent St; Mon–Fri 9am–5pm, Sat–Sun 9am–1pm; tel: 4190 5742).

Hervey Bay

The main portal to Fraser Island, **Hervey Bay** ⑬, 300km (186 miles) north of Brisbane, is another once-sleepy seaside community experiencing the impact of development, albeit limited to six storeys.

Urangan Boat Harbour, the terminus for ferries to Fraser Island, has already been girdled by modern apartments a trend reflected in the tourism-orientated villages of Torquay, Scarness and Pialba (less so at Point Vernon). Caravan parks, low-tariff motels and rental holiday homes continue to assert a presence but, assisted by direct flights from Sydney and Melbourne, Hervey Bay is redefining itself as a resort for retirees and families of more modest means.

Formerly associated with whaling (notice the harpoon mounted on the marina), Hervey Bay now provides a base for whale-watching excursions, as well as for game fishing and charter boats. The city (pop: 77,000) is also interesting for its memorial to Kanakas (the South Sea Islanders virtually kidnapped to work for low wages in the Queensland cane fields). Allow at least three-and-a-half hours for the drive from Brisbane to Hervey Bay.

QPWS camping and access permits for Fraser Island can be collected when purchasing barge tickets at the River Heads vehicular terminal.

Note that permits have to be booked in advance. This can be done by contacting the Hervey Bay Tourist and Visitors Centre, shop 2, 401 Charlton Esplanade, Torquay, Hervey Bay (tel: 4124 4050; www.herveybaytouristinfo.com.au); or the Kingfisher Bay resort (tel: 1800 072 555). Permits can also be obtained online via Smart Service Queensland (www.qld.gov.au/camping).

Fraser Island

Fraser Island ⑭ is justifiably known as one of the world's premier wilderness destinations. The burden of mass visitation has taken a toll, but conservationist John Sinclair's 1990 description of the island as "a magnificent mosaic of plant communities, lakes, swamps, sand blows, beaches and wetlands" holds true. If anything, Sinclair's rhetoric has proved too effective. Thanks to his environmental campaigns, the world's largest sand island has become an irresistible magnet to eco-tourists and 4WD aficionados.

Despite logging from 1863 until 1991, pockets of pristine rainforest survive on this 184,000-hectare

Aside from its scenic wonders, Fraser Island is famous as the scene of a tragic encounter between Aborigines and a party of mariners whose ship came to grief on the Great Barrier Reef in 1836. Eliza Fraser, after whom the island is named, survived rough treatment at the hands of her captors until rescued by a search party. She eventually wrote a book about her experiences and became a celebrity.

BELOW: shark show, Hervey Bay.

Wild dingoes roam on Fraser Island. They're undeniably part of the native fauna but they do cause problems (there was a fatality in 2001). Fences circle picnic areas, and rogue dingoes are culled. Don't be tempted to feed them.

BELOW: driving on the beach is part of the Fraser Island experience. So is getting bogged.

(455,000-acre) island. Piccabeen palms hold back the sun; satinay and brush box trees flourish amid creepers, ferns, elkhorns and orchids.

Passenger ferries for Fraser Island depart from Urangan Boat Harbour in Hervey Bay, and vehicular barges from River Heads. Both dock at Kingfisher Bay and Wonggoolba Creek on the island. At the up-market end of the spectrum, Kingfisher Bay Resort attracts mainly "green" tourists, who spend their days exploring walking paths or lazing on the beach.

Less visited than the more photogenic "blue" lakes, **Lake Boomanjin**, its water tannin-stained to the colour of strong coffee (due to minerals it collects from streams), is still one of the island's more beautiful lakes.

The island's roads, if you could call them roads, are impassable by anything other than 4WD vehicles – and, even then, motorists appear to spend most of their time extracting one another from bogs. If people always behaved as they do when mired in sand, the world would be a better place. Bogged motorists are unfailingly polite and grateful.

The ocean beach on Fraser Island is great fun in a 4WD. Salty breezes blow, terns wheel overhead and, at certain times, waders gather at the water's edge, building up strength for their annual flight to Siberia.

A driving permit is required on Fraser Island, and fees apply for the use of camping facilities. Contact Queensland Parks and Wildlife Service (tel: 5486 3160); or Smart Service Queensland (tel: 13 74 68; www.qld.gov.au/camping).

Gympie

Gympie ⑮, 90km (56 miles) south of Maryborough, falls outside the generally recognised boundaries of the Sunshine Coast, but, being roughly equidistant from Noosa Heads and Rainbow Beach, it warrants a mention here.

A rip-roaring gold-mining town until the 1920s, Gympie now functions as a service town for the surrounding agricultural area. It has historic architecture but, as destinations go, the visual impact is less than riveting. That said, it should be remembered that Queensland might

be a very different place if gold prospector James Nash had not struck it lucky in Gympie in 1867 – rescuing the then fledgling state from bankruptcy. Almost 100 million grams of gold were obtained – a bonanza chronicled in informative attractions such as the **Gympie Gold Mining and Historical Museum** (215 Brisbane Road; daily 9am–4.30pm; charge; tel: 5482 3995); and the **Gympie Woodworks Museum** on the history of forestry and timber (corner of Bruce Highway and Fraser Road; Mon–Sat 10am–4pm; charge; tel: 5483 7691).

The Hinterland

Maleny ⑯, 100km (62 miles) north of Brisbane, began as a timber-getting town in the 1870s, progressing to dairying and fruit crops as the land was cleared – finally adding tourism to its economic mix a few decades ago. At 450 metres (1,480ft) above sea level, Maleny (pop: 5,000) offers a cool hill station for the coastal lowlands around Caloundra and Maroochydore: a verdant, scenic zone supporting a bewildering array of bed-and-breakfast operators as well as a large artistic community.

The agricultural ambience of the main thoroughfare, Maple Street, is leavened by the many galleries and craft outlets, supplemented by a handicrafts market at the community hall on Sunday (9am–2pm).

For a glimpse of what Maleny was like before timber-getters began chopping their way along the Blackall Range, look for the **Mary Cairncross Reserve**, 5km (3 miles) east of Maleny in Mountain View Road. Named after the 19th-century conservationist, this 52-hectare (128-acre) patch of pristine rainforest contains a comprehensive array of native flora and fauna, including a huge strangler fig said to be 500 years old.

The Maleny Visitor Information Centre (tel: 5499 9033) has details on accommodation and can provide details of local attractions such as the Maleny Show in May and the Christmas Carnival.

Just 10km (6 miles) to the north is the quaint township of **Montville** ⑰ – a community that strives to create the impression of having been transplanted from the Swiss Alps. You half-expect the inhabitants to wear leather shorts and yodel. Judging by Montville's thriving galleries, speciality shops and tearooms, the Swiss Alps ploy is working a treat.

Two nearby settlements are so understated as sometimes to pass unnoticed. The hamlet of **Flaxton**, 4km (2½ miles) along Flaxton Road from Montville, has a winery with clear-day views to Mount Coolum and Moreton Island. **Mapleton**, a few kilometres further on, comprises a general store, a French restaurant, a tavern and a petrol station. Contact Montville Tourist Information Centre (tel: 5478 5544) for information.

The Blackall Range

There are two parks within the Blackall Range area – **Kondalilla**

TIP

When in Montville, make a detour to The Settlers Rise Vineyard and Winery (249 Western Avenue, Montville; daily 10am–5pm; tel: 5499 9606), to sample their award-winning wines.

BELOW: Gympie's Valley Rattler steam train runs on Wednesdays and at weekends.

National Park (3km/2 miles north of Montville) and **Mapleton Falls National Park** (4km/2½ miles west of Mapleton) – both with spectacular waterfalls. Kondalilla National Park has tall open eucalypt and subtropical rainforest. The Kondalilla Falls drop 90 metres (300ft) over Skene Creek into a rainforest valley. The Mapleton Falls are even more impressive, tumbling 120 metres (400ft) down an escarpment from Pencil Creek. Both have lookouts with fabulous views over the rainforest.

Eumundi and Yandina

Eumundi , 20km (12½ miles) west of Noosa, is a twice-a-week city, with up to 20,000 people rolling up for the Wednesday and Saturday markets – swelling the population 40-fold and lending this otherwise quiet hinterland city a carnival atmosphere.

The market's 500 stallholders, by themselves, double the population. It's noisy, colourful and unrelentingly jolly. All sorts of gewgaws are sold. People wear fancy dress, apparently for no better reason than that's what they like to do. Established

in 1979 in an attempt to save this former timber and dairying community from fiscal extinction, the markets have revived the area's commercial life, with cafés and speciality shops now lining the street.

Another 10km (6 miles) to the south is **Yandina** – another town that has embraced tourism. The Ginger Factory, 50 Pioneer Road (tel: 5447 8431), is the biggest producer of ginger in the world and now a tourist attraction – complete with cane train rides and a shop. There's also a pleasant garden in Fairhill Road (*see Tip left*).

Nambour

Nambour , on the Brisbane Highway between Caloundra and Noosa, stands aloof from the tourism circus – happy to fulfil its traditional role as a service centre for the surrounding sugar-cane and pineapple farms. Settled in the 1860s by disappointed gold miners from Gympie, its 15,000 citizens embody the ideals of steady industry, with no interest in joining the frantic rush for tourist gold. Go there for a blast of ordinariness. You'll probably need it. ❏

BELOW: pineapple farm, Nambour.

BEST RESTAURANTS, BARS AND CAFÉS

> Prices for a three-course dinner per person with house wine:
> **$** = A$60 and under
> **$$** = A$60–100
> **$$$** = A$100 and over

Caloundra

Alfie's Mooo Char and Bar

Otranto and Esplanade
Tel: 5492 8155
Open: L Mon–Sat, D daily. **$$**
Queensland rugby league legend Alan (Alfie) Langer's restaurant boasts excellent steaks, seafood and water views.

Coolum

Harvest

1806 David Low Way
Tel: 5446 4314
Open: D daily. **$$**
This place, created by Gary Skelton, was a magnet for foodies from day one. With new owners and chef Paul Gilligan, it is still winning awards. Great barbecued seafood antipasto.

Maroochydore

Ebb Waterfront Dining and Cellar

6 Wharf Street
Tel: 5452 7771
Open: L daily, D Thur–Sat. **$$$**
Central but with an amazing waterfront location, Ebb offers elegant dining, where dishes such as Hervey Bay scallops or wagyu beef rump are matched by superb wines.

Mooloolaba

Bella Venezia

95 The Esplanade
Tel: 5444 5844
Open: L & D daily. **$$**
Casual is the buzz word here. Cool, modern atmosphere with reassuring traditional Italian fare; think pizzas, pasta, risotto and a small selection of mouth-watering mains.

Noosa

Berardo's Restaurant and Bar

52 Hastings Street
Tel: 5447 5666
www.berardos.com.au
Open: D daily. **$$$**
New Yorker James Berardo has given his adoptive home a very classy restaurant. Food is Mod Oz with a Mediterranean edge.

Berardo's on the Beach

On the Beach, Noosa
Tel: 5448 0888
Open: L & D daily. **$$**
An enchanting location for young chef Ryan Fitzpatrick's version of Noosa cuisine. The menu offers such delights as grilled local prawns with fennel cream, and beer-battered goldband snapper.

Bistro C

49 Hastings Street
Tel: 5447 2855
www.bistroc.com.au
Open: B, L & D daily. **$$**
Overlooking Laguna Bay, this casual restaurant is much favoured by locals. There are steak, chicken and seafood dishes, best described as Mod Oz, and delicious desserts.

Lindoni's

13 Hastings Street
Tel: 5447 5111
Open: L & D daily. **$$$**
A delightfully romantic restaurant where Australia's best ingredients are given a wonderful Italian makeover, with dishes such as painted lobster with preserved lemon, chilli and vincotto risotto.

River Cottage

301 Weyba Road, Noosaville
Tel: 5449 7441
Open: L Fri, D Mon–Sat. **$$$**
River Cottage has a constantly changing menu that features the best of local produce from the sea and the hinterland. Try the gingerbread-crusted loin of venison or Moreton Bay bug spring roll. Plus there's a kids menu.

Sails

75 Hastings Street
Tel: 5447 4235
Open: L & D daily. **$$$**
A seafood-dominated Mod Oz menu and sweeping views across Laguna Bay. Sails is a fine place to watch the sun set.

Yandina

Spirit House

20 Ninderry Road
Tel: 5446 8977
www.spirithouse.com.au
Open: L daily, D Wed–Sat. **$$$**
Fragrant contemporary Thai food served beside a lily pond within a tropical jungle.

RIGHT: Thai dining at the Spirit House.

CAPRICORN COAST
AND ITS HINTERLAND

Queensland's central coast encompasses graceful resort cities, rugged national parks and dreamy islands. Here the attractions are many and varied. Go rum tasting in Bundaberg, turtle-watching on Heron Island or trekking in the Carnarvon Gorge

Brisbane

traddling the Tropic of Capricorn, Queensland's central coast extends 750km (470 miles) north from Bundaberg to just south of Mackay. It extends beyond Carnarvon Gorge to the tiny Outback town of Jericho, 550km (340 miles) west of Rockhampton. In this region, the sugar barons of 19th-century Bundaberg vied with the mining magnates of Mount Morgan to build ever more grandiose civic buildings; and also here, in contrast, away from the modern resort developments (but within easy reach of them), you'll find some of the world's most spectacular national parks. The Great Barrier Reef begins offshore from Bundaberg at Lady Elliot Island, or you could head inland for the gemfields of central Queensland.

Bundaberg

Sitting alongside the Burnett River, in the heart of sugar country, is **Bundaberg ❶**, 371km (230 miles) north of Brisbane. This little agricultural town is known for its most famous product – Bundaberg rum, distilled here since 1883. "Bundy" (as both the town and the tipple are affectionately known) is distinguished by elegant public buildings, venerable churches,

a striking monument to Bundaberg-born aviator Bert Hinkler, and a remarkable turtle hatchery at Mon Repos Beach.

Commercial tourism has yet to take root in any crass way. Young travellers who come to pick fruit seem in no hurry to leave, blending with the locals, using the city as a base for excursions to the reef.

The heritage trail

Bundaberg's unhurried pace of life sits well with the colonial splendour

Main attractions
BUNDABERG
MON REPOS TURTLE ROOKERY
LADY ELLIOT AND LADY MUSGRAVE ISLANDS
TOWN OF 1770
HERON ISLAND
ROCKHAMPTON
SAPPHIRE GEMFIELDS
CARNARVON GORGE

LEFT: a fringing reef, Lady Elliot Island.
RIGHT: a tour of the Bundaberg Distillery.

Pioneering aviator Bert Hinkler (1892–1933) spent several years in England working as a test pilot. In 1983, his English house was shifted, brick by brick from Southampton to its present location in his home town of Bundaberg, where it is now a museum (see right).

of buildings such as the **School of Arts** (1888) in Bourbong Street and the **Post Office** (1890) in Barolin Street. Its 30-metre (98ft) clock tower was built at the height of Bundaberg's prominence as a sugar town.

Here, a number of impressive churches line the streets. The **Holy Rosary Church** (1875), in Woongarra Street, is the oldest, with successive renovations resulting in a structure curiously reminiscent of a Roman temple.

Amid the cluster of heritage buildings in the city centre is the fascinating **East Water Tower** in Sussex Street (1902). Circled by actual and blind windows at each level, the eight-storey tower would not look out of place in a Tuscan hilltop town, and was considered a masterpiece of brickwork construction. Although the tower postdates many of Bundaberg's impressive civic buildings by more than a decade, it symbolises the city's importance and prosperity

during the 1880s, when the sugar industry boomed.

Botanical Gardens

Located at the city's northern entrance, on the corner of Mount Perry Road and Young Street, are the **Bundaberg Botanical Gardens** (daily 6am–6pm; free; tel: 4153 2377), comprising 28 hectares (68 acres) of lush, well-tended parkland studded with landmarks of historical significance. The centrepiece is the **Hinkler Hall of Aviation** (daily 9am–4pm; charge; tel: 4130 4400; www.hinklerhallofaviation.com), which honours Bundaberg-born aviator Bert Hinkler. Hinkler's former residence *(see left)*, containing the Hinkler House Museum, overlooks the park where, in 1928, he completed his record-breaking England-to-Australia solo flight.

Another impressive attraction within the gardens is Fairymead House, a plantation homestead

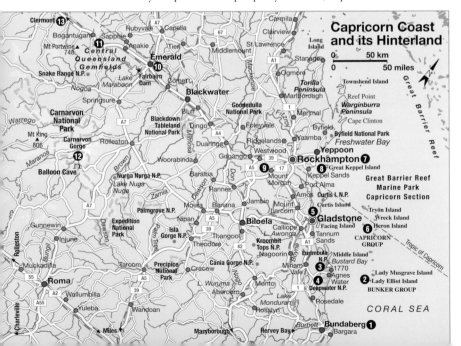

reborn as a **Sugar Museum** (Thorn-hill Street; daily 10am–4pm; charge; tel: 4153 6786). Built in 1890, the house testifies to the grand lifestyle enjoyed by Bundaberg sugar barons in the late 19th and early 20th century. Relocated from its original site in 1994, Fairymead House has been furnished in authentic style.

On Sundays and public holidays, volunteers from the Bundaberg Steam Tramway Preservation Society (tel: 4152 6609) fire up their small fleet of steam locomotives for rides around the gardens. If you want more railway memorabilia, drop in at the **Bundaberg Railway Museum**, corner of Wilmot and Station Streets (Tues and Fri 9am–3pm; Sat 8am 4pm; charge; tel: 4152 2170). Housed within the city's first railway station, displays include old rolling stock, photographs and uniforms.

Most visitors to the Botanical Gardens end up having a snack at Café 1928 (daily 9am–4pm; tel: 4153 1928), but the lily-fringed lagoons also make a delightful setting for a picnic. More than 10,000 trees and shrubs have been planted since the gardens opened in the mid-1980s, creating a habitat for many water birds.

The distillery

No visit to Bundaberg is complete without paying homage to its famous export with a one-hour tour around the **Bundaberg Rum Distillery** (Whittred Street; tours every hour on the hour Mon–Fri 10am–3pm, Sat– Sun 10am–2pm; charge; tel: 4131 2999; www.bundabergrum.com.au). During the tour, you'll peer into deep pools of molasses, pose for photographs beside an outsized rum bottle, wander among tall storage vats and, finally, head to the bar for an invigorating slug of "Dad and Mum".

Close to the rum distillery is **Schmeider's Cooperage and Craft Centre** (5 Alexandra Street; Mon–Fri 9am–5pm, Sat 9am–3pm; free; tel: 4151 8233), where in-house artisans engage in barrel-making, wood-turning, glass-blowing and pottery – as well as selling souvenirs.

Bundaberg's beaches

Southeast of Bundaberg, a 13km (8-mile) drive past cane fields leads

BELOW: Mon Repos Beach, Bundaberg.

TIP

Some 28km (17 miles) west of Bundaberg, on the Gin Gin Highway, lie the Mystery Craters (daily 8am–5pm; charge; tel: 4157 7291), so named because they're so darned mysterious. Formed more than 25 million years ago, the 35 craters are still puzzling geologists. Some think they are meteorite fragments, others say they may be the result of volcanic disturbances or the action of an underground sea.

BELOW: Lady Elliot Island.

to **Bargara**, set against a dramatic backdrop of black volcanic rock. This beach enclave has undergone swift and dramatic modernisation over recent years, with new apartments and boutiques. The dazzling bank of coral near the shore makes it very popular with divers and snorkellers.

About five minutes from Bargara is the beach at **Mon Repos**, the most accessible loggerhead-turtle rookery in Australia, where, in season, you can watch these ancient creatures struggle up the beach to nest. Until a decade ago, it was "open slather", as the locals would have it (or unrestrained free-for-all), for turtle-watchers. Queensland Parks and Wildlife Service has since formalised Mother Nature's peepshow with an information centre, video show, boardwalk and ticketing system. As a rule, turtles nest between mid-November and February. Hatchlings make their run from January to the end of March. Viewing takes place at night and is closely supervised (Bundaberg Region Tourism, 271 Bourbong Street; tel: 4153 8888; freecall: 1800 30 88 88; www.bundabergregion.org).

Southern Reef islands

Bundaberg is also a gateway to **Lady Elliot Island ❷**, one of the southernmost islands of the Great Barrier Reef, a delightful coral cay, with a low-key resort (www.ladyelliot.com.au) that provides easy access to snorkelling and diving (no camping). Flights depart daily from Bundaberg Airport (Childers Road, Kensington; tel: 4155 1238; www.bundaberg.qld. gov.au).

Nearby, **Lady Musgrave Island**, in Capricornia Cays National Park, is a beautiful, uninhabited coral cay, accessible by boat from Town of 1770 *(see below)*. It offers excellent diving and snorkelling within a brilliant-blue lagoon to day-trippers and campers; camping is only allowed with a National Parks permit, available from the boat operators and online at www.qld.gov.au/camping.

Agnes Water and Town of 1770

About 120km (75 miles) north of Bundaberg are the twin coastal resorts of Agnes Water and the Town of 1770, popular seaside destinations surrounded by national parks, great

beaches and the ocean. Although developing rapidly, they still retain a certain charm. **Agnes Water** is busier, with bustling shopping centres, coffee bars and restaurants; its main attraction is a magnificent surf beach (Queensland's most northerly), where the 1770 Longboard Classic, a major surfing competition, is held every March.

Just 5km (3 miles) up the track is the **Town of 1770**. Bounded by national parks and the Great Barrier Reef, 1770 is a popular spot for fishing and boating, and is a departure point for neighbouring national parks and the southern cays of the Great Barrier Reef. Captain James Cook anchored the *Endeavour* off this coast on 23 May 1770 before venturing ashore with botanists Sir Joseph Banks and Dr Daniel Carl Solander to collect plants. While Banks and Solander were plunging through paperbark swamps in search of new species, Cook's men brought down a plains turkey, a bird that tasted so pleasing to the great navigator that he named the inlet **Bustard Bay**.

Amphibious buses known as LARCs, the military acronym for Lighter Amphibious Re-Supply Cargo vessels (tel: 4974 7555; www.1770larctours.com.au), depart from The Marina, Captain Cook Drive, Town of 1770, for **Bustard Head Lighthouse** (Mon, Wed, Sat only). The journey is an adventure in itself, involving four tidal-creek crossings to reach the restored lighthouse, where a small but crowded cemetery underlines the hardship of a lighthouse keeper's and his family's life in the 19th century *(see box below)*.

Coastal parks

To the northwest of Agnes Water is **Eurimbula National Park ❸**, a 12,500-hectare (30,900-acre) landscape of thick mangrove, freshwater paperbark swamps and eucalypt forest. An 11km (7-mile) bush track accesses the Bustard Beach camping area at the mouth of Eurimbula Creek. Camping permits must be obtained before you arrive at the camp ground. To book a site, visit www.qld.gov.au/camping; or go to the Government Service Office, 71 Springs Road, Agnes Water (tel: 4902 1555).

The lighthouse at Bustard Head.

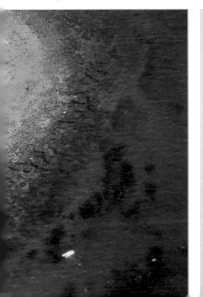

Lighthouse of Tragedy

From the moment it first lit up on 26 June 1868, a heavy burden of tragedy descended on the gloomy lighthouse at Bustard Head. In all, the adjoining cemetery contains 11 graves, two unmarked, almost all of them underscored by tragedy. First to go was a carpenter accidentally hit on the head; next, in 1887, lighthouse keeper Nils Gibson's wife Kate slit her throat; two years later, Gibson's 20-year-old daughter Mary and two others died in a boating mishap. Six years after Mary's death, Gibson passed away; two months later, assistant lighthouse keeper Ernest Waye's wife gave birth to a daughter who died at 20 months after being accidentally scalded.

Revenge, abduction, a murder, mysterious disappearances... Stephen King might have concocted the true-life tales revolving around this unhappy lighthouse. As it happens, former Bustard Head lightkeeper-turned-author Stuart Buchanan has beaten him to it. Buchanan has authored several books featuring this dramatic coastline, two about Bustard Head, most notable of which is *Lighthouse of Tragedy*, which can be purchased locally.

Gladstone's original name was Port Curtis. An attempt was made to establish a settlement here in 1847, but it failed when the ship carrying the commandant and 200 convicts became marooned on Facing Island. Renamed Gladstone in honour of the British Prime Minister, the port was opened in 1854. It remained of minor importance until 1961, when coal exports led to a dramatic increase in activity.

BELOW: green sea turtle hatching at Heron Island.

Another area of outstanding beauty is the 4,600-hectare (11,400-acre) **Deepwater National Park ❹**, 8km (5 miles) to the south of Agnes Water. Here you will encounter a mosaic of coastal vegetation, heathland fringed with dunes, and sweeping beaches studded with freshwater creeks. The park is used as a breeding ground for loggerhead turtles; you can see hatchlings emerging at night between January and April (follow the precautions recommended by the QPWS park brochure). Access to the park is by 4WD only. Camping permits may be obtained at the camp grounds, with advance bookings recommended for busy times (visit www.derm.qld.gov.au for maps of both of the parks).

Gladstone

Gladstone ❺, 175km (109 miles) north of Bundaberg, is one of the biggest ports in Australia, with more than 60 million tons of cargo passing through it each year. About two-thirds of this is coal from open-cut mines in the Bowen Basin reserve. Queensland Alumina Ltd's refinery

is one of the biggest in the world, processing 9 million tons of bauxite to produce 4 million tons of top-quality alumina (aluminium oxide), while Gladstone Power House produces 15 percent of the state's electricity. There are also cement plants, chemical plants and oil-exploration companies.

But it's not all industrial. Beyond the wharves and smokestacks lies the clear blue of the ocean, where turtles laze in the crystal-clear water, and further afield lie the coral cays on the southern Great Barrier Reef.

Gladstone's comparatively recent development means there's little history. A National Trust-listed fig tree in Roseberry Street is all that survives of the gracious 19th-century residence to which it belonged. The **Commonwealth Bank** (1929), the former **Gladstone Post Office** (1932) and the **Council Chambers** (1934) are interesting insofar as they reflect the then government's attempts to generate employment via public works programmes.

Amid thrusting industrial prosperity are Gladstone's **Tondoon**

A Load of Bull

A colourful local personality and former mayor of Rockhampton, Rex Pilbeam had a baggy-necked Brahman bull cast in concrete and erected at the northern entrance to the city (the Brahman is the breed favoured by cattlemen to the north), and a similar sculpture of a Hereford (the British breed favoured by farmers in the south) at the southern end. Anticipating playfulness by local lads, Pilbeam had several spare sets of testicles for each animal placed in storage. Souvenirhunters struck the Brahman almost immediately. They were dumbfounded when the mayor ordered his workmen to bolt on a replacement appendage the very same day.

Botanic Gardens (Glenlyon Road; Oct–Mar Mon–Fri 7am–6pm, Sat–Sun 9am–6pm; Apr–Sept Mon–Fri 7am–5.30pm, Sat–Sun 8.30am–5.30pm; free; tel: 4977 6899). This magnificent 83-hectare (205-acre) site comprises rainforest and Australian native plants, with good walking trails and lakes.

Heron Island

Heron Island ⑥, 70km (43 miles) northeast of Gladstone, is accessed by helicopter or fast catamaran (contact Gladstone Tourist Information Centre, Bryan Jordan Drive, The Marina; tel: 4972 9000 for details). This beautiful coral cay buzzes with diving enthusiasts, who stay at the Heron Island Resort; marine boffins who inhabit the university research station here; and a noisy population of mutton birds, noddy terns, herons and silver eyes, who go where they please.

One of only three resort islands positioned on the Great Barrier Reef itself (the others are Lady Elliot and Green Island, *see pages 134 and 185*), Heron Island provides spectacular snorkelling and diving, and the opportunity, between October and March, to see green turtles nesting.

Rockhampton

Only a few kilometres north of the Tropic of Capricorn (which is marked by a roadside spire), **Rockhampton ❼** is the commercial heart of central Queensland and the centre of the state's beef industry.

A sprawling city, with modern pubs and office blocks interspersed with older buildings, Rockhampton is a commercial centre for thousands of square kilometres of rich grazing country to its west, where heat, drought, floods and fires have shaped a hardy breed of survivors on the large, scattered cattle stations of the Dawson and Fitzroy River Valleys.

There's a wide range of attractions in "Rocky", and the **Customs House** in Quay Street (Mon–Fri 8.30am–4.30pm, Sat–Sun 9am–4pm; free; tel: 4922 5339) is a good place to start. Constructed in 1899, this gracious sandstone structure houses the Rockhampton Tourist and Business Information Centre and is a mine of

Rockhampton has some stunningly well-preserved old hotels and warehouses down by the river. You can pick up heritage trail brochures from any visitor centre in town.

BELOW: Customs House, Rockhampton.

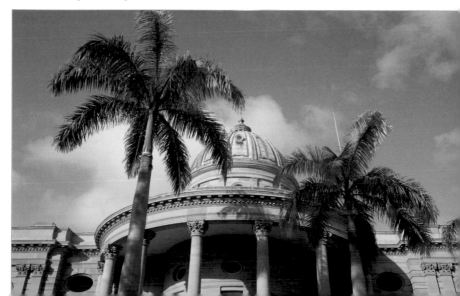

BELOW: Long Beach, Great Keppel Island.

information about the city's heritage and attractions. Here you can learn how brothers Charles and William Archer, on an expedition to the district in 1853, became the first Europeans to record and chart the Fitzroy River. The Archers built a wharf to transport wool from their property, Gracemere Station. The wharf site, dictated by rocks blocking further movement upstream, eventually became the port of Rockhampton.

Although Rockhampton's economy is agriculture-based, gold discoveries in the hinterland, most notably at Canoona in the 1860s and Mount Morgan during the 1880s, furnished the funding for the town's stately buildings. The National Estate lists an entire street – **Quay Street** – on its heritage register, and some of the state's finest colonial homes are found in **Agnes Street**.

The city is proud of its superb **Art Gallery** (62 Victoria Parade; Tues–Fri 10am–4pm, Sat–Sun 11am–4pm; free; tel: 4927 7129), which houses a collection of 20th-century works by prominent Australian artists. There is also an enchanting green oasis in the

Botanical Gardens, Spencer Street, The Range (daily 6am–6pm; free; tel: 4922 1654), with a Japanese garden, lagoons and a small zoo with koalas and other native species.

Another worthwhile stop is the **Archer Park Station and Steam Tram Museum** (corner of Denison and Cambridge streets; Sun–Fri 10am–4pm; charge; free tram rides Sun 10am–1pm; tel: 4922 2774). The station – an ornate 19th-century edifice – houses a restored steam tram salvaged from a fleet of four built in 1908 by Monsieur Valentin Purrey of Bordeaux, France, to provide Rockhampton with public transport. These four-wheeled passenger "toastrack" trams, each powered by an underfloor steam engine, with the boiler and driver on a front platform and trailers behind, carried passengers in and around the town.

Other Rockhampton attractions include an excellent 18-hole golf course and a modern theatre.

"Rocky" itself can be insufferably hot, but don't let this bother you. Just slip quietly away on a 40km (25-mile) detour to the relaxed and welcoming

township of **Yeppoon**, "Gateway to the Capricorn Coast", for a dip and some excellent local seafood.

Great Keppel Island

It's a 40-minute catamaran ride from Roslyn Bay, 7km (4.5 miles) south of Yeppoon, to **Great Keppel Island** ❽. The island's coast is blessed with astounding rock formations, pirates' caves and picture-postcard beaches. It is a sanctuary for a variety of bird species, including rainbow lorikeets and kookaburras. Great Keppel is not directly on the reef (although there is coral in most of the bays and some great snorkelling spots), so short cruises run out for divers.

The island's main resort closed in 2008, and while there are plans for it to reopen, the new development has become a contentious issue between conservationists and the developers. Meanwhile, there are several alternatives – rental beach shacks, motel-style rooms, cabins, bunkhouses, floored tents and even an offshore houseboat *(see page 256)*.

Catamarans to Great Keppel depart from Roslyn Bay Marina daily. Charter flights operate from Rockhampton Airport. Contact Rockhampton Tourist and Business Information (208 Quay Street; tel: 4922 5625; www.rockhamptoninfo.com) for details.

Inland from Rockhampton

The historic mining town of **Mount Morgan** ❾ is interesting, not so much for what it is, as for what it was. A stockman named William Mackinlay discovered gold 40km (25 miles) inland from Rockhampton, but did nothing about it because the gold was mixed not with quartz, but with ironstone. In 1882, one of Mackinlay's daughters persuaded mining expert Thomas Morgan to assess the find. Morgan realised its worth, pegged 260 hectares (640 acres) and, with borrowed capital, rushed in a crusher. Morgan and Mackinlay became wealthy and sold out. Next came a syndicate that amassed an even greater fortune. By 1889, Mount Morgan's population had reached 5,800. When gold yields diminished, they mined copper. So it went until the 1920s, when a new company returned the mine to production as an open cut.

A steam pressure valve on an exhibit outside the Mount Morgan Museum.

BELOW: the old railway station at Mount Morgan houses the visitor information centre.

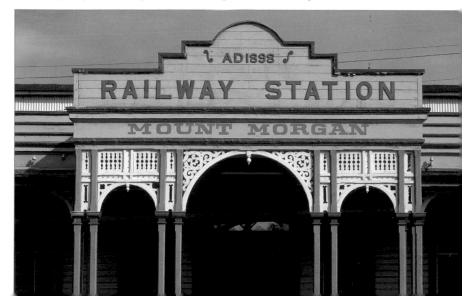

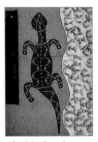

Aboriginal art decorates the walls of some of the municipal buildings in Mount Morgan.

BELOW: fossicking for gems.

Abandoned in the 1980s, the open cut has since filled with water, poisoned by waste from the mines.

A wealth of mining memorabilia is enshrined within the **Mount Morgan Museum** (daily 10am–4pm; charge; tel: 4938 2122). Tours of the town and the mine are run by TMC Tours (tel: 4938 1823). Of special interest are 150-million-year-old dinosaur footprints clearly visible on the roof of caverns unearthed by brickmakers excavating clay. At the time of writing, the clay caverns were closed until further notice.

The Mount Morgan Tourist Information Centre is housed in the Historic Rail Complex (1 Railway Parade; tel: 4938 2312).

Emerald

Emerald **⑩**, 263km (163 miles) west of Rockhampton, is a rural community of about 10,000 people who busy themselves with coal mining, grazing, agriculture (grain and cotton) and horticulture (grapes and citrus fruit). Emerald's focus shifted from grazing to agriculture in the late 1940s, a move hastened by the completion of the Fair-

bairn Dam across **Lake Maraboon** in 1972, creating a watery expanse three times the size of Sydney Harbour.

Tourism is a relatively low priority, though Emerald does possess a fine National Trust-listed **Railway Station** (*c.*1900) and, outside the town hall, two lumps of fossilised wood that are said to be 250 million years old. Beside the information centre on the Capricorn Highway stands **Emerald Pioneer Cottage and Museum**, a small historical village where exhibits include a cottage (1880), the former lock-up (1910), St Mark's Church (1884) and a vintage printing press (Mon–Fri 2–4pm; charge).

Emerald's most arresting attraction is an enormous reproduction of Van Gogh's painting, *Sunflowers*, resting on a 25-metre (82ft) easel in **Morton Park**, a reference to the Easter Sunflower Festival. Also in Morton Park is the **Federation Footpath**, a 100-metre (330ft) mosaic pieced together by Emerald artists Maxine Wild and Daryl Black in 2001 to commemorate the centenary of Federation. (Central Highlands Visitor Information Centre, Cler-

mont Street; Mon–Sat 9am–5pm, Sun 10am–2pm; tel: 4982 4142; www. centralhighlandstourism.com.au).

The Sapphire Gemfields

Emerald is also a gateway to the central Queensland **gemfields** ⑪, the largest sapphire fields in the world. Fortunes were made during the 1970s and 1980s, and the region still yields enough precious stone to sustain communities at Rubyale, Sapphire, Anakie and Willows Gemfield – as well as on the gemfields themselves *(see box)*.

Carnarvon Gorge

Lying between Emerald and Roma, in the middle of the Great Dividing Range, **Carnarvon Gorge** ⑫ is a stunning oasis in an arid landscape. Towering sandstone cliffs form a steep-sided gorge with lush, vibrantly coloured side gorges. Cabbage-tree palms, ancient cycads, ferns, flowering shrubs and gums line the main gorge. Well-maintained walking trails allow you to explore this majestic gorge, with its rare plants, wildlife and poignant Aboriginal

art; the rich indigenous artwork can be found under several rocky overhangs, with engravings, ochre stencils and freehand paintings at **Cathedral Cave**, **Balloon Cave** and the **Art Gallery**.

Camping is permitted during the Easter, June/July and September/October Queensland school holidays. Alternatively, you can stay at one of the bush resorts or lodges. Check out www.derm.qld.gov. au/parks for details.

Clermont

Clermont ⑬, 106km (66 miles) north of Emerald, is a quiet country town with a colourful past. Explored by Ludwig Leichardt in 1845, Clermont became the first inland settlement north of the Tropic of Capricorn, founded on gold, copper, sheep and cattle.

In 1916, a flood swept through, killing 65 people and convincing those who remained to drag the entire town to higher ground (where it still stands). A concrete "tree" at the southern entrance to Clermont marks the 1916 flood level.   ❑

Sapphires are gem forms of corundum (aluminium oxide) and are second only to diamonds in hardness. They can be blue, yellow, clear, pink, green, black and multicoloured. Red rubies are sapphires containing chromic oxide.

BELOW: one of the must-see destinations in Queensland is Carnarvon Gorge.

The Gemfields

In 1938, a boy found the famous "Star of Queensland" in the central Queensland gemfields. In 1979, the Centenary Stone, a 2,000-carat yellow sapphire believed to be the largest gem-quality sapphire, was found. And In 2000, some Bundaberg tourists stumbled upon the 221-carat Millennium Sapphire, which sold for a cool $87,000. Feeling lucky? There are several fossicking parks in the gemfields that sell buckets of "wash" that you sift through yourself – the gemfields' version of a lottery ticket. You'll need a licence to go fossicking, and a separate bush-camping permit if you want to camp. Contact the Central Highlands Visitor Information Centre *(see Emerald, page 140 for details).*

BEST RESTAURANTS, BARS AND CAFÉS

Prices for a three-course dinner per person with house wine:
$ = A$60 and under
$$ = A$60–100
$$$ = A$100 and over

Agnes Waters and Town of 1770

Agnes Water Tavern
Tavern Road, Agnes Waters
Tel: 4974 9469
Open: L & D daily. **$**
Informal dining in a tropical beer garden and atrium. Nothing fancy, just good steak and seafood dishes. Salad bar for lunch, vegetable bar for dinner. Sunday is roast night.

The Deck Bar and Restaurant
Captain Cook Holiday Village, Captain Cook Drive,

Town of 1770
Tel: 4974 9157
Open: L Thur–Sun, D Wed–Mon. **$$**
Fresh local seafood is given a European twist in a romantic setting. The varied menu includes Belgian specialities such as *waterzooi* (a Flemish-style chowder), prawn croquettes and an irresistible chocolate fondue.

The Tree Bar
Captain Cook Drive, 1770
Tel: 4974 7446
Open: L Tue–Sun, D daily. **$**
Unpretentious and reasonably priced Aussie tucker. Steaks and seafood by day, supplemented by pizzas in the evening. Great views across Bustard Bay to the lighthouse.

Yok Attack Agnes Waters
Endeavour Plaza, Captain Cook Drive, Agnes Waters
Tel: 4974 7454
Open: L & D Thur–Tue. **$**
Authentic Thai food – good-value soups, noodles, stir fries and seafood curries.

Bargara

Mira's Café
100 Hughes Road
Tel: 4159 1245
Open: L Wed–Sun, D Fri. **$**
Also open for breakfast, Mira's is a popular lunch spot with an inexpensive menu of unpretentious dishes. Friday nights are tapas nights' with a great variety of hot and cold tapas and home-made sangria to wash it all down.

Bundaberg

Café 1928
Botanical Gardens, Young Street, North Bundaberg
Tel: 4153 1928
Open: L daily. **$**
Family-orientated Café 1928 dishes up fish and chips, quiche, salads and Devonshire teas in a lovely outdoor setting overlooking the manicured lawns and garden of Bert Hinkler's House. A restored cane train trundles around the park at weekends. Lovely lunch spot.

H20 Bar and Bistro
Burnett Riverside Motel, 7 Quay Street
Tel: 4155 8777
Open: L & D Mon–Sat. **$$$**
Modern bistro fare – pasta, juicy steaks and locally caught fish.

Rendezvous Restaurant
220 Bourbong Street
Tel: 4153 1747
Open: D Mon–Sat. **$$**
Well-regarded and long-established à la carte restaurant serving modern Australian cuisine.

Restaurant at Rowers on the River
Corner Quay Street and Toonburra Street
Tel: 4154 4589
Open: D Tue–Sat. **$$**
The in-crowd descends on this erstwhile rowing shed with a fantastic deck overlooking the Burnett River. The menu is Mod Oz, with lots of seafood and steaks, and a decent wine list.

Spinnaker Bar and Bistro
1a Quay Street
Tel: 4152 8033
Open: L Tue–Fri, D Tue–Sat. **$$**
The emphasis in this smart Bundaberg institution is on seafood dishes such as Moreton Bay bugs with lemon risotto. The pleasant deck overlooks the Burnett River.

LEFT: freshly cooked mussels.

Thai Tulips Restaurant
47 Takalvan Street
Tel: 4153 1881
Open: L Tue–Fri, D Tue–Sun.
$
Standard Thai dishes, such as tom yum, stir-fries and curries.

Peppercorn Motel
Capricorn Street
Tel: 4983 1033
Open: D daily Mon–Sat. $$
Steak and seafood served in the restaurant or beside the swimming pool.

The Capricornian Restaurant
17 Esmond Street
Tel: 4982 1113
Open: D Mon–Sat. $$
Emerald's only stand-alone restaurant dishes up exotic Queensland dishes such as croco-dile, swordfish and soft-shell crab alongside more familiar dishes.
Emerald Explorer's Inn
Gregory Highway
Tel: 4982 2822
Open: D daily. $$
Fine dining and an extensive seasonal menu that reflects the quality of the accommodation that is also on offer.

Kapers BYO Restaurant
124b Goondoon Street
Tel: 4972 7902
Open: D Mon–Sat. $$
Mediterranean-based fare that includes such dishes as cuttlefish in beer batter with chilli plum dipping sauce, as well as traditional favourites such as Beef Wellington. Some vegetarian and coeliac-friendly dishes, too.
Scotties Bar and Restaurant
46 Goondoon Street
Tel: 4972 9999
Open: D Mon–Sat. $$
Gladstone's young crowd and professional classes mingle at the bar. Menu runs the gamut from linguine with smoked rainbow trout to local grain-fed rump steak.
Thai Classic
100 Goondoon Street
Tel: 4972 1647
Open: L Mon–Fri, D daily. $
A predictable but tasty menu of Thai curries and stir-fries.
Vino Vino
76 Goondoon Street
Tel: 4972 7555
Open: L Mon–Fri, D Mon–Sat. $$
Coffee shop by day, à la carte restaurant by night. This well-known Gladstone institution delivers an evening menu that relies on reef and beef dishes, supplemented by tapas and pasta. Wine list includes some premiums.
Yachties Bistro
Gladstone Yacht Club, 1 Goondoon Street
Tel: 4972 2294
Open: L & D daily. $
Stunning views of Auckland Inlet through to Gladstone Harbour, and a menu that encompasses à la carte service and a nightly buffet. Seafood, pasta and meat dishes.

Leichardt Hotel
52 Morgan Street
Tel: 4938 1851
Open: L & D daily. $
This 1891 hotel includes a well-presented restaurant that is famous for its pizzas and serves a wide range of traditional pub grub.
Lucky Strike
11 Central Street
Tel: 4938 2154
Open: D Wed–Mon. $$
This unpretentious and casual restaurant is noted for its fresh home-made pasta and award-winning pizzas. Simple, tasty fare prepared with care beneath the pressed-metal ceiling of historic 19th-century premises. BYO.

The Allenstown Hotel
8 Upper Dawson Road
Tel: 4922 1853
Open: L & D daily. $$
The hotel's reinvigorated bistro serves such quality pub grub as BBQ pork ribs, chicken parmigiana, and Bruer's beer-battered barramundi. But pride of place goes to the char grill, with several mouth-watering cuts of beef and sauces to match.
The Brunswick Hotel
Archer and West Street
Tel: 4922 1389
Open: L & D daily. $
Value for money at around A$10 for an over-flowing plate piled with steak or seafood served with chips and salad or vegetables. Eat in the bar, the beer garden or restaurant.
The Cambridge Hotel
Cambridge and Bolsover streets
Tel: 4922 3006
The hotel has two restaurants – one for corporate types on expense accounts, another for the more budget-conscious. The Flame Char Grill specialises in prime steaks (open: L Mon–Fri, D Mon–Sat. $$). The Overflow Bar and Bistro is a kid-friendly bistro (open: L & D daily. $).
The Coffee House
William and Bolsover streets
Tel: 4927 5722
Open: L & D daily. $$$
Owners Grant and Rebecca Cassidy deliver gourmet fare in contemporary surroundings. The signature dish is pan-roasted Angus beef served with seasonal vegetables.
Da Berto
62 Victoria Parade
Tel. 4922 3060
Open: L & D Tue–Sat. $$
Fresh Italian/Mediterranean fare. Typical dishes include gremola scallops, spice-dusted sweetlip and traditional pannacotta.
Thai Taste
635 Norman Road North
Tel: 4926 7788
Open: D Tue–Sun. $
Bangkok-style and Lao-style Thai dishes. Special Thai fried rice is a favourite with locals. Good value.

SOUTHERN REEF
AND THE WHITSUNDAYS

Heritage is sweet in the elegant sugar-boom town of Mackay, but the big attraction in this part of the state is the Whitsundays. Spectacular island idylls with pristine beaches and clear blue waters, they are nature at its very best

Brisbane ●

Main attractions

MACKAY
EUNGALLA NATIONAL PARK
AIRLIE BEACH
DAYDREAM ISLAND
SOUTH MOLLE ISLAND
HOOK ISLAND
WHITSUNDAY ISLAND
WHITEHAVEN BEACH
HAYMAN ISLAND
HAMILTON ISLAND

The area from Mackay north to the town of Bowen is a prosperous one thanks to agriculture, mining and, increasingly, tourism. The coastal stretch is a convenient springboard for the Whitsundays, an archipelago of 74 jaw-droppingly beautiful islands in the southern Great Barrier Reef. Several of the islands now feature tropical resorts, with options to suit all tastes, whether family-friendly, sports-orientated or simply that perfect island hideaway.

Mackay

Fanned by fresh breezes and surrounded by a gently rustling sea of sugar cane, **Mackay ❶**, 975km (605 miles) north of Brisbane, is an attractive city distinguished by wide streets, tropical palms, elegant buildings and flocks of raucous rainbow lorikeets that appear around dusk. It exudes an air of prosperity – partly deriving from mining and sugar production (the Mackay region supplies about half of Queensland's coal and a fifth of Australia's raw sugar), and partly from the tourism generated by its close proximity to the Great Barrier Reef.

Mackay's centre is on the southern bank of the wide Pioneer River,

where a number of heritage buildings survive in the Central Business District (CBD), but the flavour of modern Mackay is more cogently expressed by the waterfront developments north of the river, such as **Marina Village**, adjacent to Mackay Harbour, and **Harbour Beach**, which looks across the Coral Sea to the Whitsunday Islands of Brampton, Keswick, St Bees and Scawfell.

In common with other coastal towns that rose to prominence during the sugar boom of the late 1800s

LEFT: sail the Whitsundays... **RIGHT:** ...or take the ferry.

Mackay's Customs House (1902) is one of the few structures remaining in the once-busy precinct beside the Pioneer River.

and early 1900s, Mackay's CBD is blessed with imposing banks and ornate Art Deco public buildings. The most efficient way to see them is by obtaining a copy of the *Heritage Walk* booklet, which covers 22 sites, from the **Mackay Visitor Information Centre** (320 Nebo Road; Mon–Fri 9am–5pm, Sat–Sun 9am–4pm; tel: 1300 130 111); or the Town Hall (63 Sydney Road; Mon–Fri 9am–5pm, Sat–Sun 9am–noon; tel: 4951 4803).

Listed by the National Trust, the formal facade and elegant clock tower of the old **Town Hall** (1912) speak volumes about Mackay's optimism and confidence at that time. One of the few structures to weather a devastating cyclone in 1918, the Town Hall continues to dominate the streetscape, though the council has long since shifted operations to the Mackay Civic Centre. Mackay gained many Art Deco buildings in the rebuilding programme that followed the 1918 cyclone.

The city's oldest commercial edifice, the **Commonwealth Bank** (1880; 63 Victoria Street) is marked by a masonry colonnade at street level with cast-iron columns supporting an iron "lace" balustrade and veranda roof on the upper storey.

Two other venerable sites are the **Customs House** *(see left)* and the **Courthouse and Police Station** complex at the corner of Victoria and Brisbane streets.

Lending a contemporary edge to the streetscape is **Artspace Mackay** (Civic Centre Precinct, Gordon Street; Tues–Sun 10am–5pm, closed Mon; free; tel: 4961 9722; www.artspacemackay.com.au). On offer here are workshops and masterclasses by visiting artists, exhibitions and installations.

The **Mackay Regional Botanic Gardens** (Lagoon Street; daily in daylight; free; tel: 4952 7300; www.mackayregionalbotanicgardens.com.au), 3km (2 miles) south of the city centre and very close to the Mackay

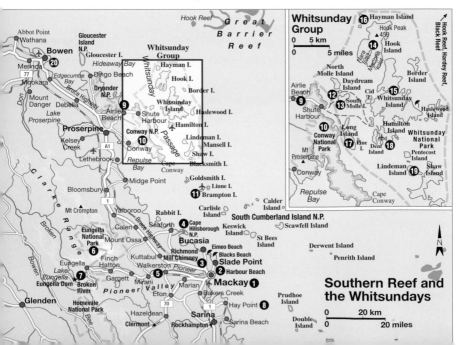

Southern Reef and the Whitsundays

Visitor Information Centre, are definitely worth a visit. Although only part way through a very long-term development project involving Mackay City Council and the State Government, these already excellent gardens promise to be amazing when completed. Set beside the banks of Eulamere Lagoon, the park's gardens are accessed by pathways, ramps and bridges – heralded by a spectacular display at the main approach to the Visitor Centre. Exhibits include a tropical shade garden (daily 9am–5pm) and an elevated deck from which to observe wetland flora and fauna. Stage two, completed in 2006, has exhibits to explain the evolution of plant life and presents displays of flora unique to the region.

Around Mackay Marina

North Mackay is blessed with excellent beaches, unfortunately blighted by box jellyfish from November to April. Public pools offer free admission on days when beaches are closed due to stingers. **Harbour Beach ②**, 6km (4 miles) north of the centre, is patrolled throughout the year, and during holiday periods surf life-savers also patrol **Lamberts**, **Eimeo** and **Blacks Beaches**, further up the coast. Town and Illawong Beaches, to the south of Mackay, are unsuitable for swimming but remain popular with locals for picnics.

Thanks to the ease of access to surrounding islands, prosperous Mackay enjoys an unusually high rate of boat ownership. **Marina Village** (at the northern end of Harbour Beach) is something of a jaw-dropper, with 500 berths – six of them designed for 60-metre (196ft) mega-yachts. Small boats are available for hire. A pleasant activity is to sail to a nearby island or follow the course of the Pioneer River through the city.

While in the vicinity of Harbour Beach, look for the white tower and red roof of the **Pine Islet Lighthouse** (1885) on the esplanade in Mulherin Drive. The lighthouse remained operational until 27 August 1985, when it was placed in storage. Reassembled on its present site in 1992, the lighthouse now enjoys National Trust listing and is in close proximity to several upmarket restaurants.

TIP

Among the more than 350 businesses operating within Mackay's CBD is the familiar mix of clubs, bars, alfresco coffee shops and brasseries. The largest concentration is on the busy main thoroughfare of Victoria Street.

BELOW: Mackay Marina.

TIP

If you're interested in learning more about how sugar is made, the Farleigh Mill, 10km (6 miles) north of Mackay, on the Bruce Highway, offers tours of its sugar mill during the crushing season (July–Nov Mon–Fri 1pm; charge; booking essential; tel: 4963 2700).

The Mackay Visitor Information Centre, to the south of town (see page 146) is marked by a replica of the tall brick chimney of the old Richmond Sugar Mill, making it easy to spot. The actual **Richmond Mill Chimney** ❸ (1881) – one of the last remaining stacks from the early sugar boom – stands in Habana Road, 14km (9 miles) north of Mackay. Richmond Mill was the district's first central mill, and became renowned for the quality of its sugar and golden syrup, but falling prices, coupled with a ban on South Sea Islander labour, led to its closure in 1895. The ruins stand on private property surrounded by canefields, but the 20-metre (65ft) tapered chimney stack is clearly visible from the road.

The **Mackay Bulk Sugar Terminal**, in Mackay Harbour, reputedly Australia's largest facility of this type, represents a more modern monument to the sugar industry – but there are no tours.

The wild green yonder

For a coastal excursion, head 50km (31 miles) north along the Bruce Highway, past pawpaw plantations and cane farms, to the sandy beaches, subtropical rainforest and mangrove-fringed wetlands of **Cape Hillsborough National Park** ❹. Kangaroos are often seen on these beaches. Fishing is allowed, but swimming is not. Estuarine crocodiles populate the waters, and box jellyfish are present from October to May.

For a glimpse of quintessential north Queensland scenery, head along the Peak Downs Highway to **Walkerston** ❺, 15km (9 miles) west of Mackay, where, in 1915, grazier Albert Cook built **Greenmount Historic Homestead** (Greenmount Road; Mon–Fri, Sun 9.30am–12.30pm; charge; tel: 4959 2250). This gracious family home stands on land that belonged originally to the city's founder, John Mackay, but he was later forced to sell it. The house retains original furniture and fittings that belonged to the Cook family, providing a real insight into the life of a prosperous grazier during the early 19th century.

From Walkerston, continue west for 65km (40 miles) along the

Below: Sugar Cane Train crossing the Pioneer River.

Mackay–Eungella Road, through the townships of Mirani (where opera singer Dame Nellie Melba once lived as the unhappy wife of a local sugar-mill manager), Gargett and Finch Hatton to **Eungella National Park** ❻ (free; tel: 4958 4552 or QPWS Mackay, tel: 4944 7800; www.derm.qld.gov.au/parks). Here, you have an excellent chance of spotting a platypus.

Essentially, the road follows the course of the Pioneer River towards its source – a journey through canefields, roadside mango trees, neat one-pub settlements, green fields and cane-train crossings. From **Finch Hatton**, at the base of the Clarke Range, a tortuous 18km (11-mile) uphill road through the Great Dividing Range leads to **Eungella** township. Here you can enjoy the surreal experience of taking refreshment at the chalet while, a few metres away, hang-gliding daredevils launch themselves into the clear blue yonder.

The best spot to spy on platypuses is from a purpose-built viewing platform at **Broken River** ❼. Reportedly, as many as eight of these duck-billed, otter-tailed, spur-legged marsupials have been seen here at one time, though sightings are not guaranteed.

Among the other weird and wonderful creatures that inhabit Eungella's mist-shrouded mountains are the Eungella gastric brooding frog, the Eungella spiny cray and Eungella honeyeater. Eungella has over 20km (12½ miles) of walking tracks, the easiest being the Sky Window circuit, which affords spectacular views of the Pioneer Valley.

Hay Point

Located 38km (24 miles) south of Mackay, **Hay Point** ❽ is one of the largest coal-export ports in the world, comprising two separate terminals – the Dalrymple Bay Coal Terminal and the Hay Point Services Coal Terminal. The DBCT wharf stretches 3.8km (2½ miles) out to sea; the Hay Point Services Terminal 1.8km (1 mile). The terminals have a combined throughput capacity of around 100 million tons per annum – delivered from coal mines in the northern Bowen Basin by trains 2km (1¼ miles) long and drawn by four locomotives. An open-

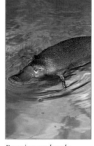

Evening and early morning are the best times to spot platypus in the water at Eungella National Park.

BELOW: the coal terminal at Hay Point.

Mackay: Sugar Central

The city is named after John Mackay, who established a pastoral run in the river valley in 1861. By 1863, the first lots of land sold. Sugar cane was planted in 1865 and quickly eclipsed pastoralism as the district's foremost activity. Plantation owners turned to Kanaka indentured labour, but the dubious methods used to recruit the South Sea Islanders, akin to kidnapping, drew fierce criticism, and the practice was banned. Subsequently, Europeans, particularly Italians, provided the labour, forming their own settlements. Improved railway access from 1924 boosted the industry. By the 1920s, Mackay had become the fastest-growing town in Queensland.

The Great Barrier Reef is one of the last remaining habitats of the dugong, or sea cow, but this statue at Airlie Beach is the closest that most visitors will get to seeing one.

BELOW: sailboats at Airlie Beach.

air viewing platform affording an overview of this remarkable operation can be accessed in the Port Administration building, Horyu Maru Drive, off Hay Point Road as you enter Hay Point township.

Airlie Beach

Airlie Beach ❾, about 140km (87 miles) north of Mackay, is the principal gateway to the Whitsunday Islands. The antics of youthful international travellers endow the place with a certain *joie de vivre*, while the trappings of the town's plutocracy lend an air of elegance and cosmopolitanism.

Airlie's location, overlooking Pioneer Bay and the Whitsunday Passage, has long marked it as a prime holiday destination. Tall resort apartment buildings occupy the streets behind the Central Business District (CBD). The CBD itself is chock-a-block with bars, restaurants, nightclubs and souvenir shops. Shops open seven days a week, and traders at the Saturday market sell fruit and getables, arts and crafts and assorted gewgaws under the coconut palms on the foreshore.

A profusion of BMWs and Mercedes line the streets, and luxurious yachts fill the **Abel Point Marina**. Abel Point and **Shute Harbour**, 8 km (5 miles) away, serve as departure points for islands in the Whitsunday group and provide a base for charter operators offering both skippered and "bareboat" yachts.

Between Airlie Beach and Shute Harbour is the 22,500-hectare (55,600-acre) **Conway National Park ❿**, where the landscape closely resembles that of the Whitsunday Islands. This is because the islands were part of the mainland until rising sea levels drowned the coastal valleys thousands of years ago. The park's rocky cliffs provide a spectacular 35km (22-mile) backdrop to the Whitsunday Passage and its islands.

To get to the national park from Airlie Beach, follow the Shute Harbour Road 2.5km (1½ miles) southeast to the QPWS Whitsunday Information Centre (tel: 4946 7022). The entrance to the park is a further 4km (2½ miles). A pleasant camping ground, complete with pebbly beach and million-dollar views, is located at

Island Camping

Looking for a back-to-nature escape? Why not go camping on one of the islands – Whitsunday, Henning, North Molle, Planton and Denman cater exclusively to campers and boaties. Scamper (Airlie Beach; tel:4946 6285; www.whitsundaycamping.com.au) provides a water-taxi service to many island camp grounds, plus you can hire all the camping gear and obtain camping permits through them. You can also book camping permits at the Airlie Beach QPWS Whitsunday Information Centre (Shute Harbour Road; tel: 4946 7022); or on www.qld.gov.au/camping. If you're feeling adventurous, you can organise a sea kayak to go island-hopping or just for cruising the pristine inshore waters around your camp.

the end of a 20-minute hike from the Swamp Bay/Mount Rooper car park. Picnic tables, a shelter shed and pit toilets are provided. Take water and a fuel stove, and ensure you have a camping permit.

THE ISLANDS

The islands covered in this chapter lie in the Southern Reef, and are mostly in the Whitsunday and Cumberland groups. Some of them are dry, barren and windy, while others are green and lush, with pockets of rainforest. The islands offer a varied combination of attractions, from snorkelling, diving, bushwalking and beachcombing to nightclubbing, alfresco dining and poolside cocktail lounging. Lodging varies from 5-star resorts to backpacker hostels and campgrounds, and access is by various means, including watercraft, seaplane and helicopter – or you can jet right into Hamilton Island.

Brampton and Carlisle islands

Brampton Island ⓫, 32km (20 miles) northeast of Mackay, is a beautiful island with rocky headlands dotted with hoop pines, sheltered bays and long sandy beaches. A 7km (4-mile) walking track through the **Brampton Islands National Park** rises from sea level to 214 metres (700ft) at Brampton Peak, offering views over nearby islands and the mainland. At low tide, you can walk across a sand spit to neighbouring **Carlisle Island**, in whose waters turtles feed.

The waters surrounding both islands are good for snorkelling and offer some excellent dive sites. There is also sailing and water-skiing in the bay. At the time of writing, the Brampton Island Resort was closed for refurbishment. For the latest information, contact Brampton Island Resort (tel: 4951 4499; www. bramptonholidays.com.au).

Non-resort visitors wishing to visit **Brampton Islands National Park** should contact Reef Star Cruises (tel: 4942 2339; www.reefstarcruises.com.au). Access to QPWS campsites on Brampton or Carlisle islands can also be arranged by charter flight or private boat (QPWS Mackay; tel: 4944 7800; www.derm.qld.gov.au).

Brampton and Carlisle Islands are part of the Cumberland Island group. Like most of the islands off the Queensland coast, they were sighted by Captain Cook in 1770. Cook named the group after the Duke of Cumberland. The island itself was named simply "M" – until 1879, when a British Royal Navy commander named each of the islands in the group after a town in England's Lake District.

BELOW: Daydream Island, the antidote to summer in the city.

The "putt your way around Australia" mini-golf course on Daydream Island is reputed to have cost over a million dollars to build.

BELOW: there are resorts within every price bracket in the Whitsundays.

Daydream Island

Daydream Island , located 5km (3 miles) northeast of Shute Harbour, is distinguished by its tiny proportions; it's just 1km (0.6 miles) long and 400 metres (437 yards) at its widest point. A shoreline boardwalk and a rainforest walk link the 17-hectare (42-acre) island's two main centres of activity. If you tire of walking, you can hitch a ride on a motorised buggy. Live-in guests inhabit a 296-room facility set in manicured gardens on the northeast of the island. The southern end is mainly for day-trippers. It has a tavern, souvenir shops, swimming pool, mini-golf and an outdoor cinema in a spectacular setting. Yachties cruise in to see new releases. The resort's A$3 million spa is reason enough to visit Daydream. The facility has 16 rooms and comes with its own naturopath (*for more information on accommodation, see page 257*).

To get there, fly to Hamilton Island's Great Barrier Reef Airport, then catch a ferry – the journey takes about 30 minutes. Alternatively, fly to Proserpine Airport (Lascelles Avenue; tel: 4945 0200. www.whitsunday.qld.gov. au) for a bus and ferry connection via Airlie Beach's Abel Point Marina.

South Molle Island

Southeast of Daydream Island is **South Molle Island** ⑬, part of the Molle Islands National Park. No longer the low-key, family-friendly destination of yore, the resort, the only one on the island, has morphed into the Adventure Island Resort (tel: 1800 466 444; www.adventureislandwhitsundays.com), a dedicated party resort popular with backpackers. Diving, swimming, sailing, golf, fishing and shopping are all offered, but, as usual, Mother Nature steals the show. In all, there are 16km (10 miles) of walking tracks. If time is limited, an easy 15-minute stroll from the resort through rainforest and grassland to Paddle Bay gives an accurate overall impression. The view from **Spion Kop** (154 metres/505ft) is spectacular, and, on the way, you'll see the remains of a quarry where local Aboriginal people dug up basaltic stones for axes and cutting tools. **Mount Jeffreys** (194 metres/635ft) and **Lamond Hill** (133 metres/435ft) also afford good views.

The island is reached by launch from Abel Point Marina, or from Hamilton Island. People wishing to bush camp on South Molle will find QPWS sites at Sandy Bay and Paddle Bays. There are other sites on North Molle, Long, Tancred, Planton and Denman islands, all of which require a QPWS permit.

Hook Island

A good way to see the Whitsundays is by boat, and charter operators in Airlie Beach offer a tantalising range of vessels, both skippered and self-sail. For many Whitsunday seafarers, the first stop is **Nara Inlet**, on the southern side of **Hook Island** ⓮, where Aboriginal cave paintings can be found at the far end of the inlet. Faded graffiti on rocks overlooking the inlet record a visit by actor Errol Flynn, who sailed his ketch *Sirocco* there in 1930.

The island's highest point is **Hook Peak**, at 459 metres (1,500ft). Another view, provided that the water is clear, is from an underwater observatory, submerged 9 metres (30ft) below the surface of the narrow passage

between Hook Island and Whitsunday Island. Just north of the observatory is the low-key Hook Island Wilderness Resort (tel: 4946 5255; www.hookislandresort.com). The ferry *Voyager* departs Abel Point Marina daily at 9am.

Whitsunday Island

Across Hook Passage is **Whitsunday Island** ⓯, at 109 sq km (42 sq miles), the biggest of the 74 Whitsunday Islands. It is notable for **Whitehaven Beach** – a pristine expanse of white sand that stretches 6km (3½ miles) along the island's eastern side. As beaches go, Whitehaven is pretty unbeatable. A popular destination for yachtsmen, day-trippers and guests on excursions from nearby resort islands, the beautiful beach is so vast that you scarcely notice the presence of others. A boardwalk leads to a lookout high on **Tongue Point**, providing a sweeping view of Whitehaven Beach and Hill Inlet.

There is no resort on Whitsunday Island. However, the QPWS maintains six camping grounds for which you will need a QPWS permit.

A plaque explains how the Whitsundays got their name.

BELOW: kayaks for hire.

Electric buggies are the popular way for tourists to get around Hamilton Island. They are available for rent beside the ferry terminal.

Hayman Island

The Whitsunday group's most exclusive resort is **Hayman** ❶❻ (tel: 4940 1234; www.hayman.com.au). The 5-star resort is a big favourite with high-flyers and Australian honeymooners *(for further details, see page 257)*.

Located 33km (20 miles) from the mainland, close to the Outer Reef, the island is circumscribed by an 8km (5-mile) bush circuit that takes around 2½ hours to complete. The sheltered waters between Hayman's sandy beach and the northern shores of Hook Island form a tranquil coral-trimmed lagoon, while Hook Island's blue-green mountains make a picture-perfect backdrop.

Day visitors are tolerated, provided they call ahead. Yachties who find it impossible to tear themselves away by dusk are expected to check in for the night.

Long Island

As its name suggests, **Long Island** ❶❼ is long and thin – about 9km (5½ miles) from end to end, narrowing at one point to only a few hundred metres. This narrow point is the location for the secluded 4½-star **Peppers Palm Bay** (tel: 1300 737 444), one of three very different resorts on the island. Its sheltered lagoon is also a favoured overnight anchorage for "bareboat" yachtsmen, who can tie up to the palm trees lining the beach.

Long Island Resort (tel: 1300 883 887), in Happy Bay, is a resort for all ages, but it's particularly popular among families with young children, with plenty of activities to keep them amused. Both resorts are just a short boat trip from the mainland.

The **Paradise Bay Eco Resort** (tel: 4946 9777), in Paradise Bay, is the smallest and most unusual of the island's resorts. It is largely self-sufficient – using solar power and natural gas where possible. Unfortunately, however, at the time of writing this resort had appointed receivers and its future was uncertain.

Hamilton Island

The Whitsunday group's largest, most aggressively marketed resort, **Hamilton Island** ❶❽ (tel: 137 333; www.hamiltonisland.com.au) is more akin

to a Gold Coast development than a traditional Whitsundays resort. The island has become the region's major transport hub, providing both a convenient airport for travellers heading to resort islands and a safe harbour for boaties seeking provisions and/or running repairs. The island's centrepiece – the 19-storey **Reef View Hotel** *(see page 257)* – is distinguished by transparent lifts that run up and down the building's exterior.

Located 13km (8 miles) south-east of Shute Harbour, Hamilton Island has everything: hotel suites, luxurious apartments, private villas and self-contained suites. The largest tourist facility in the Whitsundays, its four hotels provide 750 rooms and more than 200 apartments. There are 10 restaurants, six bars, more than 50 shops, and an array of operators covering every conceivable holiday need.

Activities include snorkelling, reef fishing, sailboard riding, tennis and squash. A fauna park is home to koalas, kangaroos, emus, wombats and various birds. There is a network of walking trails to Coral Cove, Passage Peak and Escape Beach.

Lindeman Island

At the southern end of the Whitsunday archipelago, **Lindeman Island** ⑲ was home to Australia's first Club Med. But all that changed in late 2011 when the resort was shut down and put up for sale. By the time you are reading this, new owners will hopefully have reopened the resort. Beyond the resort buildings, the island has retained the beauty of its natural setting. The 690-hectare (1,700-acre) **Lindeman Islands National Park** offers lovely walks to secluded beaches, while the summit of **Mount Oldfield** is a fine place to watch the sun set.

Lindeman is 30 minutes by launch from Hamilton Island, and can also be reached from Mackay and Proserpine.

Bowen

Back on the mainland, **Bowen** ⑳ marks the halfway point between Mackay and Townsville, covered in the next chapter. The focus here is on agriculture. The area is well known for tomatoes, producing about half the Queensland output, and mangoes. Other major industries include cattle raising, coal mining and fish processing. The visitor centre near the Big Mango *(see right)* can provide directions to the beach at **Horseshoe Bay**, north of Bowen, where reef fish and coral come to within a couple of metres of the shoreline.

For panoramic views to Edgecumbe Bay and the Gloucester Passage, drive to the summit of **Flagstaff Hill**, just beyond the Bowen Boat Harbour. The centre can also point you towards attractions such as the **Bowen Historical Museum** (22 Gordon Street; Mon–Fri; tel: 4786 2035) and the **Courthouse** (1883) in Herbert Street, Bowen's main thoroughfare. They'll also clue you in about events such as the Bowen Family Fishing Classic, held every September.　　❑

The Big Mango, proudly erected on the Bruce Highway in South Bowen, illustrates the importance of the annual crop. For information, contact the visitor centre (daily 8.30am–5pm; tel: 4786 4222).

BELOW: one of the key venues of Hamilton Island's thriving wedding industry.

BEST RESTAURANTS, BARS AND CAFÉS

Prices for a three-course
dinner per person with
house wine:
$ = A$60 and under
$$ = A$60–100
$$$ = A$100 and over

Airlie Beach

**Banjo's
Chargrill'n'Bistro**
Shute Harbour Road,
Whitsunday Shopping
Centre, Cannonvale
Tel: 4946 7220
Open: L & D daily. **$$**
Reasonably priced steak,
seafood, pasta and
salad dishes.
Déjà Vu
Golden Orchid Drive
Tel: 4948 4309
Open: L Wed–Sun,
D Wed–Sat. **$$$**
Contemporary fusion
featuring Asian and
Mediterranean themes.
Déjà Vu attracts an
appreciative crowd of

gourmets and romantic
diners. The Sunday long
lunch (fixed price) is a
"gastronomic event"
with eight courses and
live entertainment.
**Fish D'vine and Rum
Bar**
303 Shute Harbour Road
Tel: 4948 0088
Open: L & D daily. **$$**
Fresh seafood prepared
every which way, and
more than 100 different
rums available from the
bar. Of course, the signa-
ture dessert is Caribbean
rum baba.
Mangrove Jacks Café
Shute Harbour Road
Tel: 4964 1888
Open: L & D daily. **$$**
Relaxed pub-style dining,
serving everything from
Thai beef salads to suc-
culent rib fillet. Pizzas
cooked in a wood-fired
oven are a speciality.

**Whitsunday Sailing
Club**
Airlie Point
Tel: 4946 7894
Open: L & D daily. **$$**
Simple bistro meals, cold
beer and a great deck.

Bowen

Horseshoe Bay Café
Horseshoe Bay Road
Tel: 4786 2565
Open: L daily, D Thur–Sun **$$**
Well-reviewed café. Self-
service by day, table
service by night. Good
views over the bay, too.
**Sands Restaurant
at Whitsunday
Sands Resort**
Tel: 4786 3333
Open: L Sat–Sun, D daily. **$$**
Mainly seafood but steak
and curry dishes also
feature. All come with an
ocean view.
Three Sixty on the Hill
Flagstaff Hill
Tel: 4786 6360
Open: L & D Wed–Mon. **$$**
Fantastic location on the
highest point in Bowen.
And the food more than
matches the splendour
of the outlook.

Eungella National Park

**Possum's Table
Restaurant**
Broken River
Mountain Resort
Tel: 4958 4000
Open: D daily. **$**

Uncomplicated dishes,
with chicken, steak and
seafood options, all
made with regional pro-
duce. Great rainforest
setting and excellent
kids menu.

Mackay

Fast-food and budget
outlets in Mackay are
clustered at Café Court,
Caneland Central, Man-
grove Road (tel: 4944
7111), and at the food
court within the Mount
Pleasant Shopping
Centre (tel: 4969 2400).
Austral Hotel
Corner Victoria and Pell
streets
Tel: 4951 3288
Open: L & D daily. **$$**
Typical pub grub in a
busy bistro atmosphere,
with the juicy steaks
being the best value.
**Church on Palmer
Street**
15a Palmer Street
North Mackay
Tel: 4944 1477
Open: D Mon–Sat. **$$**
Stylish restaurant spe-
cialising in steak and
seafood. Modern Aus-
tralian dishes with a dis-
tinctive French influence.
Citron Brasserie
Seabreeze Resort Hotel,
72 Pacific Esplanade,
Lambert's Beach
Tel: 4955 1644
Open: L & D daily. **$$**

LEFT: mudcrab caught in the region.
RIGHT: Mussaman curry.

Casual bistro environment with a tried-and-trusted menu of reef and beef dishes.

Covers Bistro
Harrup Park Country Club
Juliet Street
Tel: 4944 0000
Open: L & D daily. $
Reasonably priced char-grilled dishes, seafood and pasta, with vegetarian options.

Fifth Floor Training Restaurant
Central Queensland Institute of TAFE, Sydney and Shakespeare streets
Tel: 4940 3281
Open: L Tue–Wed, Fri; D Thur; closed school hols. $
Supervised students prepare à la carte cuisine. An inexpensive way to experience fine dining, with great views, too.

Galleon's Restaurant
Ocean International Hotel
1 Bridge Road
Tel: 4957 2044
Open: B, L & D daily. $$$
Locally farmed barramundi, crocodile and kangaroo bolster the usual meats on the menu. House speciality is the ubiquitous seafood platter.

George's Thai on the Marina
Mulherin Drive, Mackay Marina Village
Tel: 4955 5778
Open: L & D daily. $$
Excellent authentic Thai cuisine featuring the delicious ingredients north Queensland is famous for. Try the Queensland green pawpaw salad, king prawns and cashew nuts.

Kevin's Place
Victoria and Wood streets
Tel: 4953 5835
Open: L & D daily. $
Odd name for a grand colonnaded colonial building, but Kevin dishes up sensational Singaporean stir-fries and curries. Perfect on a warm tropical night.

Latitude 21
Clarion Hotel
Mackay Marina
Tel: 4955 9400
Open: L & D daily. $$
Intelligent blending of Asian, African and European cuisine served either alfresco, with pleasant views over the marina, or in air-conditioned comfort.

Muddies
Illawong Drive
Illawong Beach Resort
Tel: 4957 8427
Open: D daily, L Sat only. $$$
As the name suggests, this restaurant specialises in locally sourced mudcrabs, delivering such flavour-packed dishes as chilli mudcrab and seafood platters.

Satchmo's at the Reef
Mackay Marina
Tel: 4955 6055
Open: L & D daily. $
Tapas-style menu includes such dishes as tamarind-, chilli- and-coconut-marinated lamb cutlets and Singapore coconut noodle cakes.

Sorbello's Italian Restaurant
166 Victoria Street
Tel: 4957 8300
Open: L & D daily. $$
Speciality pastas, pizzas

cooked in a wood-fired oven, and authentic risotto dishes, as well as a big selection of mains. Traditional Italian decor.

Toong Tong Thai Restaurant
10 Sydney Street
Tel: 4957 8051
Open: L Mon–Fri, D daily. $
Cheap and cheerful curries and stir-fried dishes from central Thailand, including a delicious Mussaman curry. BYO.

Tradewinds Bistro
Mackay Yacht Club, 9–19 Breakwater Access Road, Outer Harbour
Tel: 4955 4950
Open: L & D daily. $$
Standard steak, seafood and chicken bistro meals in a casual setting at the marina, with Harbour Beach views.

The Islands
Most island resorts welcome day guests for lunch, though it is prudent to book ahead.

Hamilton Island (tel: 4946 9999) offers everything from pizza cooked in a wood-fired oven to fine dining. The Beach Club restaurant has an

atmosphere of laid-back luxury, with a beachfront setting. Back on the marina, Romano's Restaurant delivers modern cuisine with Italian overtones –highlights are the local seafood dishes. For cheap eats and live music, head for Sails Restaurant, overlooking Catseye Beach. The island has a Kids Eat Free promotion, offering free meals to kids aged 12 and under when dining with parents. Most places offer this service, but not all.

Mermaids Restaurant, on **Daydream Island** (tel: 4948 8488), is open for lunch daily, offering café-style fare such as tropical open grilled sandwiches and salt-and-pepper calamari (average spend A$30).

Hayman Island (tel: 1800 122 339) has five restaurants but only two are open for lunch. The Hayman Pool Bar and Beach Pavilion serve light lunches daily, noon-5.30pm, including fish and chips, burgers and tapas (A$26–35).

AROUND TOWNSVILLE

From gold rush to tourist boom, the area in and around Queensland's second-largest city is rich with attractions. There's architectural heritage in Townsville, Ravenswood and Charters Towers, plus natural wonders on the doorstep – from vast waterfalls to spectacular gorges, tropical rainforest and unspoilt island beaches

The administrative headquarters for Queensland's far north and the state's second-biggest city, Townsville is the hub of a thriving tourism industry as well as a prosperous service centre for the mineral-rich hinterland. A diverse, mostly youthful mix of people keep the city's casino, nightclubs and restaurants humming. Inland lie the gold-rush towns of Ravenswood and Charters Towers. The region also offers mountainous rainforests, pretty creeks, cane and banana plantations, and, at Wallaman Falls, Australia's longest single-drop waterfall. Off the coast lie some of far-north Queensland's most spectacular islands – among them Hinchinbrook Island, Australia's biggest national park island.

Townsville

Townsville ❶ has never looked better – thanks, ironically, to two destructive cyclones that ripped the foreshore apart in 1997 and 1998, prompting a A$29 million restoration along The Strand. (Thankfully, Cyclones Larry in 2006 and Yasi in 2011 had no lasting impact on the town.) Four man-made headlands jut into the sea, breaking the waves,

and netted enclosures keep stingers at bay from November to May. This 2km (1¼-mile) stretch of white sand, swaying palms and casual restaurants has redefined workaday Townsville as a tropical resort of considerable appeal.

History and heritage

The city takes its name from Robert Towns, the entrepreneur widely credited with instigating the dubious system of importing indentured South Seas labourers to accomplish the hard

Main attractions

TOWNSVILLE
REEF HQ
MAGNETIC ISLAND
CHARTERS TOWERS
PALUMA RANGE NATIONAL PARK
WALLAMAN FALLS
HINCHINBROOK ISLAND
MISSION BEACH

LEFT: the swimming hole at Little Crystal Creek, near Paluma. RIGHT: the water park on Townsville's Strand.

Dominating the cityscape of Townsville is the silhouette of 286-metre (940ft) Castle Hill. Fine views of the city are to be had from the top. For the less energetic, the panoramic point at the top of 585-metre (1,920ft) Mount Stuart is accessed by road 2km (1¼ miles) south of Townsville.

BELOW: Townsville tower. The town centre has some impressive Art Deco buildings, along with the usual Victoriana.

work that white men could not, or would not, do. Towns spent just three days in the city that bears his name. Fortuitously, the establishment of the port of Townsville coincided with the discovery of gold at Ravenswood, the sugar-growing boom and the expansion of pastoral industries.

Townsville has a profusion of heritage buildings, 58 of which are listed by the National Trust. The City Council has mapped out a series of walks that highlight the older buildings. Contact the Townsville Visitor Information Centre (tel: 1800 801 902).

The city's picturesque, yacht-filled Ross River was named after William Ross, who opened the city's first pub, **The Criterion Hotel**, on The Strand. The splendid old **Post Office** (1861), on the corner of Flinders and Denham streets, now houses a boutique brewery called, simply, The Brewery. Opposite is the **Perc Tucker Regional Gallery** (Mon–Fri 10am–5pm, Sat and Sun 10am–2pm; free; tel: 1300 878

001; www.townsville.qld.gov.au), formerly the Union Bank of Australia, built in 1881. The gallery showcases a collection of north Queensland art and also puts on a programme of music, theatre, dance and talks.

Merely to glance at the city's **Railway Station** (1903) is to comprehend the importance of rail transport in Queensland at the turn of the 20th century. At the terminus of a track connecting the inland gold-mining centres of Ravenswood and Charters Towers, this commanding building represents 19th-century railway architecture at its most eloquent.

Modern Townsville has a cosmopolitan edge that suits the elegance of its colonial backdrop. There's a casino overlooking Cleveland Bay, and a dozen or so eating places jostle for attention in **Palmer Street**.

Wildlife watching

In and around Townsville are various places to enjoy the weird and

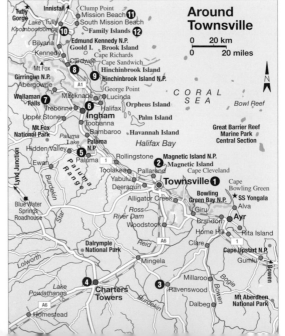

wonderful world of native Australian fauna and flora. If you can't find time to snorkel or dive on the Great Barrier Reef, pay a visit to **Reef HQ** (Flinders Street East; daily 9.30am–5pm; charge; tel: 4750 0800; www.reefhq.com.au). The world's biggest coral-reef aquarium, it contains 130 coral species, 120 fish species, plus myriad sea stars, sea urchins, sea cucumbers, sponges and assorted reef organisms. A predator tank contains reef sharks, stingrays, sea turtles and large predatory fish. There is also a replica of the bow section of the SS *Yongala*, sunk during a tropical cyclone in 1911 with 120 people on board.

At the nearby **Museum of Tropical Queensland** (daily 9.30am–5pm; charge; tel: 4726 0600; www.mtq.qld.gov.au), the gallery space is taken up by a full-size reconstruction of the bow of HMS *Pandora*, the frigate dispatched from England to track down the mutinous crew of HMS *Bounty* (see box below).

Just 17km (10 miles) south of Townsville, down the Bruce Highway, is the **Billabong Sanctuary** (daily except Christmas Day, 9am–4pm; charge; tel: 4778 8344; www.billabongsanctuary.com. au), a great wildlife park where you can cuddle a koala or feed a croc.

Magnetic Island

Backpacker-friendly **Magnetic Island** ❷ remains an inexpensive destination – blessed by a string of stunning beaches, a resilient wildlife population and an average of 300 sunny days per year. Within sight of Townsville, the island covers 5,200 hectares (12,850 acres) and rises to almost 500 metres (1,630ft) at Mount Cook – named after James Cook, who himself named Magnetic Island, in the mistaken belief that something in its geological composition had affected his compass. The island is 11km (7 miles) at its widest point, with 40km (25 miles) of coastline. Despite increased tourism numbers, "Maggie" retains its laid-back atmosphere.

A national park, crossed by 25km (15½ miles) of walking track, occupies over half of the island. An 8km (5-mile) hike from Picnic Bay to West Point takes in tidal wetlands,

HMS Pandora *was sent in 1790–1 from England to find* HMS Bounty. *The wreck of the* Bounty *was not discovered until 1957.*

BELOW: reef life in the aquariums at Reef HQ.

Search for the Mutineers

The English sent the naval frigate HMS *Pandora* to the South Pacific in search of mutineers from HMS *Bounty*, led by the legendary Fletcher Christian. Although the *Pandora*'s captain Edward Edwards was unable to find Christian, he did manage to apprehend 14 of the *Bounty* crewmen in Tahiti. He was returning to England when his ship went down east of Cape York. Christian, immortalised by Marlon Brando in the 1962 film *Mutiny on the Bounty*, is thought by some to have been killed in 1793 by a Tahitian who accompanied him to then uncharted Pitcairn Island. A more romantic theory suggests that he slipped back to England, living undetected with his lover.

Paragliding at sunset – just one of the activities available on Magnetic Island.

mangroves, saltwater swamps and creeks. Also starting from Picnic Bay is a 600-metre (2,000ft) walking track to **Hawkings Point**, with views to Townsville, Rocky Bay and Arcadia.

Fast catamaran and barge services connect Townsville Marina with Magnetic Island's Nelly Bay. Book passenger tickets through Sealink (tel: 4726 0800; www.sealinkqld.com.au); and vehicular barges (plus passengers) through Fantasea Cruising Magnetic (tel: 4796 9300; www.fantasea cruisingmagnetic.com.au).

Lying off Cape Bowling Green is the wreck of the SS *Yongala*. The 90-metre (300ft) vessel rests in about 30 metres (100ft) of water, where it has become home to a bewildering variety of marine life. (Yongala Dives, tel: 4783 1519; www.yongaladive.com.au; Adrenalin Dives, tel: 4724 0600; www.adrenalindive.com.au)

Ravenswood

It takes a stretch of the imagination to envisage the former gold-rush town of **Ravenswood** ❸, 130km (80 miles) south of Townsville, in 1871, when 30 hotels served a shanty town of about 1,000 fossickers. That was just three years after stockman Marmaduke Curr noticed specks of alluvial gold in the bottom of his pannikin after scooping up a drink of water from Elphingstone Creek.

Ravenswood's population peaked at 4,700 in 1903. From 1908, the town fell into slow decline, leaving a legacy of 19th-century buildings amid mullock heaps (waste from mines), tall chimneys and derelict machinery. During the 1920s, many of the remaining residents left. Technology enabled a modest revival in the 1930s, but by the 1960s the population had fallen to 70. It is now approximately 200.

An open-cut gold mine opened in 1987, and other underground mining has resumed nearby, but Ravenswood has been saved mainly by tourism. Everything that remains of the town has been listed by the Australian Heritage Commission and the National Trust of Queensland – to order a beer in the bar of **The Imperial Hotel**, Macrossan Street, is to understand why. Virtually nothing in this bar has changed since the early 1900s, down to the cedar-and-glass fittings, beer

BELOW: Alma Bay on Magnetic Island.

pumps and ceramic taps. One of only two hotels remaining in Ravenswood – the other is **The Railway Hotel** in Barton Street – the Imperial was owned and operated by members of the Delaney family for over 90 years, until 1994.

Charters Towers

During a gold boom that lasted almost three decades, **Charters Towers ❹**, 135km (84 miles) south-west of Townsville, became Queensland's second-largest city, after Brisbane. With a population of 27,000 at its zenith, the city operated its own stock exchange and was known to its residents as "the World", because there was nothing that couldn't be obtained there.

Gold was discovered in 1871 by an Aboriginal youth named Jupiter, in the company of three European prospectors. By the end of 1872, 3,000 hopeful prospectors had arrived, though many soon relocated to the Palmer River fields. When alluvial gold petered out, crushing machinery extracted reef gold. From 1899, yields gradually diminished, and, when the mine was declared unprofitable in 1912, many people left the city.

Private boarding schools were established in vacant heritage buildings from 1912, giving the city its second wind, and in the late 1960s, tourists began to take an interest in this world-famous goldfield. Then, as now, visitors were fascinated by the **Stock Exchange** (1888), with its glazed vault supported by ornate steel trusses above a central court. Restored in the 1970s, it is now owned by the National Trust. The ground floor, where financial business was conducted, is now occupied by shops.

Other National Trust-listed sites include the impressive **Courthouse** (1886), at 28 Hodgkinson Street, and **Thornburgh House** (1890), at 57–59 King Street, formerly the residence of the mining magnate, EHT Plant, but now a boarding school.

Behind its somewhat residential exterior, the **Civic Club**, at 36 Ryan Street, offers an intriguing insight into what it was to be a member of the Charters Towers elite in late Victorian times. It was built in 1900 to be

TIP

Exhibits in the Ravenswood's Courthouse Museum (Macrossan Street; daily 11am–1pm; tel: 4770 2047) trace the town's history. Ask for a map and a descriptive brochure.

BELOW: only one kind of "train" still comes to Ravenswood.

Charters Towers is rich in grand colonial edifices built with the proceeds of the early gold discoveries.

BELOW: the Civic Club appears mostly unchanged since its Victorian heyday.

a gentlemen's club, where the wealthy and influential might congregate to play cards or billiards. These days, the club has abandoned any all-male snootiness, and visitors are encouraged to drop by to meet the locals. Reportedly, the Friday-night steak-and-sausage sizzle is a blast.

Pains have been taken to preserve Charters Towers' 19th-century streetscape. In some cases, heritage facades hide new buildings; the Visitor Information Centre (74 Mosman Street; daily 9am–5pm; www.charterstowers.qld.gov.au) is an example of this.

Paluma

About 60km (37 miles) north of Townsville, the historic **Mount Spec Tourist Road** leaves the Bruce Highway, turning inland towards the mountains of the Paluma Range. This scenic road was built mostly by hand during the Depression of the 1930s and forms the southern gateway to the **Wet Tropics World Heritage Area**, **Paluma Range National Park**, and the tiny mountain village of **Paluma ❺**.

Along its tortuous bends are many fine examples of masonry, the most striking of which is the much-photographed stone bridge over **Little Crystal Creek**, a popular swimming hole fed by icy, crystal-clear water from the gorge.

From Paluma, walking tracks access the Mount Spec area of **Paluma Range National Park**, home to the Herbert River and the ringtail possum and the northern bettong. About 120 bird species are found here, including all four types of bowerbird.

One of north Queensland's spectacular drives is the 15km (9-mile) road connecting Paluma village with **Lake Paluma** (actually a large dam). The road, part-gravel, passes through dense rainforest in which cassowaries are sometimes seen.

Cottage accommodation is available in Paluma Rainforest Village (tel: 4770 8520; www.palumarainforest.com.au). Queensland Parks and Wildlife Service issues camping permits for Paradise Waterhole on Big Crystal Creek, at the foot of the range (tel: 13 74 68; www.qld.gov.au); and Townsville City Council issues camping permits

for Lake Paluma (tel: 4727 9000; www.
townsville.qld.gov.com.au).

Ingham

Around 60 percent of the 6,000
citizens of **Ingham ❻** are of Italian
descent, giving this northern sugar
town a touch of European zest. Italians began arriving here in the 1890s,
filling the labour shortage in the sugar
fields left by Kanaka cane cutters, who
were, by this time, being repatriated
to their South Seas homelands. Along
the main street, older Italians still talk
in their mother tongue and read the
town's Italian-language newspaper.

Located 110km (68 miles) north
of Townsville, Ingham's appeal lies in
close proximity to secluded beaches,
fishing grounds and national parks,
including one at **Orpheus Island**,
20km (12½ miles) offshore, hence
its appeal. Anglers can fish from the
shore or launch boats at **Lucinda**, a
port town with a jetty nearly 6km (4
miles) long, or at Dungeness, Forrest
Beach and Taylor's Beach. Other boat
ramps are at Mona Landing and Cas-
sady Creek.

Beware of crocodiles in these parts.

Do not clean fish at the water's edge,
stand on floating logs (they might be
crocodiles) or dangle arms or legs in
the water. The man after whom Ingham was named – Oxford-educated
adventurer William Ingham – paid
little heed to these precautions. In the
1870s, he made news in the London,
Times after wrestling and stabbing
to death a 4-metre (13ft) crocodile.
Fearless to the end, Ingham met
his demise in New Guinea in 1878,
when cannibals boarded his boat,
chopped off his hands, then roasted
and devoured him.

Wallaman Falls

It's well worth the 51km (32-mile)
drive northwest to visit the spectacular **Wallaman Falls ❼** in **Girringun
National Park**. Plunging from a
height of 268 metres (879ft), this is
Australia's longest waterfall with a
single drop, and is seen at its best following the wet season rains. You can
swim at the base of the falls. However,
resist the temptation to climb Mount
Fox, an extinct volcano within the
park, as the views from the top are dis-
appointing. For further information,

TIP

Ingham's Australian
Italian Festival in May
celebrates the cultural
rapprochement
between new and old
Australians. It's country
fun – with grape-
stomping competitions,
mud crab-tying events
and spaghetti-eating
contests. A vintage cane
train is dusted off to
carry children along the
narrow-gauge track at
Ingham's Victoria Mill,
and there's a
procession to the
singing of Italian songs.

BELOW: beneath the
canopy of Paluma's
dense rainforest.

Statue gracing the streets of laid-back Ingham, in the heart of the sugar-cane district.

BELOW: the cemetery at Ingham reflects the presence of early settlers from Italy and Spain.

contact the TYTO Visitor Information Centre (corner of Bruce Highway and Cooper Street, Ingham; Mon–Fri 8.45am–5pm, Sat–Sun 9am–4pm; tel: 4776 4792; www.tyto.com.au).

Cardwell

First settled in 1864, **Cardwell ❽**, located 160km (100 miles) north of Townsville, was envisaged as the main port for north Queensland. However, mountain ranges to the west made access difficult, and the discovery of gold at Charters Towers gave Townsville the advantage. Virtually unnoticed for most of its existence, Cardwell grabbed the headlines in the late 1990s due to a controversial development. Environmentalists were concerned about the potential impact the **Port Hinchinbrook** mega-resort could have on the nearby World Heritage-listed Hinchinbrook Island *(see opposite)*.

Opponents' arguments fell on deaf ears. That was until Cyclone Yasi struck on 3 February 2011, when all the dire warnings by experts that were dismissed by the developers came to pass. The marina became a boat "wrecking yard" and the waterfront houses were severely damaged. Nevertheless, the development was slowly resurrected and the resort (www. porthinchinbrook.com.au) reopened in 2012. In addition to the resort, private residences and marina, there are plans for a health club and golf course.

Edmund Kennedy, Girramay National Park, 4km (2½ miles) north of Cardwell, was named after the traditional owners, the Girramay people and the explorer Edmund Kennedy, who passed this way in 1848 while attempting to travel overland from Rockingham Bay to Cape York *(see page 22)*. A network of walking tracks passes through and above tropical rainforest and mangroves.

There's a spectacular lookout 2.5km (1½ miles) west of Cardwell. A 20km (12½-mile) scenic drive takes in swimming holes at **Attie Creek Falls**, **Dead Horse Creek** and the **Spa Pool**. For more information, contact the Rainforest and Reef Visitor Centre (142 Victoria Street, Cardwell; Mon–Fri 8.30am–5pm, Sat–Sun 9am–1pm; tel: 4066 8601; www.greatgreenwaytourism.com).

Hinchinbrook Island

Hinchinbrook Island ❾, 160km (100 miles) north of Townsville, is Australia's biggest national-park island, with no human presence save for a small resort at Cape Richards (www.porthinchinbrook.com.au/island-resort), currently only taking group and function bookings, and assorted bushwalkers. Within the island's 39,900 hectares (98,500 acres) are lush rainforests, heath-covered mountains, rocky headlands, and wetlands, with mangrove-fringed shores and sweeping sandy beaches.

The best time to follow the 32km (20-mile) trail along the island's east coast is during the cooler months, from April to September. Camping grounds have been established along the route. Allow three days to complete the journey, and note that this trek is for fit and experienced bushwalkers (see page 270). Limits apply to the number of walkers allowed on the trail at any one time, and bookings are required at least six months in advance.

Water taxis from Cardwell and Lucinda transfer campers and walkers to the island. Ingham Travel operates a shuttle bus between Cardwell, Ingham and Lucinda. For details on walks or access, contact the Rainforest and Reef Visitor Centre (tel: 4066 8334).

Tully

The highway north of Cardwell passes through cane farms and banana plantations interspersed with pretty creeks and swathes of rainforest. It's picturesque country, made luxuriant by tropical rainstorms. The road passes Kennedy, a tiny town with a store and a school, before crossing the Tully River and leading into the main street of **Tully** ❿.

Other Queensland cities make much of their sunny weather. Tully, about 240km (150 miles) north of Townsville, celebrates the rain. Indeed, the first thing you notice on entering the main street is a huge **Gumboot**. The boot stands 7.93 metres (26ft) high – the height the rain reached during Tully's record-breaking deluge in 1950. Inside, a spiral staircase accesses a viewing platform, with views to the Tully Sugar Mill and Mount Tyson.

Tully's 2,500 citizens compete with Babinda and Innisfail for the Golden Gumboot award for highest rainfall. It's tongue-in-cheek stuff, but rivals take genuine pleasure in putting the boot in when Tully falls behind. Undeterred, Tully hosts the annual Golden Gumboot Festival every September, when events include a gumboot-throwing competition.

BELOW: Hinchinbrook Island seen from the jetty at Cardwell.

Tully Gorge rafting operators will arange pick-ups from Mission Beach and Cairns.

BELOW: a quiet Sunday afternoon in Tully.

Originally known as Banyan, Tully was surveyed in 1883, but little happened until 1925, when the government built the (then) biggest sugar mill in Australia – now the heart of Tully. Massive expenses of sugar cane are under cultivation, and, during harvest, from June to November, the mill operates day and night, crushing over 2.4 million tons. Banana cultivation is also thriving.

Guided tours of the mill are more or less mandatory during the harvest, and hardy visitors can undertake a three-hour hike to the Mount Tyson lookout for an overview of Tully and the surrounding farms.

The main tourist attraction is the **Tully Gorge**, which descends from an escarpment to form more than 45 rapids that thunder in spectacular style through steep gorges amid World Heritage-listed rainforest.

The lure of adventure draws thousands of white-water rafters annually. The experience is open to beginners as well as more experienced rafters, under the supervision of qualified river guides. The Flip Wilson Lookout, downriver from the Cardstone

Weir, offers a good observation point for watching the rafters as they plummet past, wide-eyed and charged with adrenalin. For information on rafting and bushwalks, contact Tully Visitor and Heritage Centre, Bruce Highway, Tully; tel: 4068 2288 (www. csc.qld.gov.au).

Misty Mountains

Inland from Tully and Innisfail is Australia's first network of long-distance wilderness walks in high-altitude rainforest – the Misty Mountains (tel: 4046 6600; www.mistymountains. com.au), which can also be accessed from Cairns *(see page 184)*. More than 130km (81 miles) of tracks have been constructed along old logging trails, often following the ridgelines used by the traditional Aboriginal owners. One of the more appealing walks is the five-hour return trek through pristine rainforest to the rarely visited but serenely beautiful **Elizabeth Grant Falls**, cascading 300 metres (1,000ft) into Koolmoon Creek. The start of the walk is 40km (25 miles) from Tully, along Tully Gorge Road (also known as Cardstone Road).

Follow the signs and turn right into Cochable Creek campground. To book, tel: 13 74 68; or contact: www.qld.gov.au/camping.

Mission Beach

Turn right north of Tully for the 20km (12½-mile) drive to **Mission Beach** ⑪ – the generic name for a string of small seaside communities set amid rainforest. Mission Beach is a chic resort village with decent restaurants and an atmosphere that hovers between up-market exclusivity and backpacker *joie de vivre*.

The name derives from the Aboriginal mission established in 1914 but destroyed by a cyclone four years later. The strip runs north from Tam O'Shanter Point to South Mission Beach, Wongaling, Mission Beach, Clump Point and Bingil Bay. **Clump Point** is the departure point for cruises to the Great Barrier Reef and Dunk Island. The area has well-marked rainforest walks on which cassowary sightings are not uncommon. These flightless birds inhabit the shadowy world of the rainforest, scouring through the leaf litter for dropped fruit. Indeed, many rainforest trees rely on the cassowary to eat their fruit, then disperse and deposit the seed in a new location with a dollop of fertiliser.

The Mission Beach Visitors Information Centre (Porter Promenade; tel: 4068 7099; www.missionbeach tourism.com) can provide information on the region.

Family Islands

The **Family Islands** ⑫ are a small group of islands off the Mission Beach coast. The largest of the group is Dunk, the island chronicled by Edmund James Banfield in his book *Confessions of a Beachcomber*. These islands were severely impacted by Cyclone Yasi in 2011. Resorts on Dunk and Bedarra islands were destroyed and their future remained uncertain at the time of writing, but most of the island group is national park, and campgrounds are slowly being reopened. For the latest information check www.derm.qld.gov.au/parks/family-islands. Access is by water taxi from Mission Beach's Clump Point jetty. ❏

Cassowaries are well designed for their rainforest lifestyle, with water-shedding hairlike feathers and a horny helmet, possibly for crashing through the undergrowth. Their three-clawed feet sport a dagger-like middle claw, used for scraping the forest floor and as a weapon in fights.

BELOW: any afternoon on Mission Beach.

BEST RESTAURANTS, BARS AND CAFÉS

Prices for a three-course dinner per person with house wine:
$ = A$60 and under
$$ = A$60–100
$$$ = A$100 and over

Cardwell

Portside
Port Hinchinbrook Marina
Tel: 4066 4007
Open: L & D daily. **$$**
Portside was closed following Cyclone Yasi, but should be reopened by the time you read this. Expect a modern menu based on steak, barramundi and mud crab, and great views over to Hinchinbrook Island.

Charters Towers

Henry's Café and Restaurant
82 Mosman Street

Tel: 4787 4333
Open: L & D Tue–Sat. **$$**
Henry's comes as something of a surprise, with a Mod Oz menu incorporating Indian, Japanese and Thai influences. High ceilings, cream walls and slatted blinds lend this heritage-listed restaurant a delightfully cool ambience.

Redz Coffee House
32 Gill Street
Tel: 4787 1590
Open: L daily. **$**
A good place to while away a few hours, as it combines a café with a bookstore. Excellent coffee, juices, bruschetta, baguettes and quiches. Interesting selection of books, too.

Stock Exchange Café
1/76 Mossman Street

Tel: 4787 7954
Open: L Mon–Sat. **$**
Inside the venerable Stock Exchange building, this café is a popular breakfast and lunch spot, with an airy relaxed ambience and good coffee.

Ingham

Café Fiorellis
1 Lannercost Street
Tel: 4776 2172
Open: L & D daily. **$**
Café and restaurant with fresh seafood and an Italian influence. Geared towards locals and budget travellers.

Lou's Emporium
Lannercost Street
Tel: 4776 1587
Open: L daily. **$**
Lou's is a delicatessen, not a restaurant, but the shelves display a remarkable array of items, all connected with Italy – reflecting the substantial Italian community in Ingham. Owner Venero Cavallaro stocks everything, from cutlery to condiments.

Serenita@Tyto
24-30 Macrossan Avenue
Tel: 4776 1470
Open: L Wed–Sun, D Thur–Sun. **$$**
Features bistro-style food with an emphasis on seafood and steaks. Overlooking the Tyto wetlands, it's certainly a

serene place to chill out with a fine wine and good company.

The Olive Tree Coffee Lounge
45 Lannercost Street
Tel: 4776 5166
Open: L daily, D Fri–Sun. **$**
This is about as close as it gets to a full-on Italian restaurant in Ingham. Good coffee and Sicilian fare prepared in the traditional manner make it popular with locals, too.

Magnetic Island

Barefoot Art Food Wine
5 Pacific Drive,
Horseshoe Bay
Tel: 4758 1170
Open: L & D Thur–Mon. **$$**
There's a bit of everything here. The wine list has more than 100 entries, and the food is Mod Oz with Asian touches. Sit in a tropical garden or on the deck overlooking the sea. The art gallery is a bonus.

Mission Beach

Bibesia Beachfront restaurant
Castaways Resort and Spa,
2 Pacific Parade
Tel: 4068 7444
Open: B, L & D daily. **$$$**
The resort's centrepiece restaurant with great beach frontage delivers a wide-ranging seasonal menu that includes such

LEFT: chef at stylish Table 51.

dishes as prime eye fillet beef with prawns and prawn linguine puttanesca.

Caffè Rustica
24 Wongaling Beach Road
Tel: 4068 9111
Open: L Sun, D Wed–Sun. **$$**
Caffè Rustica is a delightful corrugated-iron trattoria with an Australian tropical ambience and authentic Italian cuisine. Excellent antipasti, pasta and pizzas, the last with traditional thin and crispy bases.

Paluma

Ivy Cottage
Mount Spec Road
Tel: 4770 8533
Open: varies – phone. **$**
This is Paluma's oldest house. It's in a great location, backing on to the rainforest, and serves light meals and traditional treats such as Devonshire teas and coffee made the old-fashioned way.

Townsville

Bennys Hot Wok Café
17–29 Palmer Street
Tel: 4724 3243
Open: L Fri–Sun,
D daily. **$$**
The food here is a modern fusion of Thai, Japanese and Chinese, including sushi, traditional soups, Asian salads, Thai curries and stir-fries.

Bistro One
30–34 Palmer Street
Tel: 4771 6333
Open: B, L & D daily. **$$**

Chic modern Australian fare with a Mediterranean influence, using very fresh ingredients. Separate menus for breakfast, lunch and dinner.

Cactus Jack's Bar and Grill
21 Palmer Street
Tel: 4721 1478
Open: D daily. **$**
If you feel like a change, try the Tex-Mex food here – fajitas, tortillas, enchiladas, nachos et al – served along with the more familiar Ozzie fare.

C Bar
Gregory Street Headland, The Strand
Tel: 4724 0333
Open: L & D daily. **$$**
Attractively situated on an artificial headland, right on the beach front, offering alfresco dining with marvellous sea views. There's a café menu by day, and more up-market restaurant-style dining by night.

Jamaica Joe's
80 Gregory Street Headland, The Strand
Tel: 4724 1234
Open: L & D daily **$$**
Joe's place is modelled on an American diner, albeit on the Queensland coast with a Caribbean menu. But it's not all rum and jerk; you can also get great Queensland beef and seafood, as well as burgers and pizza.

Ladah
Shop 1/157 Stanley Street
Tel: 4724 0402
Open: L daily. **$**

Gourmet café cuisine. Good breakfast menu, and lunch snacks such as smoked cod and potato pie.

Michels
7 Palmer Street
Tel: 4724 1460
Open: L Tue–Fri,
D Tue–Sat. **$$**
Multi-award-winning restaurant. Seafood, pastas and salads served within the restaurant or on the terrace.

Rhino Bar
3 Palmer Street
Tel: 4771 6322
Open: L Thur–Sun; D daily. **$$**
Tapas, steaks, draught beers and cocktails. The decor is fashionable; the crowd likewise.

Table 51
51 Palmer Street
Tel: 4721 0642
Open: L Tue–Fri, D Mon–Sat. **$$**
Stylish up-market restaurant with an appeal-

ing and wide-ranging modern Australian menu featuring ingredients from Tasmanian salmon to Moreton Bay bugs, local barramundi and, of course, Queensland beef.

The Rockpool Seafood Café and Bar
The Strand
Tel: 4771 6916
Open: L Fri–Sat,
D Tue–Sun. **$$**
Stunning location overlooking Townsville's Rockpool, with a modern Australian bistro menu of steak, chicken and seafood. Decent wine list, too.

Wayne and Adeles Garden of Eating
11 Allen Street
Tel: 4772 2984
Open: L Sun, D Wed–Mon. **$$**
This homely restaurant has won awards annually since 1994, including Best BYO in Queensland.

RIGHT: a local scallop dish.

TASTING QUEENSLAND

Go into any supermarket in Australia and you'll find produce from Queensland on its shelves. The state is like one giant farm, producing a bounty of tasty delights

Agriculture is central to the Queensland economy, with bananas, pineapples, sugar and beef leading the way, and a whole host of other produce following on, including peanuts, cotton, wool and countless fruit and vegetables, some tropical, some temperate. It is almost impossible to travel within the state without seeing evidence of this, whether it's the quaint narrow-gauge trains holding up traffic as they transport sugar cane to the mills, or cattle wandering across the road in the dusty Outback.

You can visit a sugar mill during the processing season, or see the sugar cane being turned into the famous Bundaberg rum. But if you want the full hands-on experience, consider a farm-stay, where you may find yourself rounding up cattle on horseback or picking your own pineapples. Most visitors, however, are happy simply to make the most of the produce further down the line, whether picking up a box of mangoes at a roadside stall, or a range of exotic fruit at one of the markets. Better still, seek out the many fine restaurants that make the most of seasonal produce to create tasty dishes for the gourmet.

ABOVE: inland is cattle country, where drovers have to muster stock on huge stations that can extend over thousands and thousands of square kilometres. Eventually the cattle will be sold at market, as here at Cloncurry.

ABOVE: pineapples, along with other tropical fruit such as mangoes and pawpaws, are shipped across Australia but tend to be cheaper locally.

LEFT: Furphy's water carts were found on farms from the 1870s onwards. They were also used in World War I. It's believed the colloquial usage of 'furphy' for a lie or rumour derives from this early equivalent of "water-cooler" gossip.

TASTE BUD-TEMPTING TOURS

Anyone travelling through Queensland, particularly the north, at the height of the sugar season (June to November) will find it hard to avoid sugar's sweet, sticky presence. Visitors to Tully can join a tour of the sugar mill and, in an hour-and-a-half with a guide, gain a basic knowledge of the crushing and processing of sugar cane. All this sugar has myriad uses, but none more associated with Queensland than that of Bundaberg Rum. A tour of the distillery is a must for connoisseurs.

In Mareeba, a short drive west of Cairns on the fertile Atherton Tableland, you can see how Australian coffee is grown and roasted. There are also orchards here where you can sample tropical-fruit wines. South of here, and still only a short drive from Cairns, near Malanda, is Australia's largest tea garden, Nerada Estate. Here you can learn about the

history of the plantation, taste the product and tour the factory. Meanwhile, there are more traditional cellar-door tastings in the Granite Belt vineyards of Stanthorpe and Ballandean; and look out for farms selling macadamia nuts, either roasted or whipped into superb ice-cream concoctions.

RIGHT: a small but successful coffee industry feeds the booming café market. Specialist flavours include this example, featuring the *de facto* national nut of Australia.

ABOVE: in June to December, sugar cane is harvested in northern Queensland and loaded on to railtrucks that trundle slowly along narrow-gauge lines to the nearest mill. During this period it's pretty much certain that if you're driving, you will get held up at some point as the trains meander backwards and forwards across the roads.
RIGHT: rich soil and a generally predictable climate means that Queensland's farmers are producing fruit and vegetables for the rest of the country all year round.

ABOVE: bananas are a key product, and, with imports barred, Australia is dependent on northern Queensland for them. This became only too evident in 2006, when Cyclone Larry devastated the crop and within weeks no bananas could be found.

CAIRNS TO CAPE TRIBULATION

Cairns is perfectly placed for exploring everything the tropical north has to offer, both on- and offshore. It's the gateway to the Great Barrier Reef and the Wet Tropics rainforest, and is backed by the lush, cool plateau of the Atherton Tableland

All roads may lead to Rome, but it can seem as if all roads lead away from Cairns. With its own international airport, the premier city of tropical far-north Queensland attracts visitors from all over the world – only to wave them goodbye as they head off to the myriad attractions of the Great Barrier Reef (see page 53), the beaches and Atherton Tableland. Choppers and catamarans speed to reef platforms. Cable cars and a scenic railway connect with Kuranda's souvenir shops in the mountains beyond. There are reef excursions, journeys aboard underwater contraptions, hair-raising experiences on rapids, sybaritic champagne sessions aboard charter yachts. Visitors join 4WD safaris to Cape York, tackle marlin in the Coral Sea, or embark on bushwalking expeditions. Even the food trail veers away from Cairns, plunging deep into the wilds of the Atherton Tableland.

Gateway to paradise

The reputation of **Cairns ❶** as a "tropical gateway" deters many visitors from devoting any length of time to exploring the city itself. Yet there is much of interest in this cosmopolitan hub. Restaurants and clubs are kept busy by a passing parade of mature

travellers and fun-seeking backpackers. So much happens there now that it's hard to believe that when the late Hollywood actor and game-fishing enthusiast Lee Marvin "discovered" Cairns in the 1970s, it was a sleepy backwater with ramshackle pubs, colourful characters and plenty of marlin swimming off the coast.

Change was slow until the development boom of the 1980s introduced modern hotels and high-rise blocks. These days, Cairns presents a sophisticated face while still exud-

Main attractions

CAIRNS
KURANDA SKYRAIL AND SCENIC RAILWAY
MAREEBA
CHILLAGOE
THE WATERFALLS CIRCUIT
GREEN ISLAND
TJAPUKAI ABORIGINAL CULTURAL PARK
PORT DOUGLAS
MOSSMAN GORGE
DAINTREE
CAPE TRIBULATION

LEFT: view of Barron Falls, Kuranda.
RIGHT: taking it easy on Marlin Marina.

Night-market shopping in Cairns.

ing an atmosphere of tropical ease from the shady verandas of its old-fashioned pubs and timber-and-tin stilt houses. The mosquito-infested swamps that blighted pioneers in the gold- and tin-rush eras have long since been reclaimed – but you can still see how Cairns used to be as you pass through steamy mangroves and verdant cane fields on the short drive from Cairns International Airport to the city centre.

With a population of 150,000, modern Cairns enjoys the benefits of air-conditioned malls and international tourism. Japanese signage adorns boutiques and gift shops; hotel clocks are set to London, New York and Tokyo time. Along The Esplanade, backpackers gather in bars lining the strip, or sunbathe, minimally clad, on the lawns of an **artificial lagoon** – rather incongruous amid locals picnicking beneath Moreton Bay figs and palm trees. Nearby, a cluster of ritzy hotels dominates the waterfront. Completing the picture of tropical languor is The Pier Marketplace shopping complex, open daily, with weekend markets, and a marina for Cairns' marlin-fishing fleet and pleasure boats.

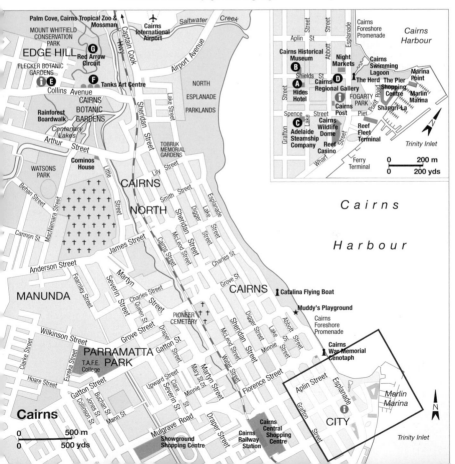

At high tide, the ocean laps the narrow beach along the shoreline. At low tide, primeval mudflats extend to the distant blue of the sea. Cairns' affection for its mudflats became apparent some years ago when environmentalists successfully fought a scheme to inundate them.

History, art and botany

Much of the city's original architecture has been demolished, but enough remains to give an idea of how it used to be, particularly around the Wharf Road, Abbott Street and Lake Street precincts.

The row of rough-and-ready pubs that once made up the Barbary Coast Wharf precinct has been reduced to just one – the much sanitised Reef Hotel (35–41 Wharf Street), which houses a casino and, under its glass dome, an enchanting zoo (Cairns Rainforest Dome; daily 9am–6pm; charge; tel: 4031 7250; www.cairnsdome.com.au), with the usual kookaburras and koalas, and a giant croc called Goliath.

Hides Hotel A, in Lake Street, dates from the 1920s, when it was the epitome of tropical elegance. Opposite is the splendid School of Arts, built in 1907, now home to the **Cairns Historical Museum B** (Mon–Sat 10am–4pm; charge; tel: 4051 5582; www.cairnsmuseum.org.au). The museum traces the city's genesis from mosquito-infested swamp to sugar town, railway terminus, port, and its current incarnation as international tourist destination.

Also on Lake Street, at No. 37, stands the former headquarters of the **Adelaide Steamship Company C** (1910), still adorned with a sculpture of one of the company's vessels.

The elegant **Cairns Regional Gallery D** (corner of Abbott and Shield streets; Mon–Sat 10am–5pm, Sun 1pm–5pm; charge; tel: 4046 4800 www.cairnsregionalgallery.com.au) presents interstate and international exhibitions, as well as showing works by internationally respected local artists such as Ray Crooke and Rosella Namok.

One of Cairns' less-visited treasures is the **Flecker Botanic Gardens E** (Collins Avenue, Edge Hill; Mon–Fri 7.30am–5.30pm, Sat–Sun 8.30am–

Didgeridoos for sale in Cairns.

BELOW LEFT: the Esplanade at Cairns. **BELOW RIGHT:** Cairns Regional Gallery.

Barron Falls is one of the main stops on the trip up to Kuranda. The falls can also be seen from the Skyrail.

BELOW: Kuranda's scenic railway.

5.30pm; free; tel: 4044 3398). About five minutes' drive from the city centre, the main gardens are a rainforest in miniature, with tall trees and palms covered by lianas and tropical climbers, orchids, bromeliads and ferns. Boardwalks weave through lowland swamp forest and melaleuca wetland. Within the gardens is a section devoted to flora used by local Aborigines for medicine, food, weapons and shelter.

While you're in the Botanic cultural precinct, the **Tank Arts Centre** ❺ (Collins Avenue; Mon–Fri 8.30am–5pm; tel: 4032 6600) is worth a visit. Ingenious use of converted World War II fuel tanks has created space for art and photography exhibitions, jazz concerts and markets.

Walk along Collins Avenue to a small off-street parking bay, which is the beginning of the **Red Arrow Walk** ❻. A well-made but steep walking track leads you to tranquil gullies, through virgin rainforest, and to sweeping viewpoints that look out over the town centre, Trinity Bay, the airport, and the mangrove creeks and swamps along the coast.

Palm Cove

North of Cairns is a string of pretty, laid-back beaches, all clearly indicated on the Captain Cook Highway. Up-market **Palm Cove** is the largest of these northern beach resort areas before reaching Port Douglas, and is where many visitors base themselves. Unlike Cairns, it has a white-sand beach and usually clear waters. On the highway just south of Palm Cove is **Cairns Tropical Zoo** (8.30am–4pm daily; charge; www.cairnstropical-zoo.com.au), which exhibits a variety of north Queensland and more exotic animals. You can even join the zoo critters for breakfast on one of the special tours.

Kuranda

These days, most tourists split the pleasant 44km (27-mile) return trip from Cairns to **Kuranda** ❷ (pop. 1,500) into two experiences. A train, with vintage coaches, takes you in one direction, climbing tortuously amid spectacular scenery, through tunnels and past impressive waterfalls; the return half of the journey is by **Skyrail**, a 7.5km (4½-mile) aerial tramway

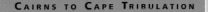

that glides over the treetops of the **Barron Gorge National Park**. This ingenious piece of engineering allows you to see the gorge's eucalyptus woodlands and vine-clad rainforests without the inconvenience of skinned shins or tick bites. The journey takes 90 minutes and includes stops at Red Peak, where a boardwalk ventures into the rainforest, and Barron Falls, where you can see the remains of a 1930s hydroelectricity plant.

At ground level, the **Scenic Railway** winds through the gorge to the flower-decked Kuranda Railway Station, a heritage-listed building. Between 1887 and 1891, a workforce of 1,500 men built the 24km (15 miles) of track between Redlynch and Kuranda, which entailed the construction of no fewer than 15 tunnels and 40 bridges – all by hand. The Christmas Creek bridge is a rare example of wrought iron construction.

At the Kuranda Railway Station, there's a free bus to the village, where tourism has taken over. Among Kuranda's attractions are the **Heritage Markets** (Rob Veiver's Drive; daily 9am–3pm), selling a cheerful jumble of arts and crafts and produce. Nearby is the popular **Australian Butterfly Sanctuary** (www.australianbutterflies. com), home to 1,500 magnificent tropical butterfly species, as well as a koala park and an aviary (complete with resident cassowary). There's even a fruitbat rehabilitation centre, Batreach (www.batreach.com).

A third way to reach Kuranda is by bus from the terminus in Lake Street, Cairns. Contact TransNorth (tel: 4061 7944) for schedules. For more information, contact the Kuranda Information Centre (daily 10am–4pm; tel: 4093 9311; www.kuranda.org).

Mareeba

It's a 64km (40-mile) drive from Cairns to **Mareeba** ❸ – famous as a tobacco town until anti-smoking campaigns made the crop unviable,

Mareeba is a service centre for the Cape York and Gulf Country cattle stations. Huge "road trains" bring beasts from outlying stations each week to be auctioned. Every July, ringers and stockmen converge for Mareeba's rodeo.

BELOW: mango grower in Mareeba.

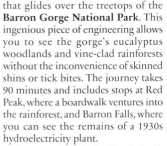

Cairns to Cape Tribulation

Chillagoe

For an interesting detour from the usual tourist route, head to this ill-fated mining town surrounded by mysterious limestone caverns

The former mining settlement of Chillagoe is an archetypal Outback town. The ruins and relics of boilers, steam engines and tall chimney stacks set against jagged limestone outcrops, chiaroscuro caves and ancient Aboriginal rock paintings present a surreal and captivating landscape. Located 215km (134 miles) west of Cairns, via Mareeba and Dimbulah, Chillagoe can be visited on a day trip from Cairns, but an overnight stay will give you more time to absorb this fascinating place. The Hub Interpretive Centre (Queen Street; tel: 4094 7111) is a good place to get your bearings, and provides an overview of Chillagoe's mining history.

Chillagoe's life as a mining town began in 1887, when magnate John Moffat pegged claims in the area and built a private railway between Chillagoe and Mareeba. Construction of his Chillagoe smelter began in 1900,

setting the scene for a sorry saga of ineptitude, scandal and plain bad luck. First, a series of mishaps resulted in the smelter standing idle for the duration of the World War I metals boom. Through the 1930s, the then state-owned smelters made stupendous losses in a noble but futile bid to alleviate the Great Depression. In 1943, the works closed for the final time. In all their history, the Chillagoe smelters never once turned a profit. Today, the main chimney still dominates the township.

There are about 150 derelict copper and lead mines in the area, but the township's main attraction is the limestone caves that surround it. The Chillagoe caves were formed 400 million years ago, when receding sea levels exposed ancient coral reefs. Today stalactites, stalagmites and flowstones embellish the caverns and passages. Above ground, a belt of soaring limestone pinnacles 45km (28 miles) long and 5km (3 miles) wide extends to the south and northwest. Up to 70 metres (230ft) high, these eerie towers are an unforgettable sight.

Among the most impressive caves in the Chillagoe–Mungana National Park is Royal Arch Cave, a 1.5km (1-mile) passage punctuated by 13 side chambers, random tree roots and intermittent shafts of light. Walking paths connect Royal Arch with Donna, Pompeii, Bauhinia and Trezkinn caves – and also join with another marvel called Balancing Rock, a gravity-defying boulder balanced on its end. Another absorbing cave is The Archways, 16km (10 miles) northwest of Chillagoe, where daylight filters through passages edged with maidenhair fern, and Aboriginal art adorns the smaller galleries.

It is permissible to explore The Archways, Pompeii and Bauhinia caves without a guide. However, if you do so go it alone, QPWS advises you to take at least two torches and always go accompanied. For maps and/or a copy of *Rocks and Landscapes of the Chillagoe District*, go to The Hub or download maps from www.derm.qld. gov.au. Guided tours of the Royal Arch, Trezkinn and Donna caves can be booked at The Hub. ❏

LEFT: derelict smelter in Chillagoe.

now better known for sugar, coffee, mangoes and other tropical fruits. It's possible to sample coffee and tropical-fruit wines at local plantations. One of the biggest operations is the Nastasi family's Golden Drop Winery (227 Bilwon Road; daily 8am–6.30pm; tel: 4093 2750), which specialises in mango wine. More diverse is the **Mount Uncle Distillery** (1819 Chewko Road, Walkamin; daily 10am–5pm; tel: 4086 8008), a working banana, avocado and macadamia-nut farm where visitors are invited to taste home-made banana, coffee, mulberry and mango liqueurs. North Queensland Gold Coffee Plantation (Dimbulah Road, via Mareeba; tel: 4093 2269) offers plantation tours and coffee tastings. Another "food trail" stop is **The Coffee Works** (136 Mason Street, Mareeba; tel: 4092 4101), where visitors are shown through the blending factory before being invited to sample house specialities such as macadamia-flavoured coffee, coffee liqueur and chocolate-coated macadamia nuts.

North of Mareeba, at the end of an unsealed road that winds for 7.5km (4½ miles) through sugarcane fields, is the **Mareeba Tropical Savannah and Wetland Reserve** (Pickford Road; April–Dec, Wed–Sun, 9am–4.30pm; free; tel: 4093 2514; www.jabirusafarilodge.com.au), home to countless birds and an up-market eco lodge. This is a gateway to the Cape York peninsula and the Gulf Savannah region, presenting a superb introduction to the wonderful biodiversity along the Savannah Way, the route that stretches across the top of Australia, from Mareeba to Broome 3,200km (2,000 miles) away (see page 207). **Clancy's Lagoon**, fed by excess irrigation water, attracts a high concentration of regional wildlife such as brolgas, sarus, cranes, red-tailed black cockatoos and the strikingly elegant jabiru, Australia's only stork. You can do several walks on your own, but guided boat tours and twilight wildlife safaris are available.

Military hardware enthusiasts will enjoy the **Beck Museum** (Kennedy Highway; daily 10am–5pm; charge; tel: 4092 3979) on the southern edge of Mareeba. Its extensive collection

BELOW: historic church in Yungaburra.

TIP

Spend a tranquil afternoon at Lake Eacham, a volcanic crater lake in the rainforest, not far from Yungaburra. You can swim in the placid water or follow signs to the ranger station to pick up trail maps. There is a 3km (2-mile) circuit around the lake, which is a cassowary habitat, and you're also likely to see scrub turkeys, yellow robins and a range of water birds.

BELOW: Mungalli Falls.

includes 1940s aircraft and other vehicles and weaponry, most of it housed in a huge hangar.

Head south on the highway for the township of Tolga and the **Big Peanut**, where you can sample hot, freshly roasted peanuts right beside the plantation.

Tyrconnell

Southwest of Mareeba lies Dimbulah and the **Tyrconnell Historic Mine** (charge; tel: 4093 5177; www.tyrconnell.com.au), a well-preserved remnant of 19th-century gold fever. The highlight of the mine site tour, taken either on a day trip or during an overnight stay in one of the cabins, is the firing up of the quartz-crushing machine. Despite a century of neglect, this steam-age antique clatters into action, with a great whirring of flywheels and the crack of mechanical hammers.

A few kilometres away is **Thornborough**, a once-roistering gold town of 22 hotels and 10,000 souls, now reduced to a decayed scattering of rusty tin shacks and a cemetery where early settlers are buried.

Atherton and Yungaburra

Sandwiched between the Cairns coast and the Outback, at the edge of the Great Dividing Range is the lush and elevated sweep of the Atherton Tableland. It's a rain-soaked area of fertile pastures, dairy farms, country towns, scenic lakes, tropical forests and waterfalls. Handy to local attractions is the country town of **Atherton ④**, where the Atherton Tableland Information Centre (corner of Main Street and Silo Road; daily 9am–5pm; tel: 4091 4022; www.athertoninformationcentre.com.au) provides maps and brochures and makes bookings.

The main point of interest in the town itself is the **Hou Wang Temple** (Herberton Road; 10am–4pm; www.houwang.org.au). Built in 1903, it was once the spiritual heart of a thriving Chinatown. When tin was discovered on the Wild River in 1880, Chinese labourers established a separate settlement across the creek from the Europeans at Prior's Pocket, later renamed after prospector John Atherton. At its height, in 1909, Chinatown comprised a short main street lined with 100 shops and houses. After World War I, when Chinese farm leases were made over to soldier-settlers, the Chinese population dwindled to a handful of elderly men, who used the temple intermittently until the 1970s. Restored by the National Trust, the temple is decorated with ornate carvings embellished with vermilion and gold.

Another of Atherton's attractions is the **Crystal Caves** (69 Main Street; Mon–Fri 8.30am–5pm, Sat 8.30am–4pm, Sun 10am–4pm; charge; tel: 4091 2365; www.crystalcaves.com.au), where the owner has built a substantial artificial cave to house his collection of crystals, fossils and gems.

Yungaburra ⑤, 12km (7½ miles) east of Atherton, is a cheerful town renowned for its heritage houses (the National Trust has listed 23 sites), picturesque crater lake (*see Tip left*)

and the 500-year-old Curtain Fig Tree, an amazing natural "sculpture" with long aerial roots resembling a hanging curtain. The town has a range of decent restaurants, and the Tableland's biggest market is held here on the fourth Saturday of every month. A lively two-day folk festival is held every October (www.yungabur-rafolkfestival.org).

The Waterfalls Circuit

A 15km (9-mile) drive southeast of Yungaburra through lush green hillside pastures dotted with black-and-white Friesian cows, leads to **Malanda**, where dairying has been the town's main occupation since the early 1900s. A detour before Malanda takes you to the **Nerada Tea Estate** (Glen Allyn Road; charge; tel: 4096 8328), Australia's largest tea plantation with a visitor centre, tasting room and factory tours.

Neighbouring **Millaa Millaa** ❻, 25km (15 miles) to the south, is another dairy town – memorable because it is ringed by some of the Tableland's most spectacular waterfalls. Enter the waterfall circuit by

taking the Theresa Creek Road, 1km (⅔ mile) east of Millaa Millaa on the Palmerston Highway. **Millaa Millaa Falls** is the most photogenic, with the best swimming hole, a picnic area and teahouse. But **Zillie Falls** and **Ellinjaa Falls** are also attractive (the latter also has a swimming hole). Back on the Palmerston Highway, 5km (3 miles) towards Innisfail, there's a turn-off to the **Mungalli Falls**.

Ravenshoe

At 920 metres (3,000ft) above sea level, **Ravenshoe** ❼, 25km (15 miles) southwest of Millaa Millaa, is the highest town in Queensland. The town at the top of the Great Dividing Range came into being around 1900 as a centre for the timber industry. Logging was outlawed in the 1980s when the surrounding 2.2 million acres (880,000 hectares) of rainforest were declared a World Heritage Site.

Today, Ravenshoe provides a more sustainable resource in the form of wind-generated power. About 5km (3miles) outside town, the 20 graceful turbines of Windy Hill Wind Farm swish musically in the breeze,

The Ravenshoe and Atherton Insteam Locomotion Company, runs trains along a 7km (4-mile) section of track every Sunday at 1.30pm.

BELOW: the aftermath of Cyclone Yasi in Tully Heads.

Cyclone Fury

It's impossible to comprehend the power of a tropical cyclone unless you have experienced one. Winds in excess of 250km/hour (155mph) can wrench huge trees from the ground and anything that comes loose, such as roofing iron, outdoor furniture and tree branches, immediately become lethal missiles.

Cyclone season in tropical Queensland is between November and April, and, on average, there are around five cyclones per year. Although most cyclone activity occurs in northern Queensland, destructive cyclones have also affected Brisbane and southern Queensland. Cyclone Yasi, which crossed Queensland's coast on 3 February 2011, was the largest and most powerful cyclone in living memory.

This mosaic plaque in Gordonvale bemoans the blight of the cane toad, introduced from Hawaii in 1935 in the mistaken belief that it would eat the beetles that were destroying the cane crop.

generating enough electricity to supply about 3,500 homes.

Ravenshoe is the main entry point for the Millstream Falls and the Misty Mountains trails. **Millstream Falls** are the widest falls in Australia, spilling over an ancient lava flow. In the rain shadow of the eastern dividing ranges, the dry, open woodland offers a stark contrast to the nearby rainforest. To get there, drive 3.5km (2 miles) past Ravenshoe on the Kennedy Highway towards Mount Garnet and look for the sign. A 400-metre/yd track descends from the car park through eucalypt forest to the falls.

The **Misty Mountains Trails**, a network of long-distance walking tracks through high-altitude rainforest, and the **Tully Gorge National Park** are within easy reach. For detailed information and maps of all these natural attractions, visit the **Ravenshoe Visitor Centre** (24 Moore Street; daily 9am–5pm; tel: 4097 7700; www.ravenshoevisitorcentre.com.au).

Innisfail

BELOW: following a rainforest trail.

Cyclones are a fact of life in Queensland's far north, but few have matched the fury of Cyclone Yasi, which swept through the town of **Innisfail** ❽, 85km (53 miles) south of Cairns, on 3 February 2011, smashing houses and destroying crops *(see box page 183)*.

The sugar town of Innisfail has a strong Italian presence as successive waves of immigrants settled here from 1907 onwards. Hard-working and frugal, the first Italians helped one another to progress from cutting cane to owning their farms. Throughout the last century, immigrants from other countries joined the community. Today, Innisfail's population is a cosmopolitan mix of Spanish, Greek, Slavic, Maltese and Chinese.

The district's most romantic landmark is the ruin of **Paronella Park** (daily 9am–7.30pm; free; tel: 4065 0000; www.paronellapark.com.au), 20km (12 miles) southwest of Innisfail, where, in the 1930s, a Spanish dreamer named José Paronella built a "Spanish-style *castillo*". Inspired by the Moorish architecture and gardens of Spain, Paronella Park was one of north Queensland's earliest tourist attractions – a pleasure palace where visitors sipped tea, played tennis or danced in the ballroom. Despite flood, fire and weathering, you can see what it used to be. If anything, the place is more successful as a ruin than in its heyday. It now offers guided walks, bush-tucker lectures and Aboriginal dancing.

For more information about what to see and do in the region, visit the **Innisfail Information Centre** in Mourilyan, 6km (4 miles) south of Innisfail on the Bruce Highway (open Mon–Fri 9am–5pm, Sat–Sun 10am–3pm; tel: 4063 2655; www.innisfailtourism.com.au).

Babinda and the Josephine Falls

Motoring north from Innisfail along a scenic stretch of the Bruce Highway, the next town is **Babinda** ❾. Before

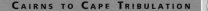
you get there, look for the turn-off that leads to **Josephine Falls** (20km/ 12 miles from Innisfail), at the eastern approach to Mount Bartle Frere, Queensland's highest mountain *(see Tip, right)*. This is rugged country. Rainfall often tops 10,000mm (395ins), sending rivers and creeks plunging through the lush, dense rainforest that covers the landscape. It's unusual to find so much natural beauty concentrated in a rural community so close to a major urban centre. (Cairns is just 50km/31 miles to the north.)

The falls are 8km (5 miles) off the main highway and extremely beautiful, with tumbling cascades of water splashing over rocks amid lush tropical rainforest. You can swim in the natural pools, but the rocks are slippery and flash flooding is an ever-present possibility; there have been instances of fatality and serious injury. The safe option is to observe Josephine Creek from one of the viewing platforms accessed via a 600-metre (1,950ft) walking track leading from the car park through tropical rainforest.

The Boulders, 7km (4 miles) west of Babinda, is another stunning location – a Wet Tropics World Heritage area with a nature reserve, visitor facilities and well-marked trails. Parts of the park are occasionally closed due to flooding damage to bridges and walkways, so find out the latest news at Babinda before you set off.

Gordonvale

Gordonvale ❿, 24km (15 miles) south of Cairns, is a benign, solid town of old-fashioned shops, well-preserved streetscapes, historic buildings and a huge sugar mill, all overlooked by **Walsh's Pyramid**, the highest free-standing peak in the world. Rising 922 metres (3,000ft), this symmetrical mountain is the venue of the Great Pyramid Race, held in Gordonvale every August, when competitors clamber to the summit and back for a trophy.

Gordonvale's other claim to fame is that it was the first town to release cane toads into the wild, in the ill-conceived plan to rid the sugar crops of beetles. The toads devoured everything but beetles, and being toxic, inflicted death on native species. Even worse, they proved to be prolific breeders.

The route from Gordonvale to Cairns takes the Bruce Highway for 23km (14 miles), an easy but sometimes busy road.

Green Island

Cairns is the gateway to some of the most popular destinations on the Great Barrier Reef *(see page 53)*. The 2,300km (1,430-mile) stretch of reefs, coral cays and islands comes closest to the shore up here in the tropical north. Diving is extremely popular, but it's not the only way to experience the beauty of the reef. There are plenty of day cruises to the islands, with opportunities to go snorkelling or view the marine life from the comfort of a glass-bottomed boat.

The closest island to Cairns, lying 27km (17 miles) offshore, is **Green**

TIP

For those who can't see a mountain without wanting to climb it, the track up 1,622-metre (5,322ft) Mount Bartle Frere is irresistible. Provided the summit is not shrouded in cloud (as often happens), your efforts will be rewarded with panoramic views of the Bellenden Ker Range, the coastal lowlands and the Tableland.

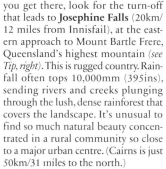

BELOW: narrow-gauge sugar trains crisscross the roads.

Aboriginal Culture

Seeking out a taste of the rich and living heritage of the original inhabitants of the rainforests and islands is an invaluable means to appreciating this country

Far-north Queensland is home to several Aboriginal tribes, collectively called Murri, as well as the Torres Strait Islanders, inhabitants of the islands between Cape York and New Guinea. Great expanses of Cape York are designated Aboriginal Land, and small and large communities dot the cape. Despite two centuries of cultural repression, the indigenous peoples of north Queensland retain their connection to the land, uphold their timeless traditions and care for sacred sites.

Adventurers should seek out the famous **Quinkan rock-art sites,** north of Cooktown, near the township of Laura, which hosts an annual Aboriginal Dance and Culture festival. But you don't need to embark on a 4WD expedition for a taste of indigenous culture. On the outskirts of Cairns, at Caravonica, the **Tjapukai Aboriginal Cul-**

tural Park (Cairns Western Arterial Road; daily 9am–5pm, 7–9.30pm; charge; tel: 4042 9900; www.tjapukai.com.au) showcases the history and culture of the rainforest people of tropical north Queensland through high-tech theatrical performances full of dazzling special effects. As you might expect of a show that has been in continuous performance since the mid-1980s (with an entry in the *Guinness Book of Records* to prove it), it runs smoothly, if routinely. A cinema within the complex screens archival footage of life on an Aboriginal mission in the 1950s, with sobering depictions of massacres and photographs of Aboriginal people in chains. Allow at least four hours for a daytime visit, where, apart from the entertainment that includes spectacular dance and theatre, you can learn to play a didgeridoo and throw a spear and a boomerang. During the evening performance with dinner, the Dreamtime legends come to life with a traditional corroboree, story-telling and a fire-making show. You can expand the experience by going on walkabout on the beaches and through the mangroves with an indigenous guide to learn about bush tucker and medicines, traditional hunting methods, and local customs and ceremonies.

In Kuranda, the **Rainforestation Nature Park** (Kennedy Highway; daily 9am–4pm; charge; tel: 4085 5008; www.rainforest.com.au) hosts the Pamagirri Aboriginal Experience (10.30am, noon and 2pm). The one-hour show takes the form of a corroboree with dances depicting Dreamtime legends. You can further immerse yourself in the culture by taking a Dreamtime Walk into the rainforest and having a go at throwing a boomerang and playing a didgeridoo.

When souvenir-hunting, it's worth seeking out Aboriginal-owned enterprises so you can be sure that you are getting the real deal. Tjapukai has its own gift shop in Kuranda. Check out also Boongar Art Gallery (Kuranda Village Centre) and Djurri Dadagal Art Enterprises (9 Coondoo Street, Kuranda). ❑

Left: playing the didgeridoo at Tjapukai Cultural Park.

Island **⓫**, an alluring place edged with white sand and ringed by reefs. Somewhat overrun by trippers during the day, the island's population shrinks dramatically at nightfall when it becomes the preserve of guests staying at the upmarket resort and a handful of residents. Old-timers will tell you that the reef at Green Island isn't what it used to be. Others say it's never been better. Either way, it's worth going for a snorkel or taking a trip on one of the glass-bottomed boats operating beside the pier.

In the middle of the island is a reptile park and tribal-art museum, **Marineland Melanesia** (tel: 4051 4032 for times; charge; www.marine landgreenisland.com). The museum is owned by retired crocodile-hunter George Craig, who spent 20 years in the Northern Territory and Papua New Guinea gathering his collection of reptiles, rare fish and primitive art. George's crocs earn their keep with twice-daily performances.

Port Douglas

A scenic coastal road heads 80km (50 miles) north from Cairns to **Port Douglas ⓬**, a chic resort notable for its great restaurants and its proximity to the northern end of the Great Barrier Reef. Like most of the coastal settlements, it was founded after a gold rush in the 1870s, when the Gugu-Yulangi people were forced from their land. What began as a tent city of grog shops and boarding houses burgeoned into a boom town of 8,000 residents, with 20 permanent hotels, an unrecorded number of brothels, a regular postal service and a local newspaper. By 1886, gold was on the wane and miners moved to new fields in Papua New Guinea. When Cairns became the regional railhead, Port Douglas drifted into the long hibernation that prevailed until a couple of decades ago. These days it's a vibrant place, surrounded by glitzy resorts.

The approach from the main road is an early clue to the town's evolution. It is lined by an avenue of about 450 huge African oil palms, and as many again are planted around the Sheraton Mirage Resort and the Marina Mirage – part of the extravagant vision of former multi-millionaire Christopher

TIP

Tropical north Queensland's unique cuisine is based on local seafood, exotic fruits, nuts, tea, coffee, sugar, Asian vegetables and herbs and spices. One of the best places to sample this cuisine is in Port Douglas, where at least 40 restaurants compete for your custom. The Nautilus Restaurant is an institution. So is the Salsa Bar and Grill. But the most interesting of them – Flames of the Forest – has no known address, appearing and disappearing like a conjurer's rabbit (see page 191).

BELOW: the up-market Marina Mirage Resort in Port Douglas.

TIP

Heading north from Port Douglas, travellers pass cane farms and exotic fruit plantations en route to Miallo, famous as the place where the late actor Diane Cilento established her 500-seat Karnak Playhouse (tel: 4098 8111; www.karnakplayhouse.com.au) with husband, playwright Anthony Shaffer. It's worth a look for the setting alone.

Skase, who went spectacularly bust in a series of media and leisure ventures.

A casually elegant throng promenades along Macrossan Street's landscaped boulevard of ritzy restaurants and swanky boutiques. Buildings from Port Douglas's frontier days remain. On the foreshore stands the **Courthouse** (1879), now a museum, and near by is historic **St Mary's by the Sea** church, with its dramatic open window to the ocean.

The **Four Mile Beach** is among the region's most beautiful. Once backed by nothing but hinterland swamp, it retains an air of spacious solitude (the southern end is the least crowded part – or you could stroll the 4km/2½ miles to the northern end). Avoid swimming during the stinger season (Oct–May) when venomous box jellyfish infest the waters. If the water proves irresistible, swim inside the nets.

Every morning dozens of boats head out for day trips on the reef: just offshore are the highly popular Low Isles, while a string of excellent snorkelling spots is only an hour away. Operators range from tiny sailships catering for only a dozen passengers to the massive catamarans that can shuttle several hundred people at a time to a well-equipped pontoon moored on the Outer Reef.

The Mossman Gorge

Heading north on the Captain Cook Highway, about 10km (6 miles) beyond the turn-off to Port Douglas you'll pick up signs to **Mossman Gorge** ⑱ (about 5km/3 miles west of the pleasant town of Mossman) at the southeastern edge of Daintree Wilderness National Park. From the car park you can access the swimming area a little way upstream. Exercise caution if you decide to swim among the rocks, especially after it's rained. Just a little further up the path is a suspension bridge leading to a 3km (2-mile) walking circuit past mountain streams and lush, dripping foliage.

Daintree

Slightly further north, past rich sugar-cane country, is the village of **Daintree** ⑭ (55km/34 miles from Port Douglas). Side roads on the way lead to small seaside communities at **Newell Beach** and **Wonga Beach**.

BELOW: Daintree River cruise boats.

Daintree stands on the southern bank of the Daintree River, framed by rainforested mountains and an undulating landscape of lush farmland and cattle properties. Settled in the late 1870s by cedar fellers, Daintree enjoyed a brief incarnation as an inland port. Today, its small community thrives on tourism, offering guided walks, eco-tours and, most successfully, river cruises. The tours take you up- or downstream, depending on weather and tide, through narrow reaches lined with mangroves or rainforests that are rich in wildlife. It's unusual not to spot a crocodile at a safe distance, especially in the cooler months when the huge reptiles come out of the water to sun themselves on the river banks.

Cape Tribulation

The rainforested mountains and long sandy beaches of **Cape Tribulation** ⓑ are accessed via ferry at the Daintree River Crossing, about 15km (9 miles) back from Daintree village. Beyond the ferry, conventional two-wheel-drive access is possible as far as Cape Tribulation. High clearance is useful, and caravans are not recommended since the road is narrow and winding. The imperfect road is compensated by one of the most beautiful and biologically diverse areas in the world, where ancient plants and animals thrive in forest-covered mountains that rise steeply from the coast. Part of the Wet Tropics World Heritage Area, this is one of Australia's last extensive areas of tropical lowland rainforest. No matter what the weather, it's an awe-inspiring sight.

The Cape Tribulation Road area is scattered with lovely places to eat and sleep – high-quality eco-lodges nestle in the forested hills and beaches. Before proceeding north, it's worth stopping at the **Alexandra Range Lookout** for sweeping views back across the wide mouth of the Daintree River, Snapper Island and

the cane fields and ranges beyond. Nearby, the **Daintree Discovery Centre** (daily 8.30am–5pm; charge; tel: 4098 9171; www.daintree-rec.com. au) provides ample information. An aerial walkway leads up to the 23-metre (76ft) Canopy Tower for a bird's-eye view of the forest floor.

Other worthwhile stop-offs are the picturesque **Cow Bay Beach** and **Thornton Beach**. At the end of the road, **Cape Tribulation** itself has a host of accommodation and dining options, from the rustic to the chic, but the focus is on the glorious mangrove-fringed **Myall Beach**.

Beyond the headland, at the southern end of Emmegen Beach, is the beginning of the **Mount Sorrow Trail**, a challenging climb to the ridge of Mount Sorrow. Less demanding is the Dubuji Boardwalk through mangroves beside Myall Beach. Contacts: Tourism Tropical North Queensland (Cairns; tel. 4031 7676) for general information; QPWS (Cape Tribulation; tel: 4098 0052) regarding walking trails and permits. The Daintree Cape Tribulation website www.daintree coast.com is a useful resource. ❏

Cape Tribulation is an incongruous name for one of Australia's most serene corners, but then, James Cook was in a bad mood after his ship, Endeavour, was holed on a reef in 1770: "I named...the north point Cape Tribulation because here began all our troubles." His choices for Mount Misery, Cape Sorrow and the like confirm that he wasn't having a relaxing voyage.

BELOW: swimming in Mossman Gorge.

BEST RESTAURANTS, BARS AND CAFÉS

Restaurants

Prices for a three-course dinner per person with house wine:
$ = A$60 and under
$$ = A$60–100
$$$ = A$100–120
$$$$ = A$120 and over

Cairns

Beethoven Café
105 Grafton Street
Tel: 4051 0292
Open: L Mon–Fri. $
Bread of all descriptions with interesting fillings, and, the clincher, spectacularly good cakes.

Botanic Gardens Café and Restaurant
Flecker Botanic Gardens, Collins Avenue, Edge Hill
Tel: 4053 7087
Open: B and L daily. $
All-day breakfasts; light lunch until 3pm (anything from Greek salad to smoked salmon). Cheap and cheerful fare in a magnificent setting.

Café China
Pullman Reef Hotel Casino, 35–41 Wharf Street
Tel: 4041 2828
Open: L & D daily. $$
Hong Kong-style cuisine with some Szechuan menu entries. Specialities include salt-and-pepper mud crab, Peking duck and steamed coral trout.

Cherry Blossom
Corner of Spence and Lake streets
Tel: 4052 1050
Open: L Wed–Fri, D Wed–Sat. $$$

Cairns' oldest and classiest Japanese restaurant. Both food, including teppanyaki (table barbecue), and decor are top quality. Not cheap.

Coral Hedge Brasserie
The Esplanade
Tel: 4031 2211
Open: D Tue–Sat. $$
The signature restaurant of Rydges Esplanade Resort. Well-presented international cuisine is complemented by a seafood buffet and steak cooked before your eyes.

Donnini's Ciao Italia
Marina at the Pier
Tel: 4051 1133
Open: L & D daily. $
Known for its excellent pizzas, but other Italian classics are also on offer. Boardwalk location with views over the marina. Good value.

Fusion Organics
135 Grafton Street
Tel: 4051 1388
Open: L Mon–Sat. $
Health-conscious eatery that uses organic and local produce. Good coffee, juices and gluten-free cakes.

Mondo Café Bar & Grill
Cairns Hilton,
34 The Esplanade
Tel: 4052 6780
Open: L & D daily. $
A popular meeting place both for its stunning views across the inlet and its well-designed

menu. Just the spot for a late-afternoon drink.

Ochre Restaurant
43 Shields Street
Tel: 4051 0100
Open: L Mon–Fri, D daily. $$$
Renowned for innovative handling of bush-tucker flavours and native game. Examples include smoked wild spice-crusted kangaroo, crocodile wonton and emu pâté.

Perrotta's at the Gallery
38 Abbott Street
Tel: 4031 5899
Open: L & D daily. $
Outside the Cairns Regional Gallery, and noted for its coffee, Perrotta's is the place to see and be seen. Good food. Wine by the glass.

Pesci's Seafood Restaurant
C1 Pier Marketplace,
The Esplanade
Tel: 4041 1133
Open: L & D daily. $$
A fine place to watch boats on the inlet while enjoying very good Mediterranean cuisine.

Salt House
6/2 Pier Point Road
Tel: 4041 7733
Open: B, L & D daily. $$
With a prime location at Marina Point, the gorgeous Salt House delivers excellent steak and seafood grills and tapas; great breakfasts as well.

Tandoori Oven
62B Shields Street
Tel: 4031 0043

Open: D Mon–Sat. $
This pleasant café serves mostly North Indian food. The curries and breads are good, but the dishes from the tandoori oven are special. BYO.

Cape Tribulation

Café-on-Sea
Thornton Beach
Tel: 4098 9118
www.cafeonsea.com
Open: L & D daily. $
Casual café about 24km (15 miles) north of the Daintree River ferry offering fresh salad-based meals. The beach-front location makes it a fine place for a light, affordable lunch.

Heritage Lodge Restaurant
Turpentine Road, Diwan
Tel: 4098 9321
www.heritagelodge.net.au
Open: L and D daily. $$
Heritage Lodge is about 19km (11 miles) north of the Daintree River ferry. Bordered by Cooper Creek and set in pristine rainforest, evening meals at this airy restaurant focus on game dishes such as crocodile, kangaroo and wild boar.

Chillagoe

Chillagoe Observatory and Eco-Lodge
1 Hospital Avenue
Tel: 4094 7155
Open: D daily. $
The observatory is open between April and

November, the restaurant all year round. It offers bistro fare surrounded by greenery and birdlife.

Post Office Hotel
17 Queen Street
Tel: 4094 7119
Open: L daily, D Mon–Sat. $
Country-style pub grub served at the bar or in the beer garden.

Daintree
Julaymba Restaurant and Gallery
Daintree Eco-Lodge and Spa
20 Daintree Road
Tel: 4098 6100
Open: L & D daily. $$$
Overlooks a peaceful freshwater lagoon within the rainforest. The menu incorporates bush-tucker flavours; typical of the dishes are red-claw yabbies wok-tossed in lemon myrtle and rainforest liqueur, and barramundi wrapped in paper bark with bush herbs.

Green Island
Emeralds Restaurant
Green Island Resort
Tel: 4031 3300
Open: L & D daily. $$$
This restaurant leaves no stone unturned in its effort to present fabulously luxurious cuisine. Service is flawless, the setting superb. The Green Island seafood platter tops out the menu.

Millaa Millaa
Out of the Whey Cheesery & Teahouse
Brooks Road, Mungalli (near Millaa Millaa)
Open: L daily. $
This isn't a restaurant in

the strict sense; it's a farmhouse veranda where farmers Rob and Sally Watson serve light refreshments to visitors who've come to see cheese and yoghurt being made. The Mungalli Creek Dairy is 10km (6 miles) from Millaa Millaa (closed in February).

Palm Cove
Far Horizons Restaurant
Angsana Resort,
1 Veivers Road
Tel: 4055 3000
Open: B, L & D daily. $$
Well-reviewed restaurant in a beautiful location featuring international cuisine with an Asian influence. Dine alfresco by the beach or indoors.

Nu Nu's
Peppers Beach Club & Spa,
123 Williams Esplanade
Tel: 4059 1880
Open: L & D daily. $$$
Nu Nu's is owned by Nick Holloway (formerly head chef at Melbourne's Pearl restaurant. Cairns foodies go into raptures about his use of Asian and Mediterranean flavours. Everything is made from scratch – from breads and jams through to coconut creams.

Palm Cove Tavern
Veivers Road
Tel: 4059 1339
Open: L & D daily. $
Standard quality pub grub in this busy establishment where gaming machines tend to dominate the ambience.

Reef House Restaurant
99 Williams Esplanade
Tel: 4055 3633
Open: L & D daily. $$$
Chef Joel Robert's fare has a deceptive simplicity. By day, he tempts with meze plates of hummous, feta and olive, aubergine salsa and roti bread. By night, he serves entrées such as crispy fried prawns with lime, coconut, mango, soy and ginger.

Port Douglas
Flames of the Forest
Bus picks up diners from 6pm.
Tel: 4099 5983
www.flamesoftheforest.com.au
Open: D Tue, Thur–Sat. $$$
Dine in the rainforest and listen to Aboriginal tales: guests are transported from their hotels to the Mowbray Valley, where flames light a path to a clearing and candles flicker beside a stream. More candles illuminate tables, immaculately set. It's *The Lord of the Rings* meets *Alice's Adventures in Wonderland* – an original, magical experience.

Nautilus Restaurant
17 Murphy Street
Tel: 4099 5330
www.nautilus-restaurant.com.au
Open: D daily. $$$
Everybody in Port Douglas goes to the Nautilus at least once. Bill and Hillary Clinton, Rod Stewart and Mick Jagger have been – along with many thousands of less celebrated diners, who soak up the tropical

ambience while sampling such culinary offerings as wok-tossed squid with vegetables, tatsoi and lychees.

Salsa Bar and Grill
26 Wharf Street
Tel: 4099 4922
www.salsaportdouglas.com.au
Open: L & D daily. $$
If any one dish exemplifies Port Douglas, it's the chilli mud crab, and this is the best place to try it. The restaurant itself is airy, with an open deck and a view across Wharf Street to St Mary's and Dickson's Inlet.

Yungaburra
Eden House Heritage Restaurant
20 Gillies Highway
Tel: 4095 3355
www.edenhouse.com
Open: L Sun, D Thur–Mon. $$$
Highly regarded French-influenced Modern Australian menu taking full advantage of locally sourced produce. Part of the luxurious Eden House Retreat and Mountain Spa.

Nick's Swiss Italian Restaurant
33 Gillies Highway
Tel: 4095 3330
Open: L Wed, Fri–Sun, D Tue–Sun. $$
Nick has been serving Italian-Swiss cuisine and modern Australian dishes since 1986. The Alpine theme does seem a little at odds with his prize-winning tropical garden – but after a few beverages from the Yodeller's Bar, who cares?

THE RAINFOREST

Tropical or temperate, the rainforest is one of Queensland's defining characteristics, as well as a key tourist attraction

High rainfall – at least 2 metres (6½ft) – is a prerequisite for rainforest, and then it's generally a matter of latitude and proximity to the ocean which defines it as either tropical or temperate. The Australian state of Queensland is big enough to meet both of these requirements.

Rainforests are nature in *extremis*. Two-thirds of all the Earth's plant and animal species can be found within them, and in north Queensland the highest diversity of local endemic species in the world is present. It is the last bastion for many of these animals, while others are still being discovered, particularly in the upper regions under the canopy, an area only recently appreciated for the richness of its various flora and fauna.

It is estimated that the tropical rainforest stretching from just north of Cairns to Cape Tribulation and on to Cooktown is in the region of 110 million years old, and constitutes the last remnant of the forest that used to cover all of Australia and, before that, Gondwanaland. Now protected as an element of the Wet Tropics World Heritage Area, it is a key attraction for tourists. The economic rationale that has seen the destruction of forests elsewhere in Australia and round the world will probably now protect it.

ABOVE: the orange-thighed frog *(Litoria xanthomera)* is a tree frog native to a small area in tropical northern Queensland. The call of the frog is a long "aaa-rk", followed by a soft trill. They call after monsoon rain, and often congregate around ponds, or at the edge of any still water.

BELOW: when the platypus was first discovered in Australia, many European naturalists were convinced that it must be an elaborate hoax. It is the only living member of its family *(Ornithorhynchidae)* and genus *(Ornithorhynchus)*, and is one of the few monotremes.

LEFT: there are more than 520 species of lizard in Australia. The five main families are geckos, legless lizards, dragon lizards, monitor lizards, and skinks.

THE DAINTREE

Some of the most easily accessible rainforest, and therefore most visited, is in the Daintree National Park *(right)*. There's a well-worn route from Cairns or Port Douglas up to Cape Tribulation, and every tour bus or expedition will stop at least once for a walk in the woods. In several places there are short boardwalk circuits from handy parking spots, and the way is marked by a series of interpretive boards. This makes it easy for the

visitor to explore, and also helps in managing the forest by keeping tourists away from pristine areas.

The complete packaged rainforest experience can be enjoyed at the Daintree Discovery Centre (daily 8.30am–5pm; tel: 07-4098 9171; www. daintree-rec.com.au; charge), a short distance north of the Daintree ferry. Boardwalks wend along the forest floor, and a steel walkway through the canopy allows visitors to share the birds' perspective on life. Audio guides are available and there are more of the ubiquitous interpretive boards. The cassowaries here seem used to visitors.

LEFT: the cassowary (*Casuarius casuarius*) is the third-largest flightless bird, after the ostrich and the emu. Its claws are particularly sharp, and cassowaries have been known to strike out at humans, although the legend that a human can be disembowelled with a single kick by the cassowary's strong legs has never been proven.

RIGHT: the red-necked pademelon *(Thylogale thetis)* is a small, forest-dwelling marsupial. It is very shy, and typically hides in the forest during the day, only emerging to look for food at night. The pademelon was nearly hunted to extinction by imported foxes on the mainland, but can be found throughout Tasmania.

ABOVE: to see the rainforest from a different perspective, take a zip-line tour, where you can stop at several platforms perched among the tree tops.

COOKTOWN AND THE CAPE YORK PENINSULA

Historic Cooktown is the final frontier, beyond which sprawls the Cape York Peninsula, a popular destination for four-wheel-drive tours to the Outback and Australia's northernmost tip. It's an amazing journey, but not one to be undertaken lightly

Brisbane ●

ocated 350km (217 miles) by the inland route from Cairns, **Cooktown** stands at the mouth of the Endeavour River, where Captain Cook spent 48 days repairing his ship after coming to grief on the corals. Beyond lies the Cape York Peninsula, where swamps, rivers and rainforest offer sanctuary to rare wildlife species, and the vast plains, giant termite mounds and woodlands lend the intrepid traveller a delicious sense of freedom. Almost 10 percent of the Cape has been dedicated as national park. Offshore lies the Great Barrier Reef Marine Park, creating a rare confluence of protected zones on both land and sea.

Cooktown

Cooktown ❶ can be reached from the south by two roads: an inland road and a coastal road. The inland route from Cairns follows the highway via Mareeba, Mount Molloy, Mount Carbine, the Palmer River and Lakeland, and is fully paved, with year-round access to conventional vehicles. The coastal route, the Bloomfield Track, is shorter but you will need a 4WD for the stretch from Cape Tribulation to Cooktown. It's

highly inadvisable to attempt this route during the wet season, and you must watch the tide at the Bloomfield River crossing – unless you want to contribute to the crocodiles' diet as you swim downstream after your retreating vehicle.

About 25km (15 miles) from Cooktown, the inland road and the coastal route converge. Whichever route you take, be sure to call into the **Lion's Den** at Helenvale, on the coastal road near the junction. One of the oldest pubs in north Queensland,

Main attractions

Main attractions
COOKTOWN
LIZARD ISLAND
LAURA
RINYIRRU (LAKEFIELD) NATIONAL PARK
WEIPA
JARDINE RIVER NATIONAL PARK
CAPE YORK AND THE TIP
THURSDAY ISLAND AND HORN ISLAND

LEFT: Aboriginal rock art at Laura with guide.
RIGHT: one of a clutch of old hotels in Cooktown.

Cooktown and the Cape York Peninsula

it features the original wooden bar, a piano, an array of pickled snakes and some equally pickled locals.

Cooktown is one of far-north Queensland's unspoilt outposts, shielded from crass development by its very isolation. In part, the appeal of Cooktown is bound up in its frontier flavour. Although many of the rough edges have been smoothed down, the town retains a colourful cast of characters – pub raconteurs, Aboriginal ringers, ageing hippies and rugged individualists.

Captain Cook's visit has inspired a profusion of monuments around the town, but your eye is mainly drawn to the swaggering architecture residual from Cooktown's shining moment as a gold-mining port. Most of this dates from the building boom that followed prospector James Mulligan's 1873 discovery of alluvial gold in the Palmer River – a wild and woolly era when Cooktown's notorious bordello-keeper, Palmer Kate, vowed to feed rivals to the crocodiles, and thirsty miners were relieved of hardwon gold after drinking spiked whiskey. At one point, 35,000 prospectors were digging in the goldfields. By 1880, Cooktown itself contained 47 hotels, countless grog shops and a mind-boggling array of brothels, bakeries and breweries.

The town's population peaked at 4,000, but by the 1890s, the Palmer River rush was over and people began to drift away. Next, a cyclone flattened the town. An enforced military evacuation during World War II completed the depletion to just a handful of people. Revival has been slow but steady.

Cooktown landmarks

Cooktown still thrives on the memories, and it has maintained a languid charm. Poking between palm trees on the wide main street are many late 19th-century buildings, including the former **Queensland National Bank** (1891), the former **Bank of North Queensland** (1890) and the former **Post Office** (1876–7), all in Charlotte Street, and three surviving watering holes (to avoid confusion, known as the Top, Middle and Bottom pubs).

The **James Cook Museum** (Helen and Furneaux streets; daily 9.30am–4pm; charge; tel: 4069 5386), located in the former convent of St Mary (1887), is one of the best museums in Australia. Exhibits include Cook's journals and the original anchor of the *Endeavour*, retrieved from the reef. The museum also covers the indigenous Guugu Yimithirr Bama culture, the gold rush and the Chinese presence.

At the end of Charlotte Street is a seafront park where Cook brought the *Endeavour* ashore. Like Cook, you can climb **Grassy Hill**, from where there is a fabulous view of the town, the river and the ocean. The Cooktown cemetery, just north of town, is full of its own stories of the old pioneers.

Information can be obtained from the **Visitors Information Centre** (tel: 1800 174 895), part of a complex

TIP

Members of the local Guugu Yimithirr tribe offer Aboriginal experiences, from bush-tucker foraging to guided walks. The Visitors Information Centre can arrange bookings. It also supplies brochures guiding you to Cooktown's heritage, fishing and bird-watching spots, and excellent walking trails.

BELOW: Cooktown on the Endeavour River, from Grassy Hill.

TIP

Regular flights connect
Lizard Island with
Cairns. Charter flights
operate from Cairns and
Cooktown. Access is
possible by boat but,
again, only by charter.
Contact QPWS
Cooktown (tel: 4069
5777) or QPWS Cairns
(tel: 4046 6600). The
research station
conducts weekly tours
for yachties and
campers during the
winter (tel: 4060 3977).

containing an environment centre,
two galleries, a bookstore and café,
located within the 62-hectare (153-
acre) **Botanic Gardens** in Finch
Bay Road. Established in 1878, the
gardens are crossed by stone paths
leading to pretty beaches at Finch
Bay and Cherry Tree Bay (beware of
crocodiles and stingers).

Lizard Island

Lizard Island ❷, 27km (19 miles) off
the coast and about 100km (62 miles)
north of Cooktown, is a dry, rocky and
mountainous island with some superb
beaches for swimming and pristine
reef, which makes for great snorkelling
and diving. The Lizard Island group
became a national park in 1939, and
the Australian Museum established a
research station there in 1973.

The Lizard Island Resort (tel: 1300
863 248; www.lizardisland.com.au), a
playground for the rich, opened in
1975. It is geared for high-earners,
but anyone with a QPWS permit can
camp at Watson's Bay.

Captain Cook anchored in one of
Lizard Island's bays in 1770, climbing the hill now known as **Cook's**

Look to plot his passage through the
treacherous reef. It's a pleasant walk
to this, the island's highest point
(359 metres/1,178ft). Cook named
the island after one of 11 species of
lizard that live here. Green and loggerhead turtles nest in late spring,
and black flying foxes inhabit the
mangroves. Birdlife includes pheas-
ant coucals, yellow-bellied sunbirds,
white-bellied sea eagles and terns.

Black Mountain (Kalkajaka) National Park

Alarming tales are told of men and
beasts disappearing into **Black
Mountain**'s ❸ labyrinthine jumble
of smooth black rocks, 30km (19
miles) south of Cooktown. Entire
herds of cattle have allegedly been
swallowed up – presumably devoured
by the carnivorous ghost bats within.
To the Kuku Yalanji Aboriginal
people, the mountain represents an
important meeting place and is the
source of a rich mythology. More
prosaically, geologists describe the
boulders as a molten mass that solid-
ified below the Earth's surface 260
million years ago. The rocks appear

BELOW: wild oysters on
Lizard Island.

Bloomfield Lodge

For a close-to-nature experience, stay
at the serene Bloomfield Lodge (tel:
4035 9166; www.bloomfieldlodge.com.
au) in Weary Bay, south of Cooktown.
Getting there is an adventure in itself; a
bush airstrip has to be cleared of wallabies before the plane from Cairns can
land. Then there is a two-hour odyssey
along back roads and, finally, a punt
journey down the Bloomfield River. Keep
a sharp eye and you may spot a crocodile lazing in the mangroves. Civilisation
seems aeons away. Bloomfield Lodge
makes a minimal imprint on this dramatic coastline – an old jetty, a patch of
sand, a cluster of roofs peeping through
the foliage – but the luxury of this retreat
is unforgettable.

black, but are actually light grey and covered with algae. On very hot days, rain can cause them to explode. The boulders shelter three creatures found nowhere else in the world – the Black Mountain skink, the Black Mountain gecko and the Black Mountain microhylid frog.

Laura

The journey from Cooktown to Australia's northernmost tip makes for an adventurous and memorable road trip, but if you would rather not go it alone, there are plenty of tour companies that can take you.

The first leg of the journey goes via Lakeland through Quinkan Country, named after the Aboriginal spirits, or "Quinkans", who inhabit the sandstone bluffs. The first stop is **Split Rock**, 10km (6 miles) south of the tiny township of Laura. Here you'll find some of the finest examples of Aboriginal rock art, dating back 14,000 years. They can be reached via two walking tracks. The easier path takes about half an hour, the other takes up to three hours. Contact the **Quinkan and Regional Cultural Centre** (www.quinkancc.com. au) for information and to arrange local guides to some of the other, less accessible rock-painting galleries in the area. The centre itself has fascinating exhibits about the area and its people.

Laura ❹ (140km/87 miles from Cooktown) has a mainly Aboriginal population of about 200. The **Laura Dance Festival**, held at the Anggnarra Festival Ground, 15km (9 miles) south of Laura, every June in odd-numbered years, attracts up to 5,000 people.

Rinyirru (Lakefield) National Park

A right-hand turn 2km (1¼ miles) north of Laura leads to **Rinyirru (Lakefield) National Park** ❺ – a 537,000-hectare (1.33-million acre)

park characterised by mighty rivers, spectacular wetlands, water birds, barramundi and estuarine and freshwater crocodiles. There are mangroves and mudflats to the north around Princess Charlotte Bay, grasslands and paperbark woodlands on floodplains and sandstone hills to the south. The park is home to several rare species, including the golden-shouldered parrot and the spectacled hare-wallaby. Traditional owners, the Lama Lama, Kuku Warra, Kuku Yamithi and Kuku Thaypan people, take a hand in managing the park.

There are a number of designated camping areas near rivers and waterholes. Information about campsite locations can be found at www.derm. qld.gov.au. Reservations for camping pitches must be made with QPWS (www.qld.gov.au/camping; tel: 13 74 68) – there is no self-registration – or on the touch-screen computers at the ranger station (tel: 4060 3271), 82km (51 miles) along Lakefield Road towards Musgrave, below Kalpowar Crossing.

Lakefield's grazing history dates back to 1879, when a lease was

The Aboriginal Dingaal people have viewed Jiigurru (Lizard Island) as a sacred place for 3,000 years – shell middens have been found dating back that far. It was used for initiation ceremonies and as a base for collecting shellfish, fish, turtles and dugongs.

BELOW: ancient painting on Mushroom Rock, near Laura.

Here and there, you'll see signs warning of "Road Trains", huge trucks with limited manoeuvrability. If you encounter one on an unpaved road, pull over as far as you can, stop the car and wind up the windows, because they raise a great deal of dust.

granted for Laura cattle station. About 30km (22 miles) north of Laura, the old **Laura Homestead** still stands, albeit slightly the worse for wear. The Red and White Lily Lagoons, 8km (5 miles) north of Lakefield Ranger Station, are lovely.

Musgrave to Archer River

Take the Marina Plains Road past Violet Vale to rejoin the Peninsula Development Road at **Musgrave Roadhouse** ❻ (tel: 4060 3229). Built as an overland telegraph station in 1887, the station was fitted with rifle ports and interior rainwater tanks in case of attack or siege. The building is now a licensed café and roadhouse selling fuel, groceries and takeaway food, and there are also basic rooms and camping facilities.

Next is the former gold town of **Coen**, 109km (68 miles) north of Musgrave. The ruins of Coen's Great Northern Mine, established in 1892, stand on the edge of town. The town comprises a pub, two general stores, a post office, hospital, school, police station, an airstrip and an Aboriginal cultural centre. The airport is about

22km (14 miles) to the north. Skytrans (tel: 40 462 462; www.skytrans.com.au) flies from Cairns to Coen.

A little further on is the track to rugged **Mungkan Kandju National Park** (tel: 4060 1137; campsites must be booked; www.qld.gov.au/camping; tel: 13 74 68), where eucalypt woodlands and melaleuca (paperbark) swamps extend from the McIlwraith Range to the junction of the Archer and Coen rivers. The Coen Information and Inspection Centre (tel: 4060 1135) stands opposite the airport turn-off.

The **Archer River Roadhouse** (tel: 4060 3266) lies 65km (40 miles) north of Coen, along a sandy track that is relatively smooth at the start of the dry season, becoming very rough as traffic intensifies. The roadhouse represents the last chance to stock up on fuel and provisions before the 200km (124-mile) haul to Weipa.

If you have time for a detour, it's worth heading for the **Kutini-Payamu (Iron Range) National Park** ❼; turn east off the Peninsula Development Road, 22km (14 miles) north of the Archer River Roadhouse; it's another 110km (70 miles) to the ranger station (tel: 4060 7170) at King Park Homestead. This beautiful national park, where tropical rainforest meets the windy beaches of the Coral Sea, is the largest area of tropical lowland rainforest remaining in Australia, and is home to some rare flora and fauna, such as the striking green eclectus parrot. William Bligh landed here after the *Bounty* mutiny, and explorer Edmund Kennedy left a party here during his ill-fated expedition in 1848 *(see page 29)*.

The park's several bush camps (booking required) include one at Gordon Creek, where rusty mining relics remain from the 1930s and 1940s.

Weipa

The isolated mining town of **Weipa** ❽, 145km (90 miles) northwest of the Archer River Roadhouse, was built to

On the Road

Beyond Laura, you're in 4WD territory. Gung-ho drivers have been known to nurse conventional vehicles all the way to Weipa, but Coen, 108km (67 miles) north of Musgrave, is the recommended extreme. For 4WD drivers, the best time to travel to Cape York is between June and December, in the drier months. Even then, caution should be exercised. For details about road closures, contact the Queensland Traffic and Travel Information department (tel:13 19 40), or the racq Road Reports (all hours tel: 1300 130 595; www.racq.com.au).

For details of companies which hire 4WD vehicles, refer to *page 250*, where you'll also find advice on safe driving. Here are a few additional points to remember: when driving in dusty conditions, or in a convoy, especially in bulldust, clean your air filter daily. Move to the left when oncoming vehicles approach; most accidents in Cape York are head-on collisions. Be particularly understanding of road-train drivers hauling huge trailers. Before crossing a creek or river, check to see how deep it is. Make sure that it is not flowing too swiftly and that there are no holes in the bottom.

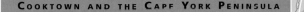

accommodate the mine workers; the town has the world's largest deposits of bauxite, the ore from which aluminium is processed. In a dramatic location and with good amenities, Weipa prides itself on its great fishing and stunning sunsets.

This area was the first stretch of Australian coastline ever to be explored by Europeans. Dutch mariner Willem Janssen anchored the vessel *Duyfken* in Albatross Bay, off present-day Weipa, in March 1606. He was unimpressed, reporting that the indigenes knew little of metals "and even less of nutmegs, cloves and pepper". Matthew Flinders noted the reddish hue of the cliffs around Albatross Bay during his circumnavigation of Australia in 1802 – but almost a century would pass before this redness would be identified as bauxite. In 1955, geologist Harry Evans, guided by Aborigines George Wilson and Old Matthew, realised the true potential of the find. Weipa is now the largest bauxite mine in the world. Mine tours are available April–Nov daily at 8.30am and 2.30pm (charge; tel: 4069 7871; www.campweipa.com).

The huge shell mounds dotted along the rivers flowing into Albatross Bay contain an estimated 200,000 tons of shells, of which more than 9,000 million are cockleshells. They are thought to have been formed between 2,000 and 400 years ago by successive generations of Aboriginal people, and they are now a protected archaeological site.

To the Cape

Returning from Weipa, look for a short cut about 70km (43 miles) out of town heading east to Batavia Downs Homestead and the Telegraph Road. This will slice 80km (50 miles) off the journey to the tip of the Cape, though you run the risk of getting bogged after wet-season rains. Locals prefer to go the long way. Check with Weipa Police (tel: 4069 9119) or Batavia Downs Stations (tel: 4060 3272) before setting out.

The final 22km (17 miles) to the Wenlock River is along a very rough road. There is now a concrete bridge over the river, but it still floods in the wet season. The 155km (96 miles) from the Wenlock River to

In 1928, two New Zealanders drove an Austin Seven from Sydney to the tip of Cape York – the first car to do so. Hector McQuarrie and Dick Matthews lashed their Austin Seven to makeshift rafts to cross swollen streams. The trip took a month.

BELOW: 4WD – the only way to travel in Cape York.

the Jardine River via the Telegraph Road take you across several challenging creek crossings, and are only for the intrepid traveller. A newer and easier route is via the Southern and Northern Bypass Roads, which avoid most of the rivers and creeks (although drivers speed along these corrugated roads far too fast, so you have another hazard to deal with).

On the northern bank of the Wenlock, **Moreton Station** (tel: 4060 3360) provides accommodation but no fuel. Alternatively, continue 40km (25 miles) from Moreton to **Bramwell Junction Roadhouse** (tel: 4060 3230), a popular stop where you'll find cabins, campsites and fuel. Here you can decide whether to take the scenic Telegraph Road, with its many river crossings, or to brave the corrugations of the Southern and Northern Bypass Roads. For advice and information, contact the **Heathlands Ranger Station**, midway along the Southern Bypass road (tel: 4060 3241), which is the base for the **Jardine River National Park** .

This vast, remote wilderness, encompassing much of the catch-

ment of the Jardine River, is the traditional country of several Aboriginal groups. At any time during the wet season, particularly after a cyclone, the park may be closed due to flooding and subsequent road damage. Contact QPWS Information Centre in Cairns (tel: 4046 6600) for up-to-date information.

Popular detours from Telegraph Road include **Twin Falls** (where you can camp) and **Fruitbat Falls** (no camping). These falls, with their crystal-clear waters, are a delightful place to stop for a swim.

There are several challenging creeks to cross over the next 23km (14 miles) to the Jardine River. If you prefer the safer route, take one of the tracks heading west to the Northern Bypass Road. At the **Jardine River Ferry and Roadhouse**, you are advised to take the ferry crossing, run by the Injinoo community, since the ford crossing is treacherous. The fee includes a camping permit for the surrounding area.

Bamaga

Bamaga ⑩, about 70km (43 miles) from the ferry crossing, is a small, laid-back community (pop. 800) mainly comprised of descendants of Saibai Islanders, who voluntarily relocated from their Torres Strait island following a tidal inundation in 1947. The town takes its name from the Saibai leader who ordered the evacuation. It has a shopping centre, a hospital, a police station and a well-equipped resort. Flights to Cairns, Horn Island and Weipa depart from Injinoo Airport, a 40-minute drive from town.

Seisia

Australia's northernmost town is **Seisia** (pronounced "Say-sia"), 6km (4 miles) up the road from Bamaga. It's a pleasant place to linger and wash off the dust of the Outback, with a small lodge, camping ground, garage, supermarket and laundry. Fast

BELOW: landing strip in the middle of the Cape York bush.

launches depart from Seisia Wharf for Thursday Island (Mon–Sat during the tourist season, less frequently at other times; contact Peddells Thursday Island Tours, tel: 4069 1551). Seisia is the departure point for 4WD pilgrims who decide to make the return journey by sea. The cargo barge *Trinity Bay* will transport vehicles; it travels weekly between Seisia, Thursday Island and Cairns (contact Seaswift, tel: 4035 1234 www.seaswift.com.au).

Cape York and the Tip

The drive north to **Cape York** ⓫ is delightful, crossed by crystal-clear creeks and bordered by ferns. Heathland and savannah make this a birdwatchers' paradise. More than 250 species have been identified so far, some of them unique to the region.

Punsand Bay (tel: 4069 1722), a fishing resort 5km (3 miles) west of the tip and 28km (17 miles) from Bamaga, offers meals and accommodation in a beautiful setting. Rainforest grows to the edge of the beach, and the sunsets are striking.

Not far from here is the former British outpost of Somerset, where notorious adventurer Frank Jardine wreaked havoc on the Aboriginal population. Apart from the grave of Jardine and his wife, there's not a lot to see.

From Pajinka Wilderness Lodge (closed after being damaged by fire), a few hundred metres from the tip of Cape York, follow the path from the old lodge through the rainforest and along Frangipani Bay. A sign on the rocks marks the end of the Australian continent. Behind you lies some of the most savagely beautiful landscape on the planet. Off the coast is Possession Island, where Captain Cook claimed the east coast of Australia for England.

Thursday Island and Horn Island

With little to do in Bamaga, most visitors take the ferry to **Thursday Island** ⓬, a multicultural island known affectionately as TI. The trip itself offers magnificent views of sheltered bays and golden beaches.

The island's rich history is evident in the older buildings; All Souls and St Bartholomew's Quetta Memorial

TIP

The Seisia Holiday Park (tel: 1800 653 243) is a popular campsite that also acts as a booking agent for local tours – guided fishing trips, pearl-farm tours, croc-spotting, 4WD tours of the Tip, and scenic flights.

BELOW: the Cape York peninsula.

Face paint and headdress of indigenous dancer from the Torres Strait Islands at the Laura Aboriginal Dance Festival.

BELOW: pearl-diving helmet exhibit at the Torres Strait Heritage Museum, Horn Island.

Church in Douglas Street was built in 1893 in memory of the victims of the *Quetta* shipwreck of 1890, one of Australia's worst maritime disasters. Another late 19th-century ecclesiastical landmark is the church of Our Lady of the Sacred Heart, with timber spires and trompe l'oeil murals by Thursday Island-born artist David Sing. The Victorian splendour of HM Customs stands intact, albeit deprived of its harbour-front prominence by a rusty warehouse. Other places to visit include Green Hill Fort, built in the 1890s to repel a feared Russian invasion, and TI's cemetery, where the graves of 700 Japanese pearl divers live beside those of Torres Strait pilots, fortune hunters, sailors and ships' passengers drowned at sea, as well as generations of islanders. A lively night out is usually guaranteed at the **Federal Hotel** (Victoria Parade; tel: 4069 1569) – it's smoky and noisy, with a band and pool tables.

The airport for the Torres Strait is located on **Horn Island ⑬**, a 10-minute ferry ride from Thursday Island. Horn Island, and its small town of Wasaga, is quiet and undeveloped, its main point of interest being the **Heritage Museum and Gallery** (charge; tel: 4069 2222) within the Gateway Torres Strait Resort, a couple of minutes' walk from the wharf. The museum explains pre-colonial culture in the Torres Strait and traces outside intrusion from the 1860s and 1870s, when bêche-de-mer crews, pearl-shellers, Protestant missionaries and government officials began to arrive. The pearl-shell industry came to a halt during World War II, when naval authorities requisitioned the boats. Horn Island became a battle zone, suffering eight air raids by the Japanese. The museum addresses the largely unrecognised contribution of Torres Strait Islanders, who joined forces with 7,000 Australian and United States military personnel during World War II.

You can visit other islands in the Torres Strait, but there is virtually no tourist infrastructure. Most inhabited islands have an airstrip for light aircraft. Contact the Torres Strait Regional Authority (tel: 4069 0700; www.tsra.gov.au). ❑

BEST RESTAURANTS, BARS AND CAFÉS

Prices for a three-course dinner per person with house wine:

$ = A$60 and under
$$ = A$60–$100
$$$ = A$100 and over

Bamaga

The Paperbark Room
Resort Bamaga, corner Lui and Adidi streets
Tel: 4069 3050
Open: D daily. **$$**
Well-appointed restaurant overlooking a tropical garden. Menu includes far-north favourites such as *barramundi*, crayfish and steak.

Cooktown

The Balcony Restaurant
Sovereign Resort, corner Charlotte and Green streets
Tel: 4069 5400
Open: L & D Apr–Nov. **$$**
Light tropical fare with a European flavour.

Restaurant 1770
Fisherman's Wharf, Webber Esplanade
Tel: 4069 5440
Open: L & D daily. **$$**
Stunning location and a mainly seafood menu, along with the usual reef and beef dishes.

River of Gold
Hope Street
Tel: 4069 5222
Open: D daily. **$$**
Serves solid country-style fare with nightly specials.

Shadows of Mount Cook
Corner of Hope and Burkitt streets
Tel: 4069 5584
Open: D Tue–Sat. **$$**
A 20-seat restaurant serving locally sourced game and seafood, overlooking gardens within a rainforest. Best to book.

Vera's Café
Nature's Powerhouse, Botanic Gardens, Walker Street
Tel: 4069 6881
Open: L daily. **$**
Healthy meals prepared from fresh, pesticide-free local ingredients.

Laura

Laura Roadhouse
Peninsula Development Rd
Tel: 4060 3419
Open: L & D daily. **$**
Hamburgers, fish and chips, steak and vegetables, fish and salad.

The Quinkin Hotel
Terminus Street
Tel: 4060 3393
Open: L & D daily. **$**
Traditional pub-counter meals in a typical Outback pub environment. Steak and *barra* dishes.

Musgrave

Musgrave Roadhouse
Peninsula Development Road. Tel: 4060 3229
Open: D daily. **$$**
Plain, mainly grilled fare. Dishes such as T-bone

with egg and chips are served at tables spread under the historic telegraph station/fortress.

Torres Strait Islands

Jardine Restaurant
Corner Normanby and Victoria parades, Thursday Island
Tel: 4069 1555
Open: D daily. **$$**
Sophisticated food and wine in an intimate restaurant. Also an affordable open-air bistro.

The Gateway Torres Strait Resort
24 Outie Street, Horn Island
Tel: 4069 2222
Open: D daily. **$**
Buffet menu changes from night to night.

Wongal Hotel
2 Wees Street, Horn Island
Tel: 4083 1100
Open: L Mon–Sat, D daily. **$**
Traditional pub food. Torres Strait Island musical legend Seaman Dan performs Wednesday nights.

Weipa

Albatross Bay Resort
Duyfken Crescent
Tel: 4090 6666
Open: L & D daily. **$**
Wide range of dishes, from upper-end cuisine to pub grub, served on a spacious deck overlooking the sea.

Barras Bar and Grill
Heritage Resort
Tel: 4069 8000
Open: D daily. **$$**
Grilled steaks and seafood served poolside or in the dining room.

RIGHT: a serving of *barramundi*.

SAVANNAH WAY

Vast distances, stark terrain and pockets of miraculous beauty mark the remarkable sweep of country that is the Savannah Way. Crossing the Gulf of Carpentaria from Cairns to Camooweal, this epic route follows in the footsteps of explorers Leichhardt, and Burke and Wills. It is also very hot and, in summer, extremely wet

Brisbane •

The Savannah Way is one of Australia's ultimate adventure drives, linking Cairns in tropical north Queensland with the historic pearling town of Broome in Western Australia. The Queensland section embraces the geological phenomenon of the Undara Lava Tubes at one end and the timeless beauty of Boodjamulla National Park (Lawn Hill) at the other. In between, there are lost mines, ghost towns, desert oases, curious limestone formations and busy gemfields. You'll meet laconic graziers, wild trawlermen and flinty fossickers. This is raw Outback, and care should be taken when driving (see page 250).

Undara Lava Tubes

"Undara" is an Aboriginal word meaning "long way" – and it's an appropriate description for the geological phenomenon that is the **Undara Lava Tubes ❶**, 55km (34 miles) east of Mount Surprise and 17km (10 miles) from the start of the Gulf Developmental Road. The longest lava flow from a single volcano in modern geological times, Undara was formed 190,000 years ago when lava from the eruption spewed down the paths of ancient river beds. The lava

at the surface cooled and hardened, forming a crust, while the molten lava drained away – leaving a series of massive basalt tubes extending underground for 100km (62 miles). Only nine of the 169 sections of the tube system can be visited. The rest are too toxic, too fragile or too difficult to enter.

The area falls under the protection of the **Undara Volcanic National Park** (tel: 4097 1485). The only way to explore the tubes is by signing up for a tour with one of the following:

Main attractions
UNDARA LAVA TUBES
MOUNT SURPRISE
GEORGETOWN
CROYDON
NORMANTON
KARUMBA
BURKETOWN
LAWN HILL GORGE

LEFT: dwarfed by the surroundings in Lawn Hill Gorge. **RIGHT:** road hazard.

Visitors who stay at Undara's Lava Lodge site are invited to gather around the campfire to be serenaded by a man with a ukelele .

Undara Experience (tel: 1800 990 992, www.undara.com.au); or Bedrock Village (tel: 4062 3193; www.bedrock village.com.au).

To enter the tubes, some as big as train tunnels, is to embrace a subterranean wilderness that has sent entomologists and biologists into raptures – more than 40 new species have been identified in Undara's dark recesses, some of them inhabiting atmospheres with carbon-dioxide levels 200 times higher than that on the surface.

Above the caves, the grassy open spaces of the savannah are interspersed with patches of dry rainforest where the tube ceilings have collapsed, forming shallow canyons.

Accommodation at Undara Lodge (booked through Undara Experience, *see above*) is in a set of restored antique railway carriages. There's also a central camping area. In summer, the lodge conducts sunset tours to the mouth of **Barker's**

Cave, where brown tree snakes and pythons make short work of bats foolish enough to venture within striking range. The bat population of Barker's Cave has been conservatively estimated at 40,000. Those who have entered the bats' domain have likened the experience to being blindfolded in a wind tunnel filled with sonic guided missiles.

QPWS has cut a self-guided trail up and around the crater rim of Kalkarni, the volcano that started it all.

Mount Surprise

Located 55km (34 miles) from the eastern end of the Gulf Developmental Road, **Mount Surprise ❷** is a go-ahead little place with a pub, two cafés, a general store, a railway station, a service station and a handful of gem shops. Its economy mainly depends on cattle grazing, gemstones and tourism. During June, July and August, the town's permanent population of just 65 doubles, as recreational fossick-

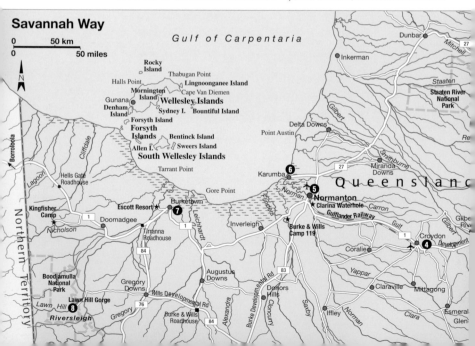

ers arrive in search of the local topaz, zircon, sapphire, aquamarine, smoky quartz and amethyst.

Mount Surprise Gems and Fossicking (Garland Street; tel: 4062 3055; www.mtsurprisegems.com.au) can supply mud maps, fossicking knowledge and equipment. Most fossickers head for the gemfield at O'Brien's Creek, renowned for its topaz. Fossickers' Licences may be obtained from the Mining Registrar in Georgetown, the BP Roadhouse, Mount Surprise or Mt Surprise Gems & Fossicking.

Georgetown

Georgetown ❸, about 100km (62 miles) west of Mount Surprise, owes its existence to the gold fever that swept Queensland in the late 19th century. Initially it was just one of several shanty towns on the Etheridge Field in 1869. Within two years, however, the township had emerged as the region's administrative centre. Georgetown's fortunes

fluctuated following discovery of gold at the Palmer River in 1873 and the Hodgkinson rush of 1876. Between 1880 and 1900, Georgetown's population hovered at around 300 – about the same as it is today. The glory days of mining are gone, but amateur prospectors continue to visit the area in the hope of stubbing their toe on a nugget.

National Trust-listed **Antbed House**, in South Street, was built in the boom years between 1880 and 1900. This former mine manager's residence was constructed of termite-mound adobe rather than the usual timber and iron. Other historic buildings include the Shire Hall (1908) in St George Street, the Masonic Temple on the corner of Haldane and Cumberland streets and the Catholic Church (1913) in High Street.

About 20km (12½ miles) west along the Croydon Road stands the **Cumberland Chimney**, marking the site of an early gold-ore crushing

BELOW: Undara Lava Tube.

TIP

It's worth planning your trip so you can take a ride on the *Gulflander*, an old train that leaves Normanton Station (www.thegulflander. com.au; tel: 4745 1391) on Wednesday at 8.30am and arrives in Croydon about five hours later, after leisurely stops for tea and mail delivery. It returns from Croydon on Thursday at 8.30am, so you'll need to stay overnight. From May to September, short 40-minute or two-hour trips are available every day except Wednesday and Thursday.

BELOW: the Gulflander.

plant. The dam built as part of the crushing plant has been colonised by water birds, making for a picturesque bush scene.

Forsayth, 40km (25 miles) south of Georgetown, is popular with gold fossickers. **Agate Creek**, about 70km (43 miles) further south, yields multi-coloured agate formations known as "thunder eggs". Professional miners and amateur "rock hounds" alike use hand tools to dig for this translucent quartz formed as a result of volcanic activity some 250 million years ago.

Conventional vehicles can traverse the gravel road that leads to Agate Creek May–September. At other times it's 4WD territory.

Intending fossickers should call into the Queensland Department of Minerals and Energy office in George-town (weekdays 9am–5pm) for information and a Fossicker's Licence.

Croydon

Croydon ❹ is connected to Normanton by the *Gulflander*, a historic train that trundles between the two towns once a week. A journey on the *Gulflander* has long been *de rigueur*

for travellers reaching the inland port of Normanton. For many, the issue of destination is eclipsed by the romance of simply being aboard this beguiling old rattler (*for detailed information, see Tip, left*).

The railway line was completed in 1891 when Croydon was a booming gold-mining town. Gold was discovered in 1885; a year later, 2,000 people were working the gold-fields, swiftly rising to 6,000. By the end of World War II, the gold had run out and Croydon had become a ghost town. Now, tourists arrive on the restored train and are guided on tours of the restored buildings on Samwell Street.

Rating high among Croydon's 19th-century treasures is the Heritage-listed **Courthouse** (1887). Flanked by the old police station on one side and the old town hall on the other, the courthouse is distinguished by its iron cladding, and a clock tower to add gravitas. These three buildings form the core of a historic precinct that includes the surgeon's house, the mining warden's office, the general store, the old butcher's shop and the

Croydon railway station. Croydon's **Visitor Information Centre** (daily 9am–4.30pm, closed Sat–Sun in wet season; tel: 4745 6125) is located in the old police sergeant's residence in Samwell Street.

Normanton

Being the terminus of the Normanton–Croydon railway, **Normanton** ❺ was accorded a more impressive station than Croydon – complete with a blacksmith's shed and carpenters' workshop. Today, the station's arched roof has become one of the far north's most photographed buildings, synonymous with Normanton's history and emblematic of the rich cast of characters among its population.

Actor Paul Hogan says he based *Crocodile Dundee* on the people he met around Normanton. At the **Purple Pub**, **Albion Hotel** or **Central Hotel**, you'll meet barracuda fishermen, stockmen, local Aborigines, kangaroo shooters, fossickers, assorted wild men and, increasingly, curious tourists. The frontier atmosphere is lent zest by historic buildings spread throughout the town – among them,

the **Carpentaria Shire Offices**, the 1886 **Bank of New South Wales** (now Westpac), the notorious Normanton **Gaol** and the **Burns Philp Building**, now the library and visitor information centre (tel: 4745 1065).

The town is situated on the banks of the Norman River, 150km (93 miles) west of Croydon. Explorer Frederick Walker discovered the river while looking for Burke and Wills. He was followed by William Landsborough who, in 1867, chose the site for a port. Normanton's boom years were during the gold rush of the 1890s, when it was the port for nearby Croydon, but, as the gold petered out, the town went into slow decline – hitting an all-time low in the late 1940s when the population fell to about 200 (it's now 1,500). The revival is partly attributable to tourism, partly to the fishing industry at Karumba, 70km (43 miles) to the north.

Outback pastimes

People come from miles around to the **Normanton Rodeo** (tel: 4745 1155), held annually during the

Taking part in the Normanton rodeo.

BELOW: Normanton's Purple Pub.

Alligator Point in Karumba.

Queen's birthday weekend in June, when hard men and women of the Outback do battle with bucking bulls and feisty horses. The **Normanton Races** (tel: 4745 1580 for dates, which vary from year to year) is another lively Outback event.

Other attractions include taking a cruise along the crocodile-infested **Norman River**, or a sport-fishing expedition to the Gulf. Norman River Fishing and Cruises (tel: 4745 1347) depart from Normanton Boat Ramp twice daily. Owner Dennis Taney is an accredited Savannah Guide who knows where to find the tidal-water barramundi, exotic birdlife and local crocodiles. His punt, which seats 12 passengers, ranges up to 30km (18 miles) upstream "depending on where the fish are biting". Fishing trips depart at 7.30am. Alternatively, sunset cruises depart at 5pm.

Karumba

Karumba ❻ sits at the mouth of the Norman River, about 70km (43 miles) northwest of Normanton on the Gulf of Carpentaria. It is a port of about 600 people mainly engaged, one way or another, with commercial prawn trawling and professional barramundi fishing. During the two prawn seasons, the fishing fleet quadruples. The rest of the time, Karumba basks quietly in the sun, uncertain if it's an Outback outpost or a fishing port. The only town on the Gulf Coast serviced by a bitumen road, it's linked via the Savannah Way from Cairns and the Matilda Highway from the south.

Older travellers, European backpackers and amateur fishermen turn up in force during the dry winter months, attracted by ripping yarns of suicidal barramundi, life-changing sunsets and the meteorological phenomenon known as "morning glories". One of the Gulf Savannah's most peculiar spectacles, this meteorological phenomenon, known as a roll cloud, is a long, low cylinder of cloud that scuds across the sky like a giant rolling pin. It can be up to 1,000km (620 miles) long, 2km (1.2 miles) high and only 200 metres (650ft) above the ground. In Karumba it usually comes through before dawn, the roar of the updraft preceding the

cloud enticing bleary-eyed campers out of their tents and vans. In Burketown, it arrives at a more civilised hour and it has become a draw card for gliding enthusiasts who can "surf" it for hundreds of kilometres.

If you've ever wondered about the mysteries of piscatorial bisexuality, or just wanted to see some big fish close up, visit the **Karumba's Barramundi Discovery Centre** (148 Yappar Street; daily 1–4.30 pm; charge; tel: 4745 9359).

A fascinating insight into local culture can be had at Karumba's **Animal Bar**, adjacent to the main boat ramp, where tattooed prawn fishermen let off steam after protracted periods at sea. If the atmosphere becomes too boisterous, you can relocate to the lounge, known as the Suave Bar. Women are in short supply in Karumba (the ratio of men to women is around seven to three), so female visitors can expect to receive a more than usually warm welcome.

Burketown

Burketown ❼ (pop. 180) is a remote settlement 30km (18 miles) from the Gulf of Carpentaria. It is named after Robert O'Hara Burke *(see page 30)*, and there is a sign about 50km (31 miles) along the road from Normanton to Burketown indicating the doomed explorer's last camp – Camp 119.

Few of Burketown's early structures have withstood the test of time, but the former post office, built in 1887, is one of them. Restored, relocated and redefined as the **Visitor Information Centre** (tel: 4745 5111), it stands at the intersection of Musgrave and Burke streets.

The **Burketown Hotel** (Beames Street; tel: 4745 5104), just to the east, is a friendly Outback pub; originally built as the customs house, it's the oldest building in Burketown. The **War Memorial** is directly outside, and the shire offices are next door.

The barramundi fishing is excellent, and this is what lures visitors to this tiny town on the flat plains of the Albert River. Burketown also happens to be an important access point for Lawn Hill National Park and the World Heritage-listed Riversleigh fossil field.

From Normanton, the Savannah Way (also known as the Gulf Track here) sweeps across the flat plains of the Gulf to Burketown. The road is unsealed, but is open to conventional vehicles during the dry season; don't attempt the journey during the wet season (November–April) as heavy rain can close the road.

BELOW: ready for fishing in Karumba.

Termite mounds are found in many parts of outback Queensland but there are subtle variations in size and shape.

Lawn Hill Gorge

Lawn Hill Gorge ❽, southwest of Burketown in the remote northwest highlands, is the scenic centrepiece of **Boodjamulla National Park**'s magnificent array of limestone escarpments, spring-fed creeks and tranquil waterholes. On Lawn Hill Creek, the gorge is a beautiful Outback oasis – a place where 60-metre (200ft) red sandstone walls reflect in green waters inhabited by turtles and freshwater crocodiles. At sunrise the call of the sandstone shrike-thrush echoes through the gorge. Wallaroos, tiny bats and ringtail possums hide among the rocky outcrops. It's a far cry from the flat plains of the Gulf.

The main problem is getting there. Detailed directions are provided at www.derm.qld.gov.au. Unsealed roads in the area provide unpredictable access, and precautionary steps should be taken before setting off (*see page 250*), as there is limited mobile-phone reception. Travelling here during the wet season (Nov–April) is not recommended.

Formerly known as Lawn Hill National Park, the park has been re-named Boodjamulla in deference to its Aboriginal owners. Boodjamulla translates as "rainbow-serpent country". Midden heaps, grinding stones and rock art scattered throughout the park are testimony to the Waanyi people's 17,000-year occupancy. Two rock-art sites have been made accessible to visitors.

The southern section of the park is occupied by the World Heritage-listed **Riversleigh** area, where bones dating back 25 million years are preserved in lime-rich sediments. Most of the significant finds are displayed at the Riversleigh Fossils Centre in Mount Isa, but D-Site, where the first fossils were found, gives visitors an opportunity to view fossilised mammals and reptiles *in situ*. Climb to the top of the hill for striking views across the plains.

There are numerous walking trails of varying lengths and difficulty through spectacular scenery, and canoeing through the gorge is wonderful. A convenient base for exploration is Adels Grove (www.adelsgrove.com.au), a short drive from the park entrance. ❑

BEST RESTAURANTS, BARS AND CAFÉS

Prices for a three-course dinner per person with house wine:

$ = A$60 and under
$$ = A$60–100
$$$ = A$100 and over

Club Hotel
Corner Sircon and
Brown streets
Tel: 4745 6184.
Open: D daily. **$**
Standard Outback pub menu is enlivened by specials such as lasagne and shepherd's pie. Traditional Wednesday-night roasts coincide with the arrival of the *Gulflander* from Normanton.

Croydon Café
Brown Street
Tel: 4745 6159
Open: 7am–7.30pm. **$**
Once, every Australian country town had a café like this – cheap and cheerful hamburgers, sandwiches and fish and chips, with groceries and fishing tackle on the side.

Midway Caravan Park Restaurant
High Street
Tel: 4062 1219
Open: daily. **$**
Plain and simple country fare served in an outdoor setting – everything from chips to chicken Kiev.

Karumba Seafoods
Corner Yappar and
Massey streets
Tel: 4745 9192
Open: L and D daily. Sometimes closed during the wet season (Nov–Feb). **$**
Bistro near the Norman River, where you can get a decent cup of coffee and very fresh seafood, all served on an elevated deck amid tropical greenery. BYO.

The Sunset Tavern
2 Ward Street,
Karumba Point
Tel: 4745 9183
Open: L and D daily. **$**
This a great place to sip a beer while watching the sun set on the Gulf of Carpentaria. Bill of fare runs from snacks through to steaks and the ubiquitous seafood platters.

Mt Surprise Café
Garland Street
Tel: 4062 3055
Open: B, L & D daily Apr–Sept. **$**
Owners Pete and Pam Blackburn serve real coffee (as distinct from the instant coffee so prevalent in the Outback) and also give gem-faceting demonstrations.

Undara Iron Pot Bistro
Undara Lodge,
Gulf Development Road via
Mount Surprise
Tel: 4097 1900
Open: L and D. **$$**
As well as buffet lunches and three-course dinners, the lodge puts on a slap-up bush breakfast – a round-the-campfire affair that takes place about 200 metres (660ft) from the main complex.

Albion Hotel
Haig Street
Tel: 4745 1218
Open: L and D. **$**
Country-style pub food with few surprises but easy on the pocket. Eat at the bar or on the deck.

The Purple Pub
94 Landsborough Highway
Tel: 4745 1324
Open: L & D Mon–Sat. **$**
Predictably, given the pub's location near the Gulf, the menu focuses on barramundi. Generous helpings in a typical Outback dining room.

RIGHT: bush tucker.

MOUNT ISA AND THE WEST

For true Outback grit, the Mount Isa region has it all: Aboriginal bravery in the face of incredible odds; the rise of a desert city of silver and copper; the humble beginnings of that most Australian of institutions, the Royal Flying Doctor Service; and the murky origins of the unofficial national anthem, *Waltzing Matilda*

Brisbane ●

The mining city of **Mount Isa ❶** erupts like a post-apocalyptic mirage from the stony plateaux and escarpments of the Selwyn Range, leaving a powerful, almost surreal, first impression. Once in the city, you'll discover a prosperous, down-to-earth community that takes work and relaxation seriously.

While Mount Isa functions as a service centre for surrounding districts, it's a mining community at core, owing its existence to the rich deposits of lead, zinc, silver and copper ore to the west of the city. A high proportion of the 23,000 inhabitants earn their living from the mine in one way or another – making for an intriguing combination of professions and nationalities. Add several cosmopolitan social clubs, around 20 restaurants and a couple of man-made lakes to the mix and you have a desert metropolis like no other.

The **Mount Isa Mine** (owned and operated by Swiss company Xstrata since 2003) continues as one of the most highly mechanised and cost-effective mines on the planet. At 2,000 metres (6,560ft) beneath the surface, the Enterprise copper mine is the deepest in Australia. For an idea of the sheer scale of operations, you can take a surface tour (Mon–Sat 11am; charge; tel: 4743 2006; www.campbells travel.com.au).

Around the town

Most of the city's attractions are grouped at the **Outback at Isa** complex in Marian Street (tel: 1300 659 660; www.outbackatisa.com. au), where you'll find the Visitor Information Centre, the Hard Times Mine, the Isa Experience Gallery, the Riversleigh Fossil Centre and a landscaped park that mimics Lawn Hill Gorge (*see*

LEFT: the Ernest Henry Mine, near Cloncurry.
RIGHT: the public viewing area.

The detour across dusty plains from Hughenden is amply rewarded by views over Porcupine Gorge (see page 222).

page 214). Exhibits at the complex cover a wide spectrum of historical, cultural and social issues. Set aside at least two hours to complete a circuit of the **Hard Times Mine** (named after the horse ridden by prospector John Campbell Miles, who discovered a rich lode of lead, silver, copper and zinc here in 1923). This A$5 million mock-up of the real thing comes complete with 1.2km (¾ mile) of tunnels, hands-on drilling, massive machinery and a miner's "crib room". Expect to don overalls, boots, miner's cap, lamp and earmuffs before descending in a shaft cage to the mine floor.

The **Isa Experience Gallery** uses a range of electronic media to illustrate the district's past and present, supplemented by historic photographs, illustrative dioramas and other exhibits. The **Riversleigh Fossil Centre** is a fascinating recreation of Australia's prehistoric fauna, with actual fossils and a working laboratory.

More recent history is enshrined at the nearby **Kalkadoon Tribal Council and Cultural Keeping Place** (Marion Street; Mon–Fri 9am–5pm; charge; tel: 4749 1001). The territory on which Mount Isa stands formerly belonged to the Kalkadoons, an Aboriginal tribe that resisted white settlement long after their brethren elsewhere had been demoralised or slain. The Kalkadoons engaged native police and squatters in wily guerrilla warfare for more than a decade, striking unexpectedly then melting into the hills. Lured into open conflict at Battle Mount, north of Cloncurry, in 1884, they were mown down by native police with carbines. Descendants of the Kalkadoons staff their brightly decorated building, telling stories and explaining the use and meaning of tribal artefacts.

The National Trust-listed **Tent House** (Fourth Avenue; Apr–Sept daily 10am–2pm; charge) is one

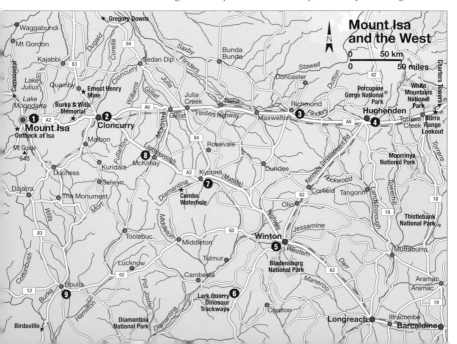

of 200 such houses that provided inexpensive but comfortable miners' with accommodation during the 1930s and 1940s. Designed for coolness in a harsh climate, these houses were built of hessian, canvas, wood and corrugated iron with a double roof to allow breezes through.

The **Underground Hospital Museum** (Joan Street; Apr–Sept daily 10am–2pm; charge; tel: 4743 3853) is a telling reminder of World War II. With the threat of bombing by the Japanese, Mount Isa hospital decided to go underground; it has been preserved much as it was in the 1940s.

For a fascinating insight into how children in remote communities are educated, visit the **School of the Air** (Kalkadoon High School, Abel Smith Parade; tours Mon–Fri 9am and 10am in term time; tel: 4744 9100), where qualified teachers educate Outback children via a digital network.

The town really comes alive on the second weekend in August, when the annual **Mount Isa Rodeo** (www.isarodeo.com.au) – the biggest rodeo in Australia – is held. The city centre shuts down for a Friday-night "Mardi Gras" parade and fireworks. Accommodation is scarce to non-existent, so it pays to bring a tent.

Away from the mines, the people of Mount Isa relax at the artificial **Lake Moondarra**, 20km (12½ miles) north of the town – a popular spot for swimming, boating, water-skiing, fishing and bird-watching.

Cloncurry

Cloncurry ❷, 125km (78 miles) east of Mount Isa, is a pleasant Outback town of about 3,000 people, with several worthwhile attractions. Prominent among them is **John Flynn Place** (corner Daintree and King streets; Mon–Fri 8.30am–4.30pm year round, Sat–Sun 9am–3pm May–Sept; charge; tel: 4742 2778). This modern museum celebrates the visionary bush clergyman John Flynn, who began **the Royal Flying Doctor Service** here in 1928. Exhibits include the actual Traeger pedal wireless used by Flynn's aviators and medicos, plus a model of the *Victory*, the first RFDS aircraft. The museum forms part of a complex incorporating an art gallery, cultural centre

TIP

For a scenic overview of Mount Isa, head for the **City Lookout** (a short drive off Hilary Street), preferably at dusk when the mine lights up. You can see the whole city sprawled out across a flat valley, backed by low hills, and all dominated by the mine.

BELOW: sunset on Mount Isa.

The Royal Flying Doctor Service was started in Cloncurry in 1928 by the Rev John Flynn to provide "a mantle of safety" over the Outback. Its first plane was supplied by the Queensland and Northern Territory Aerial Service (QANTAS).

BELOW: bareback riding in the Mount Isa rodeo.

and outdoor theatre. Flynn chose Cloncurry because of its location in a region where remote mining and grazing communities were poorly served by medical help.

Cloncurry was founded when Ernest Henry discovered copper in 1867. The **Post Office** (1895; 47 Scarr Street) and **Courthouse** (1897; 42 Daintree Street) reflect the prosperity of the era.

Around Cloncurry

The pioneering prospector's name is honoured at the **Ernest Henry Mine** – a modern open-cut and underground copper and gold mine 36km (22 miles) north of Cloncurry. The mineral fields around Cloncurry contain several interesting old mine sites and towns – among them Kuridalla, Selwyn, Kajabbi, Duchess and Dobbyn.

About 20km (12 miles) south of Cloncurry is the **Bower Bird Creek Battery**, listed by the National Trust. The battery, which is remarkably intact, stands near the ghost town of Bower Bird, which, in 1895, comprised three stores, two hotels and a post office.

Located on a spinifex-covered hill, the site contains a number of early surface workings, and there's a campsite about 100 metres (330ft) east of the battery. If you want to inspect the mine, first call into the Cloncurry Information Centre, McIlwraith Street (tel: 4742 1361) for directions and advice.

The **Mary Kathleen Memorial Museum and Park** (McIlwraith Street; Mon–Fri 8am–4.30pm, Sat–Sun 9am–3pm Feb–Sept; charge; tel: 4742 1361) contains the Cloncurry Information Centre and has some interesting relics from the Burke and Wills expedition (the prize exhibit is a water bottle allegedly belonging to explorer Robert O'Hara Burke). Other displays include rare Aboriginal artefacts, a collection of old mining machinery and the Rail Ambulance used from 1956 to 1971. The museum's information centre is an exhibit in itself, having been used as a police station in the early mining towns of Oona and Dobbyn, and, later, in Mary Kathleen. Now little more than a memory, Mary Kathleen, halfway between Mount Isa and Cloncurry,

was constructed in 1954 by the Rio Tinto Mining Company to house its uranium miners.

More fragments of the past linger at the **Afghan and Chinese Cemeteries**, although, unfortunately, most of the graves have been washed away by floods. Afghans helped to build roads and railways in the Outback; accustomed to desert conditions, many then became traders and married Aboriginal women. The Chinese, who arrived en masse during the gold-rush era, also intermarried with the local population. The sole surviving headstone in the Muslim section marks the final resting place of Cloncurry mullah Syid O Mar, who died in 1915, aged 45. Only one grave remains of the original 50 in the Chinese cemetery.

Richmond

Incredible though it may seem, Queensland's dry and dusty Outback was once a verdant floodplain. Huge winged reptiles glided in air currents. Sharks and lungfish swam in its lakes. Dinosaurs roamed its forests and shorelines. The proof resides in the small Outback town of **Richmond** ❸, 287km (178 miles) east of Cloncurry, where a marine-fossil museum at **Kronosaurus Korner** (91–93 Goldring Street; daily 8.30am–4pm; charge; tel: 4741 3429; www.kronosauruskorner.com.au) showcases 200 exhibits. The region has yielded several important finds – most recently in 1989, when a local grazier unearthed the skeleton of a Pliosaur, which swam in the inland sea 100 million years ago. Also among the museum's exhibits is Australia's most complete and best-preserved dinosaur skeleton, the Minmi, unique because much of its fossilised skin remains.

Richmond was explored by William Landsborough in 1862 while searching for doomed expeditionists Burke and Wills. Pastoralists who read Landsborough's glowing reports soon followed. The **Pioneer Heritage Walk** traces the town's history through its landmarks, taking in the unusual Roman Catholic church, the corrugated-iron Strand Theatre and restored Cobb & Co. stagecoach *(see right)*. In **Lions Park**, on Goldring Street, there's a monument made of "moonrocks" – variously shaped limestone rocks, which often contain fossilised remnants of fish and shells.

Hughenden

Hughenden ❹, about 100km (62 miles) east of Richmond, is the centre of the large Flinders River pastoral district. Its main tourist draw is the Muttaburrasaurus – the replica of a virtually complete dinosaur skeleton. Measuring 7 metres (23ft) from snout to tail, Muttaburrasaurus would have been a fearsome critter in his prime. He can be seen at the **Flinders Discovery Centre** (37 Gray Street; daily 9am–5pm; charge; tel: 4741 1021).

Among the centre's displays is an exhibit explaining the genesis

Firm of Cobb & Co.

The 1880 discovery of gold at Woolgar, 113km (70 miles) north of Richmond, led to the town becoming a staging post for Cobb & Co. – a link recalled by a beautifully restored coach in Goldring Street.

BELOW: one of the last Afghan gravestones in Cloncurry's cemetery.

At Kronosaurus Korner in Richmond, the Marine Fossil Museum displays some of the finest examples of local marine fossils from the long-gone Cretaceous Inland Sea. They also offer guidance on local sites to fossick for your own fossils.

BELOW: what put Hughenden on the map.

of **Porcupine Gorge** – a spectacular national park, 61km (38 miles) north of Hughenden, where towering sandstone cliffs and lush green vine forests fringe permanent waterholes lined with casuarinas and paperbarks. A permit is required to camp at the park's Pyramid Lookout (contact the QPWS; tel: 13 74 68; www.derm.qld.gov.au). A scenic 1.2km (¾-mile) walk leads into the gorge; however, anyone planning an extended excursion on foot should notify the ranger at Hughenden (tel: 4741 1113).

The same ranger fields enquiries about **White Mountains National Park**, 80km (50 miles) northeast of Hughenden on the Flinders Highway. The park's name derives from its spectacular white sandstone bluffs and gorges, though the terrain varies widely, from spinifex grasslands to sand dunes. Conventional access is possible to **Burra Range Lookout**, but a 4WD is recommended to reach the campground at Cann's Camp Creek. During the wet season between October and April the road can be closed.

Winton

Tourism has taken root in the Australian Outback – and, in many ways **Winton** ❺, 1,400km (870 miles) northwest of Brisbane, led the way. When the drought of the 1960s threatened to turn Outback centres into ghost towns, Winton pharmacist Peter Evert and his brother Vince opened an opal museum, revived Winton's historic open-air cinema and ran minibus tours to nearby stations to give city slickers a taste of rural life. Peter Evert helped found Winton's Outback Festival in 1972, and took tourist groups in his six-seater charter plane to historic sites and Outback places previously accessible only to 4WD vehicles.

Winton inspired a verse of Australia's most famous song, and in 1995 the Waltzing Matilda Centenary marked a turning point in its fortunes, when more than 14,000 people surged into the town for an eight-day festival. Businesses did roaring trade. Cattle stations opened up for homestays. Shopkeepers spruced up their acts. Now Winton is barely recognisable from the down-at-heel

Digging Out Dinosaurs

About 100 million years ago, the vast plains of western Queensland were an inland sea bordered by lush rainforests. This sea was inhabited by ferocious carnivores, such as the famous *Kronosaurus queenslandicus*, a 10-metre (33ft) marine reptile unearthed in 1931. The township of Richmond is roughly in the centre of the ancient sea, and its Kronosaurus Korner displays fossils of several marine reptiles that inhabited this warm sea. At nearby Winton, at the Australian Age of Dinosaurs Museum (www.australianageofdinosaurs.com), you can watch paleontologists at work or even join a dinosaur dig. From Winton, head to Lark Quarry Dinosaur Trackway to witness a frozen-in-time dinosaur stampede.

settlement of 30 years ago. Footpaths have been paved, streets landscaped, gaudy signage replaced.

Winton's **Waltzing Matilda Centre** (50 Elderslie Street; daily 8.30am–5pm; public holidays 10am–4pm; charge; tel: 4657 1466; www.matilda centre.com.au) is a high-tech museum, complete with a computer-generated swagman relating his role in Australia's most famous song.

Winton's other claim to fame is that it is where, in 1920, QANTAS was born, and you will find a number of displays on the first Australian airline at the Waltzing Matilda Centre.

Another Winton landmark is the **Corfield & Fitzmaurice Building** (63 Elderslie Street; tel: 4657 1486), a retail outlet that traded more or less continuously from 1878 to 1987. The present building, listed by the National Trust, was built in 1916 and houses a craft co-operative and gem collection. It retains such features as long timber counters and a "flying fox", for transferring cash and receipts between the counter and a central office at mezzanine level.

Lark Quarry

At **Lark Quarry Dinosaur Trackways** ❻ (tours 10am, noon, 2pm; charge; tel: 4657 1812; www.dinosaurtrackways. com.au), 110km (68 miles) southwest of Winton, fossilised footprints record the stampede of a herd of dinosaurs pursued by a larger dinosaur across a prehistoric mudflat 100 million years ago. As the inland sea receded, the tracks turned to stone, creating an indelible record of pursuit and flight. Almost 4,000 dinosaur footprints are clearly visible in an area of just 210 sq metres (2,260 sq ft).

Despite exposure to the elements and visitors for many years, the footprints have remained intact. They are now shielded within a modern interpretative centre. The road from Winton is less than ideal, but the journey is worth it. Fuel up before you leave and carry food and water.

Kynuna and McKinlay

From Winton, it's 160km (100 miles) northwest on the Landsborough Highway to **Kynuna** ❼, a small settlement best known for the **Blue Heeler Pub** (tel: 4746 8650), where station

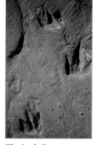

The Lark Quarry dinosaur tracks came to light in the 1960s, when a local station manager digging for opal discovered what he thought to be fossilised bird spoors.

Map on page 218

TIP

To experience Outback life at first hand, spend a night or two at Carisbrooke Station, 85km (53 miles) southwest of Winton, where graziers Charlie and Penny Phillott have converted their shearers' quarters in to tourist accommodation (tel: 4657 0084).

BELOW: camel racing in Boulia.

hands, truckies, shearers and bush characters rub shoulders with nomads and 4WD pilgrims. A former Cobb & Co. staging post, it has become an almost mandatory stop for travellers on the Matilda Highway.

Nearby is the billabong mentioned in *Waltzing Matilda*, also known as the **Combo Waterhole**, accessed from a turn-off 13km (8 miles) south of Kynuna. One of a string of semi-permanent coolibah-lined lagoons on the Diamantina River, the site is lent romance by the stone causeways built by Chinese labourers from 1883. From the car park, it's a 40-minute return walk to the waterhole. Camping is not permitted here.

McKinlay ❽, 76km (47 miles) northwest of Kynuna, has never been quite the same since Australian actor Paul Hogan used the former McKinlay Federal Hotel as a set for his film, *Crocodile Dundee*. Locals shook their heads as the film's set designers worked over the old place, replacing aluminium windows and doors with old-fashioned joinery. Renamed the **Walkabout Creek Hotel** (tel: 4746

8424), the building now represents McKinlay's one and only tourist attraction.

Boulia

Boulia ❾ is a small township in far-western Queensland, 303km (188 miles) south of Mount Isa and 366km (227 miles) west of Winton. The population stands at approximately 300 – with another 300 or so people scattered over the shire's 61,000 sq km (23,500 sq miles), whose boundaries skirt the Northern Territory border and the edge of the Simpson Desert.

Boulia's main celebration is the annual Camel Races in mid-July. The "Ute Muster", held at the same time, is an opportunity for Outback petrol heads to see who has the fastest and fanciest "ute" (farm truck).

The district is famous for an inexplicable and peculiarly Queensland phenomenon known as the Min Min Lights. Weird and luminous, these lights appear, hover, disappear and reappear with no apparent cause or pattern. The lights were first reported in 1912 following a fire in the Min Min Hotel, 105km (65 miles) east of town.

Boulia has turned the phenomenon to account with **The Min Min Encounter** (Herbert Street; daily 8.30am–5pm, Sat–Sun 9am–2pm; charge; tel: 4746 3386). Supported by animatronics, fibre optics and high-tech wizardry, the 45-minute show features tales of close encounters with Min Min Lights told by those who experienced them.

Another attraction is the National Trust-listed **Stone House** (Pituri Street; daily 8am–5pm; charge; tel: 5437 6481). Built during the pastoral boom of the mid-1880s, and now Boulia's oldest surviving structure, it is the centrepiece of a museum complex which houses a collection of both Aboriginal artefacts and fossilised remains. ❑

BEST RESTAURANTS, BARS AND CAFÉS

Prices for a three-course dinner per person with house wine:
$ = A$60 and under
$$ = A$60–100
$$$ = A$100 and over

Boulia

The Australian Hotel
Herbert Street
Tel: 4746 3144
Open: L & D daily. **$**
Traditional pub menu of steak, seafood and chicken dishes in a typical Outback dining room.

Cloncurry

Gidgee Bar and Grill
Matilda Highway
Tel: 4742 1599
Open: D Mon–Sat. **$$**
Generous reef'n'beef offerings such as rib fillet with grilled bugs, prawn Béarnaise, pea purée and soufflé potatoes.

Leichhardt Hotel-Motel
11 Scarr Street
Tel: 4742 1389
Open: L & D daily. **$$**
Well-prepared bistro meals featuring premium grain-fed steak, and fresh Gulf-sourced seafood. Extensive wine list.

Wagon Wheel Motel
54 Ramsay Street
Tel: 4742 1866
Open: D daily. **$$**
A la carte menu of steak and seafood dishes, with a separate menu for pizza and pasta.

Hughenden

Great Western Hotel
14 Brodie Street
Tel: 4741 1454
Open: L & D daily. **$**
Huge T-bone steaks are the feature of this family-orientated hotel-restaurant.

Mount Isa

Dom's Italian Restaurant
79 Camooweal Street
Tel: 4743 4444
Open: L & D Tue–Sat. **$**
Eclectic, affordable Italian menu based on traditional dishes.

Frog and Toad Bar and Grill
The Buffs Club, corner Grace and Camooweal streets
Tel: 4743 2365
Open: L & D daily. **$**
Hearty fare served in a spacious room. Bistro for lunch and dinner. Coffee shop for light meals. Live entertainment Wed–Sun.

Keane's Bar and Grill
Mount Isa Irish Club, 1 Nineteenth Avenue
Tel: 4743 2577
Open: D daily. **$$**
The club also offers an all-day breakfast in the Tram Stop coffee shop and a lunch buffet in the Members' Bar.

Mount Isa RSL Club
89 Barkly Highway
Tel: 4743 2172
Open: L & D daily. **$**
Country-style meals in the club bar. Few frills but generous servings.

Rodeo Bar and Grill
Isa Hotel, Miles Street
Tel: 1800 603 488
Open: L & D daily. **$**
One of the Isa's better pub restaurants. A la carte modern Australian with fresh ingredients.

Overlander Hotel
119 Marian Street
Tel 4743 5011
Open: L & D daily. **$**
The hotel bistro delivers generous helpings of steak, seafood and chicken dishes.

Red Earth Restaurant
Red Earth Boutique Hotel, corner West Street and Rodeo Drive
Tel: 4749 8888
Open: L & D daily. **$$**
Classy and exceptionally presented fare in a stylish hotel. Book ahead.

Winton

Coolibah Café
Waltzing Matilda Centre, Elderslie Street
Tel: 4657 1466
Open: L daily. **$**
Coffee, cakes and pastries baked in-house. Salads and light meals are also available. BYO.

Tattersalls Hotel
78 Elderslie Street
Tel: 4657 1309
Open: L & D daily. **$**
In Winton's oldest hotel (1885), publicans Paul and Sanya Nielsen serve premium-quality steaks from all over Australia.

RIGHT: whistle-wetting in Winton.

SOUTHWEST QUEENSLAND

A region of vast distances, serene billabongs and diverse wildlife. Its isolation inspired both QUANTAS and the Royal Flying Doctor Service. Amid flood plains and red, sandy desert, the Outback spirit survives

Brisbane ●

The best time to see Queensland's Southwest is after rain. Wild flowers burst into bloom, corellas wheel overhead and waterholes brim with yellowbelly. The transformation is little short of miraculous. The channels and gullies of Cooper Creek join to form a brown stream 30km (19 miles) wide, and the red soil is cloaked in green.

Of course, the greening of the Outback is a comparatively rare phenomenon. For most visitors, the overriding impression is one of human fortitude amid a harsh, arid and unrelenting vastness. There's a curious appeal in this. In dry times – and times are mostly dry – the landscape expresses a kind of primeval power that is at once exhilarating and humbling. Perhaps that is what makes those who inhabit this unforgiving landscape such a flinty, independent breed – philosophical about setbacks, sanguine about prospects, laconic of wit.

The Southwest is studded with communities clinging to the ledge of existence. When Betoota's publican and last resident walked out a few years ago, the town became yet another vacant dot on the map. Other settlements have a more permanent air, Longreach among them. For visitors approaching Southwest Queensland by air, Longreach Airport is the first port of call before transferring to car or bus.

Self-drive allows independence, but a bus tour is by far the more informative experience, provided you don't mind amplified patter interspersed by repeated playings of *On the Road from Gundagai*. A competent driver/guide knows the name of every tree, flower, bird and critter that crosses your path. He or she will

THIS GATE SHOULD BE CLOSED AT ALL TIMES IF FOUND OPEN PLEASE CLOSE

WILD DOG DESTRUCTION BOARD

LEFT: cattle country, where every pub has character. **RIGHT:** the Dog Fence on the border with New South Wales.

TIP

A pleasant activity in Longreach is to embark on a sunset river cruise on the Thomson River – an experience usually involving Outback entertainment, star-gazing and bush tucker. For information, contact Kinnon & Co. (tel: 4658 1776; www.kinnonand co.com.au).

impart astounding facts about the bush and introduce you to some of its colourful characters.

Longreach

Longreach ❶ is a city of about 3,700 people in the heart of the Outback, 1,200km (746 miles) from Brisbane. The ennui that marks other Outback centres is less obvious here, possibly because Longreach retains its purpose as a service centre for the surrounding sheep and cattle runs.

Its most visible attractions are historical. Flying in, the first thing you see is the **QANTAS Founders' Outback Museum** (Landsborough Highway; daily 9am–5pm; charge; tel: 4658 3737; www.qfom.com.au), cementing Longreach's claim to being the birthplace of the airline. It's a sore point in the west. Winton and Longreach each claim the successful airline as their own – Winton, because the founders met in the Winton Club; Longreach because

this was where they based their operation. An uneven compromise has been struck: Winton kept the boardroom; Longreach has the A\$9 million aviation museum.

The 747-200B jumbo jet is hard to miss, towering over everything (you can tour inside at extra cost); it's a big advance on the open cockpit Avro 504K used for the airline's inaugural flight from Longreach to Winton in 1921. There's a replica of an Avro 504K inside the museum, along with a slew of informative interactive displays. Nearby, the original 1922 QANTAS hangar houses a replica of an Apollo biplane. The first QANTAS booking office in Eagle Street now serves as an information office for the museum.

Just beyond the museum is the **Australian Stockman's Hall of Fame and Outback Heritage Centre** (Landsborough Highway; daily 9am–5pm; charge; tel: 4658 2166; www.outbackheritage.com.au),

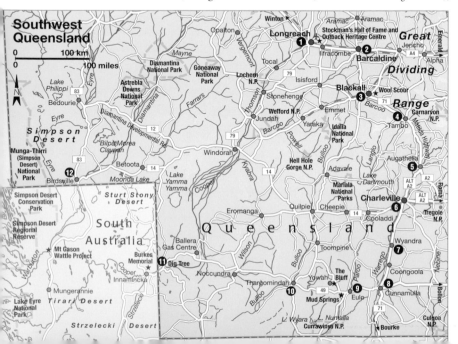

an arresting building designed as a tribute to the early explorers, stockmen and drovers of the Outback. Alongside the bush memorabilia, pioneering relics and dioramas of early Outback life, the centre has grown to incorporate themes such as Aboriginal culture and European exploration.

One Longreach legend is 19th-century cattle duffer (thief) Harry Readford, alias Captain Starlight, who, in 1870, drove 1,000 cattle stolen from Bowen Downs Station through unexplored terrain into South Australia. When a distinctive white bull sold en route gave the game away, Readford was apprehended – only to be acquitted by a jury in Roma, an Outback town well known for incomprehensible "not guilty" verdicts. Readford is commemorated in Longreach by a hill known variously as **Cassidy's Knob** and **Starlight's Lookout**. The hill overlooks the surrounding plains where, so the story goes, Readford posted a lookout to keep watch while his henchmen gathered the stolen herd.

Barcaldine

Barcaldine ❷, 107km (66 miles) east of Longreach, is a small, well-tended sheep-and-cattle town of 1,500 people, and the birthplace of the Australian Labor Party. It was here, during the strike of 1891, that shearers organised themselves into armed camps and were confronted by a military force equipped with guns. As a gesture of solidarity 1,000 striking shearers marched by torchlight to the Tree of Knowledge, where they burnt effigies of Premier Sir Samuel Griffith. When 13 of the shearers' leaders were sentenced to three years' hard labour on St Helena Island in Moreton Bay, the shearers resolved to win political power to protect the interests of working people. They met under the Tree of Knowledge to endorse shearer Tommy Ryan, who became the first Labor Party candidate to win office in the parliament, inspiring the formation of the Australian Labor Party. The iconic ghost gum in Oak Street remained alive until 2006, when vandals poisoned it.

Barcaldine was also the first town to obtain artesian-bore water, hence

Longreach was where QANTAS *(the Queensland and Northern Territory Aerial Service) set up its first operational base in 1922.*

BELOW: the Australian Stockman's Hall of Fame.

*Masonic temple in
Barcaldine.*

the oases of thriving gardens, leafy streets and orchards of citrus fruits amid desert country. Sadly, the presence of a steady water supply did not prevent conflagrations sweeping through the town. Of the six hotels that once stood in Barcaldine, only two – the **Artesian Hotel** and **The Union** – have remained unburnt.

Barcaldine's history is chronicled at the impressive **Workers' Heritage Centre** (Ash Street; Mon–Sat 9am–5pm, Sun 10am–5pm; charge; tel: 4651 2422; www.australianworkers-heritagecentre.com.au). Opened during the centenary celebrations of the Labor Party in 1991, the centre commemorates the role played by workers in the social and political development of Australia. Displays include a schoolhouse, a hospital and a powerhouse, and it's set in pleasant landscaped grounds around a central billabong.

Also worth seeing is the **Masonic Temple** (corner Yew and Beech streets). Built in 1901, and restored in 1980, the facade of this Outback gem has been painted to resemble stone blocks, pilasters and friezes.

Drop in at the Barcaldine Tourist Information Centre for a copy of the heritage trail guide (Ash Street; Mar–Sept daily 8.15am–4.30pm, Oct–Feb Mon–Fri 8.15am–4.30pm; tel: 4651 1724).

Blackall

Signs on the outskirts of **Blackall** ❸, 100km (62 miles) south of Barcaldine, announce the town as home of shearer Jackie Howe, whose record with hand blades – 321 sheep in 7hr 40min, set at Alice Downs Station in 1892 – has never been bettered. Howe died in 1920, but his bronze statue looms large outside a replica of the **Universal Hotel** that he once owned. He is depicted wearing his trademark singlet, while hefting a sheep to the board for shearing. Jackie Howe designed his singlet without sleeves to allow freedom of movement. Other shearers adopted the idea and, in time, these practical work shirts (known as "Jackie Howes") became a symbol of rugged masculinity.

Howe also influenced the future of Australian politics. In 1891, as a member of the shearers' union committee,

he contributed to the events that led to the formation of the Australian Labor Party. Barcaldine may claim to be the birthplace of the ALP, but Blackall played its part, hosting the first meeting of the shearers' union in 1886, an event marked by a memorial in Shamrock Street.

Blackall also asserts ownership of the **Black Stump** (a lump of petrified wood) that gave rise to the expression "beyond the black stump" to describe impossibly remote locations. According to historians, the Black Stump was used by surveyors to steady their surveying instruments while taking observations of latitude and longtitude around the year 1887. The original Black Stump has long since vanished, but there's a display and a mural where the stump used to be on Thistle Street.

Northeast of Blackall is the **Wool Scour**, built in 1906, and the last steam-driven wool-washing plant in Australia, which operated commercially until 1978. The wool scour runs on steam from May to September, but is powered at other times by electric motor.

Blackall's most fascinating site, **Blacks Palace**, boasts 1,000 Aboriginal drawings on sandstone cliffs. It is on privately owned Marston Station and is currently closed to the public. At the time of writing, there were no plans to reopen it, but you should check with the Blackall Visitor Centre (108 Shamrock Street; tel: 4657 4637) for the latest news.

Tambo and Augathella

From Barcaldine, the Matilda Highway heads south through Tambo and Augathella to Charleville.

Tambo ❹, 208km (129 miles) from Barcaldine, has a population of 400 served by two hotels, a general store and two post offices – one dating from 1876, the other from 1904. The 1876 building, now the **Old Telegraph Museum** (12 Arthur Street; Mon–Fri 10am–5pm, Sat 10am–2pm; tel: 4654 6133), is a rare example of late 19th-century public-works architecture, built when Tambo was the main communications point north of Charleville. It stands with other heritage buildings on the main street – the courthouse, post office and shire hall.

BELOW: the Workers' Heritage Centre in Barcaldine.

Provided you have a 4WD, Tambo is the departure point for a challenging 320km (200-mile) trip that traces early bullock routes through gorges and along rivers to the Great Dividing Range. Tambo Shire Council (21 Arthur Street; tel: 4654 6133) can provide maps and trail guides for this journey, which takes in sites of early European settlement and examples of Aboriginal rock art.

The main point of interest at **Augathella** ➎, on the Matilda Highway, 118km (73 miles) south of Tambo, resides with the town's whimsically named junior rugby team, the Augathella Meat Ants. Slightly odd wrought-iron sculptures of meat ants dot the town in support of this team. The Augathella reach of the Warrego River offers excellent fishing for Murray cod, yellowbelly, golden perch and catfish. Otherwise, not a lot happens.

Charleville

Eighty-four kilometres (52 miles) to the south is **Charleville** ➏, a classic Outback town characterised by wide streets, bottle trees and a vulnerability to flooding (on the rare occasions rain falls). Sited on the Warrego River along a stock route from New South Wales to western Queensland, Charleville was surveyed in 1867, developing as a service centre for the surrounding pastoral industry. In 1888, it became the terminus for the western railway line, confirming its strategic position, and in 1893, Cobb & Co. set up a factory for the construction of mail coaches and buggies.

Charleville's heritage architecture reflects eras of prosperity in the late 19th century and the 1920s. At the centre of one of the richest districts, the town has several substantial buildings. The Queensland National Bank (1889), now the **Historic House Museum** (Alfred Street; Mon–Fri 9am–3pm, Sat 9am–noon; charge; tel: 4654 3349), is an excellent example of early Queensland architecture, and there is an impressive collection of machinery and vehicles in the grounds, including an early fire engine and a Cobb & Co. coach. Other noteworthy structures include the **Town Hall** (1926) and **Corones Hotel** (1929).

BELOW: painting the town red in Augathella.

Charleville was at the forefront of the country's infant aviation industry; QANTAS commenced commercial services from here in 1922, taking up where Cobb & Co. had left off; Amy Johnson passed through here in the 1920s; and the US Air Force personnel commandeered Charleville Airport during the Japanese invasion scare of 1942. The Royal Flying Doctor Service (RFDS) established a base in Charleville the following year. You can visit the **RFDS Visitors Centre** in Old Cunnamulla Road (Mon–Fri 8.30am–4.30pm, Sat–Sun 10am–4.30pm; tel: 4654 1233).

One of Charleville's more innovative attractions is the **Cosmos Centre** in QANTAS Drive (Apr–Oct daily 10am–5pm, Nov–Mar closed weekends; charge; bookings essential for night time; tel: 4654 7771; www. cosmoscentre.com), an observatory that makes use of clear night skies to view planets and star clusters through its sophisticated telescopes. In the galactic theatre you can see presentations describing Aboriginal Dreamtime cosmology and the origins of the universe, while interactive displays explore the history of astronomy. The latest addition is a filter enabling visitors to look at the sun through a telescope.

The Charleville Visitor Information Centre (inside Cosmos Centre; Apr–mid Oct daily 9am–5pm, Oct–Mar Mon–Sat 10am–5pm; tel: 4654 7771) can give you details of all the attractions and activities on offer.

Wyandra and Cunnamulla

About 100km (62 miles) south of Charleville, and halfway to Cunnamulla, sits **Wyandra ❼** – a hamlet of 60 souls blessed by a pub, some old buildings, a museum and, amazingly, a beach. Call into the **Gladstone Hotel** and rub elbows with locals who may, if you show interest, reminisce about Wyandra's heyday, when the town supported two pubs, two ice works, two stores and a garage. It's very quiet in Wyandra nowadays. The best thing is the sandy beach on a picturesque bend of the **Warrego River**, where it would be easy to spend time fishing for yellowbelly or reading a book. Explorer Edmund Kennedy camped on this sandy

Every Outback town has its oddity, and Charleville's is the Steiger Gun, a rainmaking cannon introduced in 1902 by meteorologist Clement Wragge in an attempt to break a drought by blasting hot air into the sky. A battery of these devices was fired into the atmosphere but, alas, not a drop of rain fell. One of these bizarre rain guns is displayed outside the Scout hall, south of Charleville.

BELOW: bilby and baby.

Save the Bilbies

The Queensland Parks and Wildlife Service in Charleville (Park Street; Mon–Fri 8.30am–4.30pm; tel: 4654 1255) runs a breeding programme for endangered native species; you can see yellow-footed rock wallabies here. The centre is also behind the Save the Bilby Fund, a national appeal and breeding programme for bilbies, tiny marsupials whose numbers dropped to 100 at one stage. They are bred here and released into an area of Currawinya National Park surrounded by a predator-proof fence. The **Bilby Experience** (1 Park Street; Apr–Sep Mon, Wed, Fri, Sun 6–7pm; charge) provides a fascinating insight into this rare nocturnal bandicoot.

Cunnamulla's oddity is the Cyprus Pine in Stockyard Street, also known as the Robber Tree, where, in 1880, station hand Joseph Wells hid after a bank heist. Dogs tracked Wells to the tree, where he was spotted clinging to the branches. When Wells was sentenced to death, opponents of capital punishment took to the streets, but they could not save him from the gallows.

BELOW: café proprietor in Wyandra.

expanse in 1847, noting "a two-mile stretch of water 60 yards wide". He named it Camp 18. Locals prefer to call it **Wyandra Beach**. Once a busy railhead, Wyandra lives happily with its ghosts. If you're looking for the railway station, it's been moved to the racecourse, where it serves as a catering hut on race days.

So to **Cunnamulla** – an Outback town at the intersection of two major stock routes, and the southernmost town in western Queensland. With its tree-lined streets and pleasant hotels, it has old-fashioned country charm, and it lies on the Warrego River, a great place for boating, fishing and swimming.

The town was established to service the huge sheep farms that developed in the 1880s; the railway arrived in 1899, and since then Cunnamulla has been a major hub for the district. For details of what to see and do in town, visit the **Cunnamulla Information Centre** (Centenary Park, Jane Street; Apr–Nov Mon–Fri 8.30am–4.30pm, Sat–Sun 10am–2pm, Dec–Mar Mon–Fri 8.30am–4.30pm; tel: 4655 2481).

Other places of note along the Cunnamulla's heritage trail include the **Post Office** (1868), the **State School** (1885) and **St Catherine's Convent** (1914). As a respite from heat, dust and history, take time to visit the **Allan Tannock Weir**, 5km (3 miles) south of Cunnamulla. Created with flood mitigation in mind, this placid expanse provides a haven for anglers and bird-watchers – and is a boon to all who come to the Outback in search of peace.

Eulo to Noccundra

Eulo , 66km (41 miles) west of Cunnamulla, is a friendly township of about 50 people – virtually all engaged in a cottage industry of one sort or another, from opal cutters and beekeepers to artists and bush poets.

The main focus is the **Eulo Queen Hotel**, named after the original licensee, Isabel MacIntosh, whose clientele comprised opal miners slaking their thirst after a hard day's slog. So the story goes, Isabel accumulated so many opals that she became known as the Opal Queen of Eulo. The present Eulo Queen offers clean

rooms and decent food. It's a good place to meet the locals.

Nine kilometres (5 miles) west of Eulo, a sign announces the proximity of natural mud springs – fissures in the Earth's surface that act as pressure valves for the Great Artesian Basin. These mounds have a hard crust but are spongy underneath. So many bores have been sunk that pressure from below has lessened markedly, but the mounds occasionally emit loud bangs.

Yowah, a small opal-mining town, is accessed via the Quilpie turn-off, about 20km (12 miles) west of Eulo. Continue towards Quilpie for another 45km (28 miles), then turn left. Depending on the season, Yowah's population fluctuates wildly from 50 to 400 – a number that includes many amateur fossickers combining an Outback experience with the chance of finding an opal.

The town is surprisingly cosmopolitan. Sand greens and earth fairways have been shaped to form a nine-hole golf course, and there is an annual Opal Festival on the third weekend of July. **The Bluff**, 2km (1¼

miles) east of town, affords scenic views of the mine workings and a rare opportunity to take in the unrelenting and awe-inspiring vastness all around.

Getting to **Thargomindah** ⓾, 200 km (124 miles) west of Cunnamulla, is 90 percent of the fun. Aside from an old Fargo fire truck, the ruin of a disc plough and a historic house, there's not much to see or do here.

But Thargomindah does have one significant claim to fame; it is the first Australian settlement to harness bore water successfully to drive a hydroelectricity plant. In 1893, this was innovative stuff. The *Sydney Bulletin* hailed Thargomindah as a world centre for electricity, surpassed only by London and Paris. The hydroelectricity system lasted until 1951.

The first European to probe the district was grazier Vincent Dowling, who, in 1859, rode from northern New South Wales to the Bulloo River, returning three years later to establish Thargomindah Station. Gazetted in 1874, Thargomindah became a service centre for surrounding properties and, later, a stopover for people taking

BELOW: Cunnamulla.

TIP

The best times to visit Noccundra are during the second weekend of October, when local stockmen converge for the rodeo, or in the third weekend of May, when the population swells to 500 or 600 for the race meeting. Stockmen and truckies make up the core clientele of Noccundra's one pub; 4WD pilgrims, older travellers (also known as "grey nomads") and recreational aviators take up the slack.

wool to Bourke and the paddle steamers plying the Darling River.

Out here, it's the terrain – the mulga, gibber and flood plains and red sandy desert – that captures the eye… and there's plenty to observe on the 140km (87-mile) run from Thargomindah to **Noccundra**. Close up, the colour and pattern of the landscape takes on a dreamlike quality. From a light plane *(see box opposite)*, you see geometrically precise seismic oil-exploration lines crisscrossing around the Jackson Oilfield.

The road to Noccundra is sealed, inviting conventional car access. Nonetheless, it remains a one-pub township of four official residents (usually only one is present). The pub, built of stone, dates from 1882, when it served as a watering hole for drovers and later as a mail hitch for Cobb & Co. It's sufficiently remote to allow light planes to taxi to the door.

The Dig Tree

The road is rough in parts but, having come so far, it makes sense to continue 230km (143 miles) west to the **Dig Tree** ⓫ on Nappa Merrie

Station, living symbol of one of Australia's great tragedies. Here, William Brahe and three others waited more than four months at a base camp near Cooper Creek while explorers Robert Burke and William Wills made their dash to the Gulf of Carpentaria. Brahe left just seven hours before Burke, Wills and King staggered back into the camp on 21 April. The explorers found the warm ashes of a fire and, carved into a tree, the words "Dig.3ft.N.W.April.21,1861". The starving Burke drove off Aborigines who had been giving him fish as he thought them "too cheeky". Both he and Wills died soon afterwards. Only King, who had been taken in by a local tribe, survived to tell the tale. Australian history leaves fragile monuments. Yet the Dig Tree still grows beside the billabong on Cooper Creek. The carving has been grown over, but the message is partly decipherable.

On this stretch of the Cooper, pelicans glide on waterholes that echo to the calls of corellas, galahs, plovers, dotterels, herons, egrets and parrots. Bream, catfish and tortoises swim beneath the surface.

BELOW: there are oilfields in southwest Queensland.

Toompine and Quilpie

Visitors heading to Birdsville via Toompine, Quilpie and Windorah should retrace their route to the east, turning left at Thargomindah. About 75km (47 miles) north of Thargomindah, **Toompine**'s one point of interest is its pub. When built in about 1893, it was the focal point for a bustling mining settlement. Today, all it has for company is a cemetery. The building has entered a state of decay. 'Roo shooters and opal miners frequent the bar, which is adorned with signs like "The Only True Wilderness Is between a Greenie's Ears". For all that, they're a friendly mob, ready with a beer and a tale.

Another 75km (47 miles) north of Toompine is **Quilpie**, whose population stands at around 600, making it the big smoke in these parts. Tourism brochures depict Quilpie as the land of opals and oil. It is also the land of cattle and sheep, with 60,000 head passing through the railhead in a good season. Quilpie's fascination with opal – the district is a major producer of boulder opal – finds expression at **St Finbarr's Roman Catholic**

Church on Buln Buln Street, where opal lines the altar, font and lectern.

Windorah, 237km (147 miles) northwest of Quilpie, is known for its landmark of huge red sandhills just 10 minutes' drive out of town. Situated alongside Cooper Creek, it doesn't get much more "Outback" than here, with its stunning vistas and picturesque ruins. There's an old wooden pub, a general store, a post office, a service station – and not much else.

Try to time your visit to coincide with one of the events that take place here annually, when the population swells and the town comes to life; there's bronco branding, a rodeo and yabby racing (yabbies are small freshwater crayfish). The Windorah Visitor Information Centre (Maryborough Street; Apr–Oct daily 8.30am–5pm, Nov–Mar Mon–Fri 8.30am–5pm; tel: 4656 3063) can help you.

Birdsville and the Simpson Desert

Located 1,600km (1,000 miles) west of Brisbane, remote **Birdsville ⑫** clings to the edge of the Simpson Desert, close to the route that Burke and Wills

Flying Over The Outback

Air Central West (tel: 4658 9187; www.aircentralwest.com.au) offers go-anywhere charters in a six-seater from their base at Longreach Airport. They are specialists in one- and two-day tours of Lake Eyre and the Channel Country, where slow-moving flood waters have created an amazing tapestry. Check their website for the latest information on water levels. They will fly up to six passengers to almost anywhere in Outback Australia.

Outback Airtours (tel: 4654 3033; www.outbackairtours.com), based in Charleville, offers charter packages for groups of four passengers or fewer. Their tours include Birdsville, Cooper Creek, Coober Pedy (in South Australia), as well as Lake Eyre and the Channel Country.

BELOW: cattle on the plains.

The Birdsville Hotel during the annual Birdsville Races. Every September, the small town of Birdsville in southwest Queensland hosts thousands of visitors for the Birdsville Cup - one of the most famous horse-racing carnivals in Outback Australia.

BELOW: parked on the 'Big Red' sand dune in the Simpson Desert.

followed on their ill-fated expedition. On the first weekend in September its population expands from 120 to 6,000 as people converge on the town for the Birdsville Races, which celebrated 130 years of horse racing in 2011. One of Australia's most famous pubs, the National Trust-listed **Birdsville Hotel**, is booked out at race time, and is busy from March to November. Built from sandstone in 1884, the hotel has been tastefully renovated.

The town's other hotel – the **Royal Hotel**, erected in 1883 – is a relic of Birdsville's pastoral past. Now in gracious ruins, it housed the Australian Inland Mission's Nursing Home from 1923 to 1937. The town's only other surviving masonry building (apart from the Birdsville Hotel) is the **Courthouse**, built between 1888 and 1890, and still in use by the police and judiciary.

At the time of writing, the eclectic **Birdsville Working Museum** was up for sale and likely to close its doors permanently. Without a buyer, the large and interesting collection of working machinery used by early settlers is likely to be auctioned off. It

is certainly hoped that the collection will have found a new custodian by the time you read this.

Beyond Birdsville lies the **Munga-Thirri (Simpson Desert) National Park**, Queensland's largest national park. It is dominated by vast parallel dunes up to 20 metres (66ft) high and interspersed by saltpans, sand drifts and gibber-ironstone flats. This starkly beautiful environment provides the natural habitat for more than 180 bird species, and is also home to the mulgara, a rare marsupial.

If you want to cross the park in a 4WD, heed the advice on *page 250* and only travel in two-vehicle parties between April and October. Contact the ranger at Munga-Thirri National Park (tel: 4658 1761) before you go.

Conventional cars can tackle the **Birdsville Track**, which stretches south of Birdsville to Maree in South Australia, taking a desolate course of 520km (320 miles) between the Simpson Desert to the west and Sturt Stony Desert to the east. Take similar precautions as those for travelling through the national park, and notify someone of your plans prior to travelling. ❑

BEST RESTAURANTS, BARS AND CAFÉS

Prices for a three-course dinner per person with house wine:

$ = A$60 and under
$$ = A$60–100
$$$ = A$100 and over

3Ls Steakhouse
Ironbark Inn
72 Box Street
Tel: 4651 2311
Open: D daily **$**
Open-air Outback shed offering typical bistro fare such as juicy steaks.
Restaurant 1886
Shakespeare Hotel, 97 Oak Street Tel: 4651 1111
Open: L & D daily Apr–Oct. Hours vary rest of year. **$**
With a delightful court-yard and a deserving reputation for good service and great pub grub.

Big Red Café
Tel: 4656 3099
Open: L & D daily Apr–Oct. **$**
Owners Karsten John and Jackie Stallard's unique desert café offers espresso, cakes and world cuisine. Resident artist/musician Wolfgang John's paintings and CDs express the feeling of the landscape.
Birdsville Hotel
Adelaide Street
Tel: 4656 3244.
Open: L & D daily. **$**
Bistro dining daily for

RIGHT: alfresco refreshments.

lunch and dinner. Menu features organic beef from locally raised grass-fed cattle, as well as seafood and vegetarian dishes.
Birdsville Bakery
Billabong Blvd
Tel: 4656 4697
Open: L daily Apr–Oct. **$**
Baker Dusty Miller rustles up fresh bread, pies and sausage rolls in his café/bakery. Evening meals include hamburgers, pizzas and fish and chips.

Tatts Bar and Bistro
Acacia Motor Inn,
110 Shamrock Street
Tel: 4657 6022
Open: D Mon–Sat. **$**
Old-fashioned country

food – and plenty of it.

Charleville RSL Club
36 Watson Street
Tel: 4654 1449
Open: L & D daily. **$**
Bistro-style fare amid the clatter of poker and keno machines.
Outback Restaurant
Mulga Country Motor Inn,
Cunnamulla Road
Tel: 4654 3255
Open: D Mon–Sat. **$$**
Pretty standard motel fare with some unexpected exotica such as Tahitian prawns and mushroom gratin.

Jolly Jumbuck Restaurant
Sir Hudson Fysh Drive

Tel: 4658 1799
Open: L & D daily. **$$**
À la carte fare in an open restaurant set in gardens.
Longreach Club
31 Duck Street
Tel: 4658 1016
Open: L Mon–Sat, D daily. **$**
Another typical club where the cheap-and-cheerful roasts and bistro meals offer excellent value for hungry travellers.
McGinness's Restaurant
QANTAS Founders' Outback Museum, Sir Hudson Fysh Drive
Tel: 4658 3737
Open: L daily. **$**
Coffee and tasty café fare in a chic US-diner-style setting.

Outback Pubs

Step out of the glare into an Outback pub and you enter another world. A leisurely beer and good company can see that carefully planned itinerary go awry

The state's most colourful pubs survive from the pioneering days, when hotels mushroomed wherever gold was discovered or a new railhead was established. Over the years, many historic hotels have succumbed to fire and neglect – but the thirsty traveller can still savour a coldie in quirky century-old establishments that have defied the broom of progress.

Landmark pubs

Probably the most famous is the **Birdsville Hotel**, 1,600km (1,000 miles) west of Brisbane, just north of the Queensland–South Australian border. Built in 1884, it began as

a watering hole for local graziers and passing drovers. These days, it enjoys the patronage of locals and 4WD adventurers. Due to a shortage of timber, the walls are constructed of solid sandstone, keeping the bar cool and tranquil even when desert winds howl. Battered hats, stubby-holders and photographs of locals decorate the main bar. Adjacent is the Green Lizard Lounge, so named because of a beer drought that forced locals to drink crème de menthe. Despite this momentary shortage of the amber fluid, Birdsville makes no claim to be the inspiration for the late country balladeer Slim Dusty's well-known song, *The Pub with No Beer*. (That honour belongs to Lee's Hotel in Ingham, where US servicemen celebrating the Coral Sea victory literally drank the pub dry.)

Winton's **North Gregory Hotel** also enjoys popularity – partly because this is where Banjo Paterson delivered his debut performance of *Waltzing Matilda* in 1895, partly because it's a pleasant place to enjoy a cold beer on a hot day. To be precise, the present North Gregory Hotel is not the one that Banjo Paterson patronised, although it does occupy the same site. In all, there have been four North Gregory Hotels. The other three burnt down – which explains why the present hotel is built of brick.

Between Winton and Cloncurry are two more well-known bush pubs – the fair dinkum **Blue Heeler** at Kynuna, with its neon dog, and the not-so-authentic **Walkabout Creek** at McKinlay (see *Mount Isa and the West*) where Crocodile Dundee quenched a thirst. And further north again, Normanton's luridly hued **Purple Pub** holds a certain fascination with backpackers and modern-day explorers.

While many outback pubs look like they were put together in a day so that the bar could open that night, there are a few grand hotels that buck the trend. **Corones Hotel** is synonymous with Charleville – occupying nearly a block of the town's main street. Built during the economic boom of the 1920s, this famous hotel fell into disrepair during the 1960s but has since been

Left: XXXX hits the spot.

restored (though not quite to its original grandeur). For several decades, Corones Hotel was regarded as the epitome of hospitality in the west. It's worth visiting, if only to see the wood panelling and grand staircase in the foyer, not to mention the raised "pulpit" from which Harry "Poppa" Corones controlled goings-on in the bar.

The best bush pubs

Southwest of Blackall, in the foothills of the Yang Yang Ranges, the traveller comes upon the **Yaraka Hotel**, centrepiece of an idyllic Outback hamlet where, not so long ago, locals relied on a rusty hand-operated bowser for fuel and a manual telephone exchange for communication. Yaraka exists because this is where, in 1917, funding for the Great Western Railway petered out. Terminally disappointed, the rails point with abandoned hope towards their next destination, Windorah, 145km (90 miles) to the southwest. Recently, the once-a-week service to Yaraka ceased altogether, leaving Yaraka's 15 inhabitants even more isolated – but not lonesome. When the publican of the hotel throws a barbecue, the whole town turns up.

Another great bush pub is the **Wellshot Hotel**, 27km (17 miles) east of Longreach, where Ilfracombe publican Jo Scott hosts a cast of characters that includes stockmen, Maori shearers and travellers. It's a pub with plenty of Outback atmosphere – little altered since its construction over a century ago.

Other notable scrub pubs in southwest Queensland include the 1882 **Noccundra Pub**, a stone-built former mail hitch for Cobb & Co. (21km/13 miles down the turn-off at Nockatunga, along the Adventure Way); the 1893 **Toompine Pub**, gracefully decaying between Quilpie and Thargomindah; and the **Eulo Queen**, named after original licensee Isabel MacIntosh, who earned her sobriquet after accumulating a fortune in opals from sozzled prospectors.

East from Normanton, and about 400km (250 miles) inland from Cairns, is the National Trust-listed **Einasleigh Hotel**, built in 1909 during a moment of copper-mining euphoria. The hotel gained notoriety in 1994 as the focus for community protest against the proposed closing of the Cairns-to-Forsayth railway. The town's 40 residents blockaded the railway for four days, holding the Last Great Train Ride hostage. Passengers and crew were accommodated and fed in the hotel until the blockade was lifted.

Another far-north Queensland icon is the **Lion's Den Hotel**, located at Helensvale on the coastal road from Cairns to Cooktown. Set in tropical rainforest, this 1875 pub bulges with memorabilia, beginning with a welcome sign that reads: "You keep your dog outta my bar and I'll keep my bullets outta your dog." Don't be afraid. The locals are friendly, especially after a beer or two – plus you can enjoy steak and pizza, or cool off in the pub's reportedly crocodile-free swimming hole.

Cheers! ❏

RIGHT: every pub's a hotel, but not every hotel's a pub. This is both.

INSIGHT GUIDES TRAVEL TIPS

QUEENSLAND
& THE GREAT BARRIER REEF

TRANSPORT

ACCOMMODATION

ACTIVITIES

A – Z

T RANSPORT

GETTING THERE AND GETTING AROUND

By Air

About 30 international airlines fly directly to Queensland, with most bound for either Brisbane or Cairns. The QANTAS-owned Jetstar Airways also flies directly to the Gold Coast International Airport from a range of Asian cities, including Japan, Hong Kong and Singapore.

Flights between Australia and Europe take about 22 hours, but with stopovers and delays the journey could take up to 30 hours. A stopover in an Asian capital (or on the Pacific Coast or Hawaii if travelling from Canada or the US) is worth considering.

The cost of flights to Australia can be high. The peak season for travel is around December, with prices tapering off from January to April. Apex fares will reduce the flat economy fare by about 30–40 percent during the less busy periods. If you are flexible and can fly at short notice, check with discount flight centres for fares on unsold tickets. Note that with many of the heavily discounted fares, refunds and changes in flight times are generally ruled out. A small departure tax, payable in Australian dollars, is levied on all travellers leaving Australia, but this is included in the cost of an international ticket.

Travellers planning to cover several different parts of Australia in their trip will find it is probably cheaper for a travel agent to arrange flights from point to point before they leave home.

If you are planning to fly to Queensland from other parts of Australia, you will probably travel with one of the three major domestic carriers in Australia.

AIRLINES

British Airways:
Tel: 1300 767 177 (Australia)
Tel: 08444 930 787 (UK)
Tel: 1 800 247 9297 (US)
www.britishairways.com
QANTAS:
Tel: 13 13 13 (Australia)
Tel: 0845 774 7767 (UK)
Tel: 1 800 227 4500 (US)
www.qantas.com.au
United Airlines:
Tel: 13 17 77 (Australia)
Tel: 0845 844 4777 (UK)
Tel: 1 800 538 2929 (US)
www.unitedairlines.com.au
Singapore Airlines:
Tel: 13 10 11 (Australia)
Tel: 02089 616 993 (UK)
Tel: 1 800 742 3333 (US)
www.singaporeair.com.au

Apart from QANTAS, there are three "no-frills" carriers: Jetstar, Virgin Australia and Tiger Airways. They link the southern capitals with a number of points in Queensland, including Brisbane, the Gold Coast, Cairns, the Sunshine Coast, the Fraser Coast, Proserpine, Rockhampton, Mackay, Hamilton Island and Townsville. The regional airline, QANTASLink, also transports passengers from other states to some of Queensland's destinations. It links Newcastle with Townsville, and Alice Springs with Cairns, for instance.

By Sea

Sydney is generally the destination point for cruise liners travelling to Australia, but the following companies include Brisbane and Cairns and sometimes Port Douglas as a port of call on at least some of their itineraries.

Carnival Australia handles bookings for many of the cruise liners visiting Australia. Tel: 02-8424 8800 (in Australia); www.carnivalaustralia.com
Cunard Line, tel: 0845 071 0300 (UK); www.cunard.com
P&O, tel: 0845 355 5333 (UK); www.pocruises.com
Princess Cruises, tel: 1800-PRINCESS (US); www.princess.com

By Train

Countrylink has a daily XPT service between Sydney and Brisbane. The train leaves Sydney in the afternoon and travels overnight; the return trip is during the day. The trip takes about 14 hours.

There is another daily service that involves travel by the XPT to Casino in northern New South Wales and then coach travel for the remainder of the journey to Brisbane, stopping at Surfers Paradise along the way. Travel from Brisbane is during the day, while the return leg from Sydney is overnight.

Book tickets online at www.countrylink.info or tel: 132-232.

By Road

People arriving in Queensland by road will generally be travelling on one of the highways from New South Wales. The Pacific Highway is the closest to the coast and usually the fastest way to do the 970km (603-mile) trip from Sydney.

Australia's major coach company, Greyhound Australia, travels both the Pacific Highway and inland along the New England Highway from Sydney to Brisbane.

Travellers can also take a Greyhound coach from Tennant Creek in the Northern Territory to Townsville via Mount Isa. But be prepared for a long haul.

Greyhound Australia, tel: 131-499 or 4690 9950; www.greyhound.com.au

GETTING AROUND

By Air

Packed as it is with well-known attractions, it is easy to underestimate the distances in Queensland. To put it in perspective, this is a state six times the size of the United Kingdom and twice the size of Texas in the United States. The distance from Brisbane to Cairns is 1,807km (1,120 miles).

To reduce the time spent on the road, some travellers choose to treat the state as a series of short hops on a plane. Australia's three major domestic carriers are the best bet for people wanting to travel between the various destinations on the Queensland coast or to Hamilton Island. But to get any further north than Cairns, to any other islands, or to inland and Outback Queensland requires a ticket with one of the regional carriers.

The largest regional carrier in Queensland, indeed Australia, is **QantasLink**. Other regional airlines in Queensland include **Hinterland Aviation Airlines**, which flies daily between Cairns and Cooktown, except Sunday, and between Cairns and Coen on Monday, Wednesday and Friday. **Skytrans Airlines** has scheduled flights from Cairns to a range of locations further north, including Normanton, Karumba, Morningston Island, Mount Isa, Lockhardt River, Aurukun and Coen. Scheduled flights from Brisbane go to Toowoomba St George, Cunnamulla and Thargomindah.

There are a variety of airlines and charter operations servicing the islands off Queensland's coast. **Australian Helicopters** makes daily flights on demand from Gladstone, six hours north of Brisbane, to Heron Island, during daylight hours. It also makes the short trip from Mackay to Brampton Island daily on demand. Tel: 4978 1177.

An air charter service run by **Australasian Jet** flies to Brampton Island from Mackay. **Air Whitsunday** uses seaplanes to tour the Whitsunday Islands, and transfer guests to Hayman Island. It is possible to book a charter flight to unscheduled destinations with most of the regional carriers.

Air Whitsunday, tel: 4946 9111; www.airwhitsunday.com.au
Australasian Jet, tel: 1300-130

001 or 4953 3261
Australian Helicopters, tel: 4978 1177; www.ausheli.com
Hinterland Aviation, tel: 4040 1333; www.hinterlandaviation.com.au
Jetstar, tel: 131-538 or 03-8341 4901; www.jetstar.com.au
QANTAS/QANTASLink, tel: 131-131; www.qantas.com.au
Skytrans Airlines, tel: 1300-759 872 (in Australia); www.skytrans.com.au
Tiger Airways, tel: 03-9999 2888; www.tigerairways.com
Virgin Australia, tel: 136-789 or 3295 2296; www.virginaustralia.com

From the Airport

Brisbane International Airport is about 16km (9.6 miles), or a 20-minute drive, from the city centre. The domestic airport is 2km (1.2 miles) further out. The **Airtrain** service leaves the international and domestic terminals every 15 minutes in peak times and can deliver new arrivals to the city's Central Train Station, Roma Street, or a number of other destinations in about 20 minutes. Tel: 1800 119 091 or 3216 3308, www.airtrain.com.au.

An alternative for travel to the centre of Brisbane is the airport bus service run by **Coachtrans**. It meets all major flights seven days a week and ferries arrivals to the Brisbane Transit Centre at Roma Street and all central business district (CBD) hotels. The one-way fare to the Brisbane Transit Centre is A$9 per person, and to any hotel door A$11 per person. Tel: 5556 9888; www.coachtrans.com.au.

Taxis can be found outside the arrivals hall on Level 2 and will cost about A$45 for a trip to the centre of town.

People wanting to bypass Brisbane completely can travel easily from the airport the 80km (50 miles) south to the Gold Coast or 178km (107 miles) north to Noosa and the Sunshine Coast. The Airtrain runs twice-hourly express services to the Gold Coast. The journey takes about 90 minutes, and trains arrive at Nerang Station in the Gold Coast hinterland. From there it is a 15–20 minute drive to the towers of tourist accommodation that line the Gold Coast's beaches. To smooth the trip it is possible to book a 24-hour "door-to-door" service where arrivals are met at Brisbane airport by porters who assist them with getting their luggage to the station. When the train arrives at the Gold Coast they are picked up in a chauffeur-driven vehicle and transferred to their accommodation. The cost of the service, which includes the train trip, is A$50 for adults and A$25 for children one-way or A$90 for adults and A$50 for children return. The cost is reduced if there is more than one person travelling.

Coachtrans runs from the airport to the Gold Coast via the Gateway Bridge. It drops off passengers at all hotels from Sanctuary Cove to Coolangatta. Tel: 5556 9888; www.coachtrans.com.au.

To get from Brisbane Airport to the Sunshine Coast there is an hourly bus service operated by Sun-air. Buses run 5.50am– 10pm daily, and the cost is about A$51 for adults and A$34 for children one-way door-to-door, or A$35–40 for adults and A$24–27 for children to be dropped off at one of its transit stops on the Sunshine Coast, including Noosa, Noosa Heads and Coolum. Transfers can also

be arranged for people arriving outside its scheduled hours. Tel: 5477 0888; www.sunair.com.au.

The Gold Coast Airport is on the Gold Coast Highway at Bilinga, on the southern end of the Gold Coast. From there it is a five-minute drive to Coolangatta, 15 minutes to Broadbeach and 25 minutes to Surfers Paradise. If keeping costs low is important, there is a free Airport Link shuttle bus out to the Gold Coast Highway, where travellers can pick up public transport.

The **Gold Coast Tourist Shuttle** provides a door-to-door service to accommodation on the Gold Coast, charging A$19 for adults and A$10 for children one-way or A$35 and A$18 respectively for return tickets. Tel: 5574 5111 or 1300-655 655 (in Australia); www.gcshuttle.com.au.

Taxis line up at a rank outside the terminal and a trip to Coolangatta will cost about A$15, while Broadbeach will be about A$45 and Surfers Paradise A$55.

In Cairns there are two companies offering transfers from the airport. **Coral Sea Coaches** runs a shuttle bus to hotels and the city centre, as well as the northern beaches and Palm Cove. Tickets to the city centre cost A$9 per person, and children under two are free. Tel: 0417 642 943; www.coralseacoaches.com.

Sun Palm Express Coaches drops off in the centre of town and goes further afield, taking passengers to the northern beaches, Palm Cove, Port Douglas and Cape Tribulation. Prices range from A$18 for adults and A$9 for children to the northern beaches up to A$78 for adults and A$39 for children for the twice-daily trip to Cape Tribulation. Tel: 4087 2900; www.sunpalmtransport.com.

Taxis and limousines are available at the airport. The average taxi fare into the centre of Cairns is about A$27.

Public Transport in Brisbane

Public transport in southeast Queensland is divided into 23 zones, but the integrated Translink (www.translink.com.au) ticketing system makes it possible to travel on Brisbane's buses, trains and ferries from Noosa to Coolangatta on a single gocard ticket. You need to purchase the card (A$5), and then add credit. The gocard is cheaper than buying the equivalent paper ticket and provides discounts during off-peak travel.

There are various ways to explore Brisbane on the water. The inner-city ferry runs from Sydney Street Wharf to North Quay, stopping at places such as South Bank and Eagle Street Pier from 6am to midnight. There are four cross-river ferry services, running between Tenerife and Bulimba, between Holman Street and Thornton Street, between Norman Park and New Farm Park, and between Sydney Street and North Quay. They run about every 10 minutes 5.30am–11.30pm.

The Citycat runs from Bretts Wharf at Hamilton to the University of Queensland and stops at places such as New Farm Park, South Bank Parklands and West End. The full trip takes about an hour, and Citycats run 6am–11.30pm daily.

Paper tickets for the ferries may be purchased on board. Tickets and gocards can be pur-

BELOW: Queensland taxi cab.

chased from the Ferry Information Centre at the Riverside Ferry Terminal or from about 300 sellers throughout Brisbane. All ferries operate in zones one and two of Brisbane, and the maximum paper ticket price is A$4.50 for adults; for a gocard the price is A$3.05.

Brisbane's buses operate from the city, ferry wharves and railway stations. The main bus termini are in Adelaide and Queen Streets. **The Loop** is a free red-bus service that circles Brisbane's CBD, stopping at Central Station, Queen Street Mall, the Botanic Gardens, Riverside Centre and King George Square.

There is also a Brisbane City Council-operated **City Sights** tour. It takes in the CBD, South Bank, Chinatown, Spring Hill and Milton. Tickets can only be bought on the bus, and are A$35 for adults and A$20 for concessions.

Brisbane's **Citytrain** network extends from the centre of the capital city south to Beenleigh and Robina on the Gold Coast, and north to Caboolture and Gympie, east to Cleveland and west to Ipswich and Rosewood. To get to areas not serviced by the rail network there are integrated rail and bus options operating between Nerang and Surfers Paradise, linking Broadbeach and Noosa Heads. If travelling after dark, embark and alight at the areas marked with blue-and-white stripes on the platform. These areas have enhanced lighting, an emergency phone and video-camera surveillance. **Transinfo**, tel: 131-230.

Train

For those wanting to go further afield, the **Queensland Rail** network (tel: 131-617; www.queenslandrail.com.au) fans out across the state to the dry interior and northward to Cairns, offering travellers an alternative to hours of driving or sitting on coaches. Several of the long-distance trains have a vehicle car, for people wanting to

ABOVE: using the railway.

combine a driving holiday with train travel. The **Tilt Train** is the fastest way to travel the rails in Queensland. It does a 25-hour sprint from Brisbane to Cairns twice a week, leaving town on Mondays and Fridays at 6.25pm and beginning the return leg on Sundays and Wednesdays at 9.15am.

All passengers travel business class, and if the scenery isn't enough to keep boredom at bay, there's always the personal entertainment system in the back of every seat.

The Tilt Train travels more frequently between Brisbane and Rockhampton, making the nine-hour journey a dozen times a week. On this service passengers have a choice of travelling business or economy class. Fares vary depending on the time of year and whether the passenger is entitled to any concessions, but an economy ticket to Rockhampton will cost about A$120 (business class A$170), and a business class ticket to Cairns costs A$345.

The Sunlander is a slower train travelling the coastal route from Brisbane. On Sundays it leaves Brisbane at 9am, arriving in Cairns at 4.15pm the following day. On Tuesdays and Thursdays it leaves Brisbane at 1.25pm, arriving in Cairns at 7.15pm the following day. The return leg leaves Cairns on Tuesdays, Thursdays and Saturdays at 9.15am and arrives in Brisbane at 3.55pm on the following day.

Passengers travelling on The Sunlander to Cairns have a choice of making the 31-hour journey in sitting class, an economy-class berth, a first-class berth and the de luxe class known as Queenslander class. The Queenslander class includes accommodation in a twin-berth sleeping cabin and all meals, which are prepared by a chef and served in an exclusive restaurant car. Tickets range in price from around A$241 for sitting class to A$820 for Queenslander class.

Queenslander class is not available on the trips between Brisbane and Townsville.

Three trains make regular journeys into the Queensland Outback. The **Spirit of the Outback** travels the 1,300km (808 miles) between Brisbane and Longreach, following the east coast from Brisbane to Rockhampton and then heading west through Blackwater, Emerald and Barcaldine to Longreach. Trains depart Brisbane twice a week, on Tuesdays and Saturdays, and Longreach on Mondays and Thursdays, and the journey takes about 24 hours. There are three options for travel: sitting class, economy and first class, with tickets ranging from around A$210 to A$410.

To see the southwest corner of the state, take **The Westlander**. It leaves Brisbane, crosses the Great Dividing Range and travels to Charleville on Tuesdays and Thursday evenings, making the return leg on Wednesdays and Friday evenings. The trip takes about 17 hours and can be made in first-class or economy-class sleeping compartments or in seated accommodation. Full-fare adults pay about A$310 for a first-class berth, A$211 for an economy berth and A$145 for a seat.

The Inlander makes the 977km (607-mile) trip from Townsville to the mining town of Mount Isa twice a week, leaving Townsville on Sundays and Thursday afternoons and Mount Isa on Mondays and Friday afternoons.

ABOVE: travel in style.

Passengers have a choice of first-class and economy berths as well as sitting class. Fares range from about A$175 to A$358.

There are several shorter train trips that can be a wonderful way to see some of the state's sights in a day. The **Kuranda Scenic Railway** travels from Cairns through rainforest and past waterfalls to the pretty village of Kuranda in under two hours. The train departs twice daily, leaving Cairns at 8.30am and 9.30am and returning at 3.55pm and 5.25pm. Fares are A$47 for adults and A$24 for children.

The "old tin hare" is the nickname for **The Gulflander**, the train that runs from Normanton to Croydon in Gulf Country, in the north of the state *(see also page 210)*. It runs once a week, leaving Normanton at 8.30am on Wednesdays to arrive in Croydon at 1pm. The return trip is made on Thursdays at 8.30am. The one-way cost is A$65 for adults and A$33 for children.

The tongue-twisting **Savannahlander** is a 1960s train that travels at a maximum of 50kph (30mph) for its journey from Cairns up the Kuranda railway and through Savannah country to the Outback town of Forsayth. The journey leaves Cairns on Wednesdays at 6.30am and arrives in Forsayth on Thursdays at 5.45pm. The return trip is made on Fridays at 8.45am.

For tickets on the Savannahlander contact **QR Travel Centre Cairns** at the railway station in Bunda Street, tel: 4036 9250.

Boat

No visit to Queensland is complete without some time spent on at least one of its islands. In some cases it is possible to fly by seaplane or helicopter to the island, but for a more run-of-the-mill arrival, and for those with vehicles, the alternative is using one of the many ferry services. In the south of the state, **Moreton Island** and **North Stradbroke Island** are both pleasant day trips from Brisbane, and they are serviced by a number of daily vehicle- and passenger-ferry services. The Moreton Island ferries run from Eagle Farm, Lytton and Scarborough on the mainland, while the North Stradbroke ferries run from Cleveland.

To get to the sand dunes of Fraser Island there are several vehicle ferries, known as barges, operating from Rainbow Beach and Hervey Bay on the mainland to various points on the island.

With the start of the Great Barrier Reef, at Lady Elliot Island, 80km (50 miles) northeast of Bundaberg, the transport arrangements become more complicated. Some resort islands, such as Heron Island, add the cost of a high-speed catamaran in the overall charge to guests, while others, such as the popular Great Keppel and Green islands, are serviced by a multitude of ferry and tour operators based in Rosslyn Bay and Cairns respectively.

Boats to the major islands in the Whitsundays group – such as Hook, Daydream, South Molle – leave from Able Point Marina, 1 km (⅔ mile) west of Airlie Beach, or Shute Harbour, about 8 km (5 miles) east. The alternative is to travel from one of the many boats leaving Hamilton Island, an option that will suit people who fly in from other parts of Australia or Queensland.

To get from Townsville to Magnetic Island, there are frequent high-speed catamarans that take about 25 minutes to make the journey. For people who have a

hankering to see the island at the tip of Cape York, Thursday Island, there is a regular ferry service provided by Peddells Thursday Island Tour.

Here are some of the operators providing access to Queensland's islands.

Moreton Island and North Stradbroke Island

MI Cat, tel: 3909 3333; www.moretonislandadventures.com.au
Stradbroke Ferries, tel: 3488 5300; www.stradbrokeferries.com.au
Big Red Cat, tel: 3488 9777; www.bigredcat.com.au
Stradbroke Flyer, tel: 3286 1964; www.flyer.com.au

Fraser Island

Fraser Island Vehicle Barge, tel: 4120 3333 or 1800-072 555 (in Australia); www.kingfisherbay.com

Whitsunday Islands

Fantasea Cruises, tel: 4946 5455; www.fantasea.com.au

Magnetic Island

Sealink, tel: 4726 0800; www.sealinkqld.com.au

Thursday Island

Peddells Thursday Island Tours, tel: 4069 1551; www.peddellsferry.com.au
McDonald Charter Boats, tel: 4069 2246; operates between Thursday Island and Horn Island.

Cruising

Cruising is a popular way to see the Whitsunday Islands. Operators provide plenty of options, including crewed sailing boats, tours and the chance to skipper a boat yourself. Bare-boating (skippering yourself) does not require a special licence, and the operator will provide any introductory training needed. Vessels for hire include yachts, catamarans, motor cruisers and powerboats, with operators based at Airlie Beach, Hamilton Island and Shute Harbour.

Note that skippers with a boating licence must abide by the same drink-driving rules as apply to the road; their blood alcohol level must not exceed 0.05 per cent. Weather forecasts should be obtained, even for a short trip, by calling one of the following numbers: tel: 1300-360 426 (all of Queensland); 1300-360 427 (marine warnings); 1300-360 428 (southeast Queensland).

For more information on cruising, see page 271.

Coach

People without their own wheels will have no trouble getting to the major tourist destinations in Queensland by coach. **Greyhound Australia** travels the coastal route from Surfers Paradise to Cairns. Inland, it's possible to take one of its coaches west to Mount Isa and Camooweal, near the Northern Territory border. Coaches leave Brisbane for Rockhampton, Toowoomba, Long-reach, Mount Isa and Cairns.

For people planning to travel by coach to other parts of Australia, there is a range of money-saving passes to reduce travel costs. The Aussie Explorer Pass operates as a series of pre-set itineraries and is valid for travel for a fixed number of days. For instance, there's a pass that begins in Brisbane and allows travel up the coast to Cairns. It is valid for 183 days and is good for about 2,000km (1,250 miles). Backtracking is not allowed on concession passes.

A **Day Pass** is for travel on consecutive days and is available in three-, five-, seven-, 10-, 20- and 30-day options. Backtracking is allowed, but kilometres are limited.

For the greatest freedom of travel there is an **Aussie Kilometre Pass**, where a bank of km is purchased. A 10 percent discount is available on Greyhound passes for holders of various cards and memberships, including Youth Hostel Association or Hostelling International, Nomads and ISIC.

To travel beyond Cairns by coach, **Coral Reef Coaches** does a twice-daily run between Cairns and Cape Tribulation, dropping off and picking up at the Daintree, Mossman and Port Douglas.

There are plenty of coach companies running half- and one-day tours to various points of interest.

Greyhound Australia, tel: 1300-473-946; www.greyhound.com.au

Coral Reef Coaches, tel: 4098 2800; www.coralreefcoaches.com.au

Car

Visiting overseas drivers do not need a Queensland driver's licence or an International Driving Permit, provided they have an up-to-date driving licence from their home country. If the licence is not in English, it is a good idea to carry a translation.

Most of Queensland's road rules are based upon international rules, and it is simply a matter of following the signs, sticking to specified speed limits and so on. But there are a few points that drivers should be aware of:

• Australians drive on the left-hand side of the road.
• Drivers must give way to the right, unless otherwise indicated, to pedestrians (keep an eye out for zebra crossings), and to all emergency vehicles.
• The speed limit in most built-up city and suburban areas is **60kph (37mph)**, unless otherwise indicated.
• It is the responsibility of the driver to ensure restraints (including for children and babies under 12 months old) are used by passengers at all time.
• There is a 0.05 percent blood alcohol limit for drivers, which is widely enforced by the use of random breath tests carried out by the police.
• Use of hand-held mobile phones is not permitted while driving.

For safety issues, see page 250.

Vehicle Hire

Car-rental companies have offices in Brisbane, including at the airport, as well as in major tourist centres, the Gold Coast, Noosa, Cairns and Townsville. It is also possible to hire campervans, 4WD vehicles and motorbikes. If you have not already organised car hire as part of a package, you should shop around for the best deal: the smaller, independent operators tend to be cheaper.

Don't forget insurance. Many companies have an excess charge of A$800–1,500, which means that you pay that amount in the case of an accident. It is wise to pay a little extra per day to reduce the figure. When you are

BELOW: many forms of transport are available in Queensland.

RULES OF THE ROAD

Driving in Queensland can involve negotiating anything from roads that are under water during the wet season to kangaroos appearing out of nowhere. To have a problem-free holiday it is important to bear in mind the following suggestions:

• Seek local advice about road conditions, particularly in the wet season from October to April. Contact the RACQ (see below) for information prior to travelling.

• Distances between towns can be great in Queensland; always carry a spare tyre, other basic spare parts, tools, water (around 20 litres/40 pints per person) and fuel. Don't overload the vehicle and don't carry spare fuel inside the vehicle.

• Use a 4WD on unsealed roads and in remote areas, and carry communication equipment other than a mobile phone, such as a radio, a satellite phone or an emergency positioning beacon.

• Before embarking on long journeys into the Outback, you should report to the police before you leave and again when you arrive at the other end.

• Where possible, travel with other vehicles to remote locations.

• If a road is covered in water, don't cross unless you know other vehicles have done so. Use ferry crossings instead if possible. If you have to cross, ensure the road surface is firm and stay in the middle of the road.

• Allow plenty of room before overtaking road trains, and be prepared for the "windrush", which can pull smaller vehicles towards the road train.

• Animals and livestock can present a serious danger, particularly at sunrise, sunset and at night. Try to avoid driving at these times.

• Drive with your headlights on low beam during the day, as dusty conditions can make it difficult to see other vehicles on the road.

• If you run into trouble in the Outback, do not leave your vehicle. It will provide protection from the heat, and is easier to spot than an individual.

• Some areas of Outback Queensland may require permits to access Aboriginal land, and there may be restrictions on carrying alcohol into these areas.

getting a quote, ask for the full amount, including insurance and charges for items such as baby restraints. Many car-hire companies do not insure normal vehicles for off-road travel, which means that the driver is liable.

For disabled drivers, all the major hire companies have a small number of cars with hand controls. Contact them well in advance to book.

Major car-hire companies

Avis, tel: 136-333; www.avis.com.au
Budget, tel: 1300-362 848 (toll-free); www.budget.com.au
Thrifty, tel: 5570 9999 or 1300-139 009 (toll-free); www.rentthrifty.com

Campervan hire companiess

Apollo, tel: 3265 9200 or 1800-777 779 (toll-free); www.apollo camper.com
Britz, tel: 1800-331 454 (toll-free); www.britz.com
KEA Campers, tel: 1800 252 555; www.keacampers.com

For information on travel by campervan or caravan contact:
Caravaning Queensland, tel: 3862 1833; www.caravanqld.com.au
Campervan and Motorhome Club of Australia, tel: 02-4978 8788; www.cmca.net.au

Four-wheel-drive-hire companies

Britz, tel: 4032 2611 (Cairns); www.britz.com
Meteor Car and Truck Rentals, tel: 4035 2505; 1300-306 809 (toll-free); www.1300meteor.com.au

Breakdown Services

The RACQ (Royal Automobile Club of Queensland) provides roadside service to members, and has reciprocal arrangements with motoring organisations overseas. Most car-hire outlets arrange their own roadside service, but the RACQ is a good point of contact for all sorts of motoring advice.

It provides up-to-date information on road conditions on its website www.racq.com.au. For membership, insurance and emergencies, tel: 131-905; for road travel conditions (24-hour), tel: 1300-130 595. For 24-hour roadside assistance, tel: 131-111.

The Queensland Department of Transport and Main Roads is another useful source of information, including the free map, Guide to Queensland Roads, tel: 3834 2011; www.tmr.qld.gov.au.

BELOW: a Queensland road sign.

A CCOMMODATION

WHERE TO STAY

Overview

Queensland has a whole range of options when it comes to finding somewhere to stay. Generally speaking, the standard of accommodation is high. At the top of the pile are the super-luxury 5-star establishments, often on secluded tropical islands, such as Lizard and Hayman, luring the very wealthy. The ever-aspiring Gold Coast goes one star better and boasts the state's first "6-star" hotel, Palazzo Versace. Presumably on the princess-and-the-pea principle, guests sensitive enough to be able to discern the difference can choose between multiple variants of pillow.

For everyone else there's an enormous choice of conventionally starred hotels and – mainly in the beach resorts – holiday apartment blocks. Many of the latter are only let out in week-long chunks, but can be great value for families. Boutique hotels are making inroads; motels are plentiful and are often the only option in the Outback; plenty of pubs provide rooms of varying standards or have motel units, usually in a separate adjunct.

Tea- and coffee-making equipment and supplies are usually provided in accommodation of all levels. Usually it's in the bed-room; if not, try the communal room(s).

Bed-and-breakfast establishments are often found in old heritage buildings. Many of these reflect the British model, where there will be a few bedrooms within a largish house and breakfast is provided in a communal dining room. However, the term "bed and breakfast" is also applied when a few provisions are left in a guest room along with a kettle and a toaster, and the guest does the work. An interesting variation on the bed-and-breakfast option is the farmstay. Farmstay accommodation can include anything from a small dairy farm to a vast grain, cattle and sheep operation in the Outback. A good resource is Bed and Breakfast and Farmstay Australia (www.australianbedandbreakfast.com.au).

Budget travellers will find a thriving backpacker scene. Queensland has always been popular with students, who often combine surfing and sightseeing with a bit of work. In the fruit-picking season, many hostels double as employment exchanges. Farmers know that's where they will find cheap, hard workers. At these times hostels can get very busy, and it becomes even more advisable than usual to book ahead.

Privately run camping grounds are generally well maintained and spacious and, almost without exception, will have cabins to rent. National Park campsites, on the other hand, require the camper to be totally self-sufficient and are extremely popular during holiday periods, when booking is essential.

One interesting phenomenon, particularly in the bush, is the donga. It's a prefab hut with spartan furnishing – usually a bed, table and chair. Designed as temporary "workers"accommodation, they are primitive, though often include basic air-conditioning.

Visitor Information Centres can offer advice on accommodation, and some of them will book on your behalf. Many hotels offer lower rates outside peak seasons (which vary and relate to disparate factors such as school holidays). Watch out for "schoolies' week" in November, when kids who've finished their exams take over whole towns and discover that if you drink a lot, you fall over (see www.schoolies.org.au).

There are a number of clearing houses selling unsold rooms at hefty discounts, especially in the cities and main tourist centres. Check out:
www.flightcentre.com.au
www.lastminute.com.au
www.quickbeds.com.au
www.wotif.com

BRISBANE

The City

Acacia Inner City Inn
413 Upper Edward Street
Tel: 3832 1663
www.acaciainn.com
Friendly inner-city facility with off-street parking, a range of rooms and a sociable ambience. Tariff includes continental breakfast. $$

Annie's Shandon Inn
405 upper Edward Street
Tel: 3831 8684
www.babs.com.au/annies/
Annie's is a popular, budget-minded bed and breakfast (continental breakfast included in tariff) with a guest kitchen and a central location. $$

Astor Metropole
193 Wickham Terrace
Tel: 3144 4000
www.astorhotel.com.au
Right by the windmill, this is a good-value, mid-scale hotel with swimming pool, restaurant and secret covered parking. $$

Banana Benders
118 Petrie Terrace
Tel: 3367 1157
www.bananabenders.com.au
Right in the middle of town, with a range of accommodation styles. Airport shuttle, internet access and backpacker party nights. $

Brisbane Hilton
190 Elizabeth Street
Tel: 3234 2000
www.hilton.com
The levels of luxury you would expect from a five-star hotel and a plum city-centre location as well. $$$$

Central Dockside Apartments
44 Ferry Street, Kangaroo Point
Tel: 3891 6644
www.centraldockside.com.au
Each spacious apartment has a fully equipped kitchen and a balcony with a sweeping view. It's across the river from the city centre, but there's a ferry at the bottom of the garden. Can be very economical for a group or family. $$$

The Chifley at Lennons
66 Queen Street
Tel: 3222 3222
www.chifleyhotels.com.au
A 20-storey tower in the city's heart, opposite Myers on the Mall; 152 units plus suites, non-smoking floors. Good value. $$$

The Marque Brisbane
103 George Street
Tel: 3221 6044
www.marquehotels.com
Five minutes' walk to the city, casino or government district. Heated outdoor pool and gymnasium. The popular spa rooms overlook the river and South Bank. $$$

Palace Backpackers
Corner Ann and Edward streets
Tel: 3211 2433
www.palacebackpackers.com.au
Opposite Central Railway Station. Basic lodgings close to cheap eateries. Plenty of noisy entertainment in the bar, which stays open late. Good-value meals and rooftop sundeck. $

Royal on the Park
Corner Alice and Albert streets
Tel: 3221 3411
www.royalonthepark.com.au
Pleasant 4-5-star, city-centre hotel in a lovely setting opposite the City Botanic Gardens. $$$$

Rydges South Bank
9 Glenelg Street
Tel: 3364 0800
www.rydges.com
Really handy for all the attractions of the South Bank. Throw in some great views of the city to make this a sound choice if you have the budget. $$$$

The Sebel King George Square
Corner Ann and Roma streets
Tel: 3229 9111
www.mirvachotels.com
Right opposite King George Square, close to the river and central shopping district, this recently refurbished hotel is good value. $$$

Stamford Plaza
Corner Margaret and Edward streets
Tel: 3221 1999
www.stamford.com.au
The Stamford Plaza is a classy heritage hotel with good restaurants; all of its rooms have river views, and it is close to the city's main attractions. $$$$

Treasury Casino & Hotel
130 William Street
Tel: 3306 8888
www.treasurybrisbane.com.au
Makes the most of the features of the old treasury building and has a handy on-site casino. $$$$

The Suburbs

City Backpackers
380 Upper Roma Street
Tel: 3211 3221
www.citybackpackers.com
Bright and breezy operation that even runs its own pub and promises the best nightlife in the city. This doesn't

necessarily make it the most restful retreat. $

Comfort Inn & Suites Northgate Airport
186 Toombul Road, Northgate
Tel: 3256 7222
www.northgatemotel.com.au
The closest motel to the airport has good facilities. Recommended if you're hiring a car because you're far from city traffic and parking problems. $$

Kingsford Riverside Inn
114 Kingford Smith Drive, Hamilton
Tel: 1800 777590
budgetaccommodation.com.au
Bed and breakfast close to ferry and bus stops, and to the popular "Brekkie Creek" pub. Convenient for the airport. $$

Thornbury House Bed & Breakfast
1 Thornbury Street, Spring Hill
Tel: 3839 5334
www.onethornbury.com
Breathe in a bit of history in this discerningly decorated 1886 Queenslander in characterful Spring Hill. $$$

GOLD COAST

Main Beach and Southport

Harbour Side Resort
132 Marine Parade, Southport
Tel: 5591 6666
www.harboursideresort.com.au
Directly opposite the Gold Coast Broadwater, this unpretentious resort has motel-style rooms and one- or two-bedroom apartments with kitchens. Ideal for families. **$$$**

Palazzo Versace
Sea World Drive, Main Beach
Tel: 5509 8000
www.palazzoversace.com.au
Supposedly a 6-star hotel, the Versace has the style and extrava gance associated with the brand. If that's to your taste, immaculate service and standards add up to the ultimate luxury hotel. **$$$$**

Sheraton Mirage
Sea World Drive, Main Beach
Tel: 5591 1488
www.starwoodhotels.com
Across the road from the Versace and on the seaward side, the Mirage claims a mere 5 stars. All the space, pools and facilities you could possibly want, including highly rated restaurants. **$$$$**

Surfers Paradise

Broadbeach Savannah Hotel & Resort
46 Surf Parade,
Broadbeach
Tel: 5504 4444
www.savannahbroadbeach.com.au
Chic one- and two-bedroom apartments in the heart of cosmopolitan Broadbeach. **$$$**

Chateau Beachside Resort
Corner Esplanade and Elkhorn Avenue.
Tel: 5538 1022
www.chateaubeachside.com.au
Right on the beach and as good a base as any, with sizeable swimming pool and tennis court. Cheap buffet breakfasts in the café. **$$$**

Gold Coast International Backpackers Resort
28 Hamilton Avenue
Tel: 5592 5888
goldcoastbackpackers.com.au
One of the new breed of backpacker accommodation that are more like a resort, with private rooms and dorms, and a sociable atmosphere. **$**

Hotel Grand Chancellort
Corner Surfers Paradise Boulevard and Hanlan Street

Tel: 5579 3499
www.grandchancellorhotels.com
High-rise pampering just a block back from the beach, with balcony views down the coast. Ask for a room from the 20th floor upwards. **$$$**

Islander Resort Hotel
Corner Beach Road and Gold Coast Highway.
Tel: 5538 8000
www.islander.com.au
One of many hotels that are set slightly back from the beach and therefore cheaper than their high-profile neighbours. **$$**

Mermaid Beachside Bed and Breakfast
115 Seagull Avenue,
Mermaid Beach
Tel: 5572 9530
www.goldcoastbedandbreakfast.com
A friendly bed and breakfast right on the beach, with accommodation ranging from single rooms with shared bathroom to a three-bedroom luxury unit. **$$$**

Pelican Cove
Corner Back and Burrows streets, Biggera Waters.
Tel: 5537 7001
www.pelicancove.com.au
Two- and three-bedroom self-contained units right on the waterfront, 10 minutes from Wet'n'Wild and Dreamworld. **$$**

Quality Hotel Mermaid Waters
Corner Markeri and Sunshine boulevards, Mermaid Waters
Tel: 5572 2500
www.mermaidwatershotel.com.au
More than 100 rooms, some in a quiet area near casino and Pacific Fair shopping centre. A 20-minute scenic walk

to the beach. Courtesy bus to Surfers Paradise daily. **$$$**

Burleigh Heads

Aussie Resort
1917 Gold Coast Highway
Tel: 5576 2877
www.aussieresort.com.au
Straightforward apart ment accommodation with an Australia-shaped pool for the keen surfer. **$$**

Hillhaven Holiday Apartments
2 Goodwin Terrace
Tel: 5535 1055
www.hillhaven.com.au
Self-contained two- and three-bedroom, beautifully furnished holiday apartments, adjoining Burleigh Head National Park. All have ocean views from balconies. **$$$**

Outrigger Resort Gold Coast
2007 Gold Coast Highway
Tel: 5535 1111
www.outriggerresort.com.au
Balconies to all rooms, covered parking and a convenient location make this resort worth considering. **$$$**

Coolangatta

Beachcomber International Resort
122 Griffith Street
Tel: 5599 7599

BELOW: the grand Palazzo Versace.

www.beachcomberinternationalresort.com.au
High-rise block of apartments with every mod con you could want. **$$$**
Coolangatta Ocean View Motel
Corner Clark Street and Marine Parade, Greenmount
Tel: 5536 3722
www.coolangattaoceanviewmotel.com.au

Looks like an old-fashioned traditional 1960s motel next to all the glossy high-rises, but service is impeccable and it's great value. **$$**
Oaks Calypso Plaza Resort
99 Griffith Street
Tel: 5599 0000
www.oakshotelsresorts.com
Attractive, low-rise hotel

far from the high-rise strip, near the surf beach, with tropical swimming lagoon and water slide. Some special deals. **$$$**

South Stradbroke Island

Couran Point Island Beach Resort
Tel: 5501 3555

www.couranpoint.com.au
Standard and kitchenette rooms are available at this appealing island resort, which is also popular with day-trippers. Here, you can cycle from one beach to another, watch the diverse wildlife in the area and generally spoil yourself. **$$$**

DARLING DOWNS

Goondiwindi

MacIntyre Motor Inn
15 McLean Street
Tel: 4671 2447
www.macintyremotel.com.au
Tidy modern motel with pool and spa that does all that could be asked of it. **$$**
O'Shea's Royal Hotel/ Motel
48 Marshall Street
Tel: 4671 1877
www.osheasroyalhotel.com.au
Reasonable pub and motel accommodation right on the main drag. **$$**

Ipswich

Ipswich City Motel
86 Warwick Road
tel: 3281 2633
www.ipswichcitymotel.com.au
A swimming pool, play area and barbecue facilities make this a popular place for families. **$$**
Ipswich Heritage Motor Inn
51 Warwick Road
Tel: 3202 3111
www.ipswichheritage.bestwestern.com.au
Excellent motel with spotless rooms, a pool, and a restaurant where you may find the owner playing requests on the piano. **$$**

Kingaroy

Burke and Wills Motor Inn
95 Kingaroy Street
Tel: 4162 2933
www.burkeandwills.com.au
A good motel made better by the presence of a notable restaurant. **$$**
Taabinga Homestead
7 Old Taabing Road, Haly Creek.
Tel: 4164 5531
www.taabingahomestead.com
This lovingly maintained 1840s homestead, not far from Kingaroy, functions both as a working farm and bed-and-breakfast facility. **$**

Miles

Miles Outback Motel
11 Murilla Street
Tel: 4627 2100
www.milesoutbackmotel.com.au
Modern motel with all the usual facilities as well as lock-up garages. **$$**
Possum Park
36865 Leichhardt Highway
Tel: 4627 1651
www.possumpark.com.au
Remarkable old military camp, 20km north of Miles. Old bunkers, Nissen huts and railway carriages have been converted into mid-range accommodation. **$**

Roma

Overlander Homestead Motel
Warrego Highway
Tel: 4622 3555
www.overlandermotel.com.au
An ersatz colonial inn, it scores well for facilities and service. **$$**
Villa Holiday Park
Northern Road
Tel: 4622 1309
www.villaholidaypark.com.au
Just out of town, it has the standard mix of tent and van sites as well as cabins with AC. **$**

Stanthorpe

Stannum Lodge Motor Inn
12 Wallangarra Road
Tel: 4681 2000
www.stannumlodge.com.au
A swimming pool is among the many facilities at this sound option, from which you can organise winery tours. **$$**
The Vines
2 Wallangarra Road
Tel: 4681 3844
www.thevinesmotel.com.au
There are the standard motel rooms available as well as a couple of self-contained cottages. Winery tours also organised. **$$**

Toowoomba

Country Gardens Motor Inn
94 James Street
Tel: 4632 3099
countrygardensmotorinn.com.au
This winner of architectural awards combines form with a high level of comfort. **$$**

Warwick

Abbey of the Roses
8 Locke Street
Tel: 4661 9777
www.abbeyoftheroses.com
An old abbey with National Trust listing and a peaceful location. **$$**

PRICE CATEGORIES

Price categories are for a double room without breakfast:
$ = under A$80
$$ = A$80–130
$$$ = A$130–250
$$$$ = over A$250

SUNSHINE COAST

Bribie Island

Avon Lodge
132 Avon Avenue, Banksia
Beach.
Tel: 3410 7318
Well-appointed, comfortable B&B where children are discouraged. **$$$**

Caloundra

City Centre Motel
20 Orsova Terrace
Tel: 5491 3301
www.mymotel.net.au
Central stylish motel of just seven rooms that covers all the bases. **$$**

Dicky Beach Family Holiday Park
4 Beerburrum Street
Tel: 5491 3342
www.sunshinecoastholidayparks.com.au
Well-run site that combines camping and caravan pitches with on-site accommodation. **$**

Rydges Oasis Resort
Corner North and
Landsborough parades.
Tel: 5491 0333
www.rydges.com
Close to the ocean with plenty of facilities. **$$$**

Coolum

Coolum Beach Caravan Park
David Low Way
Tel: 5446 1474
www.sunshinecoastholidayparks.com.au
Right on the beach, with 133 powered van sites, 71 unpowered camping sites and six cabins. **$**

Coolum Seaside
23 Beach Road
Tel: 5455 7200
www.coolumseaside.com
Self-contained apartments, complete with a pool. **$$$$**

Surf Dance Coolum
29 Coolum Terrace
Tel: 5446 1039
www.surfdance.com
A family-friendly, self-contained apartment block only metres from a patrolled beach. **$$$**

Villa Coolum
102 Coolum Terrace
Tel: 5446 1286
www.villacoolum.com
Neat and tidy, with a fenced pool. A good holiday base for those with young children. **$$**

Eumundi

Eumundi's Hidden Valley
141 Memorial Drive
Tel: 5442 8685
www.eumundibed.com
Attractive Queenslander B&B with balconied rooms and cheaper accommodation in a couple of railway carriages. Rural, relaxed atmosphere. **$$$**

Fraser Island

Fraser Island Wilderness Retreat
Happy Valley
Tel: 4127 9144
www.tourfraserisland.com.au
Individual timber lodges sit amid landscaped gardens on the coast. **$$**

Frasers at Cathedral Beach
Happy Valley
Tel: 4127 9177
www.fraserislandco.com.au/frasers
The more economic option is to camp on this spacious site or rent one of the cabins. **$$**

Kingfisher Bay Resort & Village
North White Cliffs
Tel: 1800 072 555
www.kingfisherbay.com

Well-appointed eco-resort with wooden villas surrounded by rainforest. Gorgeous. **$$$**

Gympie

Gympie Muster Inn
21 Wickham Street
Tel: 5482 8666
gympiemusterinn.com.au
Central, well-appointed rooms. **$$**

Hilltop Motel
Bruce Highway
Tel: 5482 3577
www.hilltopmotel.com.au
Just north of Gympie, this is a simple, good-value establishment. **$**

Hervey Bay

Beachside Motor Inn
298 The Esplanade, Pialba
Tel: 4124 1999
www.beachsidemotorinn.com.au
Nicely turned-out beachside motel. **$$**

Boat Harbour Resort
651 Charlton Esplanade,
Urangan
Tel: 4125 5079
www.boatharbourresort.net
Appealing beach-front resort with wooden cabins and houses surrounding a pool. **$$**

Grange Resort
33 Elizabeth Street, Urangan
Tel: 4125 2195
www.thegrange-herveybay.com.au
Luxurious town houses with self-contained apartments. **$$$**

Maleny

Maleny Country Cottages
347 Cork's Pocket Road
Tel: 5494 27444
www.malenycottages.com.au
Get back to nature and curl up in comfort and watch the wildlife in the

woods. **$$$$**

Maleny Hills Motel
932 Montville Road
Tel: 5494 2551
www.malenyhills.com.au
Clean and comfortable units in a garden setting provide a good base for exploring. **$$**

Maroochydore

Reflections
2 Picnic Point Esplanade
Tel: 5443 9707
www.reflections-apartments.com
Right on the Maroochy River and handy for the ocean. Popular apartments with families. **$$$**

The Sebel Maroochydore
20 Aerodrome Road
Tel: 5479 8000
www.mirvachotels.com.au
Apartments in a glittering 15-storey block opposite the beach. **$$$$**

Maryborough

McNevins Parkway Motel
188 John Street
Tel: 4122 2888
www.mcnevins.com.au
Two restaurants in this comfortable modern motel give it the feel of a small resort. **$$**

Wallace Motel & Caravan Park
22 Ferry Street
Tel: 4121 3970

Brisbane

www.wallacecaravanpark.com.au
Tidy caravan park that
also has good-value cab-
ins and motel rooms. **$**

Noosa

**Breakfree French
Quarter Resort**
62 Hastings Street
Tel: 5430 7100
www.breakfreefrenchquarter.com.au
High-quality option on

the river side of
Hastings. **$$$$**
Halse Lodge
2 Halse Lane
Tel: 1800 242 567
www.halselodge.com.au
Backpackers retreat
in a rambling old
Queenslander. **$**
Noosa Blue Resort
16 Noosa Drive
Tel: 1800 463 854
www.noosablue.com.au

Sleek modern resort on
the hill overlooking the
water. **$$$$**
**Seahaven Beachfront
Resort**
13 Hastings Street
Tel: 5447 3422
www.seahavennoosa.com.au
Overlooking the beach
with facilities aplenty.
$$$
**Sheraton Noosa
Resort & Spa**

Hastings Street
Tel: 5449 4888
www.starwoodhotels.com
Five-star hotel; superla-
tive service. **$$$$**
Tingirana
25 Hastings Street
Tel: 5474 7400
www.tingirana.com.au
Stylish 5-star resort by
the beach. Home to the
renowned Seasons res-
taurant. **$$$**

CAPRICORN COAST AND ITS HINTERLAND

Agnes Water/
Town of 1770

1770 Getaway
303 Bicentennial Drive
Tel: 4974 9323
www.1770getaway.com.au
Villas, set in manicured
gardens, all designed on
a hexagonal matrix. **$$$**
Beach Shacks
578 Captain Cook Drive
Tel: 4974 9463
www.1770beachshacks.com
Well-stocked, tropical-
equipped decor bunga-
lows by the beach. **$$$**

Bundaberg

**Alexandra Park
Motor Inn**
66 Quay Street
Tel: 4152 7255
www.alexandras.com.au
A nod to colonial archi-
tecture in this roomy and
comfortable motel. **$$**
Inglebrae
17 Branyan Street
Tel: 4154 4003
www.inglebrae.com
Sumptuous bed-and-
breakfast rooms in an
old Queenslander. **$$**

Carnarvon Gorge

**Carnarvon Gorge Taka-
rakka Bush Resort**
Carnarvon Gorge Road

Tel: 4984 4535
www.takarakka.com.au
Canvas cabins sleep up
to five. Campsites, too.
$$
**Carnarvon Gorge Wil-
derness Lodge**
O'Briens Road
Tel: 4984 4503
www.carnarvon-gorge.com
Reasonable facilities in
these woodland cabins,
but expensive. **$$$**

Clermont

Peppercorn Motel
51 Capricorn Street
Tel: 4983 1033
www.peppercornmotel.com.au
Sixteen units in stand-
ard motel format with a
pool. **$$$**

Emerald

Emerald Explorers Inn
Gregory Highway
Tel: 4982 2822
www.emeraldexplorersinn.com.au
Unremarkable but com-
fortable motel on the
edge of town. **$$**
**The Emerald Meteor
Motel**
Corner Opal and Egerton
streets
Tel: 4982 1166
www.emeraldmeteormotel.com.au
Spotless, well-
maintained motel with

pool and restaurant. **$$**

Gladstone

Harbour Sails Motor Inn
23 Goondoon Street
Tel: 4972 3456
www.harboursails.com.au
Modern, bright and airy
motel in the centre of
town. **$$$**

Great Keppel
Island

**Great Keppel Island
Holiday Village**
Tel: 4939 8655
www.gkiholidayvillage.com.au
Budget resort where just
being on the island is
the attraction rather
than the facilities. **$$**

Heron Island

Heron Island Resort
Tel: 1300 863 248
www.heronisland.com
Accommodation from
comfortable to over-the-
top, priced accordingly.
Exellent diving. **$$$$**

Mount Morgan

Ferns' Miners Rest
44 Coronation Drive
Tel: 4938 2350
Modern cottage units off
the road, with everything

you might need. **$$**

Rockhampton

Criterion Hotel
150 Quay Street
Tel: 4922 1225
www.thecriterion.com.au
An iconic building of the
city, and a fine example of
a Victorian hotel. Some of
the rooms are faithful to
the style of the period. **$**
Motel 98
98 Victoria Parade
Tel: 1800 643 325
www.98.com.au
Modern, well-appointed
rooms, with pool and res-
taurant by the river. **$$**

PRICE CATEGORIES

Price categories are for
a double room without
breakfast:
$ = under A$80
$$ = A$80–130
$$$ = A$130–250
$$$$ = over A$250

SOUTHERN REEF AND THE WHITSUNDAYS

ABOVE: a beach idyll.

Airlie Beach

Airlie Beach Hotel
Corner The Esplanade and
Coconut Grove
Tel: 4964 1999
www.airliebeachhotel.com.au
Prime seafront location
and 4-star facilities
make this one of the busier hotels in town. **$$$**

Best Western Colonial Palms Motor Inn
Corner Shute Harbour Road
and Hermitage Drive
Tel: 4946 7166
www.colonialpalms.bestwestern.
com.au
Comfortable rooms looking towards the sea, and
friendly service. **$$**

Coral Point Lodge
54 Harbour Avenue,
Shute Harbour
Tel: 4946 9500
www.coralpointlodge.com.au
Gorgeous views over to
the Whitsundays from
this homely guest
house/hotel. **$$**

Coral Sea Resort
25 Oceanview Avenue
Tel: 4964 1300
www.coralsearesort.com
The only entirely waterfront resort in Airlie
Beach offers a range of
apartment-style suites,
most with spa baths,
just three minutes' walk
from the action. **$$$**

Magnums Backpackers
366 Shute Harbour Road
Tel: 4964 1199
www.magnums.com.au
The most central hostel
at Airlie has won awards
for being the friendliest. It
offers dormitory, twin
share and double accommodation. **$**

Brampton Island

Brampton Island Resort
Tel: 4951 4499
www.bramptonisland.org
Beautiful isolated resort
that was under renovation at time of writing.
$$$$

Mackay

Gecko's Rest
34 Sydney Street
Tel: 4944 1230
www.geckosrest.com.au
Busy hostel in the heart
of Mackay from which
you can organise platypus-watching tours to
Eungella. **$**

Whitsunday Hotel
176 Victoria Street
Tel: 4957 2811
www.whitsundayhotel.com.au
Simple hotel close to the
town centre that represents sound value. **$$**

Whitsundays

Daydream Island Resort & Spa
Tel: 1800 075 040
www.daydreamisland.com
Popular resort on this
tiny island offers everything for a fun family holiday, including outlandish
novelty golf. **$$$$**

Hayman Island Resort
Tel: 1800 122 339
www.hayman.com.au
One of the area's

Brisbane ●

ultimate destinations.
Offers a level of luxury
that makes it a favourite
of world leaders and film
stars. **$$$$**

Long Island Resort
Tel: 1800 075 125
www.longislandresort.com.au
Relaxed resort on its
own bay, with the
emphasis on water
sports and fun, but quiet
woodland walks if you
want to get away from it
all. **$$$$**

Reef View Hotel
Hamilton Island
Tel: 137-333
www.hamiltonisland.com.au
If you like plenty of other
people around, this is
the resort for you. There
are 382 rooms and
plenty of day-trippers
popping in to add to the
numbers. **$$$$**

AROUND TOWNSVILLE

Cardwell

Mudbrick Manor
Stoney Creek Road
Tel: 4066 2299
www.mudbrickmanor.com.au
The adobe building is a
bit gimmicky, but the
facilities and attention to
detail are what count. **$$**

Charters Towers

Park Motel

1 Mosman Street
Tel: 4787 1022
www.parkmotel.com.au
Clean and efficient motel
with old-world charm in a
quiet central street. **$$**

Royal Private Hotel
100 Mosman Street
Tel: 4787 8688
A delightful balconied
gold-rush era hotel with
inexpensive pub rooms
and comfortable en-
suite rooms. **$$**

Ingham

Herbert Valley Motel
Bruce Highway
Tel: 4776 1777
www.inghamhvmotel.com.au
Good functional place to
overnight in, with a
decent restaurant. **$$**

Palm Tree Caravan Park
Bruce Highway
Tel: 4776 2403
Caravan park with a few

Brisbane ●

cabins, as well as the
usual powered and
unpowered sites. **$**

TRANSPORT

ACCOMMODATION

ACTIVITIES

A – Z

Magnetic Island

Base Backpackers
1 Nelly Bay Road, Nelly Bay
Tel: 4778 5777
www.stayatbase.com
Well run and right by the
beach, with dorms or en
suites. Good bar and
café, too. **$**

**Magnetic Island
Tropical Resort**
56 Yates Street, Nelly Bay
Tel: 4778 5955
www.magneticislandresort.com
Simple A-frame
cottages in 8 hectares (3
acres) of forest for that
back-to-nature experi-
ence. **$$$**

Sails on Horseshoe
13 Pacific Drive
Tel: 4778 5117
www.sailsonhorsehoe.com.au
Comfortable, self-con-
tained units beside a
peaceful beach. **$$$$**

Port Hinchin-brook

**Port Hinchinbrook
Resort & Marina**
Bruce Highway
Tel: 4066 2000
www.porthinchinbrook.com.au
Huge marina and resi-
dential development
with some high-spec
cabins to rent. **$$$$**

Ravenswood

Imperial Hotel
Macrossan Street
Tel: 4770 2131
Wonderfully atmos-
pheric old hotel where
the rooms have been
carefully maintained
with fans, mosquito nets
and bathrooms along
the landing, to take you
back to its 19th-century
heyday. **$**

Townsville

Beach House Motel
66 The Strand
Tel: 4721 1333

www.beachhousemotel.com.au
A pool overlooking the
beach is the distinguish-
ing feature of this stand-
ard motel. **$$**

**Jupiters Hotel &
Casino**
Sir Leslie Thiess Drive
Tel: 1800 079 210
www.jupiterstownsville.com.au
By the water and well
placed to enjoy the reju-
venated Strand. **$$$**

Strand Park Hotel
59-60 The Strand
Tel: 4750 7888
www.strandparkhotel.com.au
Sparkling all-suite hotel
with views across to
Magnetic Island. **$$$**

CAIRNS TO CAPE TRIBULATION

Cairns

Acacia Court Hotel
223-227 The Esplanade
Tel: 4051 5011
www.acaciacourt.com
Choice of rooms with
balconies and ocean or
mountain views, or
cheaper, motel-style
accommodation. **$$$**

Floriana Guesthouse
183 The Esplanade
Tel: 4051 7886
www.florianaguesthouse.com
A delightful 1930s
guesthouse with 10 indi-
vidual, en-suite rooms. A
15-minute walk to
Cairns CBD, and good
value. **$$**

Galvins Edge Hill B&B
61 Walsh Street
Tel: 4032 1308
www.galvinsonedge.com.au
Peacefully located,
genuine old Queens-
lander. The guest
accommodation has two
bedrooms, bathroom,
lounge and breakfast
room that opens on to
the natural rock swim-
ming pool. **$$$**

**Gilligans Backpackers
Hotel & Resort**
57-89 Grafton Street
Tel: 4041 6566
www.gilligans.com.au
Only a few years old, this
luxurious backpackers'
hotel offers rooms with
air-conditioning, dorms
and private en-suites,
and ample nightlife. **$**

The Hotel Cairns
Corner Abbott and
Florence streets
Tel: 4051 6188
www.thehotelcairns.com
Very well-appointed
upper-mid-range hotel
with tropical architec-
ture and great pool and
gardens . **$$$**

Mantra Esplanade
53-57 The Esplanade
Tel: 4046 4141
www.mantraesplanadecairns.com.
au
Penthouses and luxuri-
ous one- and two-bed-
room serviced
apartments, close to the
central district and
attractions. Swimming
pool, fitness room,
sauna and spa. **$$$$**

Novotel Cairns Resort
122 Lake Street
Tel: 4080 1888
www.novotelcairnsresort.com.au
Comfortable four-star
resort-style property
with lagoon pool and
landscaped gardens. A
short walk from the
Esplanade area. **$$$**

**Pullman Reef Hotel
Casino**
35 Wharf Street
Tel: 4030 8888
www.reefcasino.com.au
Central 5-star oper-ation
with a casino down-
stairs, an animal sanctu-
ary on the roof, but little
discernible atmosphere.
$$$$

Shangri-La Marina
Pierpoint Road
Tel: 4031 1411
www.shangri-la.com
Fronting Marlin Marina
and the inlet, this hotel
set in lush tropical gar-
dens has great views
and a great location.
Luxury accommodation
with private balconies or
patio. Facilities include a
large pool. **$$$$**

Cape Tribulation

Cape Trib Beach House
Cape Tribulation Road
Tel: 4098 0030
www.capetribbeach.com.au
Dormitory and family
cabins, as close to the
beach as the National
Parks Authority will
allow. Swimming pool
and bistro/bar, as well

PRICE CATEGORIES

Price categories are for
a double room without
breakfast:
$ = under A$80
$$ = A$80–130
$$$ = A$130–250
$$$$ = over A$250

as kitchen and laundry facilities. **$$$**

Ferntree Rainforest Lodge
Camelot Close
Tel: 4098 0033
www.ferntreerainforestlodge.com.au
Set in 100 hectares (250 acres) of rainforest, with accommodation in timber villas. Attractions include excursions led by rainforest guides, 4WD tours and Great Barrier Reef cruises. **$$$$**

Daintree

Daintree Eco Lodge & Spa
20 Daintree Road
Tel: 4098 6100
www.daintree-ecolodge.com.au
Luxurious tree houses and award-winning spa. The place to come to be spoilt. **$$$$**

Kenadon Homestead Cabins
Daintree 4873
Tel: 4098 6142
www.daintreecabins.com
Comfortable cabins with great views from the back deck. **$$$**

Green Island

Green Island Resort
Tel: 1800 673 366
www.greenislandresort.com.au
If Cairns gets too much, take to the island for unmitigated luxury. **$$$$**

Lake Eacham

Crater Lakes Rainforest Cottages
Lot 17 Eacham Close
Tel: 4095 2322
www.craterlakes.com.au
Four themed cottages bordering a national park. Fully equipped, including double spa bath and wood-burning stove. **$$$$**

Malanda

The Canopy
247 Hogan Road
Tel: 4096 5364
www.canopytreehouses.com.au
Private wildlife sanctuary with half-a-dozen spectacular tree houses deep in the rainforest. **$$$$**

Malanda Falls Caravan Park
38 Park Avenue
Tel: 4096 5314
www.malandafalls.com.au
Delightful woodland setting and fine cabins right beside the falls. **$**

Mareeba

Jackaroo Motel
340 Byrnes Street
Tel: 4092 2677
www.jackaroomotel.com
Top motel accommodation with lots of facilities and helpful staff. **$$**

Mission Beach

Castaways on the Beach Resort
Corner Pacific Parade and Seaview Street
Tel: 4068 7444
www.castaways.com.au
Set on a tropical beach, with large rooms, one- and two-bedroom units, and a split-level penthouse – all with wonderful views. **$$$**

Mission Beach Ecovillage
Clump Point Road
Tel: 4068 7534
www.ecovillage.com.au
Comfortable units nestle in the trees around a lagoon-style pool in this well-run resort. **$$$**

Sanctuary Retreat at Mission Beach
72 Holt Road, Bingil Bay
Tel: 4088 6064
www.sanctuaryatmission.com
Accommodation is in simple or luxurious wooden cabins dotted through the rainforest, with an empty beach just down the road. Peaceful retreat. **$-$$$**

Scottys Beach House
167 Reid Road
Tel: 4068 8676
www.scottysbeachhouse.com.au
Popular family-run place opposite the beach, offering budget accommodation in dorms or motel-style rooms. Welcomes campervans. **$**

Mossman

Silky Oaks Lodge
Finlayvale Road
Tel: 4098 1666
www.silkyoakslodge.com.au
Rainforest hideaway on the edge of Mossman Gorge; 45 tree houses and five river houses with all creature comforts, plus a spa, restaurant, rainforest excursions and canoe trips. **$$$$**

Palm Cove

The Mango Lagoon Resort & Wellness Spa
81-85 Cedar Road
Tel: 4055 3400
www.mangolagoon.com.au
Stylish suite and apartment accommodation, set amid lush landscaped gardens, with pools and waterfalls. A vast menu of massages and therapies. **$$$$**

Palm Cove Camping Ground
149 Williams Esplanade
Tel: 4055 3824
Ideal spot for campers and campervans, just across from the beach. **$**

Paradise on the Beach Resort
119 Williams Esplanade
Tel: 4055 3300
www.paradiseonthebeach.com
High standards throughout this mid-range apartment resort, with good deals for longer stays. **$$$**

Peppers Beach Club & Spa
123 Williams Esplanade
Tel: 4059 9200
www.peppers.com.au
Striking resort. Top-floor suites have their own glass-encased pools and stunning views of the beach. **$$$$**

Reef House Resort & Spa
99 Williams Esplanade
Tel: 4055 3633
www.reefhouse.com.au
Boutique resort with elegant, oversized rooms. Lush gardens, a courtyard pool and a delightful restaurant complete the picture. **$$$$**

Port Douglas

Hibiscus Resort & Spa
22 Owens Street
Tel: 4000 5315
www.hibiscusportdouglas.com.au
In exotic gardens with two pools, this hotel has a Balinese theme, with extensive use of natural wood and terracotta. Some apartments with private spas. **$$$-$$$$**

Martinique on Macrossan
66 Macrossan Street
Tel: 4099 6222
www.martinique.com.au
Comfortable apartments with kitchenettes, plus a saltwater pool. **$$$**

Port Douglas Motel
9 Davidson Street
Tel: 4099 5248
www.portdouglasmotel.com
No views to speak of, but inexpensive by Port Douglas standards and perfectly serviceable. **$$**

Sheraton Mirage Port Douglas Resort

TRANSPORT
ACCOMMODATION
ACTIVITIES
A – Z

Davidson Street
Tel: 4099 5888
www.starwoodhotels.com
A luxurious resort on the beach, with saltwater swimming lagoons, a freshwater pool, a world-class golf course, floodlit tennis courts, gym and health centre. Accommodation is in rooms, suites or villas with up to four bedrooms. **$$$$**

Ravenshoe

Kool Moon Motel
6 Moore Street
Tel: 4097 6047
Standard, unpretentious motel rooms representing very good value. **$**
Pond Cottage B&B
844 Tully Falls Road
Tel: 4097 7189
www.bnbnq.com.au/pondcottage
Platypuses, wallabies and possums are among the inhabitants you're likely to encounter at this secluded resort, 10km (6 miles) from Ravenshoe in the heart of the Misty Mountains. **$$$**

Yungaburra

Curtain Fig Motel
28 Gillies Highway
Tel: 4095 3168
www.curtainfig.com
Far above the average motel, with all the usual features and extremely helpful owners. **$$**
Eden House Retreat & Mountain Spa
20 Gillies Highway
Tel: 4089 7000
www.edenhouse.com.au
Sumptuous cottages in the grounds of a historic Queenslander. **$$$**

Kookaburra Lodge
Corner Oak Street and Eacham Road
Tel: 4095 3222
www.kookaburra-lodge.com
Comfortable and homely motel rooms set in verdant gardens. **$$**
Mount Quincan Crater Retreat
Peeramon Road
Tel: 4095 2255
www.mtquincan.com.au
Luxurious log cabins with wood-burning fireplace and a double spa bath with a view. Isolated location. **$$$$**

COOKTOWN AND THE CAPE YORK PENINSULA

Bamaga

Resort Bamaga
Corner Lui and Adidi streets
Tel: 4069 3050
resortbamaga.com.au
Good resort with 4-star accommodation and restaurant. **$$$**

Chillagoe

Chillagoe Cabins
Queen Street
Tel: 4094 7206
www.chillagoe.com
Three well-equipped cabins in lush gardens. **$$**
Chillagoe Observatory and Eco Lodge
Hospital Avenue
Tel: 4094 7155
www.coel.com.au
A high-quality set-up to enhance that Outback experience. **$**

Cooktown

Pam's Place
Corner of Charlotte and Boundary streets
Tel: 4069 5166
www.cooktownhostel.com
Motel rooms and self-contained cabins. **$$**

Peninsula Caravan Park
Howard Street
Tel: 4069 5107
A well-equipped caravan park. It also has some rather luxurious cabins. **$**
Seaview Motel
178 Charlotte Street
Tel: 4069 5377
www.cooktownseaviewmotel.com.au
Central motel offering a wide range of accommodation. **$$**
Sovereign Resort Hotel
Corner Charlotte and Green streets
Tel: 4043 0500
www.sovereignresort.com.au
Top of the range in Cooktown, lovely pool and balcony restaurant. **$$$**

Horn Island

Gateway Torres Strait Resort
24 Outie Street
Tel: 4069 2222
www.torresstrait.com.au
Hard to get excited about these units, but the only option on Horn Island. **$$$**

Laura

Quinkan Hotel
Tel: 4060 3255
The only pub, and very much the social centre of the settlement, can provide a cheap room at the back, shady camping ground and meals. **$**

Lizard Island

Lizard Island Resort
Anchor Bay
Tel: 1300 863 248
www.lizardisland.com.au
A luxurious resort fulfilling the role of playground for the rich and famous. Access is by plane from Cairns unless you spend hundreds of dollars on chartering your own boat from Cooktown. **$$$$**

Mount Surprise

Bedrock Village Caravan Park
Garnett Street
Tel: 4062 3193
www.bedrockvillage.com.au
One-stop shop with tent and caravan sites plus cabins. Mini-golf, pools

Brisbane ●

and barbecues. **$**
Mount Surprise Hotel
Garland Street
Tel: 4062 3118
The standard pub option in town. **$**
Mount Surprise Tourist Caravan Park
23 Garland Street
Tel: 1800 447 982
Caravan park, motel, café, gem shop and service station. The owners raise miniature horses and native birds. **$**

PRICE CATEGORIES

Price categories are for a double room without breakfast:
$ = under A$80
$$ = A$80–130
$$$ = A$130–250
$$$$ = over A$250

TRANSPORT

Thursday Island

Federal Hotel
Corner Victoria Parade and
Jardine Street
Tel: 4069 1569
www.federalhotelti.com.au
Historic hotel with latest
facilities. $$$

Jardine Motel
Corner Normanby Street and
Victoria Parade
Tel: 4069 1555
www.jardinemotel.com.au
This pleasant beach
resort is set within
beautiful tropical gar-
dens. $$$

Weipa

Heritage Resort
Corner Commercial Avenue
and Kerr Point Drive
Tel: 4069 8000
www.heritageresort.com.au
Fine, modern rooms.
Caters for anglers. $$$

**Weipa Camping
Ground**
Newbold Drive
Tel: 4069 7871
www.weipa.biz
Camp under the trees on
the shore of Albatross
Bay or take one of the
cabins. $$

SAVANNAH WAY

ACCOMMODATION

Burketown

Burketown Pub
Musgrave and Beames Streets
Tel: 4745 5104
www.burketownpub.com
Focal point of the town,
with some motel units. $
Caravan Park
Sloman Street
Tel: 4745 5118
Adequate cabins or
pitch a tent. $

Croydon

Club Hotel
Corner Brown and Sircom
streets
Tel: 4745 6184
www.clubhotelcroydon.com.au
A terrific atmospheric
old pub with reasonable
modern units. $$

Georgetown

Latara Motel
Gulf Developmental Road
Tel: 4062 1190

www.georgetownaccommodation.
com
Don't be put off by the
pink Savannah-style
façade. Good rooms and
attractive grounds. $$

Gregory Downs

Gregory Downs Hotel
Tel: 4748 5566
Basic rooms in a friendly
Outback pub. $

Karumba

End of the Road Motel
26 Palmer Street, Karumba
Point
Tel: 4745 9599
www.endoftheroadmotel.com.au
Out at the end of the
road, by the beach, is
Karumba's best accom-
modation in one- and
two-bedroom apart-
ments. $$$
Gulf Country Van Park
69 Yappar Street
Tel: 4745 9148

www.karumbavanparks.com.au
The usual mixture of tent
and van sites along with
some old cabins. $

Lawn Hill Gorge

Adels Grove
Lawn Hill Creek
Tel: 4748 5502
www.adelsgrove.com.au
Choice of a campsite,
pre-erected tents or very
basic rooms. There is
also a campsite in Bood-
jamulla National Park.
Book in advance. $

Normanton

Gulfland Motel
11 Landsborough Street
Tel: 4745 1290
www.gulflandmotel.com.au
Standard motel in midst
of tropical greenery. $$
**The Purple Pub and
Brolga Palms Motel**
Corner Landsborough and
Brown streets

Tel: 4745 1324
Some good-quality
motel rooms behind this
landmark pub. $$

Undara Volcanic
National Park

Undara Experience
Savannah Way
Tel: 4097 1900
www.undara.com.au
There's a campground,
but the stylish choice is
to take a room in one of a
row of cosily converted
old railway carriages.
Plenty of Outback activi-
ties laid on. $$

ACTIVITIES

MOUNT ISA AND THE WEST

A – Z

Boulia

Desert Sands Motel
Herbert Street
Tel: 4746 3000
Unpretentious, but per-
fectly serviceable motel
with everything you
would expect in its 12
units. $$

Cloncurry

Gidgee Inn
Matilda Highway
Tel: 4742 1599
www.gidgeeinn.com.au
The most salubrious of
Cloncurry's places to
stay is built of rammed
red earth. $$

**Gilbert Park Tourist
Village**
McIlwraith Street
Tel: 4742 2300
www.toptouristparks.com.au
A well-organised camp-
site that also rents out
some spotless cabins. $
Wagon Wheel Motel
54 Ramsay Street

Tel: 4742 1866
A strip of 1960s motel rooms behind this busy pub provide all the necessaries. **$**

Hughenden

Allen Terry Caravan Park
2 Resolution Street
Tel: 4741 1190
Caravan park with air-conditioned cabins and a heated swimming pool. **$**

Royal Hotel Resort
21 Moran Street
Tel: 4741 1183
Perfectly decent if not distinctive motel rooms. Swimming pool available. **$**

Mount Isa

All Seasons Verona Hotel
Corner Marian and Camooweal Streets
Tel: 4743 3024
www.all-seasons-hotels.com
Sound choice for comfort and efficiency. Popular restaurant. **$$$**

Argylla Caravan Village
Barkly Highway
Tel: 4743 4733
www.discoveryholidayparks.com.au
Neat, well-maintained, shady site with decent cabins and a pool. **$$**

Inland Oasis Motel
195 Barkly Highway
Tel: 4743 3433
www.inlandoasismotel.com.au
A well-presented mod-

ern motel. Like all accommodation in Mount Isa, it can fill up quickly on days when extra workers have been shipped in for shifts at the mine. **$$**

Richmond

Ammonite Inn
88 Goldring Street
Tel: 4741 3932
Plenty of good units as well as reasonable pub rooms. **$$**

Winton

Matilda Country Tourist Park
43 Chirnside Street
Tel: 4657 1607

www.matildacountrytouristpark.com
Sixty powered sites and fine cabins make this a good budget choice. Tours of Lake Quarry and bush-poetry evenings. **$**

North Gregory Hotel
67 Elderslie Street
Tel: 4657 0647
www.northgregoryhotel.com
Standard pub rooms and motel rooms in a later incarnation of the hotel where Banjo Paterson first performed *Waltzing Matilda*. **$**

Winton Outback Motel
95 Elderslie Street
Tel: 4657 1422
www.wintonoutbackmotel.com
Clean, well-maintained and handily placed for the centre of town. **$$**

SOUTHWEST QUEENSLAND

Barcaldine

Ironbark Inn
Landsborough Highway
Tel: 4651 2311
Reasonable motel rooms in this friendly establishment, which features a large open-air dining room. **$$**

Shakespeare Hotel
95 Oak Street
Tel: 4651 1111
In a street full of old-style country pubs, this one offers good-value basic rooms. **$**

Birdsville

Birdsville Caravan Park
Florence Street
Tel: 4656 3214
www.birdsvillecaravanpark.com
Various levels of comfort in the cabins here, but all in a scenic setting. **$**

Birdsville Hotel
Adelaide Street
Tel: 4656 3244

theoutback.com.au/birdsvillehotel
Many actually go to Birdsville just to see this historic pub, so it makes sense to stay in one of its comfortable units. **$$**

Blackall

Acacia Motor Inn
Corner Shamrock and Short streets
Tel: 4657 6022
www.blackallacaciamotorinn.com.au
High-class units and a restaurant in this central motel. **$$**

Blackall Caravan Park
53 Garden Street
Tel: 4657 4816
www.blackallcaravanpark.com.au
Friendly site where guests are encouraged to mingle round the campfire. There are a handful of units. **$**

Charleville

Corones Hotel
33 Wills Street

Tel: 4654 1022
hotelcorones.com.au
Terrific old wooden pub with first-floor verandas, lots of atmosphere and reasonable rooms. **$$**

Warrego Motel Charleville
73 Wills Street
Tel: 4654 1299
www.warregomotel.com
Standard units that do the job without fuss or flair. **$$**

Cunnamulla

Country Way Motor Inn
17 Emma Street
Tel: 4655 0555
We're in standard motel territory, but done well. **$$**

Longreach

Albert Park Motor Inn
Sir Hudson Fysh Drive
Tel: 4658 3181
Lots of room, and grounds teeming with

wildlife. The most luxurious place in town. **$$**

Longreach Motor Inn
84 Galah Street
Tel: 4658 2322
www.outbacklongreach.com.au
Another fairly large enterprise that scores with attention to detail. Local tours available. **$$**

ACTIVITIES

FESTIVALS, THE ARTS, NIGHTLIFE, SHOPPING AND SPORTS

FESTIVALS AND EVENTS

Autumn (Mar–May)

Australian Surf Life-Saving Championships, Mar/Apr, the peak event for Australia's 34,000 surf life-savers, on the Gold Coast. www.sls.com.au/aussies

Kilkivan Great Horse Ride, April, an annual event that draws more than 1,000 riders.

Australian-Italian Festival, May, one of northern Queensland's biggest events, held in Ingham near Townsville www.australianitalianfestival.com.au

Winter (June–Aug)

Cooktown Discovery Festival, mid-June. An annual re-enactment of Captain Cook's emergency landing on the banks of the Endeavour River, includes a gala ball, and a "ute" and 4WD muster. www.cooktowndiscoveryfestival.com.au.

Laura Aboriginal Dance Festival, mid-June odd-numbered years. Highlighting the diversity of indigenous culture in song and dance. www.laurafestival.tv.

Gold Coast Airport Marathon, early July. www.goldcoastmarathon.com.au

Cairns Festival, Aug. Arts, music, dance and theatre take centre stage at this annual festival. www.cairnsfest.com.au

Mount Isa Rodeo, mid-Aug. Australia's biggest and richest rodeo. www.isarodeo.com.au

The Ekka, mid-Aug. City meets country at the Royal Queensland Show in Brisbane. www.ekka.com.au

Noosa Jazz Festival, late Aug/early Sept. www.noosajazz.com.au

Spring (Sept–Nov)

Birdsville Races, first weekend in September. Annual racing event held to raise money for the Royal Flying Doctor Service. www.birdsvilleraces.com.

Brisbane Festival, early Sept. A celebration of Brisbane's arts, culture and environment. www.brisbanefestival.com.au

Brisbane Writers' Festival, mid-Sept. A five-day festival to celebrate reading and writing, at South Bank. www.brisbanewritersfestival.com.au

Valley Fiesta, Oct. Brisbane's biggest and best street festival held in its most cosmopolitan precinct, Fortitude Valley. www.valleyfiesta.com

Coolangatta Gold, mid-Oct. Iconic Ironman competition involving a series of endurance events in and out of the surf. www.sls.com.au/coolangattagold

Noosa Triathlon, late Oct. A week-long festival of multi-sport events, including the Noosa Triathlon. Tel: 5449 0711.

Schoolies, Nov–early Dec. A period when high-school graduates from Australia's eastern states converge on Surfers Paradise to celebrate the end of their exams. Best avoided if possible. www.schoolies.org.au

Summer (Dec–Feb)

Australian PGA Championship, mid-December. Australia's oldest professional golf championship is held at the Hyatt Regency Coolum. www.championship.pga.org.au.

Woodford Folk Festival, late-Dec–1 Jan. Hundreds of folk music-lovers gather to bring in the new year. www.woodfordfolkfestival.com.

Big Day Out, Jan. An annual rock, electronic and contemporary outdoor music event held on the Gold Coast. www.bigdayout.com

Australia Day, 26 Jan. Celebrations held all over Queensland. www.australiaday.gov.au/qld/

Tropfest, Feb. International short-film festival comes to Brisbane for a day. www.tropfest.com/au/brisbane

THE ARTS

Art Galleries

The best way to find out what's on in Queensland's art galleries is to buy a copy of *Art Almanac*, a monthly booklet that lists galleries and their current exhibitions. It costs A$4 and is available at good bookshops and galleries. Brunswick Street, in Brisbane's Fortitude Valley, is a good starting point for gallery-hopping, and includes Craft Queensland, an incubator for up-and-coming artists. There are also galleries aplenty in neighbouring suburbs such as Newstead and New Farm. Some of Queensland's public and commercial galleries are listed below.

Fireworks Gallery
52a Doggett Street
Newstead, Brisbane
Tel: 3216 1250
www.fireworksgallery.com.au
A mixture of indigenous and other contemporary artworks. Tue–Fri 10am–6pm, Sat 10am–4pm.

Heiser Gallery
90B Arthur Street
Fortitude Valley, Brisbane
Tel: 3254 2849
www.heisergallery.com.au
Tue–Sat 10.30am–6pm.

Institute of Modern Art
420 Brunswick Street
Fortitude Valley, Brisbane
Tel: 3252 5750; www.ima.org.au
Housed inside the Judith Wright Centre of Contemporary Arts. Tue–Sat 11am–5pm, Thur until 8pm.

Jan Murphy Gallery
486 Brunswick Street
Fortitude Valley, Brisbane
Tel: 07 3254 1855
www.janmurphygallery.com.au
Represents contemporary Australian artists such as Ben Quilty and Marina Strocchi. Tue–Sat 10am–5pm.

Philip Bacon Art Galleries
2 Arthur Street
Fortitude Valley
Brisbane
Tel: 3358 3555
www.philipbacongalleries.com.au
One of Australia's best-known private galleries. Tue–Sat 10am–5pm.

Queensland Art Gallery
Melbourne Street
South Brisbane
Tel: 3840 7303

ABOVE: Cairns Museum.

www.qag.qld.gov.au
The state art gallery has an extensive collection of Australian art, including contemporary and indigenous artworks. Mon–Fri 10am–5pm, Sat–Sun 9am–5pm.

Queensland Gallery of Modern Art
Melbourne Street
South Brisbane
Tel: 3840 7303
www.qag.qld.gov.au
The impressive modern-art gallery, known as GoMA, is 150 metres/yds from the original Queensland Art Gallery. Mon–Fri 10am–5pm and weekends 9am–5pm.

Suzanne O'Connell Gallery
93 James Street
New Farm, Brisbane
Tel: 3358 5811
www.suzanneoconnell.com
Australian indigenous-art specialist, including paintings and woodcarvings. Wed–Sat 11am–4pm.

Gold Coast

The Arts Centre Gold Coast
135 Bundall Road
Surfers Paradise
Tel: 5581 6567
www.theartscentregc.com.au
An outdoor sculpture walk with work by Australian and international artists is part of the permanent display here. Mon–Fri 10am–5pm, Sat–Sun 11am–5pm.

Ipswich Art Gallery
D'Arcy Doyle Place
Nicholas Street, Ipswich
Tel: 3813 9222
www.ipswichartgallery.qld.gov.au
Queensland's largest regional gallery. Daily 10am–5pm.

Art Gallery Schubert
Marina Mirage, Seaworld Drive
Main Beach, Gold Coast
Tel: 07 5571 0077
www.schubertcontemporary.com.au
Deals in some of the biggest names in Australian art. Daily 10am–5.30pm.

Sunshine Coast

Keep an eye out for galleries in the Sunshine Coast hinterland villages of Montville, Maleny and Eumundi.

Noosa Regional Gallery
Pelican Street, Tewantin
Tel: 5449 5340
www.noosaregional gallery.org
An annual exhibition of artists' books is one of the innovative programmes at this regional gallery. Wed–Sun 10am–4pm.

Cairns & Further North

Cairns Regional Gallery
Corner Abbott and Shields streets
Tel: 4046 4800
www.cairnsregionalgallery.com.au
Displaying visual arts of tropical north Queensland. Mon–Sat 10am–5pm, Sun 1pm–5pm.

Daintree Timber Gallery
12 Stewart Street, Daintree
Tel: 4098 6224; www.daintreetimber-gallery.com.
Local timber art. Daily 10am–4pm.

Concerts and Opera

The **Queensland Symphony Orchestra** is the state's only professional symphony orchestra. It gives concerts throughout the year, ranging from classics to new commissions and Baroque music. The Concert Hall at the Queensland Performing Arts Centre in Brisbane is home base, but the orchestra also tours to other towns in the state, as well as to regional areas.

For a special insight into specific members of the orchestra, go along to one of the Sunday afternoon performances by the **Ferry Road Chamber Players**. The chamber-music series is a collaboration between orchestra members and local musicians at the orchestra's Ferry Road studio.

Opera Queensland is the second-largest opera company in Australia. It presents three major operatic productions in Brisbane each year at the Queensland Performing Arts Centre.

Opera Queensland
16 Russell Street
South Bank, Brisbane
Tel: 3735 3030
www.operaqueensland.com.au

Queensland Symphony Orchestra
53 Ferry Road
West End, Brisbane
Tel: 3377 5000 or 136 246
(bookings); qso.com.au

Dance

The **Queensland Ballet** stages more than 100 performances a year, from a repertoire that extends from classic ballets to modern dance. The company of 26 dancers has its home in the Thomas Dixon Centre for Dance in Brisbane's West End, a building that started life in the 1900s as a shoe factory.

The **Australian Ballet**, the main classical dance company, is based in Melbourne, but has two seasons each year in Sydney and brings some performances to the Lyric Theatre at Brisbane's Queensland Performing Arts Centre.

A trip to Brisbane can also offer the chance to catch the latest performance by some of Australia's best contemporary dance companies on tour.

Queensland Ballet
Thomas Dixon Centre
Corner of Drake Street and Montague Road
West End, Brisbane
Tel: 3013 6666
www.queenslandballet.com.au

Theatre

The **Queensland Theatre Company** (QTC) is the state's most prominent drama company. Established in 1970, the company caters to a broad range of theatrical tastes, staging a main-stage season of nine plays a year. Under the artistic direction of award-win-

ning playwright and director, Wesley Enoch, it presents everything from classic comedies to Christmas crowd-pleasers for families. Part of its vision is to assist in the development of new writing and actors, and it does this by staging a week of professional play readings annually, which includes new plays by local talent.

The banner for developing new and emerging Queensland theatrical talent is also held by **La Boite Theatre Company**, a company that was founded in 1925. Known for performing in the round, the company continues its tradition of providing intimate and accessible performances at the **Roundhouse Theatre** in Kelvin Grove.

Blockbuster musicals, operas and concerts are usually performed in the Lyric Theatre or the Concert Hall at the **Queensland Performing Arts Centre** on the river at South Bank. The Queensland Theatre Company often performs in its Playhouse Theatre, with smaller, less mainstream productions put on in the Cremorne Theatre in the same complex.

The **Judith Wright Centre of Contemporary Arts** and the **Brisbane Powerhouse** are multi-function arts venues, hosting plays, dance and art exhibitions at the edgy end of the scale.

Brisbane Powerhouse
119 Lamington Street
New Farm
Tel: 3358 8600
www.brisbanepowerhouse.org
Judith Wright Centre of

Contemporary Arts
420 Brunswick Street
Fortitude Valley, Brisbane
Tel: 3872 9000
www.jwcoca.qld.gov.au

La Boite Theatre Company
6–8 Musk Avenue
Kelvin Grove, Brisbane
Tel: 3007 8600
www.laboite.com.au

Queensland Performing Arts Centre
Corner of Grey and Melbourne Streets, South Brisbane
Tel: 3840 7444 or 136 246
www.qpac.com.au
Includes the Lyric Theatre, the Playhouse and the Cremorne Theatre (which seats just 315).

Queensland Theatre Company
78 Montague Road
South Brisbane
Tel: 3010 7600
www.qldtheatreco.com.au

NIGHTLIFE

Casinos

Queensland is home to four casinos.

Treasury Casino & Hotel
Queen Street Mall
Brisbane
Tel: 3306 8888

Jupiters Hotel & Casino
Broadbeach Island
Gold Coast Highway
Tel: 5592 8100

Pullman Reef Casino
35–41 Wharf Street

SIGHTSEEING TOURS AND EXCURSIONS

Queensland boasts a huge number of possibilities when it comes to expertly guided experiences. Here are just some options you will find more details under the appropriate place names in this book. From August to October you can go **whale-watching** in Hervey Bay, or there is **dolphin feeding** on Moreton Island all year round. You can be walked through an

eerie **lava tube** at Undarra, west of Cairns, or lowered into a **mine shaft** at Mount Isa – claustrophobics need not attend! **Trainspotters** will enjoy the quirky *Gulflander* that rattles between Croydon and Normanton.

For information on the myriad sightseeing activities that are available on the **Great Barrier Reef**, *see page 53*.

see page 53.

TRANSPORT

ACCOMMODATION

ACTIVITIES

A – Z

Cairns
Tel: 4030 8888
Jupiters Townsville
Sir Leslie Thiess Drive
Townsville
Tel: 4722 2373

Comedy Venues

Albion Comedy Club & Restaurant
281 Sandgate Rd
Albion, Brisbane
Tel: 3262 7308
Sit Down Comedy Club
Paddington Tavern
186 Given Terrace
Paddington, Brisbane
Tel: 3369 4466

Live Music

Brisbane has a well-deserved reputation for its live-music scene. The cluster of venues in Fortitude Valley makes it easy to wander from one to another, checking out the latest bands.
Arena Entertainment Complex
210 Brunswick Street
Fortitude Valley, Brisbane
Tel: 3252 5690
The Beat Megaclub
677 Ann Street, Brisbane
Tel: 3852 2661
Brisbane Convention & Exhibition Centre
Corner Merivale and Glenelg streets
South Bank, Brisbane
Tel: 3303 3063

Brisbane Entertainment Centre
Melaleuca Drive, Boondall
Tel: 3265 8111; www.brisent.com.au
Brisbane Jazz Club
1 Annie Street
Kangaroo Point, Brisbane
Tel: 3391 2006
The Hi-Fi
125 Boundary Street
West End, Brisbane
Tel: 1300 843 443
The Music Kafe
185 Boundary Street
West End, Brisbane
www.themusickafe.com
The Tivoli
52 Costin Street
Fortitude Valley, Brisbane
Tel: 3852 1711
X&Y Bar
648 Ann Street
Fortitude Valley, Brisbane
Tel: 3257 1259
Zoo
711 Ann Street
Fortitude Valley, Brisbane
Tel: 3854 1381
www.thezoo.com.au
The Zoo is Brisbane's oldest live-music venue and is the place to discover previously hidden talent. Expect any type of music ranging from hip-hop to jazz and rock to reggae.
Open Wed and Thur 7.30am–1am; Fri and Sat 8pm–2am.

Outside Brisbane

The Arts Centre Gold Coast
135 Bundall Road
Surfers Paradise

Tel: 5588 4000
Village Theatre Sanctuary Cove
Masthead Way
Sanctuary Cove
Tel: 5577 8999

Cinema

Check the daily newspaper for cinema listings, and the weekend newspapers for the best film reviews.
  For mainstream films in Brisbane, try the **Regent**, at 167 Queen Street (tel: 3027 9999), or the cinemas in the Myer Centre. Arthouse films are screened at the **Palace Centro Cinema**, at 39 James Street, Fortitude Valley (tel: 3852 4488), and the **Dendy Cinema**, at 346 George Street, Brisbane (tel: 3211 3244).
  Look out for listings for outdoor cinemas in the summer. The following are just some of Queensland's cinemas.

Gold Coast

Coolangatta BCC
Showcase on the Beach
Tel: 5536 9300
Gold Coast Arts Centre
135 Bundall Road
Surfers Paradise
Tel: 5581 6515
Pacific Fair BCC
Pacific Fair Shopping Centre
Broadbeach
Tel: 5572 2666

Sunshine Coast

Noosa
29 Sunshine Beach Road
Noosa Heads
Tel: 5447 5130
Townsville
Townsville Event Cinemas
Sturt Street (corner of Blackwood Street)
Tel: 4771 4101
Cairns
Cairns BCC
108 Grafton Street
Tel: 4051 1222
Cairns Central
Cairns Central Shopping Centre
Tel: 4052 1166
Mount Isa
Cinema Mount Isa

BELOW: independent cinema in Queensland.

22 Marian Street
Tel: 4743 2043

Pubs and Bars

The Bowery
676 Ann Street
Fortitude Valley, Brisbane
Tel: 3252 0202
www.thebowery.com.au
Craggy brick walls and plush banquettes make this converted terrace a cosy place for a drink. Live jazz week nights and live DJs at weekends.

Cru Bar and Cellar
22 James Street
Fortitude Valley, Brisbane
Tel: 3252 2400
www.crubar.com.au
Open-air seating and a stellar wine list draw Brisbane's beautiful. Daily 11.30–1am.

Glass
420 Brunswick Street
Fortitude Valley, Brisbane
Tel: 3252 0533
www.glassjazz.com.au
Crowds cluster around the yellow light-box bars in this drinking hole in the Judith Wright Contemporary Art Centre.

Old Favourites

Breakfast Creek Hotel
2 Kingsford Smith Drive
Breakfast Creek, Brisbane
Tel: 3262 5988
www.breakfastcreekhotel.com
Well known for its steaks, this historic pub has an interesting twist with Substation No. 41, its cocktail bar housed in a former substation on the hotel premises.

Friday's
Riverside Centre
123 Eagle Street, Brisbane
Tel: 3832 2122
Bar, restaurant, club in iconic setting. An institution.

Press Club (Empire Hotel)
339 Brunswick Street
Fortitude Valley, Brisbane
Tel: 3852 1216
Watch the Valley's passing parade from the verandas of this local favourite. Live DJs.

Regatta Hotel

543 Coronation Drive
Toowong, Brisbane
Tel: 3871 9595
One of Queensland's oldest pubs, built in 1874.

Story Bridge Hotel
200 Main Street
Kangaroo Point, Brisbane
Tel: 3391 2266
This revamped hotel under the bridge is a well-known place for a tipple.

SHOPPING

What to Buy

Aboriginal Art

Aboriginal artists sell their work in art centres, specialist galleries and craft retailers, and through agents. Each traditional artist owns the rights to his or her particular stories, motifs and tokens. Indigenous fabric designs by artists such as Jimmy Pike are eagerly sought. Dark paintings are the most common form of Koori (Aboriginal) art, but look out for contemporary works on board, boomerangs and didgeridoos.

Clothing

A distinct style of clothing has evolved in rural Australia (an area collectively known as "the Bush"). Driza-Bone oilskin coats, Akubra hats (wide-brimmed and usually made of felt) and the R. M. Williams range of bushwear (including boots and moleskin trousers) are good examples.

Food and Drink

Local delicacies include macadamia nuts, bush honey, royal jelly, chocolates and the inevitable Vegemite, a savoury spread. Australian wines can be bought at any pub or bottle shop, with fair-quality wines starting at A$15 a bottle.

Gemstones

Australia is the source of about 95 percent of the world's opals.

ABOVE: Aboriginal design.

"Boulder"opals – bright and vibrant – come from Quilpie.

Where to Shop

Australiana

Australian Geographic Shop
Shop 248, Myer Centre
Queen Street, Brisbane
Tel: 3220 0341
Many excellent Australian products for the great outdoors.

Opals Down Under
11 Ballantyne Court, Glenview
Sunshine Coast
Tel: 5494 5400
A wide range of opals including local boulder opals and the renowned black opal.

Quilpie Opals
Queen Street Mall
Brisbane
Tel: 3221 7369
One of Queensland's opal specialists.

R. M. Williams
Airport Drive
Eagle Farm, Brisbane
Tel: 3860 6600
Domestic Airport, Cairns
Tel: 4035 9702
Suppliers of bush gear including riding boots, Akubras (see Clothing) and oilskin bushmen's coats. Also at Cairns Airport.

Tjapukai Aboriginal Cultural Park
Kamerunga Road, Smithfield, Cairns
Tel: 4042 9999
Aboriginal art and crafts from Queensland and elsewhere.

TRANSPORT

ACCOMMODATION

ACTIVITIES

A – Z

International Brands

Queensland's Gold Coast has a variety of big-name international designer stores, and a number of others have moved into the newest addition to the Queen Street Mall in Brisbane, Queens Plaza.

These are some of Queensland's most exclusive designer outlets:

Cartier
Shop 3, The Moroccan Centre
9 Elkhorn Avenue
Surfers Paradise
Tel: 5529 3744

Gucci
Shop 6, Elkhorn Avenue
Surfers Paradise
Tel: 5531 6966

Hermès
Shop 154, 74 Seaworld Drive
Main Beach
Tel: 5532 4959
9–11 Elkhorn Avenue
Surfers Paradise
Tel: 5538 4388

Louis Vuitton
Ground Level, Queens Plaza
Queen Street Mall
Brisbane
Tel: 1300 883 880
Corner Orchid Avenue and
Elkhorn Avenue
Surfers Paradise
Tel: 5539 0026
18 Abbott Street
Cairns
Tel: 4031 5600

Prada
Shop 1, The Moroccan
11 Elkhorn Avenue
Surfers Paradise
Tel: 5539 8858

Tiffany & Co.
Ground level, Queens Plaza
Queen Street Mall
Brisbane
Tel: 1800 731 131

Books

Major bookstores such as **Dymocks Booksellers** and the Queensland chain **QBD** (www.qbd.com.au) can be found in the main centres. There are also numerous smaller, independent bookshops.

Brisbane
American Book Store
197 Elizabeth Street
Brisbane
Tel: 3229 4677
Originally specialising in stocking US titles not generally distributed in Australia, this bookshop still makes a business of selling the hard-to-get titles.

Archives Fine Books
40 Charlotte Street
Brisbane
Tel: 3221 0491
Massive collection of second-hand tomes.

Avid Reader Bookshop & Café
193 Boundary Street
West End, Brisbane
Tel: 3846 3422

Bent Books
205 Boundary Street
West End, Brisbane
Tel: 3846 5004
A second-hand bookshop stocking a wide range of genres, including gay and lesbian history and fiction.

Coaldrake's Bookshop
Shop 16, The Barracks
61 Petrie Terrace, Brisbane
Tel: 3367 8526.
100 Ann Street, Fortitude Valley,
Brisbane
Tel: 3854 0188.
Specialises in literature, history, travel and children's books.

Folio Books
80 Albert Street, Brisbane
Tel: 07 3221 1368
Architecture, design and graphic-arts book specialist.

Noosa
Written Dimension Bookshop
Shop 2, Cinema Centre
Beach Road, Noosa Heads
Tel: 5447 4433

Port Douglas
Whileaway Bookshop & Coffeeshop
43 Macrossan Street
Tel: 4099 4066

Townsville
Ancient Wisdom
390 Flinders Street Mall
Tel: 4771 2434

Shopping Centres

Brisbane
The main shopping action in Brisbane can be found on the Queen Street Mall. The half-kilometre retail precinct has five major shopping centres, two department stores and four shopping arcades. **Queens Plaza** is the latest addition, bringing some international brands to Queensland for the first time, while the **Myer Centre**'s six levels of speciality shops include many of Australia's fashion favourites. The 1920s **Brisbane Arcade** has fashion designers, antique dealers, jewellers and tea shops.

Nearby **Fortitude Valley** is home to edgy fashion designers (check out Ann and Brunswick Streets), stylish homeware shops and gourmet eateries (James Street). For an interesting wander around gift shops, antique stores and boutiques, try Latrobe Terrace in the suburb of Paddington.

Direct Factory Outlet
1 Airport Drive
Brisbane Airport
Tel: 3305 9250
The factory outlets for many of Australia's favourite fashion and homeware chains all under one roof. Daily 10am–6pm.

Toowong Village Shopping Centre
9 Sherwood Road
Toowong
Tel: 3870 7177
David Jones and Kmart, plus 80 speciality shops in Brisbane's west.

Westfield Shopping Centre
Corner Gympie and Hamilton roads, Chermside
Tel: 3359 0755
One of six big Westfield Malls in southeast Queensland, this one is accessible by public transport and offers all the major stores.

Gold Coast
Centro Surfers Paradise
Cavill Mall
Surfers Paradise
Tel: 5592 0155
Pick up anything from food supplies to sunglasses at this centre in the heart of Surfers.

Marina Mirage
74 Seaworld Drive
Main Beach
Tel: 5577 0088
Australian and international fash-

ion designers feature among the 80 luxurious speciality shops in this waterfront collection.

Pacific Fair Shopping Centre
Corner of Gold Coast Highway and Hooker Boulevard
Broadbeach
Tel: 5581 5117
The Gold Coast's largest shopping centre, with 270 speciality shops and Myer department store.

Cairns

Cairns Central
Corner of McLeod and Spence streets
Tel: 4041 4111
More than 180 speciality shops and department stores.

Department Stores

Queensland's main department stores are Myer and David Jones. They offer an extensive range of goods from hardware to homeware. Target and Kmart are variety stores at the lower end of the price spectrum.

David Jones, Queens Plaza, 149 Adelaide Street, Brisbane; tel: 07 3243 9000 or 13 33 57 for general enquiries; www.davidjones.com.au

Myer, 91 Queen Street, Brisbane, tel: 3232 0121; www.myer.com.au. Other locations include suburban Brisbane, Broadbeach, Cairns, Strathpine and Toowoomba.

Target, Brisbane Myer Centre, corner of Elizabeth and Albert streets; tel: 3231 6700; www.target.com.au. Other locations in suburban Brisbane, Broadbeach, Cairns, Hervey Bay, Mackay, Maroochydore, Rockhampton and Townsville.

Kmart, tel: 1800 634 251 (customer enquiries); www.kmart.com.au. There are no stores in Brisbane city, but several in suburban Brisbane and others in Broadbeach, Bundaberg, Cairns, Gladstone, Innisfail, Mackay, Maroochydore, Mount Isa, Rockhampton and Toowoomba.

Markets

Queensland's markets offer myriad buying opportunities, from organic produce to wonderful creations by local artists.

While some markets are open weekly, other "community" and "farmers'" markets only open a couple of days each month, and in the tropical north of the state, some markets only take place at certain times of the year. Most stallholders handle cash only.

Brisbane

Brisbane Marketplace
250 Sherwood Road, Rocklea
On Saturdays, this location, 11km (7 miles) from the CBD, is a fresh-food market selling everything from seafood to deli products, and on Sundays a flea market. Sat–Sun 6am–12pm, Wed 3pm–7.30pm.

Jan Power's Farmers' Market
Brisbane Powerhouse
119 Lamington Street, New Farm
One for the foodies, this organic market includes cooking demonstrations and visiting chefs. Second and 4th Saturday of the month. 6am–noon.

Queen Street Farmers' Market
Queens Street Mall (bridge end)
Great mix of good food, wine and produce. Wed 10am–6pm.

Riverside Markets
Riverside Centre and Eagle Street, Brisbane
Started by a handful of artists a couple of decades ago, there are now hundreds of stalls selling arts, crafts and gourmet goodies. Free, live performances add to the atmosphere. Sun 3am–7pm.

South Bank Markets
Stanley Street Plaza
South Bank Parklands
See these outdoor art-and-craft markets in full swing on a Friday evening. Fri 5pm–10pm; Sat 10am–5pm; Sun 9am–5pm.

Valley Markets
Brunswick Street
Fortitude Valley
Join locals in discovering the next up-and-coming jewellery design ers or get a quick massage at this Brisbane institution. Sat–Sun 8am–4pm.

Cairns

Cairns Night Market
71–75 The Esplanade
Housed in a permanent building, these markets cater to the

souvenir shopper. Daily 5pm–11pm.

Kuranda Markets
Time a day trip to this rainforest village for a day when the two markets are open. The original markets are open Sun, Wed, Thur and Fri 9am–3pm, and the Heritage Markets daily 9am–3pm.

Gold Coast

Carrara Markets
Nerang–Broadbeach Road, Carrara
The biggest markets on the Gold Coast offer everything from fruit and vegetables to clothing and plants. Sat–Sun 7am–4pm.

Surfers Paradise

Beachfront Markets
The Esplanade
Surfers Paradise
About 70 stalls selling locally made art, accessories and homeware at these night markets. Wed and Fri 5.30pm–10pm.

Noosa

Eumundi Markets
Memorial Drive
Eumundi
About 15 minutes from Noosa, this pretty village draws throngs of tourists and locals to its twice-weekly markets. Go there to enjoy the relaxed hinterland vibe. Sat 7am–2pm; Wed 8am–1.30pm.

Noosa Farmers' Market
Weyba Road, Noosa
Popular with locals, all the produce sold at this thriving market is produced by the stallholders. Sun and Wed 7am–noon.

Townsville

Cotters Market

BELOW: shopping in a market.

Flinders Street Mall
Stallholders sell pottery, jewellery and fresh produce from the Flinders Mall. Sun 8.30am–1pm. From May to December in Townsville, there are night markets on Fridays at Strand Park, 5.30–9.30pm.

SPORT

Spectator Sports

If you are keen to see one of the big football or cricket games, you'd be well advised to ask your travel agent to find out about tickets prior to arrival. The ticket agency, **Ticketek** (tel: 13 28 49; premier.ticketek.com.au), handles ticketing for most of the big games in Queensland. The main spectator-sports sites are as follows:

The Gabba
Vulture Street
Woolloongabba
Tel: 1300 843 422
 www.thegabba.com.au
Hosts the major cricket matches and Australian Rules Football.

Suncorp Stadium
Tel: 3331 5000
www.suncorpstadium.com.au
Hosts Queensland's rugby league, rugby union and soccer matches.

Dairy Farmers Stadium
Golf Links Drive
Kirwan (near Townsville)
Tel: 4722 7777
www.dairyfarmersstadium.com.au
Home ground to the North Queensland Cowboys national rugby league team.

Horse Racing

The principal thoroughbred racing club in Queensland is the **Brisbane Racing Club** (tel: 3268 2171; www.brc.com.au), which races at Brisbane's Eagle Farm and Doomben Racecourses.

The winter carnival in June is the main event in the racing calendar, featuring the Queensland Oaks Day, Stradbroke Day and the Brisbane Cup, all held at Eagle Farm.

Doomben Racecourse

Hampden Street, Ascot
Tel: 3268 6800
Eagle Farm Racecourse
Lancaster Road
Ascot
Tel: 3268 2171

Outdoor Activities

Bushwalking

Visitors wanting to "go bush" while they are touring Queensland have plenty of choices. There are about 220 national parks and state forests. The subtropical rainforest of Lamington National Park near the NSW border; the Aboriginal rock art in the Carnarvon National Park, in the Rockhampton area; and Eungella, near Mackay, are some of the most frequently visited areas. The Queensland government has been progressively establishing walking tracks through some of the most beautiful parts of the state as part of its "Great Walks" programme. The walks range from a couple of hours of walking to multi-day trips, and are located on Fraser Island, in the Conway Range near Airlie Beach, and the Mackay Highlands. More information about these walks is available from the Queensland Parks and Wildlife Service within the Department of Environment and Resource Management (www.derm.qld.gov.au).

For advice on bushwalks in general, see the Queensland Walks website (www.queenslandwalks.com.au). It includes regional information, links to bushwalking clubs and advice on how to prepare for a bushwalk.

Queensland Parks and Wildlife Service
Campsite bookings
Tel: 13 74 68; www.qld.gov.au/camping

Cycling

As long as you avoid the humidity and downpours of the height of summer, cycling in Queensland is to be recommended. A first point of contact should be the state's advocacy organisation, **Bicycle Queensland** (28 Vulture Street,

Performance venues often sell tickets through ticket agencies such as Ticketek and Ticketmaster. Names and numbers of venues are published in all listings of what's on.
Ticketek
Brisbane Myer City Box Office
Shop 95, Elizabeth Street, Brisbane. Also in other locations, including Cairns, Surfers Paradise and Townsville.
http://premier.ticketek.com.au
Ticketmaster
Record Exchange
Level 1, 65 Adelaide Street (opp City Hall), Brisbane. Also at Nerang, Surfers Paradise and the Gabba (Brisbane Cricket Ground).
Tel: 13 61 00
www.ticketmaster.com.au

West End; tel: 3844 1144; www.bq.org.au). Its website contains information on cycle shops and bicycle-user groups – local groups that often have regular ride programmes. The **Queensland Transport and Main Roads** website (www.tmrt.qld.gov.au/cycling) carries information on cycle routes and maps published by local councils from the Gold Coast to Townsville.

To make a relatively easy start, pedal some of the 400km (? miles) of cycling track in Brisbane.

Golf

Golf Queensland (tel: 3252 8155; www.golfqueensland.org.au) is a good starting point for golf players from abroad looking for information on public-access courses. Queensland has built a reputation for its golf-resort courses, with more than 10 on the Gold Coast and others on the Sunshine Coast and further north near the Whitsundays and Port Douglas.

The following list of some of Queensland's high-quality courses includes a number of resort courses.
Brisbane
Brookwater Golf Club

Tournament Drive
Springfield
Tel: 3814 5500
North Lakes Resort Course
Bridgeport Drive
North Lakes
Tel: 3480 9200
Royal Queensland
Curtin Avenue West
Eagle Farm
Tel: 3633 6500
Gold Coast
The Glades
Glades Drive
Robina
Tel: 5569 1900
Hope Island
Hope Island Resort
Hope Island Road
Hope Island
Tel: 5530 9000
The Pines
Sanctuary Cove Resort
Caseys Road
Sanctuary Cove
Tel: 5699 9050
Sunshine Coast
Hyatt Regency Coolum
1 Warran Road
Coolum Beach
Tel: 5446 1234
Noosa Springs
Links Drive
Noosa Heads
Tel: 5447 4600
North Queensland
The Links at Port Douglas
Off Old Port Road
Port Douglas
Tel: 4087 2222
Paradise Palms Golf Course
Captain Cook Highway
Near Cairns
Tel: 4059 9900
Turtle Point Golf Course
Laguna Whitsundays Resort
Kunapipi Springs Road
Whitsundays
Tel: 4947 7777

Snorkelling and Diving

Seeing the Great Barrier Reef up close and personal through either diving or snorkelling is a must for any Queensland holiday-maker. Apart from the 2,900 individual reefs and 70 coral cays that make up the Great Barrier Reef, there are also dive sites near ship-wrecks and outcrops off the southern coastline that can be explored from the Fraser Coast, Sunshine Coast or Gold Coast. Water temperatures stay warm all year round, and August through to January generally offers the best visibility for divers.

Snorkelling is a great introduction to the reef's fascinating underwater world and simply requires the ability to swim and a reasonable level of fitness. Most day trips from Cairns offer some instruction and, in some cases, a guided safari for snorkellers. While snorkelling may involve jumping out of a boat in some places, including the Low Isles, Green Island and Heron Island, it is possible to walk into the water. Less confident swimmers can also ask about using a "float coat" to provide extra buoyancy while snorkelling.

Operators in Cairns, Port Douglas, Townsville and the Whitsunday Islands offer a range of options to holiday-makers keen to do some diving. At the lowest level is the introductory dive. It doesn't require scuba-diving certification, and after some initial instruction, the diver will be accompanied by a qualified instructor on a single dive. Any other diving trips require certification, and the dive courses offered by dive companies make it possible to acquire initial open-water certification while on holiday.

Day trips from Cairns to reefs like Hastings, Saxon and Norman are usually the domain of less experienced divers, while the experienced diver is likely to opt for live-aboard boats doing four-to seven-day trips. Cod Hole is the most famous dive site off Cairns and is often included in an extended trip to the Ribbon Reefs or the Coral Sea for experienced divers.

As a starting point for planning a trip, have a look at the Dive Queensland website (www.dive-queensland.com.au). This is an association of dive-tourism operators and includes information on day trips, extended diving trips, diving insurance and training institutions.
Dive Queensland
PO Box 5120
Cairns, Queensland 4870
Tel: 4051 4298

Sailing & Sea Kayaking

Boating enthusiasts will find Queensland offers plenty of opportunities to indulge in their sport. Most are drawn to the 74 islands of the Whitsundays, where even novices are permitted to go "bareboating", cruising the calm waters without any crew.

There are dozens of operators hiring yachts, catamarans, tall ships and sea kayaks at Airlie Beach and Shute Harbour. To begin arranging a boat charter before leaving home, see the **Whitsunday Tourism** website (www.tourismwhitsundays.com.au) or contact the **Whitsunday Central**

BELOW: boat tours are a great way to see the reef.

Reservation Centre (tel: 4946 5299).

To get in touch with fellow sailors and participate in local events, contact the **Whitsunday Sailing Club** at Airlie Beach (tel: 4946 6138; www.whitsundaysailing club.com.au).

Swimming and Surfing

Queensland's surf beaches are concentrated in the southern corner of the state. Surf schools have become something of a boom industry, with lots of newcomers entering the business. Surfing Australia runs coaching accreditation courses, and also accredits surf schools. Some unaccredited schools may still be excellent, and some accredited ones may not be. Generally, the ex-professional surfers offer very good services, and there is no denying the value of their years of experience. But beware – there are some surf coaches around who can barely surf themselves. It's worth doing a bit of research and asking around before deciding where to go. Some schools worth checking out:

Cheyne Horan's School of Surf
Surfers Paradise
Tel: 1800 227873
www.cheynehoran.com.au
With world champion Cheyne Horan

Godfathers of the Ocean
Surfers Paradise
Tel: 61 7 5593 5661
www.godfathersoftheocean.com.au
With ex-professional surfer Michael Munga Barry

Gold Coast Surfing Centre
Coolangatta
Tel: 0417 191 629
With former pro surfer Dave Davidson

North Stradbroke Island Surf School
North Stradbroke Island
Tel: 0407 642 616
www.northstradbrokeislandsurfschool.com.au

Walkin' On Water
Coolangatta
Tel: 0418 780 311
www.walkinonwater.com

Noosa Surf Lessons

Noosa Heads
Tel: 0400 182 614
www.noosasurflessons.com.au
Multi-lesson packages and board hire.

Intermediate to serious surfers should try Burleigh Heads, Surfers Paradise and Coolangatta, while surfers of all skill levels will find something to like about Noosa Heads, and Noosa Main Beach is ideal for beginners. Airlie Beach marks the beginning of the Great Barrier Reef, which means calm-water beaches only for the rest of the coastline. *For recommended surf schools, see left.*

Visitors looking to cool down in Brisbane could take advantage of **Streets Beach** at South Bank, a man-made beach complete with white sand, palm trees and its own year-round life-saving patrol. Major hotels and resorts have their own pools, but many serious lappers find that these are a bit short for a good workout. There are six public pools in Brisbane that are open year-round and heated, including the 50-metre Centenary Pool (400 Gregory Terrace, Spring Hill) and the 50-metre Fortitude Valley Pool (432 Wickham Street; tel: 3257 1240).

Tennis

Play in the early morning and/or late afternoon to avoid the sun. Ask about equipment hire when ringing to book a court. A good stop for information is **Tennis Queensland** (tel: 3120 7900). Its website (www.tennis.com.au/qld) will also let you search for a tennis club in the area.

There are plenty of exciting attractions aimed at children in Queensland. Theme parks on the Gold Coast have everything from water slides at **Wet'n'Wild Water World** and **Whitewater World** to movie sets at **Warner Brothers Movie World**. Dolphins and polar bears keep smaller kids amused at **Sea**

ABOVE: a Queensland koala.

World, while the rides at **Dreamworld** cater to older children.

Australia Zoo (tel: 5436 2000) on the Sunshine Coast is the place made famous by the late Steve Irwin, otherwise known as the Crocodile Hunter. There are numerous shows throughout the day, and although crocodiles may be the main attraction, the zoo allows visitors to feed the Asian elephants and cuddle koalas. Cuddly koalas can also be found at the **Lone Pine Sanctuary** (tel: 3378 1366), near Brisbane.

The **Queensland Museum** (tel: 3840 7555) on Brisbane's South Bank is full of inspiring interactive exhibitions for kids. At the hands-on **Sciencentre** they can learn how to measure an earthquake, play a thongophone and piece together a human jigsaw. At the **Cobb & Co. Museum**, at Toowoomba, there are examples of transport from the horse-drawn era.

Budding paleontologists will enjoy the dinosaur circuit, taking in Richmond's **Kronosaurus Korner**, Hughenden's **Flinders Discovery Centre**, and the **Lark Dinosaur Trackway**, near Winton. The excitement of huge cattle sales can be seen on Wednesdays at **Dalrymple Sales Yards** (tel: 4761 5300) on the Flinders Highway at Charters Towers.

At **Tjapukai Aboriginal Cultural Park**, in Cairns (tel: 4042 9999), kids of all ages can learn to throw a boomerang, while the exciting night show includes an evening of corroboree around a campfire.

TRANSPORT

A – Z

ACCOMMODATION

AN ALPHABETICAL SUMMARY OF PRACTICAL INFORMATION

ACTIVITIES

A – Z

A dmission Charges

Entry to attractions in Queensland varies widely. The "worlds" – Dreamworld, Whitewater World, Warner Bros Movie World and Sea World – have some of the highest admission charges: for example, at Dreamworld adults pay A$80 and children A$50. There are passes that allow you multiple visits (over several weeks) to both Dreamworld and its affiliated Whitewater World for not much more than the cost of a day pass. Wet'n'Wild Water World is more expensive at A$60 for adults and A$32 for children. If you're planning to go to Sea World, Wet'n'Wild Water World and Warner Bros Movie World, there is a money-saving pass that entitles holders to entry to all three attractions. It is valid until a pre-

scribed date and so is costed according to when you buy it. Regardless of when you purchase the pass, it will be a huge saving if you are visiting all three parks.

While some attractions, such as Australia Zoo, Curumbin Bird Sanctuary and the Daintree Discovery Centre, can also be relatively pricey, they all offer family tickets, which can help keep a lid on costs if travelling with children. There are also plenty of museums and art galleries where entry is free or A$5–10 for adults and a couple of dollars for children. The Brisbane website, www.ourbrisbane. com, has an excellent section pointing out attractions and activities that are free.

B udgeting for Your Trip

Australia has low inflation, and the basics – food, accommoda-

tion, admission charges – are still comparatively inexpensive. A plate of noodles or pasta in an average restaurant costs about A$15; for fine dining expect to pay A$30–50 for a main course. A reasonable bottle of Australian wine from a liquor store starts at about A$15, a 260ml glass of beer (about half a pint) costs from A$4, and a cup of coffee or tea about the same.

Hiring (renting) a small car costs from A$60 per day. Petrol (gasoline) costs around A$1.40 per litre, more expensive than in the US but cheaper than in most European countries. A half day coach sightseeing tour is A$50–150 per person.

A dorm bed at a backpacker hostel can be as little as A$20 a night, and a double room in a motel or low-key resort from A$70–150 per night. Luxurious rooms in a 5-star hotel start at A$250 and skyrocket from there.

The cost of a taxi ride in Queensland depends on a number of factors: the flagfall, the per-kilometre rate, the per-minute rate and the booking fee. The per-kilometre rate in southeast Queensland for metered cabs is A$2.06. The waiting time or per-minute fee is 76 cents per minute. The booking fee is A$1.50. Flagfalls (minimum charges) vary according to the time of day, with the lowest, A$2.90, applying 7am–7pm Monday to Friday except for public holidays, and the highest, A$6.30, applying from midnight to 5am on Sunday.

C hildren

Queensland is a very child-friendly destination, with ample attractions ideal for kids. Moreover, there is a general policy of having reduced admission charges for children (usually half-price and usually under 14 years of age) as well as family tickets. The latter can be particularly attractive when compared with the price of individual tickets. Boredom is one factor to consider if you are contemplating a road trip or travelling Queensland's long distances. Popular coastal resorts and larger towns will certainly have baby-sitting services. Contact your accommodation or check the local Yellow Pages directory for such services and do check that they have official accreditation.

Climate

The southern half of Queensland experiences four seasons, with a warm to hot summer (December to January) and a mild winter (June to August). The inland regions of the state have the greatest range in temperature. There, temperatures can drop below 0°C (32°F) at night. In the north of the state there is a wet season from mid-December through to April, when rainfall and thunderstorms are

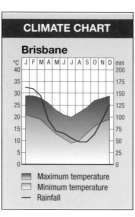

CLIMATE CHART

Brisbane

	Maximum temperature
	Minimum temperature
—	Rainfall

common and there are occasional tropical cyclones. The rest of the year in the north is noticeably dry.

Consequently, April to September during the Australian autumn and winter, when rainfall and temperatures are lower, is regarded as the best time to visit Queensland, particularly the north of the state. In Cairns the temperature range in winter is 16–26°C (55–90°F) and in summer it can exceed 36°C (125°F), when the humidity is high.

Brisbane has summer temperatures that range from 20°C to the high 30s (86°F plus) and winter temperatures of 10–20°C (35–68°F).

What to Wear

Whatever the season, you can forget your overcoat. Even a sweater may not be necessary unless you are travelling in the Outback in winter, where temperatures will be cold at night. Generally, the most you will need are shorts and long trousers and possibly skirts and/or dresses for women. Do bring some light long-sleeved shirts to protect shoulders and arms against sunburn. Comfortable walking shoes, a hat and good-quality sunglasses are essential.

Crime and Safety

Common-sense rules apply when visiting Queensland. Because of

its high tourist profile, petty theft can be an issue in popular visitor locations. Keep wallets out of sight; do not leave valuables visible in the car or luggage unattended. Take care when using ATMs to withdraw cash, particularly at night or in dimly lit areas, and keep an eye out when using public telephones to make sure someone doesn't sneak up behind you.

Drink spiking is far from commonplace, but to ensure your safety, police suggest travellers go with someone to the bar if they offer to buy you a drink, never accept a drink from a container or already opened drink that is being passed around, and avoid leaving a drink unattended. The emergency number for police, ambulance and the fire brigade is 000, or 112 from a mobile phone.

Report any theft to the police straight away, as you will need a police report if you wish to make a claim on travel insurance. The details of the closest police station will be listed in the White Pages under "Police". Non-urgent enquiries can generally be made at police stations from 8am to 4pm, but it is worth phoning first, as stations in the country may have more limited opening hours.

Customs Regulations

Australia has extremely strict regulations about what can and cannot be brought into the country. Before disembarking from the plane, visitors are asked to fill in an Incoming Passenger Card. There are heavy fines for false or inaccurate claims, so it's always best to declare an item if in doubt.

Strict quarantine laws apply in Australia to protect the agricultural industries and native Australian flora and fauna from introduced diseases. All food products, no matter how well processed and packaged, must be declared on arrival.

Overseas visitors are allowed to bring any articles for personal use into Australia free of any duty. You may also import A$900-worth of dutiable goods. Non-dutiable allowances include 2,250ml (about 4 pints) of alcohol (wine, beer or spirits); 250 cigarettes, or 250 grams of cigars or tobacco products other than cigarettes. Members of the same family who are travelling together may combine their individual duty/tax-free allowances.

There is no limit to the amount of foreign or Australian currency that you can bring into or out of the country, but cash amounts of more than A$10,000 (or its equivalent) must be declared to Customs on arrival and departure.

Customs Information Centre, tel: 1 300 363 263 (in Australia); 61 2 6275 6666 (outside Australia); www.customs.gov.au

D isabled Travellers

Queensland caters reasonably well for people with disabilities, but you would be wise to start making enquiries and arrangements before leaving home. A good place to begin is with the **National Information Communication Awareness Network** (NICAN, PO Box 407 Curtain, ACT 2605; tel: 1 800 806 769; www. nican.com.au), a national organisation that keeps a database of facilities and services with disabled access, including accommodation and tourist sights. It also keeps track of the range of publications on the subject.

The **Spinal Injuries Association** (109 Logan Road, Woolloongabba, Queensland 4102; tel: 07 3391 2044 or 1800-810 513 (in Australia); www.spinal.com. au) provides an information phone line to help link people with disabilities with service providers.

The **Queensland Holidays** website (www.queenslandholidays.com. au) is also an excellent resource. Listings for attractions include clear information about disabled access.

E lectricity

The supply is 240/250V, 50Hz. Most good hotels have universal outlets for 110V shavers and small appliances. For larger appliances such as hairdryers, you will need a converter and a flat three-pin adaptor.

Embassies and Consulates

The following are the closest contacts for travellers needing assistance when in Queensland.
British Consular Agency, Level 26 Waterfront Place, 1 Eagle Street, Brisbane; tel: 07 3223 3200; http://ukinaustralia.fco.gov.uk/en
Canadian Consulate General, Level 5, 111 Harrington Street, Sydney; tel: 02 9364 3000; recorded information: 02 9364 3050; www.canada.org.au
Consulate General of Ireland, Level 26, 1 Market Street, Sydney; tel: 02 9264 9635; www.irish-consulatesydney.net
US Consulate General, MLC Centre, Level 59, 19–29 Martin Place, Sydney; tel: 02 9373 9200; after-hours emergencies, tel: 02 4422 2201; http://sydney. usconsulate.gov

Overseas Missions

Canada, Australian High Commission, Suite 710, 50 O'Connor Street, Ottawa, Ontario K1P 6L2; tel: 613-236 0841 (plus consulates in Toronto and Vancouver)
Ireland, Australian Embassy, Fitzwilton House, Wilton Terrace, Dublin 2; tel: 01-664 5300;

email: austremb.dublin@dfat.gov.au
United Kingdom, Australian High Commission, Australia House, The Strand, London WC2B 4LA; tel: 020-7379 4334; www.uk. embassy.gov.au
United States, Australian Embassy, 1601 Massachusetts Avenue, Washington DC NW 20036-2273; tel: 202-797 3000; www.usa.embassy.gov.au (plus consulates in New York, Los Angeles, San Francisco, Miami, Detroit, Atlanta etc)

Emergency Numbers

The emergency number for police, ambulance and the fire brigade is 000, or 112 from a mobile phone.

G ay and Lesbian

Queensland may not be the gay mecca that you would find in Sydney, but there is a thriving gay community in the state's capital and Noosa is a favoured spot to wind down after the Sydney Gay Mardi Gras in March.

Further north there are several exclusively gay and lesbian hotels and resorts, including **Turtle Cove Resort** near Cairns (tel: 07 4059 1800) and **Pink Flamingo** in Port Douglas (tel: 07 4099 6622).

To find the rainbow edge to Brisbane's nightlife, try **The Wickham Hotel** in Fortitude Valley. There's also the **Sportsman Hotel**, which is the oldest gay bar in town. The annual **Brisbane Pride Festival** (www.pridebrisbane. org.au) is held in June. The highlight of the month-long festival is

BELOW: children playing in the sand on a Queensland beach.

generally a parade and fair day.

In Cairns there is Nu-trix Nightclub (53 Spence Street; tel: 07 4051 8223; Wed–Sun from 9pm) and Montage Bar at Skinny Dips Resort (18–24 James Street; tel: 07 4099 6622).

Check the gay press for more details about places to go and meeting spots. *Queensland Pride* is a free monthly newspaper, and *Q News* is a free fortnightly newspaper; both are based in Brisbane.

The International Gay and Lesbian Travel Association is a professional body for people involved with gay tourism. Visitors can find providers of different travel services on its consumer website. Gay and Lesbian Tourism Australia fulfils a similar function in Australia. **International Gay and Lesbian Travel Association**, tel: 02-9818 6669; www.iglta.org
Gay and Lesbian Tourism Australia, tel: 0414 446 401; www.galta.com.au

■H ealth and Medical Care

Australia has excellent medical services. For medical attention out of working hours, go to the casualty department in one of the large hospitals or, if the matter is less urgent, visit one of the seven-day medical clinics in the major towns and tourist centres. Look under "Medical Centres" or "Medical Practitioners" in the Yellow Pages, or ask at your hotel.

New Zealand, Finland, Italy, Malta, the Netherlands, Norway, Sweden, the UK and Ireland have reciprocal health-care arrangements with Australia, so visitors are entitled to free hospital treatment and medicare (the Australian national health plan) benefits for GP treatment. Taking out a travel-insurance policy that covers your health is recommended, however.

Vaccinations are not required if you are flying directly to Australia and have not passed through an epidemic zone or a yellow fever-, cholera- or typhoid-infected area

in the six days prior to your arrival.

Emergency medical assistance, tel: 000, or 112 from a mobile phone.

Pharmacies

"Chemist shops" are a great place to go for advice on minor ailments such as bites, scratches and stomach trouble. They also stock a wide range of useful products such as sunblock, nappies (diapers) and non-prescription drugs.

If you have a prescription from your doctor, and you want to take it to a pharmacist in Australia, you will need to have it endorsed by a local medical practitioner.

Local Health Hazards

The biggest danger for travellers in Australia is the sun. Even on mild, cloudy days it has the potential to burn. Wear a broad-brimmed hat and, if you are planning on being out for a while, a long-sleeved shirt made from a light fabric. Wear SPF 30+ sunblock at all times, even under a hat. Avoid sunbathing between 11am and 3pm.

Care should be taken while swimming at Queensland's surfing beaches, which stretch from Rainbow Bay in the south to Agnes Water, south of Gladstone. The best advice is to swim only at beaches that are patrolled, and to

BELOW: beware of stings.

swim between the yellow and red flags. Never swim at night after a few drinks or immediately after a heavy meal.

Dangerous Animals

Take care to swim inside stinger-resistant swimming enclosures when holidaying in the north of the state between November and April. It is during those months that the deadly box jellyfish appears in the area a couple of kilometres off the mainland beaches. A "stinger suit" or a full wetsuit can also provide the necessary protection. These may be available for hire.

For more information on marine stingers, go to: www.marinestingers.com.au.

Freshwater and saltwater crocodiles live in Queensland's waterways north of Rockhampton. They may be found close to the shore in the sea, or in rivers and creeks. Warning signs usually alert people to the areas where it is dangerous to swim. Also avoid camping, preparing food or cleaning fish within 50 metres/yds of the water's edge.

Mosquitoes can also be more than an occasional annoyance on a summer evening, carrying viruses such as dengue fever and Ross River fever. The best way to avoid contracting these viruses – which lead to high fevers, headaches and joint and muscle pains – is to cover up, use insect repellents and mosquito nets.

Dangerous snakes are part of Australia's landscape. In Queensland there are 120 species of snake and about 20 of them are considered dangerous. Most snakes will not attack unless directly provoked. Avoid trouble by wearing covered shoes when walking in the bush, and checking areas such as rock platforms and rock crevices before making yourself comfortable. Seek medical advice for any bite.

Other animals to be wary of include dingoes, as they have been known to attack humans, and the deadly redback spider.

ABOVE: the local wildlife is varied.

Internet

Internet cafés have proliferated in recent years, and travellers to Australia should have no trouble finding internet access in major cities and tourist locations. Many hotels and hostels now have facilities for people travelling with their own laptops, and local libraries fill the gap in communities where there is no commercial internet facility. Access in libraries is often free, or there may be a nominal charge.

Left Luggage

There are no left-luggage facilities at Brisbane Airport for security reasons. However, Cairns Airport has a baggage-storage facility run by Smart Carte Australia (tel: 0407 359 678). There are lockers for luggage on all three levels of Brisbane's Transit Centre in Roma Street. To check the facilities available at other Queensland train stations, see www.queensland-rail.com.au.

Lost Property

You should report loss or theft of valuables to the police immediately, as most insurance policies insist on a police report.

At Brisbane Airport, direct any enquiries about property lost in the terminal to the Visitors Information Desk on Level 2 in the arrivals hall, tel: 07 3406 3190. Enquiries about lost baggage should be directed to the airline involved.

Lost property found at a City-train station in Brisbane is held for three days at that particular station before being forwarded to Roma Street Station, tel: 07 3235 1859 between 10.15am and 2.25pm Mon – Fri. For anything left on Brisbane's ferries, tel: 07 3229 7778, 9am – 5.30pm daily.

To locate property left on a Brisbane bus, contact the Brisbane City Council call centre, tel: 07 3403 8888. The lost-property office is located at 69 Ann Street, Brisbane.

For items missing on Grey-hound Australia coaches, contact its lost-property department, tel: 07 3868 0901, or visit the nearest coach terminal.

Maps

The accredited Visitor Information Centres, indicated by the yellow "i" against a blue background, give away useful maps of their areas. The Queensland Holidays website carries a map of Queensland showing the locations of the Visitor Centres. Visit the RACQ Travel Centres (www.racq.com.au) for touring maps. They can also be mailed overseas to international visitors. For a detailed street map, look for either a UBD or Gregory's Street Directory.

Media

Publications

Australia has two national papers, *The Australian* and *The Financial Review*, both excellent publications at the serious end of the scale. Brisbane's daily newspaper is *The Courier-Mail*, an energetic tabloid that appears on Monday to Saturday. On Sunday, the major Brisbane newspaper is *The Sunday Mail*. Both are part of the News Corporation stable.

Foreign newspapers and magazines are available at news-agents in Brisbane, the airport and other major tourist districts, usually within a couple of days of publication.

Radio and Television

The Australian Broadcasting Commission (ABC) runs a couple of national television channels, including a 24-hour news channel, as well as an extensive network of radio stations. ABC Television offers excellent news and current affairs coverage, as well as local and imported drama, comedy, sports and cultural programmes. The commercial TV broadcasters, generally known by their old analogue station names – Channels 7, 9 and 10 – offer several digital channels covering news, drama, soaps, infotainment, travel shows and, between them, coverage of all the major international sporting events. Many hotels provide access to a large number of cable-television stations in addition to the free-to-air channels.

The radio stations include Triple J (107.7 FM in Brisbane and 107.5 in Cairns), rock and comment for twentysomethings; Classic FM (106.1 FM in Brisbane and 105.9 FM in Cairns), continuous classical music; and Radio National (792 FM in Brisbane and 105.1 FM in Cairns), excellent national news and events coverage. Commercial radio stations include Triple M FM (104.7 in Brisbane), for popular local and international rock; and Nova 1069, for contemporary music (106.9 FM). For frequencies in other parts of Queensland, check with locals.

Of particular interest to overseas travellers is Australia's ethnic/multicultural broadcaster, SBS. The organisation's television channel offers many foreign-language films and documentaries, and Australia's best coverage of world news. SBS Radio (93.3 FM in Brisbane) offers programmes in a variety of languages.

ABOVE: a busy news-stand in Brisbane.

which generally open 9.30am–5pm, but you'll usually get a better rate at one of the big banks.

Lost Cards

If you lose your credit card, call:
American Express, tel: 1 300 132 639
Diners Club, tel: 1 300 360 060
MasterCard, tel: 1 800 120 113 (world service puts you in contact with local authority)
Visa, tel: 1 800 450 346

Opening Hours

Banks generally open 9.30am–4pm Monday to Thursday, and 9.30am–5pm on Friday. Most shops are open 9am–5.30pm Monday to Friday, and to 5pm on Saturday. Many of the larger shops in southeast Queensland and in the major tourist centres to the north now open all day Sunday as well. Thursday night is late-night shopping, when some shops stay open until 8 or 9pm. In Surfers Paradise there is late-night shopping seven days a week, and Brisbane's Queen Street Mall stays open until 9pm on Friday nights. Major supermarkets and convenience stores also often have extended trading hours.

Postal Services

Post offices are open 9am–5pm Mon–Fri, with some branches opening Sat morning. The General Post Office (GPO) is located at 261 Queen Street in Brisbane and opens 7am–6pm weekdays.

Domestic Post

Posting a standard letter to anywhere in Australia costs 50c. The letter will reach a same-city destination overnight, but may take up to a week if it is being sent to a remote part of the country.

Yellow Express Post bags can be used to send parcels and letters overnight to Australian state capital cities and between major towns in Queensland. The cost represents very good value when

Money

Currency

The local currency is the Australian dollar (abbreviated as A$ or simply $), made up of 100 cents. Coins come in 5, 10, 20, and 50 cent units and 1 and 2 dollar units. Notes come in 5, 10, 20, 50 and 100 dollar units. Single cents still apply to many prices, and in these cases the amount will be rounded down or up to the nearest 5c amount. Carry smaller notes for tipping, taxis and payment in small shops and cafés.

Banks

The four big banks in Australia are the National, the Commonwealth, Westpac and ANZ. Trading hours are generally 9.30am–4pm Monday to Thursday and 9.30am–5pm on Friday. A few of the smaller banks and credit unions open on Saturday mornings. Most banks will have an internal board or a window display advertising exchange rates; if not, ask a teller (cashier).

Credit Cards and ATMs

Carrying a recognised credit or debit card such as Visa, Master-Card, American Express or Diners Club is always a good idea when travelling. A credit card should provide access to EFTPOS (electronic funds transfer at point of sale), which is the easiest and often the cheapest way to exchange money – amounts are automatically debited from the selected account. Many Australian businesses are connected to EFTPOS.

There are literally hundreds of ATMs around Queensland, allowing for easy withdrawal of cash, and again, a linked credit card will provide access to both credit and other bank accounts. Some of the islands do have limited banking facilities, so it is worth checking before going there for an extended period.

Exchange

Most foreign currencies can be changed at the airport, with major exchange outlets operating to fit in with flight arrival times. Queensland has many bureaux de change,

compared with courier costs.
Postal enquiries: tel: 13 76 78.

Overseas Post

The cost of overseas mail depends on the weight and size of the item. Postcards cost A$1.20 by airmail to the UK and the US. Standard overseas mail takes about a week to most destinations.

There are two types of express international mail. Express Mailing Service International Courier (EMS) will reach the UK in three to four working days. The minimum cost for a package is A$35. Express Post International (EPI) will arrive in the UK within four working days, and is priced according to weight and size. The cost of a prepaid envelope for documents or a letter starts at A$11.

EMS and EPI, tel: 13 76 78

Public Holidays

School holidays run from early December to the third week in January, and there are two weeks at Easter, late June and early July and late September to early October. It can be difficult to get discounted air fares and at these times.

1 January New Year's Day
26 January Australia Day
March/April Good Friday, Holy Saturday, Easter Monday
25 April Anzac Day
May (1st Mon) May Day
June (2nd Mon) Queen's Birthday
25 December Christmas Day
26 December Boxing Day

T elephones

Local calls in Australia are untimed, and cost about 25c from private phones and 50c from public phones. Instead of making calls from hotel rooms, which can be double or triple the price, you should aim to use public phones. Phonecards are widely available from newsagents and other outlets displaying the Telstra logo.

Most interstate (STD) and international (ISD) calls can be made using phonecards. These calls are timed and can be expensive, but cheaper rates are available after 6pm and at weekends.

Queensland has two types of telephone directory. The White Pages is an alphabetical listing of residential and business phone numbers. The Yellow Pages lists commercial operations under subject headings.

Calls made from Brisbane to other parts of Queensland are charged at STD rates, although it is no longer necessary to dial an area code first. However, you do have to dial an area code to call interstate in Australia. All regular numbers in Australia (other than toll-free or special numbers) are eight digits long. The area code for Queensland is 07.

Numbers beginning with 1 800 are toll-free. Numbers beginning with 13 are charged at a local rate, even if the call is made STD. Numbers beginning with 018, 041, 015 and 019 are mobile-phone numbers.

Directory enquiries: 1223
Overseas assistance. 1225
International calls: 0011, followed by the national code of the country you are calling.

Mobile Phones

Most of the large urban areas and major rural centres are covered by a telecoms "net". But some smaller towns and remote regions are not covered yet, which means that mobiles have limited use as a safety communications device when travelling in the Outback.

Many visitors will find that they can bring their own phones with them and use them without too much trouble. Contact your provider before leaving home to find out what is involved. To hire a phone during your stay, look under "Mobile Telephones" in the Yellow Pages, and shop around for the best deal – this is a very competitive market. There are also outlets offering mobile

phones for hire in some of the airport terminals.

Time Zone

Queensland is on Eastern Australian Standard Time (EST), which is 10 hours ahead of Greenwich Mean Time, 15 hours ahead of New York and 18 hours ahead of California. Unlike other states on Australia's east coast, Queensland does not observe daylight saving.

Tipping

Tipping is not obligatory, but a small gratuity for good service is appreciated. It is not customary to tip taxi drivers, hairdressers or porters at airports. Porters have set charges at railway terminals, but not at hotels. Restaurants do not automatically include service charges, but it is customary to tip waiters up to 10 percent of the bill for good service.

Tourist Information

For tourist information before you leave home, see the Tourism Australia website, www.australia.com
United Kingdom: Australia Centre, Australia House, The Strand, London WC2R 0LZ; tel: 020-7438 4601.
USA: 6100 Center Drive, Los Angeles CA 90045; tel: 310-695 3200.

Within Queensland, each of the major regions has its own tourist information centre.

V isitor Info Centres

The following is a list of the main tourist information centres in Queensland:
Brisbane
Corner Albert and Queen streets, Brisbane.
Tel: 07 3006 6290;
www.visitbrisbane.com.au
Cairns and Tropical North Visitor Information Centre
51 The Esplanade, Cairns.
Tel: 07 4051 3588;

www.cairnsgreatbarrierreef.org.au

Coolangatta
Shop 14B, corner Griffith and
Warner streets, Coolangatta.
Tel: 1300 309 440;
www.visitgoldcoast.com

Gladstone
Marina Ferry Terminal,
Bryan Jordan Drive, Gladstone.
Tel: 07 4972 9000;
www.gladstoneregion.info

Hervey Bay
Corner Urraween and Maryborough Hervey roads, Hervey Bay.
Tel: 07 4125 9855;
www.visitherveybay.info

Mission Beach
Porters Promenade,
Mission Beach.
Tel: 07 4068 7099;
www.missionbeachtourism.com

Mount Isa
19 Marian Street, Mount Isa.
Tel: 07 4749 1555;
www.outbackatisa.com.au

Noosa
Hastings Street, Noosa Heads.
Tel: 07 5430 5020;
www.visitnoosa.com.au

**Rockhampton Visitor Informa-
tion Centre**
Customs House, 208 Quay Street,
Rockhampton.
Tel: 07 4921 2311;
www.capricornholidays.com.au

Surfers Paradise
Cavill Avenue, Surfers Paradise.
Tel: 1300 309 440;
www.visitgoldcoast.com

**Townsville – Flinders Mall
Information Centre**
Flinders Mall, Townsville.
Tel: 07 4721 3660;
www.townsvilleonline.com.au

Whitsunday Information Centre
Bruce Highway, Prosperpine.
Tel: 07 4945 3711.
www.tourismwhitsundays.com.au

Visas and Passports

Visitors to Australia must have a
passport valid for the entire period
of their stay. Non-Australian citizens also needs a visa, which
must be obtained before leaving
home – except for New Zealand
citizens, who are issued with a visa
on arrival in Australia.

ABOVE: a leafy information centre.

eVisitor The eVisitor is a free
visa allowing visitors from 35
European countries (including
the UK, Ireland, France and Germany) to stay in Australia for up
to three months within a
12-month period. You must apply
for this visa online at www.immi.
gov.au/visitors/tourist/evisitor, and
you should allow 10 working
days for processing.
    ETA visas The Electronic Trans-
fer Authority (ETA) enables visitors
from eight countries, including
the United States of America,
Canada and Singapore, to obtain
either a visitor or business visa on
the spot from their travel agent or
airline office. ETA visas are generally valid for a 12-month period;
single stays must not exceed
three months, but return visits
within the 12-month period are
allowed. ETAs are issued free, or
you can purchase one online for
A$20 from www.eta.immi.gov.au.
    Tourist visas These are
available for continuous stays
longer than three months, and for
visitors from countries not eligible
for eVisitor or ETA visas. They
allow stays of three, six or 12
months. Tourist visas can be
applied for online at www.immi.gov.
au/visitors/tourist, if you are from one
of the 55 eligible countries. You
can also have a travel agent or
airline office lodge your applica-
tion. Otherwise, you must apply by

post; see the website for details.
A fee of A$110 applies.
    Those travelling on eVisitor,
ETA and tourist visas are not permitted to work while in Australia.
Travellers are asked on their
applications to prove that they
have an adequate source of funding while in Australia (around
A$1,000 a month).
    Working-holiday visas Visi-
tors from 19 designated countries
(including the UK, Ireland, Canada, France and Germany), who
are aged between 18 and 30, are
eligible for a Working Holiday
Visa. This entitles a stay of up to
12 months and casual employment (maximum six months with
one employer) during that time.
Your first Working Holiday Visa
must be applied for before you
enter Australia at www.immi.gov.au/
visitors/working-holiday The non-re-
fundable cost is A$270.
    **Department of Immigration
and Citizenship**, tel: 13 18 81; or
the nearest mission outside Australia; www.immi.gov.au.

Weights and Measures

Australia uses the metric system
of weights and measures. The
main conversions are as follows:

1 metre	3.28 feet
1 kilometre	0.62 mile
1 kilogram	2.2 pounds
1 litre	1.8 pints (UK)

FURTHER READING

TRANSPORT

Aboriginal Australia

Aboriginal Art of Australia: Exploring Cultural Traditions, C Finlay. Concise guide to Aboriginal art and the symbolism employed.
Australia's Living Heritage: Arts of the Dreaming, J Isaacs. Comprehensive look at indigenous art and its cultural importance.
Aboriginal Myths, Legends and Fables, AW Reed. Straightforward retelling of some of the key stories.
Tucker Track – A curious history of food in Australia, W Fahey. All about bush tucker.

Travel

Down Under, B Bryson. Entertaining and full of insights.
The Songlines, B Chatwin. Remarkable Outback journey into Aboriginal tradition and lore.
Tracks, R Davidson. The adventures of a woman crossing the continent on a camel.

History

Australia: A Biography of a Nation, P Knightley. Wide-ranging history, particularly good in its snapshots of key players.
The Explorers, ed. T Flannery. A superb collection of accounts from the days of the exploration and early settlement of Australia.
The Fatal Shore, R Hughes. Landmark book laying bare the truths of convict transportation and its lasting impact
A Concise History of Australia, S Macintyre. Reliable, readable and up-to-date account.

Natural History

Green Guide: Mammals of Australia, T Lindsey. Handbook to the country's amazing wildlife.
Discovery Guide to Outback Queensland, ed M Ryan. Comprehensive full-colour guide.

Australian Language

The Dinkum Dictionary, S Butler. Bonza sticky beak into Australian lingo.
Let stalk Strine, A Lauder. Hilarious, too-true massacre of the English language.

SEND US YOUR THOUGHTS

We do our best to ensure that the information in our books is as accurate and up-to-date as possible. The books are updated on a regular basis using local contacts, who painstakingly add, amend and correct as required. However, some details (such as telephone numbers and opening times) are liable to change, and we are ultimately reliant on our readers to put us in the picture.

We welcome your feedback, especially your experience of using the book "on the road". Maybe we recommended a hotel that you liked (or another that you didn't), or you came across a great bar or new attraction we missed.

We will acknowledge all contributions, and we'll offer an Insight Guide to the best letters received.

Please write to us at:
**Insight Guides
PO Box 7910
London SE1 1WE**
Or email us at:
insight@apaguide.co.uk

Fiction

The Bodysurfers, R Drewe. Short stories that evoke the beach and the Australian temperament.
Breath, T Winton. The powerful surf is as much the focus as the relationships in this accomplished novel.
Cloudstreet, T Winton. A family saga that mirrored the growth of the nation in the 20th century, and became an Australian classic.
For the Term of His Natural Life, M Clarke. The renowned convict potboiler first published in 1874.
It's Raining in Mango, T Astley. Saga stretching over a century, including gold prospecting in Queensland and Aboriginal dispossession.
Johnno, D Malouf. Semi-autobiographical account of growing up in Brisbane in the 1940s and 1950s.
Over the Top with Jim, H Lunn. Hilarious account of growing up in Brisbane in the 1950s.
Remembering Babylon, D Malouf. Moving story of a white youth taken in by a Queensland Aboriginal community in the 1840s.

Other Insight Guides

Titles that highlight destinations in this part of the world include:
Insight Guide: Australia, a superbly illustrated guide to all the best that Down Under has to offer.
Insight Guide: Tasmania, a comprehensive guide to Australia's smallest state.
Step by Step: Sydney, a series of walks and tours written by a local author guide you to the very best of this fantastic city.
City Guide: Melbourne, an extensive guide to this vibrant city that helps you get to know your way around like a local.

ACCOMMODATION

ACTIVITIES

A – Z

ART AND PHOTO CREDITS